PICASSO: HIS LIFE AND WORK

Pablo Picasso in his studio.

PICASSO : HIS LIFE AND WORK / ROLAND PENROSE

"Je parle de ce qui m'aide à vivre."

PAUL ELUARD: *A Pablo Picasso*

"Rien de ce qu'on peut dire de Picasso n'est exact. . . ."

GEORGES RIBÉMONT DESSAIGNES

Second Edition

1962

SCHOCKEN BOOKS · NEW YORK

All translations are by the author except where otherwise acknowledged

Library of Congress Catalog Card No. 62-20157

Manufactured in the United States of America

CONTENTS

LIST OF ILLUSTRATIONS

LIST OF PLATES

following p. 402

Note

The information given under each reproduction is as follows: title, date, medium, and size in inches (unless otherwise marked), height followed by breadth. All other information, and acknowledgements to museums, collectors and photographers, will be found below. (The abbreviation M.O.M.A. is used in every case for the Museum of Modern Art, New York.)

I. 1. The Picador. Earliest known painting by Picasso. Owned by the artist. 2. Girl with Bare Feet. Owned by the artist. 3. Diploma drawing. 4. Science and Charity. Coll. the artist's sister. *Photo: Melich, Barcelona.* 5. Self-portrait. Coll. Mrs. E. Heywood Lonsdale. 6. Scene in a Tavern. Coll. Howard Samuel, Esq., London. 7. Harlequin.

Photo: Cahiers d'Art. 8. Moulin de la Galette. Coll. Mr. and Mrs. J. K. Thannhauser, N.Y. *Photo: M.O.M.A.* 9. Burial of Casagemas (Evocation). Musée du Petit Palais, Paris. *Photo: Bulloz, Paris.*

II. 1. Portrait of Jaime Sabartès. Museums of Leningrad and Moscow. *Photo: Kohlhammer, Stuttgart.* 2. The Blue Room. The Phillips Gallery, Washington, D.C. 3. Self-portrait. Owned by the artist. *Photo: Cahiers d'Art.* 4. La Vie. Cleveland Museum of Art, Gift of Hanna Fund. 5. Two Sisters. Museums of Leningrad and Moscow. 6. Maternity. Fogg Art Museum, Harvard University. 7. The Old Jew (Blind Beggar with Boy). Museums of Leningrad and Moscow. 8. The Blind Man's Meal. Metropolitan Museum of Art, N.Y. 9. The Courtesan with a Jewelled Necklace. *Photo: Cahiers d'Art.*

III. 1. The Actor. The Metropolitan Museum of Art, N.Y. 2. Salomé. *Photo: Schumacher, Stuttgart.* 3. Meditation. Coll. Mrs. Louise Smith, N.Y. *Photo: M.O.M.A.* 4. The Jester. The Phillips Gallery, Washington, D.C. 5. The Soler Family. Musée des Beaux-Arts, Liège. 6. The Old Guitarist. The Art Institute of Chicago. 7. Acrobat's Family with Ape. Gothenburg Art Gallery. 8. Nude. Private Collection, London. 9. Boy leading a Horse. Coll. Mr. W. S. Paley, N.Y. *Photo: M.O.M.A.*

IV. 1. Portrait of Gertrude Stein. Metropolitan Museum of Art, N.Y. 2. Acrobat on a Ball. Pushkin Museum, Moscow. 3. Self-portrait. Philadelphia Museum of Art, A. E. Gallatin Collection. 4. Family of Saltimbanques. National Gallery of Art, Washington D.C., Chester Dale Collection. 5. Two Nudes. Coll. Mrs. G. David Thompson, Pittsburgh. 6. Woman with a Fan. Coll. Mr. and Mrs. W. Averell Harriman.

V. 1. Les Demoiselles d'Avignon. M.O.M.A. Lillie P. Bliss Bequest. 2. Negro Dancer. Private Collection, London. 3. Head. Coll. Mr. and Mrs. S. A. Marx, Chicago. 4. Nude with Drapery. Museums of Leningrad and Moscow. 5. House in Garden. Museums of Leningrad and Moscow. 6. Two Nudes (Friendship). Museums of Leningrad and Moscow.

VI. 1. Nude on Beach. Private Collection. 2. Fruit Dish. M.O.M.A. Lillie P. Bliss Bequest. 3. Portrait of Clovis Sagot. Kunsthalle, Hamburg. 4. Head of a Woman. M.O.M.A. 5. Seated Woman (Femme en vert). Stedelijk van Abbe-museum, Eindhoven. 6. The Reservoir, Horta. Private Collection, Paris. 7. Portrait of Vollard. Pushkin Museum, Moscow. 8. Portrait of Uhde. Private

XII. 1. Bather (Cannes). *Photo: Cahiers d'Art.* 2. On the Beach (Dinard). Coll. Mr. George L. K. Morris. 3. Woman's Head and Self-portrait. Private Collection, London. *Photo: R. B. Fleming, London.* 4. Metamorphosis. Owned by the artist. 5. Project for a Monument (Woman's Head). 6. Sculpture. Owned by the artist. 7. Crucifixion. Owned by the artist. *Photo: M.O.M.A.* 8. Painter and Model. Coll. Mr. Sidney Janis, New York.

XIII. 1. Woman in an Armchair. Owned by the artist. 2. Sculpture. Owned by the artist. *Photo: Chevojon, Paris.* 3. Seated Bather. Coll. Mrs. Meric Callery, N.Y. 4. Girl seated in a red armchair. Tate Gallery, London. 5. Girl before a Mirror. M.O.M.A. Gift of Mrs. Simon Guggenheim. 6. Nude on a Black Couch. Coll. Mrs. Meric Callery, N.Y. 7. Pitcher and Bowl of Fruit. Private Collection, N.Y. 8. Anatomy. Reproduced from *Minotaure.* 9. Composition with butterfly. *Photo: Brassai.*

XIV. 1. Head. Owned by the artist. *Photo: Chevojon, Paris.* 2. Figures. *Photo Brassai.* 3. Bullfight. Coll. Mr. and Mrs. Victor W. Ganz, N.Y. 4. Heads. *Photo: Brassai.* 5. Two Girls Reading. The Evergreen House Foundation, Baltimore. 6. Sculptor's Studio. From The Sculptor's Studio, Vollard Suite. 7. The' Muse. Musée d'Art Moderne, Paris. 8. Minotaur carousing. *Photo: Kleinhempel, Hamburg.* 9. Dying Minotaur. *Photo: Kleinhempel, Hamburg.*

XV. 1. Bathers with a Toy Boat. Coll. Mrs. Peggy Guggenheim, Venice. 2. Portrait of Dora Maar. Owned by the artist. *Photo: M.O.M.A.* 3. Portrait of Nusch. Owned by the artist. 4. Nude with Night Sky. Private Collection, Paris. 5. Portrait of Eluard. 6. Grand Air. Reproduced in the first ten copies of *Les Yeux Fertiles* by Paul Eluard. *Photo: Courtauld Institute of Art, London.* 7. Blind Minotaur. From The Minotaur, Vollard Suite. *Photo: Kleinhempel, Hamburg.* 8. Minotaur with a Boat. 9. End of a Monster. Private Collection, London. *Photo: R. B. Fleming, London.*

XVI. 1. Portrait of Marie-Thérèse. 2. Still-life, Le Tremblay. 3. Still-life with Horned God. Private Collection. 4. Woman with Cat. Coll. Mme. Marie Cuttoli, Paris. *Photo: Rossignol, Paris.* 5. Portrait of Maïa. Owned by the artist. 6. Portrait of Lee Miller. Private Collection, London. *Photo: Roger Mayne, London.* 7. Dream and Lie of Franco. 8. Signature to Dream and Lie of Franco.

XVII. 1. Guernica. On extended loan by the artist to M.O.M.A. 2. Weeping Woman. Private Collection, London. *Photo: R. B.*

Fleming, London. 3. Cat and Bird. 4. Minotauromachie. 5. Girl with a Cock. Coll. Mrs. Meric Callery, N.Y.

XVIII. 1. Woman in a Garden. Private Collection, New York. 2. Still-life with a Red Bull's Head. Coll. Mr. and Mrs. William A. M. Burden, N.Y. 3. Man with Lollipop. *Photo: Cahiers d'Art.* 4. Portrait of D.M. Coll. Mlle. Dora Maar, Paris. *Photo: M.O.M.A.* 5. Café at Royan. Owned by the artist. *Photo: Chevojon, Paris.* 6. Woman's Head. 7. Fishermen of Antibes. M.O.M.A. Mrs. Simon Guggenheim Fund. 8. Portrait of Jaime Sabartès. Coll. M. Jaime Sabartès, Paris.

XIX. 1. Page from Royan sketchbook. *Photo: Cahiers d'Art.* 2. Nude dressing her hair. Owned by the artist. 3. Head, Royan. Painted on the day the Germans entered Royan—11 June 1940. 4. Sleeping Nude. 5. Child with Pigeons. *Photo: Chevojon, Paris.* 6. Still-life with Sausage. Coll. Mr. and Mrs. Victor W. Ganz, N.Y. *Photo: M.O.M.A.* 7. Self-portrait from *Desire Caught by the Tail.* 8. Skull and Leeks. Galerie Louise Leiris, Paris. 9. Portrait of D.M. as a bird. Drawn on a blank leaf of Buffon's *Natural History.*

XX. 1. Skull. *Photo: Chevojon, Paris.* 2. Man with Sheep. 3. Head of D.M. *Photo: Chevojon, Paris.* 4. Head. *Photo: Brassai.* 5. Nude. Owned by the artist. *Photo: Chevojon, Paris.* 6. Bull's Head. Owned by the artist. *Photo: Chevojon, Paris.* 7. Still-life with Candle. 8. Bacchanale after Poussin. Owned by the artist. 9. Paris Landscape. Owned by the artist. *Photo: Chevojon, Paris.*

XXI. 1. First Steps. Yale University Art Gallery. 2. Seated Woman. Private Collection. 3. Woman in a Rocking Chair. 4. Serenade. Musée d'Art Moderne, Paris. 5. Pastoral. 6. The Charnel House. Coll. Mr. Walter P. Chrysler, N.Y. 7. Massacre in Korea.

XXII. 1. Ulysses and the Sirens. Musée Picasso, Antibes. 2. Spiral Head of Faun. Reproduced, *Verve,* Vol. 5, Nos. 19, 20. 3. Mother and Children with Orange. Owned by the artist. 4. Owl and Sea Urchins. 5. Françoise. *Photo: Courtauld Institute of Art, London.* 6. Night Landscape, Vallauris. 7. Portrait of a Painter, after El Greco. Coll. Mr. Siegfried Rosengart, Lucerne. 8. Chimneys of Vallauris. Owned by the artist. 9. Portrait of Sylvette. *Photo: Galerie Louise Leiris, Paris.*

XXIII. 1. War. In the Temple of Peace, Vallauris. 2. Peace. In the Temple of Peace, Vallauris. 3. Woman Vase. *Photo: Galerie Louise Leiris, Paris.* 4. Model and Monkey Painter. Reproduced from *Verve.*

5. Vase. 6. Knights and Pages. Owned by the artist. *Photo: Galerie Louise Leiris, Paris.* 7. Three Doves. 8. Plate with Bullfight. *Photo: Müller, Paris.*

XXIV. 1. Ape with young. *Photo: Chevojon, Paris.* 2. The Women of Algiers, after Delacroix. *Photo: Galerie Louise Leiris, Paris.* 3. Goat. 4. Jacqueline Roque in the Studio. *Photo: Galerie Louise Leiris, Paris.* 5 Pregnant Woman. *Photo: Chevojon, Paris.* 6. The Studio. 7. Las Meninas, after Velasquez. Owned by the artist.

PICASSO: HIS LIFE AND WORK

CHAPTER I

ORIGINS AND YOUTH
(1881-1895)

In our time the arts have been in a state of revolution, a battle-field in which tradition has slowly yielded to the onslaughts of a vanguard of innovators who have acted with the conviction of visionaries. Already in the second half of the twentieth century it is difficult for the present generation to understand the violence of this struggle in its early days, the courage of those who led the attack, and the reasons why the battle was fought with such vigour, against such odds. The day has gone in favour of the enlightened, since it is those who had vision, those who were scorned, who have now become the accepted heroes of our age. Among them Pablo Picasso stands out as a leader of undisputed brilliance.

Many factors have combined to make him the most widely known painter alive and already his life and achievements are clothed with legends. Paradoxes are so frequent in any statement made about him that the public are bewildered and imagine that he is either a strange and evil monster or an oracle whose wisdom has occult significance. Though he is a Spaniard he has lived less than a third of his life in Spain; though he is now in his old age he is more vigorous and agile both in mind and body than many men are in their youth; though he has persistently outraged the most serious critics by work that seemed incomprehensible, they have had to admit their admiration for his talent; though his fame has spread throughout the whole world and his wealth is now incalculable he has not changed his manner of living. His main desire is still to continue his work, and though he is sur-rounded by friends and companions whose love for him is great, his magnitude is such that among them he is a solitary figure.

Although Picasso has lived as an expatriate for more than fifty

years he is still essentially Spanish. To understand him it is necessary
to know something of the country of his birth, a land of strong
contrasts, brilliant sun and black shadow, extreme heat and cold,
fertility and barrenness. It is a country notorious for violent passion in
love and fanatical ruthlessness. Its people have a capacity to exteriorise
their emotions and display in a vivid light the drama of human life.
Their love of gaiety is accompanied by an insistence on suffering and
the macabre, and they find consolation for misery and relief from
anxiety in the arts. Whether it be in the poetry of Gongora, the
flamenco music of the gypsies, the bullfight or the painting of Zurbaran, there is always sorrow in the depths of their expression. Tragedy
is a reality which must be expressed, and the artist's task is to find a form
of realism capable of making it felt acutely. To achieve this, no people
know better than the Spaniards that the tragic should be balanced by
the comic, and an equilibrium established between the two moods. By
giving them equal importance it becomes possible to indulge more
profoundly in both extremes.

The work of Picasso is a revelation of the immense variety with
which he is able to display this drama between two opposite poles.
His life however is monolithic in character because of his dedication
to a single purpose, his art. The extraordinary vigour, both mental and
physical, of Picasso at the age of seventy-six is a phenomenon similar
to the prodigious speed with which he developed in childhood. His
progress was so rapid that he denies ever having drawn as a child.
Indeed the earliest known example of his work is a painting that
contains ideas which have preoccupied him all his life. At the age of
nine he was already able to paint a scene of a bullfight in which a
lively sense of characterisation appears in the figures of a picador
seated on his nag, and of the spectators.[1] A composition which is
skilful and mature shows also the unselfconsciousness and the originality of a child. The naïve disregard for scale and perspective, the
insistence on the main image at the expense of detail, and the arbitrary
use of colour—qualities that are typical of the imagination of a child
—are to be found. These elements were to be fostered by Picasso
rather than disregarded so as to serve him in his work and help him
in his discoveries.

On the 25 October 1881, at 11.15 at night, Pablo Ruiz Picasso
was born at Malaga. At that moment both the moon and the sun
approached the nadir, and the light that shone on the white houses
of the city from the midnight sky came from a strange combination

[1] Plate I, 1.

of planets and major stars, whose conjunctions and oppositions have been the cause of much speculation on the part of astrologers. Many attempts have been made by experts to find relationships between these occult influences and the life and character of one so richly endowed with rare talents. Until recently, however, it was inevitable that their calculations should be to some degree erroneous, since none had had access to his birth certificate to verify the hour of his birth. They had all readily believed his own picturesque story that he was born at midnight.

Malaga

Although the Plaza de la Merced, where Picasso was born, is the larger of the two squares in Malaga, it is not the more central. In the past it owed its importance to its position outside the gateway to Granada. On the south-eastern side, it is shut in by two steep hills on which stood the citadel, Alcazaba, and the castle, Gibralfaro, two Moorish fortresses which dominate the city and harbour. Little that happens in the narrow streets, paved with cobbles arranged in ornamental design, could pass unnoticed from these formidable ramparts. They had been built on the foundations of a Phoenician fortress. Relics of the Phoenicians and Romans show that the site had been coveted by foreigners long before its conquest in 711 by the Moors, for whom it became the principal port of the Moorish capital, Granada. From the summits above the city a grandiose panorama stretches inland over a plain covered with vineyards to the mountains, while to the south the plain meets the sea in a graceful curve, and out across the Mediterranean can be seen the snow of the Atlas Mountains, a reminder of the nearness of Africa, and of influences much stronger in the past than they are today.

By the end of the nineteenth century the rocky heights that separate the Plaza de la Merced from the port had been covered for generations with buildings made from stones pillaged from the Moorish citadel. The terraced gardens and courtyards with their fountains had become unrecognisable. They had degenerated into little more than a huddle of ruins inhabited by gypsies, the heirs of Moorish music and dancing if not of their splendour. In later years Picasso described this region to Sabartès. "It was known," he said, "as the 'chupa y tira' "— which is Spanish for 'suck and chuck'—because the people who inhabited this slum were so poor that they lived solely on a soup made of shellfish. The ground was covered with the empty shells which the inhabitants had chucked out of the windows after sucking them clean.

From the sordid hovels that spread down the hillside almost to the tidy gardens of the Plaza de la Merced, the night would be enlivened by the sound of guitars and voices singing 'cante hondo', passionate love songs based on very ancient themes and adapted by the individual singers to the joys and pains of their own hearts.

Ancestry

The sources from which Picasso sprang have now been determined with some certainty, thanks to the work of genealogists, in particular his old friend Jaime Sabartès. The paternal branch of the family tree is not lacking in distinguished ancestors, including men honoured in civic life, on the battlefield and in the Church. It can be traced back to the noble figure of Juan de Leon, a knight whose lands were at Cogolludo, near Valladolid. Records of 1541 state that his father before him was exempt from all taxes, "not by a concession from the king nor because of bearing arms as a knight, not because of his farm lands, nor for any other reason than that he was a gentleman of well-famed nobility".[1] Chronicles also state that Don Juan set forth "in good harness as was fitting in his position as a hidalgo" for the war of Granada and Loja, from which he never returned.

Toward the end of the sixteenth century, the descendants of Juan de Leon left Castille to settle at Villafranca de Cordova. Spanish usage in the matter of surnames may cause some confusion, for it is customary to add the surname of the mother to the paternal name, and some such explanation probably accounts for the sudden appearance of the surname 'Ruiz' in this family during the seventeenth century. There is no doubt, however, that they were in direct descent from the illustrious Juan de Leon and well known in Cordova until the end of the eighteenth century. It was about 1790 that José Ruiz y de Fuentes settled in Malaga and married a lady of the noble family of de Almoguera. His son, Diego, married Maria de la Paz Blasco y Echevarria; together they became the grandparents of Picasso. There has been a persistent myth that the origins of the family on this side were predominantly Basque, but Sabartès points out that the name 'Blasco' is Aragonese, and if there is any tendency in that direction it can only be through Picasso's grandmother, Maria de la Paz Echevarria, a name which is most probably Basque.

The ancestors on the side of Picasso's great-grandmother, Maria Josefa de Almoguera, had among them two distinguished priests.

[1] Jaime Sabartès, *Picasso, Documents Inconographiques*, Pierre Cailler, Geneva, 1954.

The first, the Venerable Almoguera, descendant of a 'very noble' family from the mountains of Leon, was born in Cordova in 1605 and died in great poverty but in 'the odour of sanctity' in 1676, having in his time been appointed Bishop of Arequipa, Archbishop of Lima, Viceroy and Captain-General of the Kingdom of Peru. The second was Brother Pedro de Cristo Almoguera, who flourished some two centuries later and died in 1855 at the age of eighty-one, having lived for sixty-two years as a hermit in the Sierra de Cordova. He was a man of faith and courage, who dedicated his life to meditation and to the relief of suffering.

Twenty years after the arrival of Don José Ruiz y de Fuentes in Malaga, an incident occurred. His eldest son, Diego, one day half in play, half wilfully, threw stones at the French soldiers then occupying the city, as they marched by. He was caught by a trooper and nearly beaten to death. Throughout his life Don Diego, Picasso's grandfather, remembered the event, not from shame, but from pride that he had held up the parade. From his photo as an elderly man, tall and thin, with a sour frown and heavy eyebrows, it would be easy to misjudge his real nature, which, we are told, was "restless, nervous and intelligent, a tireless worker, witty, jovial, with sudden bursts of enthusiasm".[1] He was ingenious and tactful in overcoming difficulties, and although his business was manufacturing gloves, a trade which kept him at work without respite to provide for his family of eleven children, he managed to indulge his passion for music by playing the double bass in the orchestra of the Municipal Theatre. Also he enjoyed drawing.

Don Diego Ruiz had married Maria de la Paz Blasco in 1830. Their eldest son, Diego, became a diplomat who at one time travelled in company with the Spanish Ambassador to Russia. He also appears to have become known for his talent in making likenesses of his friends. But the son who took the brunt of caring for the less fortunate members of the family after their father's death was the fourth child, Pablo. He had become a Doctor of Theology and a Canon of the Cathedral of Malaga. He made it his duty not only to look after his four unmarried sisters, but to help to provide for his unbusinesslike younger brother, José, the ninth of the family and the future father of Pablo Ruiz y Picasso.

José, to make matters worse, had decided to become a professional painter, but unlike his elder brother Diego, he was no dilettante, and his contact with society came with less ease. Since a painter

[1] Sabartès, *Documents*, p. 294.

dedicated to his art alone was according to conventional standards a ne'er-do-well, the loyalty and generosity of his elder brother Pablo were factors of great importance to him in early days. However this situation came abruptly to an end with the death of the Canon, after which José was forced to take over his brother's responsibilities towards the unmarried sisters.

Such was the ancestry of Picasso on his father's side. Devotion, tenacity, courage, appreciation of the arts and sincerity in religion were characteristics which recurred among his ancestors, and which could be expected to form part of the inheritance of their descendants. We might hope to trace reinforcements for these virtues on the maternal side, were it not that this branch is less certain of its origins. The name 'Picasso' is not common anywhere, but in Malaga it had attained fortuitous notoriety, not because of its rarity but through an incident that had happened when General José Lachambre, a native of Malaga, in obedience to a higher command, bombarded the city from the nearby hills in order to quell a political disturbance. Such events were not uncommon in the early part of the nineteenth century, but this time the indignation of the citizens was aroused when cannon balls began to fall in the Plaza de la Merced, and on their way lifted some tiles off the house where the Picasso family lived. In popular songs they at once became heroes at the expense of the general.

The family had lived in Malaga for at least two generations. Don Francisco Picasso, maternal grandfather of Pablo, was born there, and was sent to England for his education. Later he became a civil servant in Cuba, where in 1883 he disappeared and was said to have died of yellow fever (vomito negro) on the eve of his return to Malaga. This became known to his children only after fifteen years of enquiry.

Little is known of the exact origins of the family, and speculation has centred mainly round the source of the name, which in its spelling appears to be Italian rather than Spanish. This fact has led various writers to believe that the family is linked with the artist Matteo Picasso, a native of Recco near Genoa, who made a reputation as a portrait painter. He was born in 1794 and is best known by a portrait he painted of the Duchess of Galliera, now in the Gallery of Modern Art in Genoa. Picasso himself owns a small portrait of a man painted by Matteo in a pleasing but commonplace style. Recently evidence has come to hand that the grandfather of Doña Maria Picasso was born in a small village near Recco; this would lead to the supposition of a connection between the families.

Sabartès, who has in the past been eager to explode the myths of a Basque origin for the paternal branch and an Italian origin on the maternal side, has however traced a hypothetical source which originates in Africa. He holds this to be a plausible theory and one which would help to offer an explanation for Picasso's feeling of kinship with nomads and gypsies. The chronicles of King don Pedro, son of King don Alfonso of Castille, dating from 1591, give an account of a battle fought in 1339 between Gonzalo Martinez de Oviedo, commander of the armies of the King of Andalusia, and the Prince Picaço, son of the Moorish King Albuhacen, who had arrived from Africa at the head of ten thousand knights. The battle went against the fortunes of the prince, who was defeated and slain by the Spaniards.

Since the character of Picasso is one so rare and so original, it is understandable that we should naïvely expect to find extraordinary influences in his ancestry. Spain is a country that owes much of its inspiration to the Moors and the gypsies, and more than one biographer has suggested that a distant strain either of North African or of Jewish blood is present on his mother's side. A Catalan writer seeks to establish his origin among the gold-workers of Majorca who were Moorish immigrants, and discovers, in the arabesques of their engravings and filigree, the origin of the flourishes and calligraphy that we find in the versatile hand of Picasso. A Castilian poet and early friend, Ramon Gomez de la Serna, has written: "In the great nation of the gypsies of art, Picasso is the most gypsy of all."[1] This may be taken figuratively, but there still remains an affinity between the autonomous life, the spontaneity and insight of the gypsies and the Olympian independence, the inspiration and vision of the great artist.

But leaving conjecture and the implications that we may hope to deduce from heredity, it is safe to say that the ancestors of Picasso on both sides are predominantly Andalusian and sufficiently Spanish from sufficiently far back for us to pay attention, above all, to the characteristics of these people. The artistic tastes and talent of his father's family were well known locally. In addition, a portrait has recently been discovered of a certain Manuel Harerra of Velez Malaga, seated in a chair, holding in one hand a key and in the other a scroll of verses dedicated to his son. It is signed 'Picasso-Juan' and dated 1850, which suggests that on Picasso's mother's side the family also had leanings towards painting independent of the achievements of the Genoese Matteo Picasso.

[1] R. Gomez de la Serna, 'Le Toreador de la Peinture,' *Cahiers d'Art*, Paris, 1932, 3-5.

Don José Marries

The meeting of José Ruiz Blasco and Maria Picasso Lopez was not by chance. The Picasso family had lived for many years in the Plaza de la Merced in Malaga, a large square enclosing a public garden not far from the centre of the town, whereas José had been living with his elder brother, the Canon Pablo, in the Calle de Granada nearby. All ten brothers and sisters were agreed that the time had come for José to marry, partly because no male issue had yet been born to any member of their generation, and partly because they wished to see him settle down and abandon the doubtful life of a young painter, dependent on the charity of his reverend brother. The Canon in spite of his tolerance had begun to think "that the sins of youth towards which a whimsical humour" drew his younger brother had lasted long enough.[1] Having selected a suitable young lady, known to be esteemed by him, they insisted that he should propose to her. But José showed no desire to commit himself, and after keeping the family in suspense, he decided suddenly to marry not this girl but her cousin, whom he had met in her company and who shared the same surname, Picasso. Even after the decision had been made, the suspense was again prolonged by the sudden death of his brother Pablo, and it was not until two years had passed that José Ruiz Blasco and Maria Picasso Lopez were married.

In the autumn of the following year, a son was born to them. With due ceremony he was christened in the nearby church of Santiago, and in accordance with tradition the child received the names: Pablo, Diego, José, Francisco de Paula, Juan Nepomuceno, Maria de los Remedios, Cipriano de la Santisima Trinidad. Sabartès explains that in Malaga it was customary to endow children with a rich choice of christian names, and gives the sources of them all: the only one that has been remembered, however, Pablo, was given as a tribute to his recently deceased uncle.

The tall white block of flats into which Don José Ruiz Blasco moved with his bride was on the eastern side of the Plaza de la Merced. His young wife was small and of delicate build. She had the black eyes, sparkling with vivacity and wit, and blue-black hair of the Andalusians, in contrast to her husband, the tall, gaunt painter, whose reddish hair and distinguished reserve caused his friends to call him 'the Englishman'. The jibe was apt in other ways, for he appreciated English customs and English design, especially in furniture. In proof of

[1] Sabartès, *Documents*.

this, two of a set of Chippendale chairs, which had come to Malaga by way of Gibraltar, are still used by Picasso in his house in Cannes.

The new block occupied the site of the ancient Convent of Our Lady of Peace. It had been built by a patron of the arts, Don Antonio Campos Garvin, Marquis de Ignato, who also lived in the same square and enjoyed entertaining the group of poets, painters and musicians of which Malaga could boast at that time. Generous and benign, he collected pictures bought from his friends the artists, and when a crisis arose, he was willing to accept paintings in lieu of rent from those who had become his tenants. Thus on more than one occasion Don José had reason to be grateful to his landlord. Life had never been easy, and additional cares such as his new responsibility for his unmarried sisters and his mother-in-law, as well as the arrival of his first child, forced Don José to take on an administrative post in order to add to his scant income as a painter.

Don José exchanged his freedom for a post in the School of Fine Arts and Crafts of San Telmo, and accepted the curatorship of the local museum, which was housed in the Town Hall. These duties should have secured for him an income sufficient to support his family to the end of his days, had not municipal politics caused him to lose his job within a year or two. However, understanding the fickle nature of local government, he held on to his post unpaid until the swing of the pendulum returned again to his favour.

In spite of adversity, the birth of Pablo was the cause of great rejoic- ing in the Ruiz family. He was the first male heir to have been born to any of the eleven descendants of Don Diego Ruiz de Almoguera, and therefore a triumph over destiny. The birth had been made all the more dramatic by a misjudgement, nearly fatal, on the part of the midwife. The child appeared to her to be stillborn and she abandoned it on a table, so as to give all her attention to the mother. It was due only to the fortunate presence of mind of Don Salvador, one of his uncles and a qualified doctor, that the infant was saved from asphyxia before life had begun. This story, often told to him during childhood, of how death was so forcefully present at birth, has lurked in Picasso's imagina- tion throughout life.

An Earthquake

Three years after the birth of Pablo, one evening in mid-December, Malaga was shaken violently by an earthquake, and Don José, out gossiping with friends in a chemist's shop, broke off his conversation to race home to his family. On the way he decided that he must evacuate them immediately to the house of a friend, believing that its position, backed by the rock of the Gibralfaro, would make it a safer refuge than his flat on the second floor. Sabartès tells how Picasso, some fifty years later, described to him their flight: "My mother wore a handkerchief on her head, I had never seen her like that before. My father seized his cape from the coat-stand, threw it round his shoulders, took me in his arms and rolled me in its folds, leaving only my head exposed."[1] They had not far to go to reach the house of Antonio Munoz Degrain, a painter and an intimate friend. Taking shelter there, Pablo's mother gave birth to her second child, a daughter called Lola.

Local Painters and Painting

Munoz Degrain had come to Malaga to decorate the new Cervantes Theatre. He was one of a group of painters whose work now hangs in the local museum. In his academic canvases, the subject-matter, whether it be historical, religious, maritime or picturesque, is all-important, though now seriously in retreat beneath heavy coats of varnish. Although he is best known by his conventional scenes from Spanish history, there are traces of influences from abroad in some of his Andalusian landscapes which show an inclination to use colour in a less conventional way. Blue began to find its way into the shadows. The search for light of the Impressionists, and the symbolism of the Romantic painters of the north, were beginning to make themselves felt, replacing historical pastiche even in these remote parts of the peninsula. Degrain had gained a considerable reputation in Spain, which had earned him some limited fame abroad. A story, which has been the delight of Picasso for many years, is told of how on one occasion Degrain was returning with a friend from Rome where they had achieved some renown. On their arrival they found the city of Malaga gaily decorated, and their friends at the station in ceremonial dress to meet them. The two painters, overwhelmed by the display, were brought home in triumph, covered with laurels and convinced that all had been specially arranged in their honour. But to spoil their ecstasy the King arrived by the next train on a compassionate visit to the areas ruined by the earthquake which had coincided with Lola's birth.

In the small museum where Don José worked, he had the use of a room for restoring pictures. Here he could paint undisturbed, for, it is

[1] Jaime Sabartès, *Picasso, Portraits et Souvenirs*, Louis Carré et Maximilien Vox, Paris, 1946.

said, the museum was scarcely ever open. He was a dull though
competent painter with a limited range. Dining-room pictures were
his speciality: fur and feather, pigeons and lilac, together with an
occasional landscape, completed his repertoire. He was happiest when
he could make his feathered models symbolic of moral or sentimental
drama, as in his painting of a happy couple perched on the threshold
of their pigeon house, while a third party ruffled with jealousy spies
on them from below. Recently, when a small collection of his work
was unearthed in the possession of the de Ignato family in South
America—some of those paintings that had been accepted in payment
of rent—it was found inappropriate to organise a public exhibition
owing to their banality. Don José proved however to be a teacher
whose lessons were never forgotten by his son. In spite of his traditional
outlook and his unimaginative style, he had inherited the Spanish
passion for realism, and was willing to make experiments that a more
restrained and conventional temperament would have considered to
be in bad taste. The experiments were not always successful, as may be
seen from one which is still in existence at the house of his daughter
Lola in Barcelona. Don José had bought a plaster cast of the head of a
Greek goddess whose classical beauty he had transformed into an
image of Our Lady of Sorrows by painting the face with the utmost
realism, sticking on eyebrows and adding golden tears.[1] He then
draped the hair and shoulders in cloth dipped in plaster, so that it
stuck to the cast. The head was finally set up on a small eighteenth-
century table, which he repainted periodically with shiny paint,
varying the colour according to his mood. In spite of this, it was always
very ugly, according to Picasso.

Other useful tricks were observed by the watchful eye of his son.
In his passion for painting pigeons, Don José would often attempt
ambitious compositions. In order to arrive at the happiest solution in
their arrangement, he would first paint individual birds on paper, then
having cut them out, he shifted them round until the composition
took shape. In fact, from his childhood Pablo became acquainted with
the possibilities of using material in unconventional ways, borrowing
from any source that came to hand, and making the newly discovered
substance obey his wishes. Brushes and paint were by no means the
only tools of the trade; knives, scissors, pins and paste all played their
part.

One passion above all others dominated Pablo from infancy. His
mother was fond of telling how the first noise he learned to make,

[1] See L'Œil, No. 4, 15 Avril, 1955.

"piz, piz", was an imperative demand for 'lapiz', a pencil. For hours he would sit happily drawing spirals, which he managed to explain were a symbol for a kind of sugar cake called 'torruella', a word formed from a verb which means to bewilder or entangle. He could draw long before he could speak, and many of his first pictures took their ephemeral shape in the sand where the children played in the Plaza de la Merced.

The square itself is spacious, and laid out in a formal way with plane trees, which shelter a crowd of inventive and noisy children from the violence of the sun. Even more numerous than the children in the square are the pigeons. Throughout his life these birds have been the constant companions of Picasso. Gentle and elusive, they have become the symbol of his most tender feelings and utopian desires. The dove of peace drawn by his hand has appeared on the walls of many cities and has been welcomed as a symbol of new hope. From the windows Pablo, encouraged by his father, could watch the movements of these birds in the branches of the plane trees and listen to their crooning. A picture painted by Don José that remained vivid in Picasso's memory has been described by him as "an immense canvas representing a dove-cote crammed with pigeons sitting on perches ... millions of pigeons".[1] But Sabartès, who has recently unearthed this picture in Malaga, was able to count only nine in the whole composition.

Memories of the first decade of his life in Malaga tend to become confused or incomplete, but often they contain some allusion to later life which seems to give them prophetic significance. Sabartès tells the story of how, sixty years later, when watching a child learning to walk, Picasso said, "I learnt to walk by pushing a tin of Olibet biscuits, because I knew what there was inside", and he continued to insist on the importance of this motive, priding himself on his artfulness at such a tender age. This early appreciation of simple geometric shapes combined with an interest in what lies hidden beneath is highly appropriate to the inventor of cubism.

Visually Picasso's memory remains extraordinarily clear concerning things both big and small that impressed his imagination. He has described to me in detail the amazing baroque interior of the church of La Victoria, and on a photograph of himself at the age of four, reproduced by Sabartès, he wrote for me descriptions of the colour of his clothes. They consisted of a vermilion jacket with gold buttons, a kilt, bronze boots and a white collar and bow. On another portrait of himself with Lola, in which he is dressed up as a sailor, with button

[1] Sabartès, *Portraits*.

boots and black stockings, he wrote, "Lola's costume, black, belt blue, collar white. Me, suit white, overcoat navy blue, beret blue."

What has remained of these early years, more permanent than fragmentary memories, is the hereditary and traditional influence that lies mysteriously deep and well-rooted in Picasso. Qualities that he has never forgotten are the boisterous wit of the Malaguenians, their passionate love of the glamorous parade of the bullfight or the religious processions of Holy Week. He also understands their fear of the act which completes an object or finishes an event, bringing with it an unbearable finality resembling death. It is symbolised by the unfinished cathedral that dominates the city, which is known as the 'Manco' (one-handed) because it raises one tower into the air like a one-armed man, its twin never having been completed. Strong contrasts inherent in the environment have had their indelible effect; the comparison between the fertile plain and the arid rock, intense light and heat in the open contrasted with the coolness of shaded avenues and the interiors of buildings, the stench of slums with the sweet perfume of tropical flowers, the dust and grime of the earth with the purifying freshness of the sea. All these influences were present in the heredity and the environment of this child, whose responses to the world of the senses were unusually acute.

Bullfights

The traditional centre of popular entertainment in all Spanish cities is the bull ring. At Malaga it is so close to the southern slopes of the citadel that those who cannot afford seats can get a distant view by sitting on the sun-scorched hillside. Throughout the summer the arena is filled nearly every Sunday with amateurs who come with their families and their friends to applaud the prowess of their champions in the art of tauromachy. Though superficially the crowd may resemble the spectators at a football match their interest is profoundly different. The performance they have come to see is a rite rather than a sport. Its ritual can be traced to early Mediterranean civilisations such as that of Crete; but the continuity of this aspect in Spain, when in other countries the bullfight has died out or become merely a test of agility, is a sign that it supplies something necessary to the Spanish character. Its pageantry displays to them in a form that they enjoy the fearful drama of life and death. The sacrifice of the bull becomes the symbol of the triumph of man over brute force and blind instinct. Courage and skill are balanced against the tempestuous onslaught of exasperated fury. In the wake of this encounter follow suffering,

cruelty and death. The festive costume of the toreador endows him
with the qualities of the priest and the athlete. By his courage he
becomes the hero admired and reverenced of all; he can equally earn
their merciless scorn should he show himself cowardly or incompetent
in his dangerous task. In his skill he bears a resemblance to the artist.

Like most Spanish children Picasso was taken to the bullfight
at an early age. Don José had a keen appreciation of every detail and
took a pleasure in explaining the subtleties of the fight to his son.
In Pablo there seemed to be a natural propensity for the 'corrida' which
Ramon Gomez de la Serna ascribes to his possible hereditary connection or at least to affinities with gypsies. "In Malaga, his native town",
he writes, "I found an explanation . . . of what Picasso is and I understood to what degree he is a *toreador*—gypsies are the best toreadors—
and how, whatever he may do, it is in reality bullfighting."[1] The
child watching the display imagined himself accomplishing the daring
movements of his heroes within inches of the murderous horns of the
bull, and saw with envy the victorious matador in his splendid clothes
carried high in triumph by the crowd.

In the centre of the square in sight of the flat where the Ruiz family
lived stands a tall elegant obelisk in white stone. It was set up in memory
of those who fell in two unsuccessful uprisings during the nineteenth
century against the implacable absolutism of Spanish rule. Although
Picasso played in its shadow as a child, he has no memory of any gesture
on the part of his relatives that would suggest that they were particularly interested in the reformist activities which made themselves felt
from time to time in Malaga, or that politics of any description were
their concern. The early education he was given was normal for a
child in his circumstances; his first school was an ordinary infants'
school opposite the museum. His memories confirm the impression
given by the family photographs that in politics, religion and their
way of living they were a conventional, law-abiding, provincial
family.

Departure for Corunna

Ten years after the birth of Pablo, Don José was forced to admit that
his struggle to provide for his family was not succeeding. The family
had been increased in 1887 by the birth of another daughter, which
made the overcrowding at home almost intolerable. Finally the day
came when disillusioned and temporarily defeated by financial burdens,

[1] Ramon Gomez de la Serna, *Le Toreador de la Peinture*, Cahiers d'Art,
1932, 3-5.

he sadly decided to leave his native city and accept the post of art master at the Instituto da Guarda, a school for secondary education in Corunna. This brought to an end the quiet life of well-established habits that he had enjoyed, and severed contacts on which he had come to depend for help and advice. In particular, he was to suffer from leaving his younger brother Salvador, the doctor, who had achieved an important situation as chief of the Sanitary Bureau of the Port of Malaga, and whose influence had enabled him to book a cheap passage by sea to Corunna. It was a dejected Don José who sailed with his wife and the three children in September 1891 for that remote port on the Atlantic coast.

Nor was the arrival in Corunna a happy one. The sea voyage had been so rough and tedious that Don José had decided to cut it short by landing the family at Vigo and proceeding overland. At the first sight of Corunna, he decided that he hated the place. Rain and fog replaced the Mediterranean sun, and his isolation from all that he loved in Malaga weighed heavily. Near the rugged granite of Cape Finisterre, Corunna was literally the end of the world to him. An unsurmountable sadness and sense of failure overcame him a few months later when his younger daughter, Concepcion, died of diphtheria. She was the only one of his three children who showed some physical resemblance to him, since she was blonde and slender, and he felt the blow bitterly.

But the move to the north had a very different effect on Pablo. To him it was an adventure full of possibilities. They had been fortunate in finding an apartment in the Calle Payo Gomez, which was so close to the college that his mother could watch him as he crossed from door to door, and owing to his father's position in the college he was able to spend all the time he liked drawing, painting, and learning under his father's devoted instruction. His concentration was such that in a very short time he was able to master the academic technique of charcoal drawing with its insistence on modelling from light to shade. There are in existence many drawings of this period, which achieve a perfection almost unbelievable in one so young, and also reveal his acceptance of these methods of training which are now considered obsolete.[1] The drawings are faithful copies of the repertoire of plaster casts with which every traditional art school was well furnished. The school at Malaga still displays for the pupils' benefit scores of lifeless plaster statues of Greek heroes and Egyptian goddesses; fragments of legs, arms, ears and noses, together with stuffed eagles and pigeons.

[1] See *Cahiers d'Art*, II, 1950, pp. 290-1.

At Corunna it was worse, the casts were drearier and not so varied, but being under the supervision of Don José, whatever facilities the Institute could offer were eagerly accepted by his son.

Before leaving Malaga Don José had been very worried by Pablo's backwardness in elementary education, particularly in arithmetic. He dreaded the disastrous situation which he felt would be bound to arise in the atmosphere of a strange city with unknown and unsympathetic schoolmasters. Pablo had always hated school. Even the rudiments of reading, writing and sums gave him great trouble, and he was quick to escape to his father's studio to a form of learning he loved.

Don José realised that something must be done to save his son and himself from disgrace, and approaching a man who was a very good friend and also a very indulgent schoolmaster, he arranged with him for an examination to be held. The description of this memorable event, for which we are indebted to Sabartès, was given by Picasso later and is full of wit and significance.[1] Faced by his examiner, little Pablo could only answer that he knew nothing, strictly nothing. The patient professor insisted that he should write down a column of four or five figures, but even this was impossible, and exhortations to pay attention made the boy all the more nervous and distracted. However, determined to help, the master wrote the figures on the blackboard and told Pablo to copy them. That indeed was precisely what Pablo could do, and forgetting his own way of making figures, he copied stroke for stroke the numbers on the board with delight, thinking all the time of the pleasure he would have when he returned home to his proud parents and of the paintbrush that awaited him as a prize. "I shall copy the little pigeon," he said to himself as he finished the row of figures. But his troubles were not over yet. The addition had to be made, and this again would have defeated him had he not noticed that the master, carelessly or on purpose, had written the correct answer on his blotting paper. The opportunity was quickly seized by Pablo, who with great care drew in the figures that completed the sum. "Very good," said the kind master. "You see, you did know. The rest will come in time. You see, my child! Why were you so scared?"

Pablo returned home in triumph, clutching the certificate and feverishly calculating how he would draw his picture. "The eye of the pigeon is round like zero. Under the zero a six, with a three under that. There are two eyes and two wings. The two legs placed on the table underline it and below that there is the total." The addition of figures

[1] Sabartès, *Portraits*.

was not the only lesson remembered by Pablo. He had also under-stood that a symbol can have more than one meaning, as can be seen from a pencil sketch made a year or two later in Corunna, which shows a further development in his discovery. The drawing represents two men standing together. One is a comic gawky man in peasant's costume, with wide-brimmed hat and stick, the other a small creature with an oversize baby face. The tall man's eyes are both drawn in the shape of the figure '8', while the dwarf's are in the shape of '7's. Beside them, scribbled several times, are the numbers from one to nine, and a large seven appears alone, with the stem crossed in con-tinental fashion, showing that it could also be made to represent the lines of the eyebrow and the nose.[1]

Although there may have been some justification for Don José's fears that his son might grow up almost illiterate (Picasso has confessed to me that he can never remember the sequence of the alphabet), there were at that time no official regulations to force him to educate Pablo at all, and it is interesting to speculate on what might have occurred in present conditions, when much more of the boy's time and energies would have been diverted into cramming knowledge for commercial reasons into an unreceptive brain. The result might have been a frustrated genius with the approved level of scholastic achieve-ment; in fact, an unbalanced and wasted individual. Don José had understood that where great talent is involved, conventional rules must yield. "One law for the lion and the ox is oppression."

Satisfied that his son's talent would continue to gain respect at the Instituto da Guarda, Don José welcomed the help that Pablo could now give him with his pictures. Often he would leave him to finish certain portions, particularly the feet of a still-life of dead pigeons. After dissecting these from the bird, he would pin them to the table in the required position and set Pablo to copy them.

Don José had grown morose and rarely left the house except to attend Mass. When not at work he stood at the window watching the rain. One evening, when the weather was less depressing, he set a task for his son and went out for a stroll along the Alameda. Among the crowds that pass slowly up and down, beneath the datura flowers hanging like white lanterns heavy with scent, he aired his melancholy. On his return, the pigeons were complete, and so lifelike were their legs that Don José, in a burst of emotion, abruptly gave Pablo his own palette, brushes and colours, saying that his son's talent was now mature, in fact already greater than his own, and that

[1] See Zervos, *Picasso*, Vol. VI, p. 7, No. 49.

he himself would never paint again. In this act of renunciation he found some satisfaction; it helped him to hide his own personal disappointment behind his hopes in the future of his son. His self-denial was not unlike similar gestures among his pious Andalusian ancestors.

The four years spent in Corunna were of great importance to Pablo. The sudden break with Malaga, the family, grandmother, uncles, aunts and cousins, and the climate of the Mediterranean, was a first step from the provincial to the universal, from the warm, intimate nursery to a cold testing ground, where his love of the new and the vital, his eager appreciation of anything which breaks with traditional habits, suddenly became strengthened with a sense of independence and confidence in himself. He had already triumphed over his father, and at the age of fourteen was sure of his own powers and judgement. But his confidence had to be proved daily, questioned with relentless courage, until the game of confidence versus doubt became the everyday rhythm of his creative spirit, a game in which there is no promise of final victory, and in which the future is the only judge of how well it has been played.

In the academic drawings he had done for his father, Pablo had shown that he could copy accurately, and that he enjoyed doing so. It proved to be a valuable discipline, a training in the coordination of hand and eye, which made the hand the quick and unerring interpreter of observation. It became in itself a pleasure, like the athlete's delight in well-ordered and accurate movement of the muscles, and it also prepared the way for the flow of the emotions through the same channel.

But in addition to these exercises, Pablo worked endlessly on sketches of the people and the objects that he saw around him. His subjects were the fishing boats in the harbour, bourgeois families on the beach and landscapes of the Tower of Hercules, a Roman pharos on a rocky headland above the town. His favourite sitter was his sister Lola, of whom he made many drawings. She appears dressed in schoolgirlish frocks, going about her daily chores, helping the household by fetching water, or sitting happily nursing a doll.

There are in existence a few portraits of friends of Don José, which show remarkable maturity of style and which are certainly excellent likenesses. One of them is an unfinished portrait of Don Ramon Perez Costales, a minister in the first Republican government of Spain, who happened to be a neighbour and friend.[1] The personality of the old

[1] See *Cahiers d'Art*, 25th year, II, 1950, Paris, p. 296.

politician, with his billowing moustachios, his intelligence, authority and wit, stares out from the canvas. There is no hesitation in the brush strokes, and its execution would give satisfaction to many artists as the culmination of a life's work. The most impressive picture is a small painting of a young girl, with tousled hair and bare feet, painted in the last few months in Corunna.[1] With a freshness and sureness of touch, the girl is portrayed with strong accents and contrasts that suggest Zurbaran. She is seated in front of a plain wall, gazing at us with large dark eyes. The untidy shawl on her shoulders, her plain dress and bare feet, together with the austerity of the surroundings, speak of poverty. Both feet and hands are coarse, and contrast with the innocence and wonder of her gaze, the classical symmetry of her face and the sadness of her expression. The painting is wonderfully sensitive and cannot fail to impress the most academic judge of art, but already there are elements that betray an individual trend. The exaggeration in the size of the feet, the heavy ankles enveloped by her dress, emphasise her contact with the earth and situate her as one of those born to live humbly. She is at the same time prophetic of the beggars of the Blue period, which was to follow seven years later, and the colossal nudes which Picasso was to paint in the early twenties. Picasso still keeps this picture close to him. It is one of the many with which he cannot part. In it can be seen the great Spanish tradition of Velasquez and Goya, but it must be remembered that up to this date, Pablo had never seen any paintings beyond those contained in the churches, museums and art schools of the two provincial cities in which he had spent his childhood.

It is said that before the family left Corunna, Pablo exhibited a few pictures for the first time in a shop where various kinds of merchandise were for sale, including clothes and the much-needed umbrella. But in spite of the quality of his work and a short notice in the local press, sales were very few. Connoisseurs became shy of buying when they learned that the artist was only fourteen years old, but Don Ramon Perez Costales as a friend of the family accepted some small paintings as gifts.

The deliverance from this despised Atlantic haven came to Don José by chance. A post became vacant at the Barcelona School of Fine Arts, because one of the instructors there, a native of Corunna, was anxious to return home, and an exchange, financially advantageous to Don José, was arranged.

[1] Plate I, 2.

Summer in Malaga

In the summer of 1895 the Ruiz family packed their trunks and set out for their holidays in Malaga by way of Madrid. There for the first time Pablo had a brief glimpse of some great pictures. With his father he saw the work of Velasquez, Zurbaran and Goya in the Prado.

Reunion with the family was a delight to all. Pablo was still the only boy of his generation and in addition had developed to such an extent during the past four years that everyone was now impressed by his talent. He had always been a stubborn child with a will which had been strengthened by the indulgences of his doting parents and relatives, but now his achievements demanded respect. His black hair, cropped short, his round and regular features, protruding ears and burning black eyes gave him a look of devilish vivacity, well suited to his small and compact physique.

The intensity and blackness of Picasso's eyes are noticeable in the earliest photographs, and throughout his life they have struck wonder and fascination into all whom he meets. They appear to possess a power of penetration which can see beneath the surface of things, pierce their superficial coverings and lay bare their real identity. Age has not impaired their power. At times their blackness suggests a look of fear, a fear of what they may reveal, but they are also like fireworks, throwing out flashes in a dark sky: flashes of wit or anger that strike deep into the person who meets his glance.

That other member essential to the artist, the hand, is equally significant in Picasso. Small and well shaped, his hands are the instruments of his invention and the envoys of his sensibility. They can envelop a lump of clay, and transmitting his most subtle intentions, bring it to life in the form of a woman, a bird or whatever his imagination may dictate. They can draw, rub, smudge, tear, squeeze and manipulate with or without the aid of tools, whatever material he may choose to work upon. These two features, eyes and hands, are both inherited from his mother.

Although letter writing was as irksome to Pablo in these early times as it is today, he had devised a way of keeping the family in Malaga informed and himself amused during the four years of absence. He sent them letters in the form of a minute illustrated magazine, having appointed himself director, editor, illustrator and reporter.[1] He drew out the headings and gave his journal titles such as *La Coruña* or *Azul y Blanco* (Blue and White), in the latter thinking probably of

[1] See Duncan, *The Private World of Pablo Picasso*, pp. 134-7.

the weekly illustrated magazine *Blanco y Negro* (White and Black), but substituting blue for black with his characteristic preference for this colour.

The journal was copiously illustrated, and each picture given its explanation. The drawings referred generally to the discomfort of the climate. Men and women huddled together, umbrellas and skirts flying in the tempest, are given captions such as: "The wind in its turn has begun and will continue until Corunna is no more." Another page with the title "All in revolt" shows a band of active little thugs with knives fighting each other or threatening old gentlemen whose top hats spring into the air with fright. The sheet finishes with advertisements of his invention, such as: "We buy pedigree pigeons."

As soon as he had returned, his uncle Salvador at once began to think of ways which could help to promote his nephew's talent, and hopes were raised of fame for the youthful Pablo, in which the family could share. Don Salvador had on his hands at that time an old sailor, Salmeron, who was in need of charity, and killing two birds with one benevolent stone, he offered him to Pablo as a model. In addition he gave his nephew an allowance of five pesetas a day and a room in the office of the sanitary authorities. The result of this act is a portrait which is often reproduced, and may still be seen in Picasso's studio.[1] The old sailor was very successfully portrayed, but what caused consternation to Don Salvador was that the picture was finished far too soon, and he was obliged to search for other sitters.

Josefa Ruiz Blasco, Pablo's Aunt Pepa, was the third of the eleven brothers and sisters. She was the eccentric one of the family and had lived under the protection of the Canon, Pablo, until his death. After that she had moved into Don José's apartment in the Plaza de la Merced, and subsequently found a room for herself, which she decorated strangely with religious trophies and exotic bric-à-brac, very seldom allowing any visitors to penetrate her retreat. All agreed that Don Salvador's proposal that she should sit for her portrait was excellent, and Pablo, always eager to paint, consented; the only obstacle was the refusal of Aunt Pepa, who automatically answered "No" when a question was put to her. It was decided that the request would stand its best chance of success if it came from the young artist himself. Pablo went to call, but found her as usual in interminable prayer, and her "No" came with even more finality sandwiched between two Ave Marias. However, the unexpected happened abruptly, when all hope had been abandoned. A few days later, in the intense August heat,

[1] See Zervos, *Picasso*, Vol. I, p. 1.

Aunt Pepa suddenly appeared, dressed in her finest fur coat and resplendent with all the jewellery she possessed. Pablo was summoned from the courtyard where as often happened, he was playing with his sister and cousins, and reluctantly began the portrait, finishing it with astonishing speed, it is said within an hour. This picture also is still in existence.[1] It hangs in the apartment of Lola, Señora Vilato, in Barcelona. From a canvas darkened by age the pale wrinkled face of Aunt Pepa still watches the entertainments, the singing and guitar playing that the descendants of her family offer to their friends. Her fanatical eyes and quivering lips seem still to contain the same fervour sixty years later. Also the games from which Pablo had been called to paint the portrait remained as vivid in the memory of his companions, for he could amuse them in extraordinary ways by his skill. With a pencil he could bring to life with one continuous line the figures of people, birds, animals or what you will. They appeared with startling speed and exactness of outline, leaving his onlookers filled with delight. He would then say to them, "Do you want a little horse? Here it is", and with scissors he would unhesitatingly cut out of paper the most charming and lifelike animal which he would then present to the two little girls, his cousins.

[1] See Sabartès, *Documents*, Plate 9.

CHAPTER II

BARCELONA

(1895-1901)

Catalonia and Spain

IT WAS IN October 1895 at the beginning of a new academic year
that the Ruiz family set out for the second time towards the north.
Barcelona and Corunna are about equidistant from their native city,
and both, like Malaga, are active seaports. But instead of an isolated
rock-bound harbour, looking bleakly into an uninviting ocean,
Barcelona is a Mediterranean port with easy access to France and the
rest of Europe. Surrounded by rich country, it does not only make
these two other ports appear insignificant, but even rivals Madrid
commercially, politically, and as a centre of learning and the arts. Its
geographical position gives Barcelona advantages over the capital, its
interests lie with foreign neighbours to the north and east, rather than
in an exclusive loyalty towards the sovereignty of Spain.

In the last years of the nineteenth century, the Castillian grandees
surrounding the central government had been shaken in their hereditary
power by innumerable political rivalries and disasters, such as the
Spanish-American war, but they still showed no sign of wishing to
revise their ancient and unbending customs. Catalonia, on the other
hand, having suffered less from the war, and being less rigid and
conservative in its way of life, presented a more friendly and encouraging atmosphere to those whose traditions were liberal, and whose
hopes lay in social progress. A strong separatist movement had linked
this province for centuries with Roussillon across the Pyrenees, with
which it shared a common language. As the authority of Madrid
weakened, Catalonia became rejuvenated by a closer contact with
French culture. Once more, in the last decades of the nineteenth
century, the artistic circles of Barcelona were invaded by Frenchmen,
who immediately found themselves at home, whereas many Catalan
intellectuals who made their way to Paris never returned.

The turn of the century brought with it in Barcelona a thirst for
contacts outside the frontiers of Spain, and influences that seemed
even more refreshing came from countries further north than France.
Ibsen was widely read and acted in the theatres of the Ramblas.

Performances of Wagner helped to satisfy a yearning for romance which had its counterpart in the cloud-capped towers and cypresses of the paintings of Böcklin. These influences were equally popular and as easily digested as the music of César Franck, and the painting of Puvis de Chavannes. It would be a mistake to imagine that France, because she is Spain's next-door neighbour, is necessarily her next of kin. Germanic and Flemish influences abound in Spain in architecture, painting, and sculpture. There is a kindred feeling for expressionism which is to be found in the early frescoes of the Catalan primitives. Their saints are bucolic and uncouth, and they disturb the usual decorum of the Byzantine formula by outbursts of emotion that appear in their facial expressions and their gestures. The accompanying beasts and birds convey simple emotions of love and fear, symbolising the forces of life and death, good and evil. Death and the martyrdom of mankind are intolerable, haunting thoughts to all, but the Spaniard has found a permanent way of exorcising the spectre and depriving it of its obsessional power by exteriorisation. The invisible terrors of the unknown take shape in art and ritual. Once their appearance has become known and familiar their authority is diminished and they can be greeted, even applauded, like actors in the drama of life. To look death in the face continually, to become familiar with the presence of the unknown and to come to terms with its menace, is the rôle of art throughout the ages; a contribution eagerly adopted by religion as its adjunct, and accepted by philosophy as a natural medicine for the ailments of the mind.

Throughout Spain, artists of all centuries have delighted in this rôle. Their work, whether religious or secular, shows unity in a common desire to express the drama of life and death. Symbolism often takes the form of extreme realism in an attempt to bring home with greater force the eternal theme. Precious stones form the tears that stream from the eyes of Christ, blood flows from his livid wounds, trickling over his emaciated and half putrefied body. No artifice is spared in order to bring home the horror of his suffering. Other artists with the same end in view, the expression of human suffering, have employed less obvious but not less moving methods. The angels of El Greco mount, stretching upwards in a flight which will tear them away from the agony of those below. The bitterness of the colour and the threatening contrasts of light and darkness convey the anguish of the soul, just as the *Capricios* and the *Disasters of War* of Goya demonstrate in fable the reality of doubt and suffering.

Suffering is not only a permanent reality in Spain, it becomes an essential ingredient in all forms of art and also in the ritual of the Church and the bullfight. Suffering dominates, but its contemplation becomes a channel for an exuberance of expression. The corrida, flamenco dances and singing, the processions of Holy Week with their fanatical penitents, and even the convulsions of Iberian baroque architecture are evidence of this spirit which forms a link with the martyrs and devils of the Gothic North.

The Intellectuals Revolt

In the last years of the nineteenth century, the revolt against the dead hand of Church and State was widespread. In Catalonia the 'modern' movement had suddenly gained momentum. Groups of young poets and artists were boldly making their unconventional opinions known to the public. In 1894 the little walled seaside town of Sitges staged a solemn fête in honour of César Franck, Morera, a Catalan musician, and Maeterlinck. At a time when El Greco was shown no consideration in Madrid, two of his paintings, recently purchased in Paris, were carried in solemn procession through the streets, escorted by Catalan poets and painters, and installed in the local museum. Intense excitement continued all day in an orgy of speeches and readings of poetry. Casellas read a Pre-Raphaelite fragment, *The Blessed Damozel*,[1] followed by another poet, Yxart, who delivered a piece called *Impressions of Tuberculosis*. The Catalan poet Juan Maragall then read one of his melancholy poems about the silent flowers that stripped themselves of their own petals. Finally, Santiago Rusiñol, the painter, playwright, 'intimist' poet and symbolist, who had on his own account bought and presented to Sitges the El Greco paintings, pronounced "an enflamed speech in which he made disdainful allusion to the great herd, and said, notably; 'We prefer to be symbolists and mentally unbalanced, nay, even mad and decadent, rather than debased and cowardly; common sense stifles us, prudence in our own land is in excess. . . .' "[2]

The fête of Sitges was symptomatic. Such sentiments as those of Rusiñol, prompted by the writings of Maeterlinck, Ibsen and Nietzche, and well tempered with a native taste for romanticism, anarchism and individual courage, were shared by a vigorous and not untalented group of intellectuals. It was this group that attracted the youth newly

[1] Presumably a translation of part of the poem by D. G. Rossetti.
[2] Cirici-Pellicer, *Picasso avant Picasso*, Cailler, Geneva, p. 96.

arrived from Malaga. Thirsting for company that would help him to
free himself from the conventions of the provincial society in which he
had been brought up, he was shortly to find among them his most
intimate friends.

In the last decades of the century, the arts in Spain were being
strangled by academic prejudice and incompetence, starved by the
decay of popular art and threatened by a world that was taking an
increasing interest in commerce and scientific invention at their
expense. For those who were conscious of this growing menace,
hope lay in closer contacts with northern countries. France had
produced the Symbolists and the Impressionists, while in Germany
Wagnerian romanticism was in vogue. The influence of England was
important both on political and artistic grounds. Liberalism was strong
politically, and a liberal and humanitarian tendency pervaded the
significant artistic expression of nineteenth-century England, from the
works of the Romantic poets to the activities of the Pre-Raphaelite
Brotherhood and the writings of Ruskin and Carlyle. In addition the
stability of government, much envied in a country that had known
continual political upheaval, had its effect in the growing city of
Barcelona on various levels of society. The underpaid and under-
nourished workers sought employment in England, and returned with
views on democracy which they tempered with the Spanish desire for
individual liberty of expression. A widespread popular movement that
took the form of anarcho-syndicalism, influenced by the writings of
Tolstoy, Bukharin and Kropotkin, whose works were still on sale
in every kiosk along the Ramblas in the early days of the Civil War,
grew as a parallel to the intellectual revolution and influenced the trend
of its development.

Arrival in Barcelona

The city of Barcelona, having destroyed the limitations of its
ancient walls in the last decades of the nineteenth century, was ex-
panding with extraordinary rapidity, but the great square, the Plaza
Cataluña, which is now the centre of the city, was in 1895 still a
disordered fairground where booths were set up beneath the plane
trees. On the far side of the square, among groups of buildings that
began to invade the countryside, there was a hall that harboured a
splendid collection of armour. Don José, the newly installed Professor of Fine Arts, enjoyed paying visits to these attractions and would
stop on the way to examine with envy the cages of rare pigeons always
on sale along the Ramblas. Beside him walked his son Pablo, small but

well-proportioned, his round head covered with closely cropped black hair, his sun-tanned face lit up by eager shining black eyes that left nothing unnoticed, and his ears of a schoolboy, who has not yet slept enough upon them, protruding beneath his hat.

The pair made a curious contrast, and showed little family resemblance. Don José was tall. He wore a long overcoat and a wide-brimmed felt hat. The ample flourishes of his greying whiskers and reddish beard surrounded a fine straight nose and kind eyes sunk beneath heavy eyebrows. Their expressions were even more dissimilar. The distinguished, middle-aged man, slightly stooping, had a look of disillusionment, a sad resignation, whereas the small heir to his fading talents walked erect, alert like a young lion-cub watching all round and ready to seize any objective that might be captured by his intelligence and played with, tenderly or ruthlessly, according to his mood.

The family had found lodgings in the narrow Calle Cristina, in the old part of the city near the docks. The street itself was quiet, but round the corner was the continual coming and going of mule carts, trains, fishermen and white sailing ships that trade along the coast and across to Majorca. Once more they lived near the sea and, since Don José did not like walking, within a hundred yards of the School of Fine Arts.

The school occupied the top floors of an imposing building called the Casa Lonja, the Exchange. It was built on the site of a Gothic palace round a courtyard crowded with groups of statuary and fountains. Though larger and of greater prestige than the school in Malaga, it was no more advanced in its methods. The most rigid traditions and fustian gloom reigned throughout. The outside world was excluded so that the study of the antique, presented to the student in countless plaster casts, could receive all his attention. In the early stages, the pupil would sit on a wooden stool in front of a cast hung at eye level above his drawing board, on a wooden screen painted dirty brown. Day after day, hours would be spent in making laborious copies in charcoal on white paper of a fig leaf or a detail of classical architecture, until after weeks of careful application, the paper worn thin with continual erasures, he would be allowed to turn his attention to another cast. Finally the reward would be permission to graduate to the life class and full-size plaster statues. This deadly routine could be relied on to destroy the imagination and the talent of any student who was not a genius.

When Don José Ruiz arrived to take up his post in the school,

Pablo was scarcely fourteen, but although much under age he was allowed, owing to his father's pleas, to skip the boring initial stages and try his hand at the examination which would give him entrance to the higher class, known as "Antique, Life, Model and Painting".

The results were startling. The test, for which one month was prescribed, was completed by him in exactly one day, and so successfully that in his finished drawings from life he proved to be in advance of mature students who often found difficulty in reaching the required standards. Pablo's drawings for the examination, on paper bearing the official stamp, are still in existence. The undeniable technical ability they show is enhanced by a brutal disregard for the idealised classical canons of human proportions. As in earlier days, when drawing pigeons for his father, he had copied what he saw accurately and with no thought of flattering his model. The tousle-headed, black-jowled, muscle-bound, squat-legged little model is drawn with simple realism in all his pathetic nakedness.[1] There could be no hesitation on the part of the jury. They were at once convinced that they were faced, for the first and perhaps the last time, with a prodigy. Pablo was admitted. But to quote Molière, "to know all without having learnt it was one of the characteristics of great artists", and those who expected that a steady and methodical career as a student would follow this brilliant start were to be disappointed. A fever of drawing and painting had taken hold of him, and though he was willing to learn, what more had these conventional professors to teach? Without effort he had proved himself capable of mastering the academic standards required of a fully fledged art student, but the apprenticeship under the rod of academism that they proposed was no more than a step backwards for Pablo Picasso, who began life as a master. His friend Kahnweiler tells us: "He has confided to me that he does not like his pictures of this period, and considers them inferior to those he made in Corunna under the sole advice of his father."[2]

Science and Charity

The family soon moved from the Calle Cristina to another house in the same quarter, No. 3, Calle de la Merced, and Don José, always vigilant over his son's progress, found a studio for him nearby, in the

[1] Plate I, 3.

[2] D-H. Kahnweiler, *Picasso: Dessins 1903-1907*, Berggruen et Cie., Paris, 1954.

Calle de la Plata. For the first time, Pablo had a room of his own where
he could work undisturbed. The first picture he painted there is said
by some to have been called *The Bayonet Attack*, but if this is the case,
there is no knowing how the future author of the great paintings *War*
and *Peace* treated this subject in the first flush of juvenile enthusiasm,
for it has totally disappeared.[1]

However, another early painting, the first important work from the
new studio, exists in the apartment of his sister Lola in Barcelona.[2]
The finished picture has sometimes been given the title *The Visit to
the Sick*, but more correctly it is known as *Science and Charity*.[3] At a
time when the subject-matter of a picture was held to be more important than any other factor, Don José chose with care a theme which
would do his son credit, and so as to be closely associated with the
progress of the picture he sat as a model for a doctor at his patient's
bedside. The composition is completed by a nun holding a child in one
arm, and offering a cup of comfort to the sick woman. The dimensions of the picture are imposing. Its size and the consistency of its
accomplished execution are astonishing in one so young. There is,
however, little in the picture to distinguish it, except for its restraint,
from a competent work by an academic painter of the period. Other
painters of his time would have drenched the same subject in sentimentality. Pablo's version is a triumph of poise and discretion. One
touch at least is prophetic of later work. The limp, elongated and
graceful hand of the sick woman, against the white sheets, speaks in
advance of Picasso's feeling for hands, which emerged in the Blue
period and has remained characteristic of his work throughout. As so
often happens when one detail reveals more of an artist's originality
than others, it was this hand that was singled out by a scornful critic,
who wrote the following verse:

[1] One biographer describes this as a large canvas, so big that it had to be
lowered into the street from the attic windows with ropes, but Picasso cannot
remember this happening, and I agree with Barr that it seems probable that it
may have been a small picture, inspired by the frequent illustrations in the
press of those years, showing scenes from the early stages of fighting in Cuba.
But all that can be found to support this is a minute drawing of a soldier armed
with a bayonet, in the corner of a sheet covered with sketches.

[2] Here again, a legend has spread to the effect that it was painted over *The
Bayonet Attack*. This is proved to be incorrect, since the family well remember
the story of the arrival of an immense roll of fresh canvas, and the consequent
jealousy of Lola which was only cured when her parents offered her a handsome
doll as a consolation.

[3] Plate I, 4.

"I regret before such sorrow
To laugh like a brigand;
But the reason is overwhelming,
For does one ever see the doctor
Take the pulse of a glove?"[1]

Science and Charity earned for itself this doggerel, and also an honourable mention when it was sent to Madrid to the National Exhibition of Fine Arts of 1897. Later it went to Malaga, where it was awarded a gold medal, and afterwards found a home in the main hall of the house of Pablo's uncle, Don Salvador. There it remained for many years until it was installed in the apartment of Señora Lola Vilato, Picasso's sister, in Barcelona.

Between the ages of fifteen and sixteen, still influenced by his father and the academic background of his father's friends and colleagues in Malaga and Barcelona, Pablo painted several more subject pictures. *The First Communion*, which was shown in the Municipal Exhibition of 1896 in Barcelona, is now also in the possession of his sister Lola. In it, as in another large painting, *The Choir Boy*, the influence of his milieu is obvious. *The Choir Boy*[2] resembles in several ways a pompous canvas called *Acolytes' Pranks* painted by Don Rafael Murillo Carreras, the director of the Museum in Malaga who succeeded Don José. When a comparison is made it can be seen how the youthful Pablo knew how to purge his subjects of fashionable anecdote and sententious bigotry. Unlike Carreras' painting, Pablo's choir boy stands at the altar with no facetious hints or elaborate detail. He looks you in the eyes instead of glancing with sentimental piety at the altar, and he is clothed in a plain surplice and a red cassock too short to hide a pair of clumping black boots. Pablo has taken Carreras' subject and stripped it to essentials. The figure of the boy stands in the centre of the canvas in a way that recalls the *Expolio* of El Greco, and foreshadows the insistence on a central feature that we find in cubist paintings of fifteen years later.

Independence and New Influences

Pablo soon discovered that the studio of the Calle de la Plata was too close to the influences from which it was necessary to escape. Don José could drop in too often and give advice on his way to and from La Lonja. It was not long before he managed to move further afield

[1] Sabartès, *Documents*, p. 300 (translation).
[2] See Zervos, *Picasso*, Vol. I, p. 2.

and develop his own independence in his work. The first outstanding
example of a new style is a small painting of 1897. It is a sketch of the
interior of a tavern, painted early that summer.[1] The murky atmosphere of the room is lighted only by a small and distant window
against which the huddled groups of figures are silhouetted. The
picture clearly shows new influences from further afield, probably
gathered from reproductions of Daumier, and though there was little
chance of his being conscious of it at that time, there is an affinity to
the early painting of Van Gogh.

The work of a young and enterprising artist is bound to show
the influence of other artists. Such influences will multiply with his
desire to find new means of expression, and with the degree of his
understanding of what he sees. It is in no way derogatory that we
should try to link his work with the styles of other painters. Since the
beginning of this century a flood of reproductions has widened the
field greatly. The history of art is now available to an extent
that did not exist at the time of which we are speaking. Sources were
then more limited and discoveries of styles hitherto unknown were
continually being made. With his insatiable appetite for examining the
work of others, Picasso became conscious of new influences. Selecting
those that moved him most deeply, he did not hesitate to take from
them those elements which he needed, but in his expression the hall-
mark of his personality dominated. The stolen ideas were transformed
and assimilated so thoroughly that there was little occasion for them to
be claimed by their originator.

Besides those artists and styles that we know to have been admired
by Picasso all his life, there is a host of lesser influences which have been
seized on by him because of the way in which they have been a
stimulus to his mood. During the period we are speaking of, before he
first went to Paris, he knew little of the great movement in art that had
been going on for some years in France. What knowledge he had
came from a few friends who could talk about what they had seen in
Paris, and from magazines that printed the graphic work of artists
such as Steinlen and Toulouse-Lautrec. The painting of the French
Impressionists, such as Degas and Seurat, remained unknown except
from verbal descriptions until he reached Paris. There had, however,
been a considerable vogue in Barcelona for the Pre-Raphaelites, and
the young Andalusian had been fascinated in particular by the white-
skinned maidens of Burne-Jones, whom he had seen in reproduction.
The drawings of Beardsley, Walter Crane and William Morris were

[1] Plate I, 6.

also known to him through art journals, and slight flickers of their influences are occasionally to be found in drawings of these years.

In the early summer of 1897, some of Pablo's work was exhibited in Barcelona. Canvases such as the portrait of the *Man in a Cap*,[1] painted in Corunna, and more recent work were shown, but although the press gave notice of the exhibition there was no marked enthusiasm. He was still too young to be taken seriously, a fact which hindered the sales that his father eagerly anticipated.

Visit to Malaga

With great rejoicing, Don José and Doña Maria packed their trunks for their return to Malaga for the summer of 1897. Andalusian at heart, Don José had never really taken to Barcelona, where the Catalan language annoyed him, and the general behaviour of the people was too busy and casual in comparison to the leisurely warmth of the Malagueñan.

They were accompanied by Pablo and Lola, who went to stay with their grandmother. The young painter's success at La Lonja had already become known among his relatives. His uncle Salvador again saw the possibility of making him into a successful artist, and at the same time a respectable citizen, who would be a credit to the Ruiz family.

It was soon noticed that he took pleasure in walking out in the cool of the summer evenings under the trees on the Caleta near the beach with his cousin, Carmen Blasco. Smartly dressed, he wore with a flourish a black hat, from beneath which shone eyes so black that they appeared to burn with the reflected lamplight. He carried a cane under his arm with a swagger he had learnt in Barcelona. It seemed to all that he must be in love, and hopes that this, and his loyalty to Malaga, would persuade him to settle down in his native town ran high. The climax came when he presented Carmen with a superb bouquet, not bought at the florist but painted specially for her on a tambourine.

But the family was to be disillusioned. Pablo never did what was expected of him, and in October, when the holidays came to an end, so did the happy idyll. Pablo left his home alone for the first time, bound for Madrid. He wanted to see what this city could provide in the way of new experience, and whether life in the capital could offer more promise than in Barcelona or his native Malaga. This in fact was the last time he was to spend a summer in Andalusia, surrounded by the family circle.

[1] See Zervos, *Picasso*, Vol. I, p. 4.

During his stay it was made clear that it was not only his relatives who were impressed by his unusual talents. A fête was organised by a group of Don José's friends who met regularly at a club called El Lyceo. Don Joaquin Martinez de la Vega, a successful painter, had been told of the honours paid to the picture, *Science and Charity*, in Madrid. Another admirer was the old friend of the family, Antonio Muñoz Degrain, who had received as a Christmas present from Pablo two years before a remarkably lifelike water-colour portrait of Don José[1] which, with its inscription in the hand of the young painter, can now be seen in the museum in Malaga. In the elegant eighteenth-century décor of El Lyceo, beneath its painted ceilings and chandeliers, they assembled to baptise Pablo Ruiz Picasso, painter, with libations from a bottle of champagne.

Madrid

The Royal Academy of San Fernando is an austere and pompous building in the centre of Madrid. Its galleries contain several of Goya's great portraits and some superb small paintings by him of dramatic scenes of Spanish life, such as the bullfight, the Inquisition, the madhouse and a riotous procession of masquerading peasants. Velasquez, Zurbaran and other Spanish masters also are represented. The overwhelming weight of Spanish tradition, the forbidding darkness of the corridors, were no more in keeping with the visions of new forms of art than had been the provincial incompetence of the schools which the impatient youth from Malaga had already spurned.

Again his entrance to the Academy was marked by a performance of equal brilliance to that on his arrival at La Lonja. In a single day he executed drawings that satisfied the most obstinate of his examiners. By doing so he had, at the age of sixteen, exhausted all the academic tests that the official art schools of Spain could apply.

His arrival in the capital in October 1897 was his second visit to this city. On their return from Corunna two years before, Don José had found sufficient time to take Pablo round the Prado and point out some of its major treasures. But now for the first time he was alone, and desperately restricted in his means. He found humble lodgings at first in the Calle San Pedro Martin, in the centre of the city. The life of the streets and the riches of the Prado proved to be of far greater interest to him than the course laid down by his professors of the Academy. "Why should I have gone there? Why?" he asked his friend Sabartès in later years.

[1] See Sabartès, *Documents*, Plate 15.

That he worked is certain. Picasso has always worked with the same urgency that he breathes, but his poverty restricted his purchase of painting materials, and in fact, very few of the drawings and paintings he made during this stay have survived. It is possible that there may lie buried deep in academic dust, somewhere in the cellars of San Fernando, the works with which he passed his entrance tests, since it was only recently that the Madrid Museum of Modern Art discovered, hidden in its storerooms, a portrait of a girl by Picasso which had won a third prize about 1900.

Lacking further evidence, we can still gather an image of his surroundings and his poverty from a few sheets covered so completely with drawings that it is difficult to disentangle the figures of gypsies, pompous bourgeois, clowns, dogs, horses and scenes of café life. On one sheet, in the centre of which is a sketch of two men preparing for a duel with swords, he has written eight times, "Madrid 14 di Diciembre" in delicate flourishes, as though he were setting himself an exercise in calligraphy.[1] Perhaps this was the result of a moment of boredom, but it again reveals his interest in forming letters and figures, and his delight in watching a well-controlled pen make extravagant flourishes and curlicues. Also the date, which he usually adds to drawings before he signs them, has a special significance for Picasso. It records the movement of time and adds the recognition of another dimension to his art.

In another of these rare sketches there is a wooden stool and a makeshift round table on which stand two glasses,[2] set against a bare wall, evocative of the series of attics in which he lived, moving from one to another in the busy quarter round the Plaza del Progresso.

In the spring of the following year funds were running very low. His ambitious uncle in Malaga did not like the offhand way in which he believed Pablo had shirked his studies. For him, painting should be a profession which would lead to a position of honour among painters and society. What better start could there be to a successful career than the blessing of the Academy of San Fernando? He had before him the splendid examples of his old friends, Moreno, Carbonero and Muñoz Degrain, whose lifelike portraits of the aristocracy and colossal scenes depicting the glories of Spanish history had already won them fame which, he considered, should be eternal. Madrid was recognised to be the only place where an artist could attain the highest glory and fortune. In consequence, since his nephew refused to profit by his

[1] See Zervos, *Picasso*, Vol. VI, p. 11, No. 83.
[2] Ibid., Vol. VI, p. 7, No. 53.

generosity in the way he had planned, he showed his disapproval by stopping his allowance. The result was that the hard-pressed Don José deprived himself still further to keep his son alive.

But neither threats nor financial worries could disturb Pablo. Continuing to absent himself from the Academy, he enjoyed his liberty and the life around him in the streets and cafés. He became intrigued by the menacing darkness of narrow alleys and doorways frequented by a mixed Bohemian population, men and women who were undaunted by the state of misery in which they lived precariously. Their vitality was such that they were able to laugh, dance and sing in spite of the filth and hunger that would otherwise have swallowed up their lives. The poet Ramon Gomez de la Serna gives us this description: "Picasso wanders on the raging pavements of Madrid, penetrates it with the soles of his feet, discovers there that which will afterwards be the essential base of all his rebirths, the plasticity of the visible, whose hard entrails he will express in the first cubist nightmare."[1] In the streets where Goya watched and painted the revolt of the people against French tyranny, Picasso made his first lonely contact with the grim reality of poverty. Goya, a hundred years before, had witnessed revolutions and the end of a period. "He [Goya] had seen this terrestrial eminence which is Madrid, subtly lit up by the light of two centuries: the eighteenth century coming to an end, while the nineteenth was already announced, and from this he acquired a keener clairvoyance, a kind of double sight. . . . Picasso at the meeting of the nineteenth and twentieth centuries knows the ancient paths and from there discovers new ones."[1]

The winter had been hard and full of privation. In the spring Pablo fell ill with scarlet fever, and as soon as he was able he left Madrid and returned to his parents in Barcelona.

Though the exact date of his departure is uncertain, it could not have been before 12 June, because he remembers having been present at the celebrations which take place yearly on the eve of the feast of St. Anthony. The terraces between the river and the shrine of San Antonio de la Florida are crowded all night with a noisy throng of revellers. The dome of the little chapel had been decorated by Goya with groups of graceful and desirable angels whose models were the ladies of the court of Charles IV, and beneath it lies the artist's grave. Pablo's first exacting separation from his family and his friends, in harsh surroundings and the loneliness of the capital, at least finished

[1] Ramon Gomez de la Serna, *Le Toreador de la Peinture*. Cahiers d'Art, 1932, pp. 3-5.

with communal festivity in an atmosphere which recalled memories
of his great compatriot.

Horta de San Juan, Summer 1898

In Barcelona Pablo had met a youth, Manuel Pallarès, from the
borders of Aragon, who, although he was an indifferent painter,
had become a good friend, and has been remembered as such by
Picasso throughout life. The family of Pallarès lived in a village
of stone-built houses, crowded round the massive sunbaked walls of
the church. The surrounding country is rich in vegetation; wherever
irrigation can bring water to the parched soil it becomes a luxuriant
garden. Elsewhere vines and olive trees cover the hills that rise gently
from the valley of the Ebro. They are dominated by the angular
barren peaks of limestone mountains standing against the sky like the
walls of ancient fortresses. The sun relentlessly bakes and gilds the
rocks. Lying among foot-hills near the great river, the village of Horta
de San Juan[1] (Horta in Catalan means garden) enjoys the contrasts of
this marriage of fertility and sterile drought. In these surroundings,
which were to provide themes, ten years later, for some of the early
cubist landscapes, Pablo found the welcome he needed after the
privations and illness he had suffered in Madrid. Here he made the
acquaintance of the countryside for the first time, and came into
contact with a different kind of struggle for life, the enemy now being
the relentless and incalculable behaviour of nature, instead of the
severity and dishonesty of man. But the background of poverty was
much the same. Thrift and endless labour, the only means of survival,
had bred the taciturn race of peasants who now became his companions.

Pablo understood and even relished the healthy change in his
surroundings. He was eager to learn the crafts of farming. The skill
required to load a mule or yoke oxen, and the knowledge necessary
for the growing of crops or making of wine intrigued him. Owing to
his willingness to lend a hand in routine jobs he was able to boast later,
"all that I know, I learnt in the village of Pallarès".

At Horta he felt thoroughly at home, and he stayed on long after
his convalescence was complete. Many sketches are in existence of
peasants seated by the roadside, gypsies with shawls and flowers in
their hair, playing the guitar, and men and women at work in the

---

[1] There is some confusion about the name of this village. It was called
Horta de Ebro in Picasso's letters to Kahnweiler in 1909, but it is now known
officially as Horta de San Juan.

fields. They are drawn in fluent curves, with a feeling of tranquil assurance. There is one charming head of a girl, with her name, Joceta Sebastia Mendra, Horta de Ebro, Noviembre 1898, inscribed below.[1] It may well be that she was the cause of his long expeditions on foot to the only shop in the neighbourhood that could provide him with sufficiently elegant black velvet trousers.

When the heat became intolerable the two young painters found their way high up into the mountain where they lived together in a cave, buying food from a nearby farmhouse and making sketches of the pine forests while they enjoyed their isolation.

Return to Barcelona

It was shortly after Picasso's return to Barcelona in the early spring of 1899 that Sabartès, according to his own account, first met him at No. 1 Calle de Escudillero Blanco, a narrow street in the heart of the old part of the city. Pablo was using as a studio a small room in the apartment of the brother of the young sculptor, Josef Cardona. The other rooms were occupied as workshops for making ladies' underwear. Sabartès describes how "Picasso, in idle moments, enjoyed making eyelet holes in the corsets with the appropriate machines".[2]

Into the small room was crowded a mass of canvases, not only *Science and Charity* with its generous dimensions, recently returned from Madrid, but also another important work called *Aragonese Customs*, painted on the suggestion of Pallarès at Horta de San Juan. This picture has totally disappeared for the simple reason that like so many others it was painted over again and again, partly to save the cost of new canvases and partly because in his eagerness to realise a new idea Pablo could not waste the time needed to go out and buy new material. We know, however, that the painting was awarded a third prize in Madrid, and again a gold medal in Malaga, but the only remaining evidence is a caricature of it which appeared in a Madrid paper. The cartoonist had seized on the fact that in the picture a peasant with an axe looks dangerously as though he were about to decapitate a woman bending meekly beside him, and concluded that this was the reason for the title, *Aragonese Customs*.

More than eighteen months had passed since Pablo had been resident in Barcelona, and during that time he had greatly widened his acquaintance with the world by the extreme contrasts of life in the

[1] See Zervos, *Picasso*, Vol. VI, p. 17, No. 136.
[2] Jaime Sabartès, *Picasso*, *Portraits et Souvenirs*, p. 20.

metropolis and life in the depths of the country. He was now ready to start work in earnest and make his way among the seasoned intelligentsia of the modern movement in Barcelona. The everyday life of the city with the ceaseless activity of its harbour again provided him with an endless supply of subject-matter. He was living in the heart of a world intensely alive both day and night.

Beyond the Ramblas with their flower markets, cafés and endless stream of people, passing slowly up and down in animated discussion, is the so-called Chinatown of Barcelona, though the Chinese themselves are noticeably absent. On the contrary, nothing could be more Spanish than the narrow streets, crowded with various kinds of necessities, entertainments and temptations. There are restaurants where the smell of rancid olive oil and garlic perfumes the air with an odour peculiar to Spain; bodegas where the low vaults, packed with casks, ring with the passionate voices of the impromptu singers of cante hondo and the sharp punctuating notes of the guitar; cabarets that open their doors well after midnight, and fill at once to suffocation with those who love to bask in the sentiment of popular songs accompanied by a pianist; music-halls where the girls in low-cut dresses and high pearl chokers, or naked except for an embroidered shawl and jewelry, stand close to the footlights to put across the combined provocation of their voices and actions to a turbulent male audience; and, finally, brothels where in silence, without the accompaniment of song and dance, the most intimate desires can be fulfilled at the smallest cost to the purse if not to the health.

It was to these gay and sordid regions that artists and poets were naturally attracted, and in addition a revolutionary urge made it impossible for them to be indifferent to the lurid drama of life which was present all the time in an intensive form. The intellectual climate also was tumultuous, and above it could be heard the voice of Rusiñol exhorting his companions "to tear out from human life, not direct scenes, not vulgar phrases, but brilliant visions, unbridled, paroxysmal; to translate into mad paradoxes the eternal evidences; to live by the abnormal and the strange, to arrive at the tragic by frequenting the mysterious; to divine the unknown; to foretell destiny, giving to the cataclysms of the soul and to the anxieties of the world an expression excited by terror; such is the aesthetic form of this art of our time, splendid and nebulous, prosaic and great, mystic and sensual, refined and barbarous, medieval and modern".[1] These torments were in favour, rather than a carefully balanced, ordered approach to the

[1] A. Cirici-Pellicer, *Picasso avant Picasso*.

problem of life. The enemies were common sense and reason. In the belief that a new form of art should be born from the exaltation of anarchy, the Catalan modernist intellectuals echoed the cry of Rimbaud for a "dérèglement totale des sens". At the same time his challenge aimed at all existing values and his desire to transform life at its roots became confused in a romantic nostalgia, a "mal du fin de siècle". Rimbaud's anger at injustice and incomprehension became immersed in a torrent of words that bred ridicule rather than terror. The under-lying disquietude of the Catalan intellectuals was founded on the reality of a widening gulf between them and an unresponsive society that they felt bound to condemn. The role of the 'Poète maudit' spread both to those whose suffering was their fate and to the dilettanti alike. The poet and bohemian took as their chosen companions the political rebel and the starving tramp.

"Els Quatre Gats"

A group of paintings surrounded by sketches was the first exhibition to hang on the walls of a new artistic and literary tavern, which was opened in a small street near the Plaza Cataluña in 1897 by the genial Pere Romeu. The painter of these works was Isidro Nonell and the tavern was to become the famous cabaret of the Four Cats, in Catalan Els Quatre Gats. Both events were innovations of importance. Nonell's pictures formed a series which he called The Cretins. They were studies influenced by Daumier, of the old peasant women who were to be seen every day squatting on the steps of churches or queuing for alms, their faces shrivelled and their hands worn by hunger and drudgery. That they should appear on the walls at the opening was ominous of the trend for which the tavern was to become famous. They symbolised a new tendency in the art circles of Barcelona.

When Pere Romeu returned from a long trip, which included both Chicago and Paris, he did so with the intention of opening an establish-ment that would cater for the varied tastes of his intellectual friends. In Chicago, while learning about Sport, he had been greatly impressed by the possibilities of that symbol of the new age, the bicycle. Later in Paris, after an apprenticeship in the night life of Montmartre and the Latin quarter, he had evolved the idea of creating in his native city a cabaret on the lines of Le Chat Noir of Aristide Bruant, calculated to foster the most unconventional and creative spirits among poets, painters, sculptors, playwrights and musicians.

He chose for this purpose a new building in the Neo-Gothic style, with heavy beams and elaborations in carved stone and wrought iron.

The large room was to serve as a beer garden, cabaret, and concert hall, and also as a theatre for marionettes and shadow-plays directed by Miguel Utrillo. (His name has become more widely known in recent years through his adopted son, the artist Maurice Utrillo.) The painter Ramon Casas and Utrillo were joint editors of the art journals *Pel y Ploma* (Brush and Pen) and *Forma*. Small exhibitions were arranged. In the early days they were chiefly of drawings by Nonell, and clever portrait drawings, in the style of Steinlen, by Casas. The main decoration in the hall was a large mural by Casas of two bearded men, himself and Romeu, in white suits and black stockings riding a tandem.

The tavern advertised itself as a "Gothic beer-hall for those amorous of the North and Andalusian patio for amateurs of the South, a house of healing". The founders of the activities for which it became famous were men of Rusiñol's generation. His closest friends were Utrillo, Casas and the Basque painter, Zuloaga. Picasso, who was away at the time it opened, joined the group later as its "Benjamin" when its leadership had already passed into the hands of a younger generation. His talent more than filled the gap in years between him and his friends, and they at once pushed him into competition with artists of established reputation, in particular Casas, who was the accepted portraitist of the time with no limit to his clientèle. As a challenge, Picasso's unflattering but startling sketches of artists, poets and musicians were pinned up on the walls. The spontaneity and strength of his line, the unexpected flourishes, blots and scribbles, so convincing and so revealing of the character of the sitter, filled his friends with admiration. They realised that Picasso could easily surpass the painstaking work of artists ten to twenty years older than himself. But this early demonstration of his powers passed unnoticed by the outside world.

There is in existence a poster for the 4 Gats signed P. Ruiz Picasso which shows a group of elegant customers, ladies dressed in crinolines and gentlemen in frock-coats and top hats, seated with their mugs of beer on the terrace in front of the Gothic façade.[1] It is somewhat in the style of Walter Crane, and a figure resembling John Bull sits with ladies in the background. It is an elegant dream of a Bohemia, deliberately northern in feeling and very unlike the anarchist realism that was coming to birth in the paintings of Nonell. Later, in 1902, a much less stylised version was to appear, signed more discreetly with the initial P.[2] It is a pen drawing of a group of the real habitués, seated drinking

[1] See Zervos, *Picasso*, Vol. VI, p. 24, No. 193.

[2] Ibid., Vol. VI, p. 24, No. 190.

and smoking pipes around a table. In the foreground sits Picasso him-self, with black dishevelled hair, an untidy beard, large hat, overcoat and stick. Behind him is the long, sad face of Pere Romeu, smoking a large twisted pipe, and accompanied by the painter Angel F. de Soto, Jaime Sabartès and two others. A large dog completes the group, and above is written "Drink and Food served at all hours". Undoubtedly this gives a more accurate picture of the 4 Gats and those who so eagerly visited it, than the earlier version. The style of dress favoured by them was a proletarian dandyism. It consisted of a black hat, stock and high-cut waistcoat, loose dark jacket, and trousers that narrowed towards the ankle, and was derived from the costume of the anarchist agitators who were the heroes of the working class. There is a well-known portrait by Casas of Picasso dressed in this way, for although he was far too preoccupied with his work to take much interest in politics, a form of dress which distinguished him from the bourgeoisie was to his taste. From his earliest days Picasso nurtured a compassionate tendency which united him with the common people and led him to seek the company of those who were dissatisfied with a social system character-ised, as they saw it, by the greed and vanity of the rich and the misery of the poor. Beyond this, politics for him belonged to another sphere, and the language of politicians was as foreign to him as the speech of distant tribes. The political theories expounded by those who fre-quented the 4 Gats were based largely on Catalan separatism. For this reason alone they failed to interest one recently arrived from another province, and Picasso found that the anarchist doctrines which cor-responded more closely to his instinctive desires lacked sincerity when they came from a rich dilettante such as Rusiñol who risked nothing by his inflammatory talk.

The words of Jaime Brossa, a young anarchist writer, however, carried more weight. He called for a "courageous anti-snobism in art and life" which would defeat the "bourgeois and the philistine". In the review L'Avenue of January 1893 he wrote: "Man . . . comes to the point when he can no longer admit any hindrance to his speculations, and from this exaltation of the individual, no myth, idol or entity, divine or human, remains capable of opposing the absolute liberation of individuality—theories qualified by some as disruptive, but in which a negative spirit joins a positive spirit reconstructing and renewing lost forces." An echo to this war-cry may be heard forty years later in Picasso's remark: "My works are a summary of destruction."

In such theories lay the germ of convictions that in later years led the intellectuals of Barcelona to throw in their lot with the Republicans when their ideals became threatened at the outbreak of the disastrous Civil War of 1936, and also induced Picasso to declare his solidarity with them. When revolutions, dictatorships and war became realities he no longer wanted to retain his Olympian independence.

The position of Picasso among his friends of the 4 Gats became firmly established. He is "said to have been uncommunicative but of rare precision in his judgements. Those who knew him at once became his admirers or his enemies."[1] His shrewd wit could be devastating but he could also laugh boisterously at good-humoured jokes. Among the younger painters his closest friends were the painter Sebastia Junyer-Vidal, of whom he did many drawings,[2] "the vigorous and very talented" Nonell, the collector Carlos Junyer, the sculptor Manolo Hugué, the brothers Angel and Mateo Fernandez de Soto, the archi-tect and writer Reventos, the poet Jaime Sabartès, and Carlos Casage-mas, who was shortly to accompany him on his first visit to Paris.

The 4 Gats lasted only six years, but during its life it earned a great reputation, not only for the artists who were attracted by its atmo-sphere, but also for Utrillo's puppet shows and the concerts given by such distinguished young musicians as Albeniz, Granados and Morera. In 1903, after the departure of Rusiñol for Paris, Pere Romeu, who had married an English girl of whom Picasso made a very fine portrait,[3] gave up the management and returned to his passion for the bicycle. Although much loved he did not prosper, and died of tuberculosis in poverty a few years later. His tavern will be remembered for the turbulent and brilliant activity that centred round it and in which an unforgettable factor was the youthful presence of Pablo Picasso.

In this circle of young intellectuals robustness of spirit was not necessarily accompanied by good health. The distant examples of Baudelaire, Verlaine and Rimbaud had convinced their generation that the artist must of necessity be the prey of poverty and disease. Poverty was by no means unusual but disease was a commonplace and was suffered proudly, particularly when it took the form of tuberculosis or venereal diseases which carried with them a romantic aura. They were all the more likely to be contracted by those who were deter-mined to live passionately with little consideration for the con-sequences, and who accepted such doubtful rewards with pride. Neither was the aid of drugs left untried, the aim being to heighten the pitch of the imagination at all costs and if necessary at the expense of all else.

[1] Cirici-Pellicer, *Picasso avant Picasso*, p. 41.

[2] See Zervos, *Picasso*, Vol. VI, pp. 30, 31 and 33.   [3] Ibid., Vol. I, p. 63.

Sketchbooks

Ever since his return from the borders of Aragon, Picasso had continued to paint with increasing energy. Above all, his appetite for drawing was insatiable and kept him in a fever of excitement all day long; his hand, with amazing precision, was the constant interpreter of the vision of his greedy eyes. His sketchbooks contain an incredible variety of street scenes, bullfights, studies of cart horses, dock workers, men in boats, toreadors, beggars, coachmen; together with sketches made in cabarets, dance halls, cafés and brothels.[1] There are a few landscapes and views of house-tops, some nudes and great quantities of portraits and caricatures of his friends, most of them bearded bohemians, drawn with vigour and undoubtedly extremely lifelike. There are also many portraits of his family; his sister drawn with tender affection as she stands arranging her hair before the dressing-table, or poses seated in a chair; or his father, tall, bearded, elegant and distinguished. There are others where he questioned his own face in the mirror or from imagination saw himself standing in the street with friends. From an early date he was not content to see himself only as the reverse image in the glass, and anxious to know how he looked to others, he studied his own appearance from all angles. He knew himself and could describe what he knew. Sometimes he delighted in making himself look absurd. In this way some event that had wounded his pride could be laughed off by a caricature. He once drew in pastel a scene in the antechamber of a brothel where he shows himself, hat and stick in hand, presenting his excuses to a monstrous harridan seated on a couch, but there is no further explanation of why he should be doing so.

In addition to sketches rapidly taken from life, there are occasional studies for compositions in the classical style, set pieces which were suggested either by his father or his father's colleagues. But the desire to translate these subjects into large-scale paintings had passed, and on the occasions when he was tempted to start on themes such as "The Last Supper"[2] they were not carried further than preliminary sketches. A scene that never ceased to interest him, however, was the bullfight. Alive with the dramatic movement of men and beasts, the brilliant colour and strong contrasts of sunlight and shade, and the hysteria of the crowd, the arena seemed to contain, framed like a cameo in so small a space and limited time, the actions, the passions and the fears of

[1] See Zervos, *Picasso*, Vol. VI, pp. 32, 34 and 35.

[2] Ibid., Vol. VI, p. 10, No. 77.

daily life. Its appeal to Picasso was irresistible. "People think," he told me, "that I painted pictures of bullfights in those days after they were over. Not at all, I painted them the day before and sold them to anyone so as to have enough money to buy a ticket."

Some of the sketches of these years in which he was still not entirely free of his apprenticeship show evidence of the prevailing sentimentality of the time. Subjects such as the poor girl in a garret, kneeling beside the bed of a sick child, in his hands gain, however, by a tenseness in the pose of the girl and a severity of atmosphere.[1] Poverty, anxiety and sickness were real to him, and the reality he could give them as it grew in strength reappeared in his paintings of the beggars and the half-starved mothers with their children of the Blue period. On looking at sketches and paintings of these early years in Barcelona we find signs of an increasing awareness of the painting of others. The styles that attracted him, whether they belonged to the past or the present, were those which were unknown or despised in academic circles. Already in Madrid he had been deeply impressed by El Greco, and the interest that Rusiñol and Utrillo saw in his work added to Picasso's appreciation. In charcoal drawings such as the *Old Man with a Sick Girl*,[2] his adaptation of El Greco's characteristic elongations of limbs and heads becomes clearly visible.

Miguel Utrillo was an art historian as well as a critic with advanced ideas. He had travelled in Italy and at home he had discovered the Catalan primitive, Huguet. Picasso's interest in Gothic or Romanesque frescoes and polychrome sculpture, in which Catalonia is so prolific, dates from the period when Utrillo's enthusiasm was at its height.

About the same time, another influence came into Picasso's work. Barr suggests that Casas, "a clever and prolific artist in the line of Steinlen and Toulouse-Lautrec . . . encouraged Picasso and passed on to him the influence of the great French draughtsmen of the end of the century long before the young artist saw their work in Paris".[3] He also knew, through reproductions from magazines such as *Gil Blas*, the *Studio* and later the *Assiette au Beurre*, *Le Rire* and *Simplicissimus*, a great deal about the minor painters of France, England and Germany.

First Illustrations

In July 1900 a modest periodical, *Juventud* (Youth), which represented extreme "modernist and Catalan" views in literature, science

---

[1] See Zervos, *Picasso*, Vol. VI, p. 23, Nos. 180, 182, 184 and 186.
[2] Ibid., Vol. I, p. 183.   [3] Barr, *Picasso: Fifty Years of His Art*, p. 16.

and art, reproduced for the first time a drawing by Picasso. Very few illustrations appeared in this paper, and this one was done to accompany a symbolist poem by the now almost forgotten poet, Joan Oliva Bridgman, entitled *The Call of the Virgins*.[1] In the foreground of the charcoal drawing, signed P. Ruiz Picasso, reclines a rather matron-like semi-nude virgin, while there appears in a mist above her the ghostlike visitation of a muscular and desirable male. The following month, another drawing appeared illustrating a new poem, *To Be or Not To Be*,[2] by the same author. Here, in a stormy sea a man stands alone, steering his boat with a long oar through the tempest. The interest of these youthful drawings, the one symbolic and the other transcendental, lies in the fact that they are the first of so many drawings made by Picasso in later years in collaboration with his friends the poets. Whether or not he was inhibited in this first attempt by the sentimentality of the poems, both drawings are feeble in comparison with other work of the same period which remained unpublished and little known at that time.

Another review, *Cataluña Artistica*, on 6th September 1900 published a charcoal portrait of the poet Antoni Busquets i Punset, and a few weeks later, another illustration to a romantic and melancholy story by Surinac Senties appeared, with the title of the story in Picasso's own lettering and his drawing *La Boja* (the mad woman).

Life was not easy, and the small sums that these illustrations could contribute to his finances were welcome. But, unlike most of his companions, it was very rare that he helped himself out with commercial work. It is recorded that on one occasion he decorated the front of a grocer's shop in the Calle Conde del Asalto, and another time he made a poster for a patent medicine. Its qualities, advertised as an infallible cure for "lymphatism and weakening of the bones", were made unexpectedly attractive by a beautiful drawing of a wasting girl poised beside a seated pierrot.

Gaudi

A large and active circle of friends and a steadily growing reputation did not imply a comparable increase in wealth. On the contrary, even in a city where living was cheap, only bare necessities could be afforded. Picasso moved from one studio to another, seeking cheap accommodation for his work, and usually sharing it with a friend. There is a story of how he invaded the studio which was rented by a group including his

[1] See Zervos, *Picasso*, Vol. VI, p. 30, No. 245.
[2] Ibid., Vol. VI, p. 39, No. 317.

friend the painter Ramon Pichot, former pupil of Casas and Rusiñol. In a very short time after Picasso moved in the place became full of his materials, and his friends, including the owner, gave way before the urgency of his desire to paint and his indisputable authority. It became Picasso's studio. On that occasion all went well, but his ego-centric ways did not please all, and murmurings about his obstinacy and his disregard for the work of painters around him came from those who were jealous of his talent.

Later he settled in the Calle Conde del Asalto with the sculptor, Mateo Fernandez de Soto, who it is said contributed the greater part of the rent. In this narrow thoroughfare near the Central Ramblas, bordering on the Chinese quarter, the architect Antoni Gaudi had ten years before finished a palace of peculiar design that he had built for the Count de Guell, his most devoted patron. Gaudi is best known as the fanatical architect of the gigantic but still unfinished Cathedral of the Holy Family that towers over the modern part of the city. He designed his apartment houses, palaces, churches and parks with a desire to free architecture from the imposed rigidity of classical rules. Nature could give him, he believed, direct guidance in the construction and ornament of his buildings. Palm trees with their upright thrust and spreading branches, and snails with the structural economy of their spiral shells, became his models. From their example he devised highly original forms. His early work, such as the Guell palace, is heavily overlaid with decorative art nouveau ornament. Stone, wood, ironwork and mosaic are carved, moulded, beaten and twisted into the shapes of vegetable growth. The parabolic arches of its entrance are filled with heavy wrought-iron screens that suggest seaweed, and above, in the apartments and lofty music-room, there is an atmosphere of a magic palace, isolated from the busy street below. It is lit by windows that are screened from the interior by avenues of columns, and richly decorated in a style that suggests Venetian palaces or the harems of Istanbul. But Gaudi never travelled, and these in-fluences must have reached him through his patron, or more probably Ruskin, who was much read and appreciated by the intelligentsia of Barcelona.

Picasso had no particular love of Gaudi, though he admired his work, and he never met him personally. Gaudi belonged to another set and was thirty years his senior. He was a devout, even bigoted, Catholic, highly conventional in all ideas that did not touch directly on his art. As a member of the rival Cercle di San-Luc he disapproved strongly of the atheist, anarchist trends of the Bohemian 4 Gats. By

1900 his reputation was at its height, and so were his fees. An aura of snobism cut him off at that time from the younger generation, but in recent years he has been rediscovered as a great inventor by some of the most advanced architects, such as José-Luis Sert and a circle of admirers in Barcelona. It might therefore seem strange that he did not exert more influence over the young painters of his time. We must remember, however, that for painters influences do not usually originate in architecture but in painting. It happens more frequently that architects find inspiration in styles invented by painters. The art nouveau style of which Gaudi is one of the greatest exponents sprang from Ruskin and his views on painting, and later the cubists and the geometrical abstractionists were to be the source of inspiration for an international style in architecture. To Picasso, Gaudi whose work still dominates the skyline in Barcelona, is no more than a curiosity. The architect's problems are not necessarily the painter's problems.

Departure

As time passed and another summer came to an end, Picasso felt more strongly than ever an urge to escape from the surroundings of which he was again feeling the limitations. But there were serious difficulties in the way. Although he had liberated himself effectively from his family ever since he set out alone for Madrid, he still had a deep affection for his parents and his sister. He saw them almost daily, and would often stay to eat with them, making drawings of Lola and the assembled company seated round the table. They were unwilling to see him disappear abroad, thinking of the many painters who had left for Paris never to return, and what was more serious, his departure would mean a financial sacrifice they could ill afford. To the middle-aged Don José, who had by this time ceased to follow his son's restless search for something he himself found incomprehensible, the project was not encouraging.

However, among Pablo's numerous friends was a young painter, Carlos Casagemas, whose strange appearance can be judged from numerous caricatures. Tall, thin, with an enormous pointed nose dominating a chinless profile, adorned by scruffy side-whiskers sticking out from a high stiff collar, he is seen in one of Picasso's sketches, shambling along beside his friend, both well wrapped in overcoats.[1] After leaving the Calle del Asalto early in 1900 Picasso shared his third studio since his return from Horta with this awkward friend in the Calle Riera de San Juan, and finding its whitewashed emptiness

[1] See Zervos, *Picasso*, Vol. VI, p. 27, No. 219.

intolerably severe, he decided that they should have every possible comfort and luxury painted realistically on the walls. Appearing with magical speed, sumptuous furnishing soon provided for all their needs and desires. The bookcases were filled with rare volumes, cupboards, tables and easy chairs were spread around, a good-looking maid and a page stood waiting for orders, and fruit and flowers covered the sideboard on which coins had been scattered negligently. All this magnificence however was soon forgotten. In October the two friends decided to set out together towards the north to see and to conquer. Not long afterwards the studio was pulled down.

Unlike most of his companions Casagemas had private means which helped to provide for the expenses of their trip, and there is no doubt that Picasso, at least, left Barcelona in high spirits. Convinced of his talents, he had drawn a portrait of himself shortly before, adorning his own brow with the words YO EL REY (I the King) repeated three times.

I say their departure was towards the north, because Picasso assured me, when he was staying in London in 1950, that for him Paris was to be merely a halt on a journey which would take him further north, to London. The chief reason for this plan was that he had conceived a great admiration for England, partly because he appreciated his father's taste in English furniture and clothes, and partly because some English painters, especially Burne-Jones and the Pre-Raphaelites, whose work he had seen in reproductions, had a romantic attraction for him. Above all the project was due to the idea he had formed of English women, whose beauty, strength of character and courage had grown in his imagination to heroic stature. When living in Corunna he had come across the grave of Sir John Moore, and had learned that he died with the name of his love, Lady Hester Stanhope, on his lips. He had read her life, and finding a woman of a type so different from any he had ever met, a woman who had conquered her own liberty and also the hearts of men, he decided that he must investigate the country which fostered women of this admirable breed. History would undoubtedly have been very different had he held to this intention, or had the magic of Paris been less potent.

Paris

The visit to Paris, the first to take him into a foreign country, began within a few days of Picasso's nineteenth birthday. It was to be of short duration but of great importance. For the first time he made the acquaintance of the city in which he was to live the greater part of his life, and as usual, first impressions had that incisive quality which lingers for many years. Montmartre, where he was eventually to settle for nearly ten years, was his destination. He was guided by the simple reason that a colony of his friends in voluntary exile had settled there already, and contact with them not only helped to solve the language problem, but also gave him the information he needed to find his way about Paris. They knew the museums and the dealers' galleries, as well as the cafés and the streets. The painters Canals and Sunyer, and the sculptor Manolo quickly introduced him to the exuberant, untidy group of artists that frequented the cafés of La Butte. Manolo, whose wit was irrepressible and ruthless, delighted in introducing his silent young friend as his daughter, and Picasso's vehement protests were inevitably drowned by the chorus of applause that followed.

The studio where Picasso settled down to paint in Paris had belonged formerly to Nonell, who had reached Paris a year or two before. It was in a narrow street[1] near the summit of the hill on which stands Montmartre. This small detached community, which still prides itself on its own customs and its own patois, was in process of being absorbed into the metropolis. Recently crowned with the stark whiteness of the Sacré Coeur, it was slowly being robbed of its independence. The old vineyards, the worked-out quarries and paralysed windmills were vanishing, the slopes were being terraced for apartment houses, hotels, cafés and amusement halls, to accommodate the increasing crowd ot visitors who had been attracted to Paris by the great exhibition of 1900. However, La Butte de Montmartre still remained relatively detached and remote from the great city lying at its feet, a refuge for artists, poets and those of all nationalities who valued their independence and enjoyed the unconventional freedom they found there.

The life of Paris by day and by night, the streets glittering under the warm autumn rain, the din from market stalls and the clatter of horse-drawn traffic on the stones, enchanted Picasso and made him feel at home. Except for the climate these new surroundings were not unlike Barcelona and Madrid, but richer in their variety, more vital and more cosmospolitan. Here he recognised an atmosphere which would foster his development. He had come from Barcelona to escape the cramping influence of his family and the burden of provincial life. He was in search of a society which would in the widest sense nourish his ambitions as a painter, and he wished to see for himself the achievements of the past and promise for the future that this much talked-of Mecca of the arts had to offer.

[1] 49 rue Gabrielle.

Visits to museums and to dealers' galleries gave him for the first time an opportunity to see the work of Ingres and Delacroix, and to form his opinions on the Impressionists and their successors. He examined eagerly the paintings of Degas, Van Gogh, Gauguin and Toulouse-Lautrec. In spite of the shortness of his visit and innumerable distractions, he found time to paint several pictures which bear signs of the speed with which he could assimilate these new influences.

A few days after his arrival, Picasso paid a visit to Mlle. Berthe Weill, who ran a small gallery and who was to become Matisse's first dealer two years later. He was fortunate in meeting there a Catalan industrialist called Mañach, who had recently developed a dealer's interest in drawings. Mañach was immediately struck by the talent and character of the young Andalusian and offered him 150 francs a month for all the work he produced. In addition, Picasso succeeded in selling to Mlle. Weill three canvases of bullfights that he had brought with him from Spain. She gave him 100 francs for all three, and was glad to make a quick profit of 50 francs by selling them at once to a publisher, Adolphe Brissen.

Mañach's financial backing, though small, meant a great deal to Picasso, for at least it gave him a small degree of independence and allowed him to return to Spain when he wanted. Before he left, he painted several pictures of the life of gaiety and elegant debauch he saw around him. The Can-Can[1] and more important, Le Moulin de la Galette,[2] are paintings which show the influence of Toulouse-Lautrec. Since this was his territory, it was particularly difficult to see the same scenes he had painted with such verve without falling under his spell.

The Moulin de la Galette is a painting in the impressionist tradition. The subject, a hall crowded with dancers, with ladies wearing large flowery hats, is treated with flowing brushwork as a lively pattern of colour. The light seems to have its source not only in the festoons of gas lamps, but also in the colour of the dancers' gowns and the shine of well-brushed top hats. The techniques of the 'painters of light' had been seen and understood at a glance. Picasso had at once shown his ability to master a new style.

New Year in Malaga

In December the visit came abruptly to an end, though the reasons for the return to Spain remain somewhat obscure. Picasso himself has said that the main cause was his companion's despair. On arrival in Paris, Casagemas had fallen in love with a girl who in spite of all his efforts

[1] See Zervos, Picasso, Vol. I, p. 20.   [2] Plate I, 8.

Pablo aged 7 with his sister Lola.

(Translation of note written by Picasso: "Lola's dress, black, blue belt, white collar. Myself, white suit, navy-blue overcoat, blue beret.")

Picasso in his studio, 5 bis rue Schoelcher, Paris, 1915.

Picasso and Fernande Olivier in Montmartre, *c.* 1906.

Picasso and Olga Koklova in Paris, 1917.

Picasso as a Matador at a ball given by Comte Etienne de Beaumont.
Paris, 1924.

showed no interest in him. Believing that the sunshine of Andalusia might have a good influence, Picasso hastened his melancholy friend by way of Barcelona to Malaga, where they arrived on 30 December.

The New Year celebrations with the assembled family did not have the salutary effect that Picasso had hoped for. From the start everything went wrong. The inn of the *Tres Naciones* took exception to the two long-haired, uncouth Bohemians and refused to admit them. Picasso was humiliated by having to ask his paternal aunt, who lived nearby, to intercede with the landlord and act as guarantor. The next blow was when his former patron, his uncle Salvador, expressed violent disapproval of the appearance of his nephew. The long, dishevelled hair and the hat of an eccentric art student filled him with disgust. Picasso was quick to realise that a barrier had once and for all blocked the way between the conventional respectability of his family and his own ideas of how he wished to shape his life. He could see also in his father's attitude that there was no further hope of an understanding. The last disillusionment had come for Don José. His son had finally broken loose and would no longer accept the guidance that he felt he ought to give. His last rôle as a parent had come to an end, and he relapsed into old age, disillusioned and sad.

The last and deciding factor with Picasso was the conduct of his friend, who showed no inclination to be shaken from his suicidal gloom by the healing rays of the Mediterranean sun. On the contrary, he sought solace but failed to find it in the obscure depths of taverns, where nothing could remove him from the bottle.

At the end of a fortnight, all hope that any good thing could come from this situation had disappeared. Malaga had lost its charms and the memories of his past delights and flirtations had faded. Picasso once again took the train for Madrid.

That even in this short and unsatisfying visit he found time to draw, is proved by a charcoal sketch published six months later in *Pel y Ploma* of peasants sitting in a café-concert, enthralled by the music of cante hondo. It was in this tavern that he left Casagemas, hoping that the seduction of the guitar might eventually divert his thoughts. Nothing however could succeed and Casagemas, still absorbed in his unyielding misery, returned to Paris and ended the tragedy upon which he could not cease to meditate by shooting himself in a café.

Sabartès has commented on the restlessness that had taken hold of Picasso at this time.[1] He suggests that a reason for leaving Paris so

[1] Sabartès, *Picasso: Documents Iconographiques*, Pierre Cailler, Geneva, 1954, p. 51.

abruptly, deeper than his concern for Casagemas or his former promise to rejoin his parents for Christmas, was his hope that Barcelona, Malaga or Madrid might supply his need of somewhere to settle for a while. He had not yet thought of Paris except as a place to visit; it still seemed too foreign and remote. The climate and his memories had drawn him first to Malaga his native city. He now wanted to see if Madrid would yield more promise than it had done during his former visit. Whatever his motives, however, the result was a final break with the family in Malaga, whither he was never to return.

Madrid: Arte Joven

Picasso returned to Madrid no longer a student, but a young man who could already speak with the authority of one who has travelled to Paris. Finding there a friend from Barcelona, Francisco de Assis Soler, he entered into association with him in a short-lived literary project. With Soler as literary editor and himself as art editor, they set to work to produce a review to which they gave the title *Arte Joven* (Young Art). The first number was published on 10 March 1901, and on its first page it announced "*Arte Joven* will be a journal that is sincere". Soler had managed to become the representative for an invention of his father's, an 'electric' belt which was calculated to cure all ailments. The commissions from this life-giving source were sufficient to launch the review but not to sustain it for long. The last issue, which appeared in June, printed an announcement with a drawing by Picasso of a further joint publication, *Madrid, Notes on Art*. Unfortunately it never matured, for by then funds were exhausted and Picasso, abandoning the project, returned to Barcelona. From there he soon hurried back to Paris in response to the complaints of Mañach, who for some months had not received his promised pictures.

The review, of which only five numbers were published, was copiously illustrated with drawings by the art editor. The sketchbooks that he had filled in rapid succession in Paris during the previous autumn, and to which he was adding constantly, served to decorate almost every page. Throughout, the style was reminiscent of Steinlen and Toulouse-Lautrec. There were two self-portraits in charcoal.[1] In both he has kept his long untidy hair, and a lean, hungry appearance. With hands deep in his pockets he looks straight into our eyes with a sad, questioning regard.

The avowed purpose of *Arte Joven* was to implant in Madrid the Catalan modernist movement. It adopted the form laid down by

[1] See Zervos, *Picasso*, Vol. I, p. 22.

Miguel Utrillo in *Pel y Ploma*, which had also been liberally illustrated by its art director, Casas. His clever portraits, highly esteemed by the young modernists, were however now made to look conventional in comparison with those of his younger rival. In *Arte Joven* there was great variety in the subject-matter. It contained caricatures of friends, including a rapid sketch of a group standing together like conspirators,[1] and another of listeners to an after-dinner narration by the poet, Pio Baroja. There were scenes from the streets and cafés, with stiff, fashionable ladies in muffs and furs, gypsy girls and groups of peasants. The women ranged from the idealised Pre-Raphaelite virgin with flowers in her hair to the realism of the whore wrapped in shawls, waiting at the door of her squalid den.

The editors kept a close link with Catalonia. Translations into Castillian from the works of Rusiñol were published, together with a drawing by Picasso of the venerated poet-painter walking in his garden. In addition there were announcements of the activities of the 4 Gats. The tone throughout was revolutionary. Contributions came not only from Catalonia but also from writers such as Miguel Unamuno. A letter by Ramon Reventos to the intellectuals of Madrid was printed, as well as articles, nihilist in tendency, by Martinez Ruiz who advocated an abstention from the polls with "Kill the Law" as his slogan. *Arte Joven* proclaimed the revolt of a new generation, who prided themselves on their idealism and violence.

Barcelona: Exhibition at the Sala Parès

In Barcelona the impression that Picasso's talent and the force of his character had left had not been forgotten. Sabartès describes the days after his return in these picturesque words: "He withdraws for a few days into the calm of his home. He takes the opportunity, meanwhile, of disquieting us, his Catalan friends, who listen to him all agape. He goes around, up and down the Rambla, he gossips and makes plans. Like fireworks, he lights up imaginary constructions and shows new perspectives to our expectations."[2]

During this explosive visit, his friends, the editors of the review *Pel y Ploma*, organised an exhibition at the Sala Parès, a spacious gallery dedicated to the modern movement. The exhibits were all pastel drawings, most of which he had brought with him from Paris or Madrid. In June, the following month, Miguel Utrillo, the champion of the younger generation, wrote an enthusiastic article in *Pel y Ploma* signing himself 'Pincell'. It was illustrated with a portrait of Picasso by

[1] See Zervos, *Picasso*, Vol. I, p. 18.   [2] Sabartès, *Portraits*, p. 57.

Ramon Casas, which according to Utrillo describes accurately the personality of his young friend. He stands with the skyline of La Butte as his background. "Under a 'pavero's'[1] big hat", wrote Utrillo, "faded by the intemperate climate of Montmartre, with the quick eyes of a Southerner who knows self-control . . . his personality has suggested admirably to his French fellow artists the name of 'Little Goya' with which they have christened him." The editor of *Pel y Ploma* speaks with approval of Picasso's having left the autumnal influences of "the ardent country of dried grapes" and of having abandoned the lessons of the School of Fine Arts in Barcelona. "The art of Picasso", he continues, "is very young; the child of his observing spirit which does not pardon the weaknesses of the youth of our time and reveals even the beauty of the horrible, which he notes with the sobriety of one who draws because he sees and not because he can draw a nose from memory." Having spoken of Picasso's work in Madrid and the attraction of Paris, Utrillo ends his article in this way: "Paris, criticised for its febrile way of life, has again attracted him, not to make a conquest with the flourish dreamt of when he made his first visit, but rather with the ardent hope of learning from that centre where all the arts definitely flower with more fertility."[2] At the moment when this appeared in print, Picasso was already installed in Paris and a new epoch had begun for him.

The pastels shown at the Sala Parès had again a warm reception from the small group centred round the 4 Gats. They were mostly remarkable for a light spontaneous touch, and the deep glow of their colour. The fin de siècle atmosphere that dominates, suggesting above all the influence of Toulouse-Lautrec, is inclined to blind critics to the ingenuity and originality apparent in a variety of techniques. There is a pastel of a singer just stepping into the picture to make her bow before the footlights (now in the Museum in Barcelona), in which the background, composition and atmosphere suggest Degas as much as Lautrec, but the way in which he uses as colour for the long gloves of the girl the grey of the untouched paper, shows an ingenuity prophetic of future inventions.[3] There is a wonderful luminosity of colour in these drawings, which are usually focused on a single patch of light. In the *Woman before the Mirror*, the light, which is the mirror itself, glows with brilliant blue, whereas in the *Embrace*, a drawing in which two lovers stand united like one solid tree-trunk, it is

[1] One who feeds turkeys.

[2] Miguel Utrillo ('Pincell'), *Pel y Ploma*, Barcelona, June 1901, No. 77.

[3] See Zervos, *Picasso*, Vol. I, p. 15.

the blouse of the girl that lights the whole picture with its ardent red.

Most of the pictures are signed P. R. Picasso, for it was at this time that Pablo decided no longer to sign in the conventional Spanish way, with his father's surname followed by that of his mother. He preferred to drop Ruiz, which is by no means an uncommon name throughout the country, and use only the more unusual Picasso of his mother's family. This gesture also showed a disregard for the feelings of his father, and even more, those of his uncle Salvador. Both, not without reason, were proud of their family and wished to give its name every chance to become even more illustrious. But Pablo's affections leaned more naturally towards his mother. From her he had inherited his small well-proportioned and alert physique, his coal-black eyes, and hands so sensitive that they seem the perfect emissaries of his sensibility, receptive and creative, female and male. With a more subtle understanding of the extraordinary powers of her son, she refrained from advising and cajoling him. She combined patience and understanding with a fiery conviction that he would prove that he was right whatever he might attempt to do, and however mad it might appear. When his urge took him away again to Paris, his mother at least raised no objection.

CHAPTER III

THE BLUE PERIOD
(1901-1904)

Return to Paris

THERE IS SOME confusion as to the exact date of Picasso's return to Paris in the spring of 1901, but a drawing by him of his arrival accompanied by his friend, Jaime Andreu Bonsons, shows them standing together on the quay.[1] A bridge crowded with traffic, the Eiffel Tower and a passing Parisian lady form the background. The bearded Bonsons wearing a check cap carries a handbag, and Picasso holds a walking stick and a large portfolio under his arm. The way in which both are heavily clothed in overcoats—in fact nothing but Picasso's eyes and shaggy black hair can be seen beneath the brim of his black hat—suggests that the weather was still chilly.

The portfolio contained the drawings that were owing to Mañach. He had decided that rather than write letters of explanation he would bring them himself in return for the hundred and fifty francs which, in principle, he was to receive each month. Mañach, delighted to see his newly discovered protégé, welcomed him and offered to share with him his minute apartment at 130ter boulevard de Clichy. The flat, on the top floor looking south over the plane trees across the wide street, consisted of two rooms. The larger of them was to be occupied for the next few months by Picasso.

Thanks not only to a description by Sabartès but also to two paintings by Picasso, we can gain a good idea of the interior of this room and the view from its window. The canvas known as *Boulevard de Clichy*[2] is painted in a free impressionist style. The tall houses at the corner of the rue de Douai, reflecting the evening sunlight, are visible above the heads of little groups of people sauntering between the trees in the wide boulevard. There is space and life in the great thoroughfare below, but it is obvious from the other painting that inside the attic everything happened in a very constricted area.

This picture is known as *The Blue Room*,[3] because of a predominantly blue tone throughout; walls, bath-tub, water jugs, furniture, the shadows in the bedclothes and round the window are all blue. As we

[1] See Zervos, *Picasso*, Vol. VI, p. 42, No. 342.
[2] Ibid., Vol. I, p. 35.   [3] Plate II, 2.

see from the painting, as well as being a studio, the attic was a living room, bedroom and bathroom, often shared by Picasso with his model or his friends. On the walls above the bed hung pictures; a seascape and a painting copied closely from a poster by Toulouse-Lautrec of the dancer May Milton. A bowl of flowers stands on a small oval table; but the two chairs that Sabartès mentions as completing the furniture are not shown, neither is the disorder which he tells us grew steadily on the floor. Everything that found its way up the six flights of stairs stayed where it was put and each time it was necessary to clear the table for meals, more went on to the floor. The walls were lined with an ever-increasing number of canvases propped against them. None of this, however, appears in Picasso's painting of his room, which leads us to think either that it was painted before the disorder reached such overwhelming proportions or that the sense of order prevailing in his work has dominated in the picture in a way which did not entirely correspond with reality.

Disorder in fact is to him a happier breeding ground for ideas than the perfection of a tidy room in which nothing upsets the equilibrium by being out of place. As soon as an object has a place assigned to it, it loses its independence and becomes part of a decorative or utilitarian scheme, but when it is left just where chance has placed it, it can more readily call for attention and startle the onlooker into recognising its significance. These are the advantages to the observant eye of a practice which is considered slovenly by most people. Once when visiting Picasso in his apartment in the rue la Boètie I happened to notice that a large Renoir hanging over the fireplace was crooked. "It's better like that," he said, "if you want to kill a picture all you have to do is to hang it beautifully on a nail and soon you will see nothing of it but the frame. When it's out of place you see it better."

Exhibition with Vollard: June 1901

Mañach took the first opportunity of introducing his young prodigy to a dealer named Vollard, who had a shop in the rue Lafitte, a street that had become known for galleries devoted to the more advanced painters. Two years before, he had exhibited the work of Picasso's compatriot, Nonell. Born in the island of La Réunion, Ambroise Vollard had rapidly made a reputation as a friend of painters whose names are among the most illustrious of the time and whose works in many cases he was the first to show. He is probably best known for sponsoring Cézanne. Many others, however, such as Degas, Renoir, Odilon Redon, Gauguin, Bonnard and Rodin were among those who dined with him in his cellar, where he entertained with good wines and exotic créole cooking. His activity during his long life was not limited to the plastic arts, and among his visitors there were not only distinguished clients from many European countries and the United States, but also writers and poets such as Mallarmé, Zola, Alfred Jarry and Apollinaire.

Vollard speaks in his memoirs of a visit he received from his friend Mañach, whose factory he had visited in Barcelona. He brought with him he tells us, a young unknown Spaniard, Pablo Picasso, "dressed with the most studied elegance". Though this youth was only eighteen, Vollard says he had finished about a hundred paintings which he brought with him with a view to an exhibition. When he saw them his usual caution disappeared and he agreed without hesitation. But this time, in spite of the prestige that accompanied exhibitions in his gallery, the experiment was not a success, and, he adds, "for a long time Picasso got no better reception from the public. . . . I have had in my shop many of his pictures which are the most sought-after today, but for which the artist at that time could not obtain the price of a stretcher."

For this exhibition, which opened on 24 June, the gallery was shared with a Basque painter of no great interest, named Iturrino, who was nearly twenty years Picasso's senior and whose name preceded his on the printed announcements. However, the works of the younger artist, which numbered seventy-five, were noticed by Felicien Fagus, the critic for *La Gazette d'Art*.

"Picasso is a painter, absolutely and beautifully; his power of divining the substance of things should suffice to prove it", he wrote appreciatively. "Like all pure painters he adores colour in itself and to him each substance has its own colour. Also he is in love with every subject and to him everything is a subject; the flowers that gush forth furiously from a vase towards the light, the vase alone, and the table that carries the vase and the luminous air that dances around; the multicoloured seething crowds backed by the verdure of a racecourse or the sunlit sand of an arena; the nudity of the bodies of women . . . there are discoveries: three little girls dancing, the practical green skirt over white underclothes which are so exactly that stiff boyish white of little girls' starched petticoats; the yellow and white of a woman's hat, etc. . . . Thus just as in a subject everything is his subject, so everything is worth translating, even slang, a Gongorism—that other form of slang—or the neighbour's dictionary. One can easily perceive many a probable influence apart from that of his own great ancestry: Delacroix,

Manet, Monet, Van Gogh, Pissarro, Toulouse-Lautrec, Degas, Forain, Rops, others perhaps. . . . Each one a passing phase, taking flight again as soon as caught. It is evident that his passionate surge forward has not yet left him the leisure to forge for himself a personal style; his personality exists in this passion, this juvenile impetuous spontaneity (they say that he is not yet twenty and that he covers as many as three canvases a day). Danger lies for him in this very impetuosity which can easily lead him into a facile virtuosity. The prolific and the fecund are two different things, like violence and energy. This would be much to be regretted since we are in the presence of such brilliant virility."[1]

The enthusiasm of Fagus led him to judge the work of the young painter from the standards he knew and loved best, which were based on the impressionist point of view. He talks of the "luminous air" that surrounds the flowers in the numerous flower pieces, a phrase that came direct from his love of atmospheric effects cherished by the "painters of light". The shadows he noticed were made mysterious with blue transparency. But also he remarks that Picasso's love of colour led him to insist that "each substance has its own colour". The green lawns of Longchamp or the red blouse of a woman were vivid, glowing patches that radiate from their local source a light which permeates the whole picture, reminding us rather of the discoveries of Van Gogh and Gauguin than the cloudy depths of Monet.

Picasso had seized eagerly on a mixture of techniques and exploited each in his own way. In the portrait of The Dwarf Dancer[2] of 1901 he had applied colour in small spots in a manner that recalls 'pointillism', but the painstaking atmospheric modulations of Seurat were sacrificed for a cloud of speckled brilliance which enlivens the colours of the dwarf's dress and falls in cascades around her, giving both depth and movement to her background. With this the borrowed pointillist discipline was abandoned. In the same picture the face, arms and legs are painted in another style, more in the manner of Toulouse-Lautrec. The result might be expected to present disastrous inconsistencies and surprisingly it does not. Picasso had shown his ability to steal what interested him from different styles and put the loot together so that it became his own harmonious creation.

In the paintings of this period influences abound. Sometimes it is the subject-matter of Degas, the racecourse or the nude girl washing in a zinc bath tub that he has seized upon; or an interior that recalls

[1] Felicien Fagus, Gazette d'Art, quoted in Cahiers d'Art, 1932, Nos. 3-5, with reference to first Picasso Exhibition, Vollard Gallery, June 1901.
[2] See Zervos, Picasso, Vol. I, p. 31.

Vuillard; or a cabaret scene with dancers in swirling skirts, their black stockings kicking wildly, which inevitably brings to mind the manner of Toulouse-Lautrec; but always, mixed with his feverish spontaneity, there is a control by which he is able to accentuate contrasts and a sense of order with which he places the accents. Our pleasure is divided between surprise at the originality of their position and satisfaction in the arrangement of the composition.

Work of the Cabaret Period

On his return, Picasso had begun where he had broken off six months before, but with more assurance. The people among whom he lived furnished him with an inexhaustible source of material which he sought to express with tenderness or with cynicism. He made sketches of children sailing their boats, leisurely crowds enjoying the Luxembourg Gardens, the brilliant fashions of ladies on the racecourse, or the prim midinette seated on the deck of a bateau mouche, and produced pictures full of an atmosphere of pleasant ease.

A more lurid world of night life also attracted his prying eye and many paintings of the early months of this visit are a continuation of the scenes in cafés and cabarets begun in Barcelona, though with a more developed critical sense and a cynicism which attacked the frivolous orgies of the rich. There are several versions of a dinner table scene with an over-fed opulent rake, seated with a bejewelled woman whose splendour seems to overpower her benefactor. There are scenes in theatres where rows of gaping starched shirt-fronts are faced by the charms of a fragile siren, and many portraits of ladies of the demi-monde and young girls. These were often started from rapid sketches made back-stage between the acts in the popular music-halls, becoming later magnificent portraits such as the *Courtesan with the Jewelled Necklace*.[1] Between the splendid arabesque of her feathered hat and the low-cut curve of the dress, he painted an expressionless mask with drowsy sensuous eyelids. The head is poised on a trelliswork tower made of gaudy jewelry encircling her long neck. With plump fingers, rounded like the teats of a cow and crowded with rings, she caresses her own bare shoulder. Although there seems no doubt about the apparent firmness of her flesh, Picasso has arrived at this effect without the use of modelling. The roundness of the form is conveyed by the bold sweep of the curved outline set between the elliptical shapes of the hat above and the décolleté below. Bold heavy brushwork and outlining show here and in many other paintings of

[1] Plate II, 9.

this period that, as Picasso has himself said, the influence of Van Gogh was then stronger than that of any other painter. The simplicity with which the head is treated conveys by understatement the arrogance of the lady. Her vulgar beauty, flattered by its adornments, is treated by the artist with a harshness which gives her an appearance of superb self-assurance—a brazen look amounting almost to innocence.

This capacity to depict character in surprisingly unconventional ways recurs in other portraits. Thanks to the Vollard exhibition, Picasso had met Gustave Coquiot, a shrewd critic and enthusiastic collector, and shortly afterwards he painted two portraits of him.[1] In one, Coquiot is seated in front of pictures from his own collection; and in the other, dressed for debauchery, he sits in front of a mirror reflecting a bacchanalian cabaret show. Two other friends of Picasso's also served as models for remarkable character studies, Mateo F. de Soto and Jaime Sabartès. Both had followed him from Barcelona and were his constant companions. The portrait of de Soto is extraordinary for the severity of the expression of the young painter.[2] His eyes, deep, sad and thoughtful, the severe ascetic frown beneath his neatly trimmed moustache and his small pointed beard give him the sad fanatical expression of Zurbaran's monks.

Sabartès has described at length the painting of two portraits of himself during this visit to Paris. The first, soon after his arrival, came as a surprise. Picasso, arriving late for the rendez-vous, had come upon Sabartès without his friend's seeing him from where he sat waiting at a café table, shortsighted and embarrassed. On returning to his studio Picasso painted a portrait[3] which was later bought by Sergei Shchukine, the Russian collector. It is Sabartès, the young poet in a foreign land, nervously fingering his mug of beer while his myopic gaze searches the café for his friends. The portrait was an admirable likeness, but, as has happened so often, it was painted by Picasso while the model was absent.

Sabartès had arrived in Paris in the late autumn, some six months after Picasso. When he first climbed to the top floor of the house in the boulevard de Clichy, he was astonished at the quantity of canvases he found there in a style which he could not fathom. When Picasso asked him what he thought, he answered loyally, "I shall get used to it . . .". There was a greater distinction between these paintings and the former work done in Spain than any of his former changes of domicile had brought about. "The canvases that he showed me", Sabartès explains, "had violent contrasts in tone and in colour, like the shades of playing

[1] See Zervos, *Picasso*, Vol. I, p. 42.   [2] Ibid., Vol. I, p. 43.   [3] Plate II, 1.

cards."[1] In particular Sabartès was struck by the vivid colouring in the portrait of Coquiot.

Picasso did not let his work exclude visits to the museums, which were one of his chief amusements during these early days in Paris. By this time he knew his way round most of them. He spent long hours with the Impressionist paintings in the Luxembourg and he was often seen in the Louvre, where he was much intrigued by the Egyptian and Phoenician art styles, which in those days were generally considered barbaric. The Gothic sculpture of the Musée de Cluny called for careful scrutiny and he was aware in a more distant way of the charm of Japanese prints. They had already been in vogue for some years and therefore interested him less. It gave him greater satisfaction to discover things not yet noticed by others.

The summer and autumn of 1901 had been a period of fruitful exploration and experiments in the adaptation of borrowed techniques. He had learned much by copying indirectly and by transposing the work of masters he admired. By the time his twentieth birthday arrived in October he had already accomplished a vast quantity of work of remarkable quality. The stage was now set for the development for the first time of a style which would be thoroughly personal.

Max Jacob

The exhibition at Vollard's gallery, even if it had pleased no more than a few critics and collectors, was the source of new friendships. A young man, whose immaculate top hat and conventional elegance served as an effective disguise for extreme poverty, had called at the gallery. Max Jacob, the poet, painter and art critic, born in Brittany of Jewish parents, was immediately struck by the brilliance of the work of this young and unknown foreigner. He described years later the beginning that same day of an extraordinary friendship between them, which was to continue until his death in 1944 in a Nazi concentration camp. "At the time of his great and first exhibition, as a professional art critic I had been so struck with wonder at his production that I left a word of admiration with Ambroise Vollard. And the same day I received from M. Mañach, who looked after his interests, an invitation to visit him. Already this first day, we felt for each other a great sympathy." Max Jacob continues: "He was surrounded by a swarm of poor Spanish painters, who sat on the floor eating and chatting. He painted two or three pictures a day, wore a top hat like me and spent his evenings in the coulisses of the music halls of those days, drawing

[1] Sabartès, *Portraits*, p. 68.

portraits of the stars. . . . He talked very little French and I no Spanish but we shook hands."[1]

From that moment a friendship united these two men who were in many ways so unlike, but who found in each other a fundamental and instinctive understanding. Max Jacob, the mystic, was a man stricken with an overwhelming desire to enjoy life and a compensating sense of sin that led him to the severest penances and a final renunciation of the world in a monastery. He was moreover endowed with a sensibility which responded both in poetry and painting to the same human drama which was tormenting the spirit of the young Spaniard. His friend, André Billy, describes the character of Max Jacob in these words: "Malice, ingenuity, covetousness, melancholy, irony, sweetness, goodness, cruelty, salaciousness; all that you will, except innocence, simplicity, lightheartedness, true gaiety, severity, incapacity to understand. Except saintliness, I should be tempted to add if I relied only on my most distant memories."[2]

At the first meeting a return visit was planned, and Max eagerly welcomed the boisterous crowd of Spaniards to his small hotel room. By this encounter 'la bande Picasso' had enlisted a new member, one who brought with him the element of French culture which had formerly been lacking. In rooms hermetically sealed against the cold and filled with smoke, he would read to them late into the night his own poems and also those of poets of the nineteenth century, almost unknown to them except by their reputation—Baudelaire, Verlaine and Rimbaud. The barriers of language melted rapidly before their enthusiasm and his eloquence.

Decoration of Le Zut

At night there were frequent visits to the cabarets of Montmartre such as the Chat Noir, and, when tickets could be found, to the Moulin Rouge. Paris seduced the lawless Spaniards by its frivolity and its elegance. The ladies of all classes tried to outdo each other in the width of their hats and the narrowness of their waists, while the men considered themselves dishonoured to be seen without top hats. Max Jacob tells us that Picasso wore a top hat like him, and this is borne out by a self-portrait sketch in which Picasso tries the effect of his evening clothes, complete with hat, silk scarf and camellia, on a bevy of half-nude young ladies. But such extravagances were rare, the establishments

[1] *Correspondance de Max Jacob*, Editions de Paris, Paris, 1953, p. 29.

[2] *Max Jacob*, by André Billy, Pierre Seghers, Paris, 1953.

where Picasso could usually be found with his friends were extremely modest. For a while the headquarters of 'la bande' was a small bohemian cabaret in the place Ravignan, called Le Zut. Its dim passages and stained walls lit with candles attracted a mixed bag of artists of all descriptions, pimps, and girls of varied occupations. Sabartès describes how night after night they would meet in a small room where the amiable *patron* Fredé would serve their drinks, usually beer or cherries in brandy, on a barrel, and entertain them with his songs and the guitar. They remained aloof from the Parisian sociability that went on noisily in the room beyond, peering round the corner to watch when some unusually exciting dancing or fighting drew their attention away from their own interminable discussions. Picasso would sit and listen, taking part only when some terse remark of his could give a startling explanation or add a provocative paradox.

Eventually the squalor of the sweating walls and the cobwebs brought about a revolt and the Spaniards decided to decorate the room, which they had named the Hall of the Stalactites. After the walls had been whitewashed, they each decorated a panel exactly as they felt inclined. Pichot drew the Eiffel Tower with the dirigible of Santos-Dumont flying above it, and Picasso rapidly sketched in some female nudes. "The temptation of St. Anthony!" shouted someone as a bright guess at what was coming. The interruption had the effect of stopping Picasso. The composition interested him no longer.

Sabartès tells how later he finished the panel by improvising something quite different with extraordinary speed. His description of Picasso at work is not the only one given by him or by friends who have watched him. In general he does not allow others to be present when he is painting, but all who have been admitted have been impressed by the completeness of his concentration, whether the work in question is of importance or relatively trivial. The line becomes visible in the exact place where it is required with such certainty that it is as though he were communing with a presence already there. Maurice Raynal, his lifelong friend, speaks of how, in a trancelike state, he "injects his very life-blood" into the lines drawn by his brush, and Sabartès says, "he is so wrapped in thought and so intensely plunged into silence that anyone seeing him, from near or from far, understands and is silent".

Departure for Barcelona

As winter approached Picasso's friends noticed a change in his humour, he became morose. With or without excuses he would

disappear from their company, and a coldness between him and Mañach
appeared, inexplicable but ominous. Paris was losing its initial charm.
He had tasted its glamour and its squalor, and, quick to appreciate the
value of such experience without becoming saturated, Picasso decided
he needed a change. One day his usual practice of hiding his intentions
from even his closest friends—often because he is himself undecided
up to the very last moment—broke down, and he announced that he
was planning to leave Paris shortly. All he was waiting for was a letter
from his father. The moment this arrived and the way was open for his
departure he no longer tried to hide his dissatisfaction with the overcrowded lodgings provided by Mañach. Much to his friend's distress,
this brought to an end their close association and Picasso's second visit
to Paris.

The Blue Period

The picture called *The Blue Room* to which I have referred is one
of the first in which Picasso's natural predilection for blue led him,
over a period of several years, to choose this colour for the leading
rôle in his palette. About the same time he painted a composition
important both in size and content. The subject was one that had been
haunting him for some months. It has since been given the title
Evocation, but to his friends it was known as *The Burial of Casagemas*.[1]
Sabartés says that when he arrived in Paris this canvas, owing to its
ample dimensions, was used as a screen to hide a pile of miscellaneous
objects in the corner of the attic studio. It was in consequence the most
conspicuous picture in the room and the most permanently on view.

A study for this painting, nearly as large, also exists. The subject is a
group of mourners with bowed heads standing round the shrouded
corpse of a man laid out in the foreground. In the larger picture this
group, while similar in arrangement, has dwindled in importance, and
a stone sepulchre has been added on the right. The grief-stricken figures
and the corpse in its winding-sheet, however, are dwarfed by a great
expanse of sky. In a vaporous turmoil that recalls El Greco, allegorical
figures float among the clouds. The central position is occupied by a
white horse, which echoes the whiteness of the shroud below. It carries
a shadowy rider, almost entirely hidden by a woman who supports
him in her arms. Round about are three detached groups of women: a
mother accompanied by her children; two women united in a close
embrace; and seated on a cloud, a group of girls naked but for their
red and black stockings. Apart from the contradictory manner in which

[1] Plate I, 9.

the transcendental trends of the picture are contradicted by details reminiscent of the circus or the brothel, and the awkwardness of the disjointed composition, in which the groups are held together only by the rhythmic turbulence of the background, a feature of more subtle interest is the treatment of the heavily-draped figures of the mourners. In both versions their statuesque shapes announce the emergence of a new and more personal style. Their restricted gestures, smothered within the dark blue folds of their robes, emphasise the depths of their sorrow. Static, monolithic, they have the appearance of spirits imprisoned in rocks and trees. The shimmering atmospheric light of the impressionists has given place to a representation of solid form.

These two pictures are the first that show Picasso's new discovery of plastic form and the beginnings of a symbolism of his own. They mark the final crisis of his adolescence and his triumph over the influences of his family. The subject was one that had affected him personally and deeply. He had watched closely a drama which gave him a brutal sense of the conflict between life and death and raised the question of a resurrection. He had lived through his friend's tragedy so closely that it had become his own, and his new problem was to find adequate ways of expression. Already he knew the pitfalls of sentimentality and romantic symbolism. To avoid them in the painting he had introduced the bawdy detail of the coloured stockings for the celestial chorus girls. As a check to the transcendental flight of his imagination he kept an anchor firmly fixed in mundane reality, using his sense of the comic as a life-line. Since he had been led to descend into Hades it was essential for him to discover his own salvation. The rider on the white horse mounting into the clouds and the huddled mourner below were both subconsciously symbols of himself.

The marked duality of his character was early noticed by his friend Maurice Raynal, whom he met in Paris the following year. Years later Raynal wrote: "Unfamiliar as we were with the Spanish turn of mind, Picasso seemed to us to move within an aura of mystery. We marvelled at the contrast between the gravity of his art, now brooding, now flaring up dramatically, and the genial good nature of the man himself, his effervescent sense of humour and love of a good joke. It was known, of course, that now and then he fell prey to those typical Spanish fits of depression that usually came when least expected; but not realising how deep they went, we put them down to the vicissitudes of bohemian life in Paris."[1] The exuberance of his vitality coupled with the depth of his sensibility made it possible for him to live through

[1] Maurice Raynal, *Picasso*, Editions d'Art Albert Skira, Geneva, 1953.

misery and create the style which in the next four years was to begin to bring him universal fame.

Certain writers, such as Gertrude Stein, have attributed the change in Picasso's style which resulted in the Blue period to his return to Barcelona and to purely Spanish influences. When they do so, they overlook the fact that besides *Evocation* several important works had been painted during his stay in Paris in 1901. These include some versions of the theme of Mother and Child; the painting *Harlequin leaning on his elbow*;[1] the portrait of the *Woman with a Chignon*,[2] with her head resting wearily on both hands; the *Child holding a dove*,[3] fresh and tender in its allusions; and also a remarkable *Self-portrait*[4] in which, hungry, muffled to the chin in his overcoat, Picasso looks straight out with eyes that are sad, disillusioned, but still passionate.

In the autumn, during the period of transition, he reverted at times to impressionist techniques without entirely sacrificing the new direction of his work. There is a very expressive portrait of *Bibi la Purée*,[5] in which we perceive the facial gymnastics of the small-time bohemian actor, and are left no illusions as to the pathetic banality of his personality. It is one of Picasso's most brilliant works of virtuosity, but it is also the last of its kind, and perhaps it is not irrelevant that Toulouse-Lautrec died in the same year.

It had become necessary not only to change the technique of his painting and to abandon the gaudy colours derived from the frivolous night-clubs of Montmartre, but also to take a more adult view of society. To quote Professor Boeck: "The painter has evidently been chastened by his own experience: his earlier irreverent and critical attitude towards society has yielded to one of deep compassion for suffering mankind."[6]

Barcelona, January 1902

Picasso's return to Barcelona brought with it soothing influences and physical nourishment of which he was in need. Earlier causes of irritation were smoothed over by a recognition of his independence, and he settled again into his home in the calle de la Merced. A room with a terrace where he could work was found in the calle del Conde del Asalto near the corner of the Rambla del Centro. By means of an agreement with Angel Fernandez de Soto to whom it belonged, and a painter, Roquerol, to whom it had been rented, he found a corner where

---

[1] See Zervos, *Picasso*, Vol. I, p. 39.   [2] Ibid., Vol. I, p. 47.   [3] Ibid., Vol. I, p. 41.
[4] Plate II, 3.   [5] *Cahiers d'Art*, 25th year, II, 1950, p. 313.
[6] Boeck and Sarbartès, *Pablo Picasso*, Thames and Hudson, p. 123.

he could paint without being disturbed, although the sun streamed in perpetually on one side or the other, and the heat in summer was overpowering. With his unfailing capacity for concentration divided only between his canvas and his palette placed on the floor, Picasso began again to develop the themes of the Blue period. The sodden harlot, the penniless but devoted mother, the figures with bowed heads and a look of bewildered resignation that we associate with his work of this period, existed all round him, in Barcelona more persistently than in Paris. It was in the crowded streets of the Catalan capital that he had first become conscious of their eternal presence. But as usual he was not tied to one subject or even one set of subjects. He was intrigued once more by the view from his windows and by the changing effects of light on the house tops. There is a painting[1] of roofs, terraces and chimneys seen from his studio which is severely architectural and formal in comparison with the earlier impressionist view, the *Blue Roofs* of the boulevard de Clichy.

In spite of the spontaneity and unpredictable nature of his actions and his apparent disregard for time, Picasso organised his day with a minimum of complications. A monotonous regularity in his working hours has always been characteristic of his way of living. Like all Spaniards he went to bed late, sometimes very late, and was not up very early unless, as was not unusual, he had not been to bed at all. His usual round would start from his home; on foot he would pass through the narrow streets of the old city to his studio where he would arrive during the morning round about eleven o'clock. After a late midday visit to the 4 Gats and a lunch accompanied by prolonged and excited talk, he would take leave of his friends and return to his studio. There everything irrelevant to his work was forgotten until the hour came for him to leave his painting and make his way home, stopping at various cafés along the Ramblas or to talk to friends in the street. At night he would walk out again, and if he were alone he would amuse himself by watching the passers-by or by trying his luck at the penny slot-machines. Or he would fall in with friends, and become involved in long passionate conversations at café tables or sauntering under the plane trees that line the Ramblas. These would often leave him in a state of excitement which could only be calmed by noting his impressions in sketches on any scrap of paper that came to hand, or in prolonged hours of reading.

Distractions in Barcelona were less absorbing than in Paris. The only dealer's gallery of interest was the Sala Parès, and its exhibitions were

[1] See Zervos, *Picasso*, Vol. VI, p. 31, No. 250.

insignificant beside the rich variety of the rue Lafitte. The inexhaustible riches of the Paris museums could scarcely be replaced even by the paintings and polychrome sculptures of the Catalan primitives, which in those days had not been collected together in the museum in Barcelona. To see them it was necessary to make long excursions into the mountains, where they could be discovered, dimly lit, on the walls and ceilings of the churches. But to Picasso, well stocked at that time with recent memories, this was not important. All he wanted was to be able to paint, and this he continued to do daily, stimulated by the brilliant Mediterranean light and helped by the unfailing though limited support of his family in his material needs.

During Picasso's absence from Paris, Mañach organised an exhibition at the gallery of Berthe Weill. Some thirty paintings and pastels that he had finished the year before were shown. Mlle. Berthe Weill was a courageous little woman, "as tall as three apples", who thanks to her flair for spotting talent, was in those days in advance of other dealers. She had managed to get the critic Adrien Farge to write a preface to the catalogue. In it he mentioned several pictures such as the *Luxembourg*, the *Still-Life*, the *Courtesan with the Collar of Gems*, and he praised these works "in which our eyes delight, captivated by brilliant painting in tones sometimes crudely brutal, sometimes knowingly restrained".

As had happened at Vollard's gallery, his friends came and were lavish in expressions of enthusiasm, but no one bought the pictures. The exhibition brought no hope of alleviating the poverty in which he was forced to live. Extravagant living was out of the question, and Picasso's moderate tastes as a dandy were difficult to satisfy. His style of dress remained unchanged, but he enjoyed indulging his fantasy where ties and waistcoats were concerned. Some sartorial improvements were however made possible by his friendship with a tailor named Soler who was later to receive a magnificent portrait of himself and his family in payment. A final and essential adornment to his person was the fashionable walking stick which in Picasso's hands became a rapier to be used in playful tilting with the plane trees.

His energy never faltered and his wit flowed out in rapid, pitiless sketches of his friends at the 4 Gats. Several drawings were often crowded on to the same sheet—friends and enemies were pilloried with equal vigour. Rusiñol and Casas appeared as bearded old women, but the most persistent teasing was reserved as usual for one of his closest friends at that time, Sebastia Junyer, a painter with whom Picasso was to make his next trip to Paris the following autumn. He was made easily recognisable by a high forehead crowned with black hair and a black bushy moustache—which seemed too big for his small round face —against his pale skin. He is made to appear ludicrous as a toreador,[1] as a romantic painter clad in classical robes and seated on a rock seeing visions of the naiads,[2] or with a harp and scroll declaiming poems to the gulls. In another drawing Picasso parodies the *Olympia* of Manet, in which the odalisque has become a negress of immense volume to whom the white and willowy Junyer is bringing a dish of fruit. Picasso has added himself to the scene, seated on the near side of the bed; all three are suitably naked.[3]

There is another sheet from a sketchbook on which Picasso had already drawn with unhesitating line some female nudes of extraordinary grace.[4] One of them is lying prostrate with a skull appearing over her heart and a red flower growing between her legs. But the main theme on the page is a drawing of a beggar seated cross-legged with his dog, to whom a grotesquely fat bourgeois, with top hat, spats and diamond rings, gives a coin as he passes. The drawing has written across it *Caridad* (charity). At the bottom left hand corner he has added another strange cloaked figure with a straight black wig crowned with the crown of Egypt, which does not appear to connect in any way with the other drawings. Probably the appearance of these figures all on the same sheet is fortuitous, but the profile, surprisingly, is that of Picasso himself, made unmistakable by the small untidy moustache he wore at that time.

Sabartès tells a story which fits well with allusions to the lighter side of Picasso's life in Barcelona. There was, it seems, a beauty of the music halls on the Paralelo, "la belle Chelito", who was much praised for the grace which "resided in her gestures, the line of her body, the tints of her complexion and of her hair, her glances and her voice . . . and when she undressed the public went mad".[5] Picasso hearing of her from his enthusiastic friends went to see her for himself. When Sabartès called for him at his house next day at noon, his mother showed him into the room where Picasso lay still asleep among a great litter of paper covered with drawings of "la belle Chelito". A precise flowing line had caught the poise of her graceful body from all angles and he had not slept until he had exhausted every memory of her charms.

During this period of eight or nine months in Barcelona Picasso

[1] See Zervos, *Picasso*, Vol. VI, p. 61, No. 499.
[2] Ibid., Vol. VI, p. 61, No. 495.   [3] Ibid., Vol. VI, p. 42, No. 344.
[4] Ibid., Vol. VI, p. 54, No. 438.   [5] Sabartès, *Portraits*, p. 99.

continued to paint pictures predominantly blue in tone, with a subject-matter deeply tinged with pathos. Although there is a tendency for the colouring to be brighter, and for the sea rather than the café to be used as a background, there is no discontinuity between pictures such as *Mother and Child on the Shore*,[1] or those of lonely figures seated against the bare walls of the taverns of Barcelona, and their predecessors painted the autumn before in Paris.

It is particularly in drawings that a new freedom and strength appear, with a growing feeling for sculptural form. Apart from wilful caricatures, these sketches have less of obvious cynicism and show a deeper research into the meaning beneath the external expression of the human face. A theme which recurs many times is the meeting of two people, sometimes with decorous gestures of greeting, and sometimes, clothed, or naked, locked together in a passionate embrace which is so close that they stand joined as one living trunk.[2]

As the months passed a desire to return to Paris descended again on Picasso. His dissatisfaction with the lack of understanding he found in Barcelona was augmented by the memory that friends in France, such as Max Jacob, not only understood him and his work but provided him with a new stimulus. He had been quick to understand the difference between the level of intelligence of the painters of Barcelona and of the poets and critics of Paris. Language was rapidly ceasing to form a barrier, as may be seen from the letter he wrote to Max Jacob in an idiom which though it savours strongly of Spanish is clearly recognisable as French. It is illustrated copiously with drawings of incidents at the bullfight, and a self-portrait with wide black hat, tapering trousers and the inevitable cane. The bull ring forms the background. The letter as usual begins with apologies for not writing more often and the excuse that it was because he was working, and when not working "one enjoys oneself or one is bored stiff". In confidence he writes to Max: "I show what I do to my friends the 'artists' here; but they find that there is too much soul and not enough form, which is very funny. You know how to talk to people like that; but they write very bad books and paint imbecile pictures. That is life, that's it! Fontbona works a lot; but he does nothing. I want to make a picture of this drawing that I send you (*The Two Sisters*).[3] It is a picture that I am making of a whore of St. Lazare and a nun. Send me something written by you for Pel y Ploma. Adieu, my friend, write to me. Your friend, Picasso. Calle de Merced 3, Barcelona, Spain."[4]

[1] See Zervos, *Picasso*, Vol. I, p. 184.   [2] Ibid., Vol. I, p. 13.
[3] Plate II, 5.   [4] See Penrose, *Portrait of Picasso*, p. 28.

Both the drawing and a painting of the *Two Sisters* are in existence. The picture is a composition of two women facing each other, and similar in this respect to many other encounters of two figures, painted earlier and later. Here the contact is not the meeting of lovers or ladies in feathered hats. In anguish the prostitute with closed eyes and bowed head seeks the sympathy of her more serene sister. Both figures are draped, both have bare feet, and their attitudes suggest the simple imagery of the Catalan primitives. There is a restrained pathos in the picture which borders on the sentimental, saved only by the severity of their pose. The idea came to Picasso, however, from a close contact with reality in its crudest form. His curiosity had led him to make frequent visits while he was in Paris to the St. Lazare hospital for venereal diseases. He happened to know one of the doctors, who arranged for him to visit the wards as a member of the staff whenever he liked and make drawings of the inmates. The patients were given hoods like Phrygian bonnets, a shape which reappears in many canvases of this period. But Picasso's interest in the women of the street who were constant inmates continued after he had officially left the premises and washed his hands in disinfectant. He would then go to a nearby café which was frequented by the out-patients. There he could watch them and talk to them in a different atmosphere.

Paris

It is clear from the letter to Max Jacob that Picasso was ready again to cross the frontier to a more inspiring climate. For some months he hesitated, and it was not until the end of the summer of 1902 that he returned to Paris for the third time. At first he took a room in the little Hôtel des Ecoles, in the Latin quarter, but he soon moved to a cheaper room which he shared with a Spanish sculptor known as Sisket. It was a small attic on the top floor of a seventeenth-century house which had become the Hôtel de Maroc—now the Hôtel Louis XV—in the rue de Seine. This is a narrow street near the boulevard St. Germain, crowded with bookshops and art dealers. One of the artists was forced to stay in bed most of the time because an enormous iron bedstead occupied almost the whole room. At other times the bed was covered with Picasso's prolific production, but neither of them ever had a square meal.

Before long Max Jacob, who was appalled at Picasso's poverty-stricken way of living, rescued him from this sordid attic. Max had recently been able to ease his own precarious existence by taking a job in a department store. This allowed him to invite his friend to take shelter in a more spacious but otherwise equally modest room that he had rented on a fifth floor in the boulevard Voltaire near the industrial centre of the city. There was only one bed and only one top hat; both had to be shared between them. But Picasso accepted gladly. The company of Max and enough room to work made it worth while. They arranged matters between them in such a way that the bed was never unoccupied. Max slept there by night while Pablo worked, and by day, while Max was away at the store, it was Pablo's turn to sleep.

The simplest necessities were often more than they could afford and although Max Jacob's heart was warm, all that he could offer was a fair share of his poverty. An anecdote frequently retold by Picasso illustrates the real poverty through which they lived. He tells how one day with their last farthings they bought a sausage. It looked so big and satisfying that they hurried back to their attic to cook it. Suddenly as it was warming in the pan, the sausage exploded leaving no trace of any substance, only stinking air, which in no way satisfied their hunger. Some six months later, when Picasso had returned to Barcelona, he wrote to Max, saying with a touch of nostalgia: "I think of the room in the boulevard Voltaire, of the omelettes, the beans, the Brie and the fried potatoes and I think also of those days of poverty and I become sad."

During his youth Picasso had known many moments of discouragement. Doubt about the ultimate value of his work had often tortured him, but never did he taste the combined cruelty of poverty and disillusionment more acutely than during these months. By the end of the year the exhilaration of Paris had faded; the price it demanded seemed unnecessarily high. No one wanted his work. And as a final disaster, Max Jacob, whose temperamental character always made regular employment precarious, lost his job.

On the eve of his third departure from Paris Picasso managed to sell a pastel *Mother and Child on the Shore*[1] for 200 francs, and took all the rest of his pictures, which he would in desperation have sacrificed for the same sum, up to Montmartre to be stored by Pichot. Even so they were nearly lost, for when Picasso returned to claim them, they could only be found after a long search, under a cupboard where they had been too successfully hidden. So great was his distress that on the last night Picasso remembers burning a great quantity of drawings in order to keep warm.

The pictures that Picasso had painted during this short visit were not important in size, owing to his circumstances, but a picture such as

[1] See Zervos, *Picasso*, Vol. I, p. 184.

the *Mother and Child on the Shore*, which was painted in the over-crowded attic of the Hôtel du Maroc, is of a high quality and deeply moving. Limited by lack of funds and lack of space, he had found drawing the most suitable means of expression. The irresistible desire to make sketches like short visual messages concerning the essential features of what he saw was unimpeded. It seems most probable that the drawings that were sacrificed to warm him must have been an eloquent part of his production during these months.

Barcelona, January 1903-April 1904: Blindness and Vision

The letter to Max Jacob, with its nostalgic reference to the meagre fare they had shared, was written from Angel de Soto's studio in Barcelona. The letter is headed with a drawing of the towers of the Cathedral, which could be seen over the house tops. The studio was the same room in the Riera de San Juan that Picasso had occupied in 1900. Again he was forced to share it with his friend, and it was not until the beginning of 1904 that he at last found himself in a position to take a studio on his own in the calle del Commercio.

The rapid changes of domicile during these years between Barcelona and Paris are attributed by Sabartès to the restlessness that continued to pursue him. Between 1900 and 1904 he crossed the Pyrenees eight times. He had also visited Malaga and Madrid in the hope of finding a spiritual climate which would provide him with the inspiration and the stability necessary for his work.

The solitude of those who realise that they must make their path alone, and the doubt that seizes all who venture into the unknown, were already familiar to Picasso. But on this occasion he had decided not to waste his time on fruitless journeys, with the hope of finding more suitable surroundings. As he says at the end of his letter to Max Jacob, he intended to stay in Barcelona through the following winter "so as to do something".

The visit lasted over a year, into the spring of 1904, and became memorable for the production of some of the most admirable and most moving of the paintings of the Blue period. Among the many that are typical of this style in their subject and colour, there are two large and exceptional paintings. One is a family group. It shows us the tailor, Soler, out picnicking on the grass with his wife, four children and the dog.[1] The gun and the dead hare placed on the cloth before them with wine and fruit show that it was a good picnic. The attitudes of parents and children, halted momentarily in their enjoyment to face

[1] Plate III, 5.

the painter and conscious of being watched, seem to give a timelessness to the group without robbing it of its animation. In this way it is not unlike Courbet's portrait groups, intimate and realistic.

After many years this picture has finally found its way to the Liège Museum. The upper region of the picture had been left as bare canvas by Picasso. He had asked a friend to finish it for him with the result that the family found themselves seated in a conventional wooded grove. Nearly ten years later Kahnweiler bought the painting and before he sold it he showed it to Picasso, who on seeing it again, objected to the background. Painting out the trees, he replaced them with cubist rhythms in keeping with his style at that time. But this failed to please him, and sweeping all other solutions aside, he painted in a simple uniform background which does not detract from the interest of the figures.

The other picture, _La Vie_, also painted in 1903 and also of large dimensions, is in some ways the most ambitious painting of this year.[1] It is certainly impressive in its size, and it is a carefully planned composition, the outcome of many studies. The picture contains a symbolism which links it to the _Evocation_. The allegory that is intended is not easily understood and critics have sometimes been content to dismiss it as a 'problem picture'. The rigid pose of the three figures suggests that they are intended to expound some principle such as the incompatibility of sexual love and life. The composition is simple. A naked woman leaning her body against a man is balanced by the draped figure of a woman carrying a child, at whom the man points enigmatically. In the background between the figures two studies of nudes are propped up as though in a studio. The figures in both are huddled up and apparently in great distress. The drawings are placed there, it would seem, as a means of adding symbols of suffering to the picture. This adding of images has a suggestion of the 'collage' technique which led later to the introduction of real objects stuck to the painting in order to introduce different kinds of reality. The picture shows throughout signs of the self-conscious development of a complicated theme which has led the artist away from his original intentions. In a preliminary drawing, we find that the two figures on the left are both stark naked and that the man's face is clearly a self-portrait.[2] In the picture, Picasso has changed the likeness to that of one of his friends and clothed him in a slip. Both these details point to hesitation and a departure from the first spontaneous idea, in a search for an imagery that has not gained in process of elaboration.

[1] Plate II, 4.   [2] See Penrose, _Portrait of Picasso_, p. 34.

But apart from these two large pictures, there are many others, some of which are more successful and certainly more moving. Although they are closely related in style and saturated with the mysterious influence of their blue colour, there is a great variety among them and it is possible to find the first appearances of many elements that recur in later periods. There is, for instance, the *Old Guitarist*,[1] whose elongated limbs, twisted pose and affected gestures recall the 'mannerist' style of El Greco, but the geometric pattern of the human figure built round the central axis of the guitar points forward to the composition that we find in still-lifes of the cubist period.

Again, the *Woman with arms crossed* is an example of the dramatic effect produced by a deliberate distortion of limbs.[2] Here, as throughout the Blue period, there is a marked interest in the treatment of the hands. The fingers are elongated and sensitive. They seem to be remarkably endowed with power to feel like antennae and to clutch with the swiftness and the strength of an ape.

The emphasis Picasso places on hands has special significance, since it appears at the same time as a series of pictures which show very clearly his speculations about blindness. A case in point is *The Blind Man's Meal*.[3] Here a hungry man whose eye-sockets have become lifeless caverns sits at a table, feeling with long sensitive fingers the bread and the jug set before him. His hand caressing the jug compensates for a contact with the outer world of which he has been robbed. His visual sense finds a substitute in the touch of his hand, and in the secluded depths of his mind he again sees clearly with his own inner vision untroubled by the vagaries of changing effects of light and colour.

In considering the act of perception, Picasso has always been amazed at the discrepancy between seeing an object and knowing it. Its superficial appearance is to him absurdly inadequate. Seeing is not enough, neither is the aid that the other senses can bring. There are other faculties of the mind which must be brought into play if perception is to lead to understanding. It is somewhere at the point of junction between sensual perception and the deeper regions of the mind that there is a metaphorical inner eye that sees and feels emotionally. Through this eye of the imagination it is possible to see, to understand and to love even without sight in the physical sense, and this inner seeing may be all the more intense when the windows on the outer world are closed.

[1] Plate III, 6.   [2] See Zervos, *Picasso*, Vol. I, p. 48.   [3] Plate II, 8.

Recently I have heard Picasso reaffirm an enigmatic statement made by him some twenty years ago when he said: "There is in fact only love that matters. Whatever it may be. And they should put out the eyes of painters as they do to goldfinches to make them sing better." Picasso was speaking as one who has desired all his life, without counting the cost, a greater intensity in expression and a deeper understanding of the world in which we live. In brutal terms his saying echoes an idea expressed by Pascal: "Jesus Christ came to blind those who see clearly and give sight to the blind."

The allegory of the blinded man has pursued Picasso throughout life like a shadow, as though reproaching him for his unique gift of vision. It is a paradox that a man who lives so predominantly by his eyes should consider even for a moment the advantages of blindness; but it is also true that love itself is blind, above all in the act of creation, with its unpredictable consequences. In Barcelona, Picasso found models at almost every street corner for his paintings of the blind, and he produced many very moving pictures. The *Old Jew* for instance sits expressionless with hollow eyes that have long ceased to be a means of communication.[1] Beside him a small keen-eyed boy has been recruited to watch for him and add those essential banalities, money and food, to the self-contained world of the old dreamer. Another painting shows the pathetic detachment of a lonely outcast seated with his hands clutching his knees, staring upward into a sightless void. His pose seems reminiscent of the seated statues of Egyptian gods, and suggests that he has perhaps a greater gift of sight in him than others who have never known his affliction. In an etching, *The Frugal Repast*, made in Paris a year later, there is the same idea of the blind man using the eyes of his companion, in this case a woman.[2] He holds her tenderly in his long bony hands, sensing her sleeve with his finger tips, while his futile gaze is turned towards a distant corner of the room.

The Blue period also contains other themes less full of pathos; it abounds in pictures of children. Picasso has always shown his affection for children of all ages, beginning with his awed fascination by the baby at the breast. His love seems never to have been more acute than at this time, when his other preoccupations were poverty, disease and monstrous deformities. An example is the *Child holding a dove*,[3] in the collection of the Dowager Lady Aberconway. His treatment of a subject in which the pitfalls of sentimentality are so obvious is saved by the bold-

[1] Plate II, 7.
[2] See Barr, *Picasso: Fifty Years of His Art*, p. 31.
[3] See Zervos, *Picasso*, Vol. I, p. 41.

ness of the brushwork and the heavy outlines, characteristics which again evoke the vigour of Van Gogh. The surfaces are free of modelling and there are no shadows in which to introduce a complicated play of colour. By depriving himself of the obvious means of giving solidity to the image he has ironed out those gentle contours that could lead to sentimentality. An apparent harshness of treatment has brought about a marriage of opposites in the technique and the subject. The same process redeems another painting, *The Greedy Child*,[1] where a little girl is helping herself to the bottom of a pudding bowl. Again the subject, without a masterly vigour in the technique, could well merit the reproach made by certain critics that the Blue period is marred by sentimentality.

Certainly some of these pictures, those, for example, of the blind beggars, and a well-known one, now in the Chicago Art Institute, of the *Old Guitarist*,[2] come within range of this charge. Yet there is a dramatic sense of pathos based on observation of reality which saves them throughout. Picasso's preoccupation was always not how to exclude psychological interest but to discover how it could be included without the usual pitfalls of overstressed and unbalanced sentiment.

The portraits of this period, however, escape any such reproach. Beginning with the *Man in Blue*,[3] the portrait of the wife of Pere Romeu and the portraits of Sabartès[4] and Mateo de Soto, he painted later other superb likenesses. These include the portrait of Angel de Soto,[5] in which face, hands and a glass on the table make a succession of incidents admirably contrasted in form and texture. There are two portraits of Sebastia Junyer. In the larger painting of his artist friend he has placed, seated on a café bench behind Junyer, a street-walker, pallid, with heavy eyelids and holding a flower between her thin lips.[6] She haunts the background like a temptation that it would be inhuman to avoid and unwise to accept, alluding to a conflict which is not visible in the smooth, well-groomed face of Junyer. This is the only portrait which is complicated by symbolic allusions. In the others Picasso found sufficient psychological interest in his sitter alone. He enjoyed his mastery of the art of portrait painting as the dancer or the athlete enjoys the ease with which he can accomplish dazzling feats with the controlled strength of his muscles.

It was in the spring of 1904 that Picasso, needing more privacy and more space, moved into a new studio in the calle del Commercio.

---

[1] See Zervos, *Picasso*, Vol. I, p. 23.   [2] Plate III, 6.
[3] See Zervos, *Picasso*, Vol. I, p. 69.   [4] Ibid., Vol. I, p. 43.
[5] Ibid., Vol. I, p. 90.   [6] Ibid., Vol. I, p. 81.

Thanks to Sabartès, who rented two attic rooms in the same street, we know that he started work at once. His father had carefully prepared a large panel for him with the hope of watching the development of some definitive masterpiece. But Picasso treated it with no more respect than an ordinary canvas and left it with a few rapidly sketched figures and nothing more. His newly acquired seclusion was however exactly what was needed for a fresh burst of creative work. In addition, he visited Sabartès with paints and brushes and decorated his walls with murals "in the spirit of Assyrian reliefs and of the pictures of the series 1901-1904". On another wall opposite the window he drew a macabre scene in which a half-naked Moor was hanged from a tree while below him a young and entirely nude couple abandoned themselves "to the passionate game of love". Then, using a round window high in the wall as part of his design, he converted it with a few lines into an all-seeing eye with an inscription below that read: "The hairs of my beard, although separated from me, are gods just as much as I." The phrase "just as much as I" reveals both his ambition and the doubt which troubled him. As he had done years before when sharing the studio in the Riera de San Juan with Casagemas, he added an inscription invented on the spot to complete the image he had just sketched out.

Before he left Barcelona, he changed his studio once more for a more suitable room in the calle del Commercio. But good accommodation was not enough to satisfy him. Barcelona was not the equivalent of Paris, and in April 1904 he left Catalonia for the last time.

CHAPTER IV

AU RENDEZ-VOUS DES POÈTES
(1904-1906)

The Bateau Lavoir: The Final Move to Paris

ON THE SOUTH-WESTERN slopes of the heights of Montmartre there still exists in a small square, now named place Emile-Goudeau, a strange dilapidated building which more than fifty years ago was christened by Max Jacob the Bateau Lavoir, possibly because of the many ways in which it was unlike the laundry barges anchored along the Seine. It resembles a boat only in that a visitor arriving from street level must embark on the top deck and go down complicated stairways and dark passages to reach the lower floors. Otherwise it is totally unlike a floating laundry owing to the almost complete absence of water and hygiene both outside and within. On the side facing away from the square, large glazed windows announce that the whole building, perilously hanging to the slope of the hill, is in reality a hive of studios.

This strange dwelling, composed it seemed of nothing but lofts and cellars, all in such a sad state of repair that no insurance company would ever accept it as a risk, had become well known at the turn of the century as a centre of bohemian life. It had housed artists and writers of the generation of Gauguin and the symbolists. It was now to be the destination for which Picasso and Sebastia Junyer y Vidal set out from Barcelona in April 1904. Their progress by rail in the third class and their first encounters with the French are described in a series of lighthearted sketches, called by Picasso 'Alleluias'.[1] With the arrival of the two travellers, Junyer is seen in the first sketch carrying a large trunk under his arm. "And at nine o'clock they arrive in Paris at last" is the explanation below. The climax comes in the last drawing, which shows Junyer appearing bareheaded and alone, with a framed picture which he exchanges for a bag of gold offered by a bald little man in a frock coat. The explanation written below is, "I summon Duran-Rouel [*sic*] and he gives me a lot of cash". 'Alleluias', it should be explained, is the name given to nineteenth-century Spanish broadsheets, covered with woodcuts describing pictorially a pious anecdote

[1] See Zervos, *Picasso*, Vol. VI, p. 60, Nos. 485-9.

illustrating the adversity of human life. In Spain such tales invariably end in disaster. Skulls, coffins and funerals finish the story with an 'alleluia'. But Picasso's version, ending with a successful visit to the wealthiest dealer in contemporary art of the day, was according to such traditions outrageously optimistic.

Picasso's earlier visits to Paris had been made with the intention of staying no more than a few weeks, but on this occasion cases of paintings and canvases had been sent on ahead to the new address, known in those days as 13 rue Ravignan. It was possible, therefore, to settle at once into the studio on the top floor, that is to say ground floor of the Bateau Lavoir, where for the next five years he was to live, work and receive his friends.

Experience had warned him of the cruel disregard that the great city could show to a young artist, however talented and full of conviction he might be. This time "Picasso did not come to Paris to conquer it, nor even to seduce it",[1] writes Maurice Raynal, "he came there to find a cure for life".

Not all writers are in agreement as to Picasso's motives in making a move which was to have such far-reaching consequences and was, in effect, to be the beginning of his exile from his own country. From that time onwards he became virtually a French artist. Slowly and timorously, as his fame began to increase, even the official world was to acclaim his presence as an honour to France and her traditions. Outside Spain, however, Picasso has always felt himself to be a stranger. He has never asked for French nationality, but he has accepted France as his country of adoption at first willingly, and later, since his return to Spain has been made impossible by political events, with good grace.

Certain Spanish writers cannot admit statements such as that made by the poet Pierre Reverdy, when he wrote: "All his [Picasso's] career as a painter unfolded itself in Paris, and the multiple manifestations of his talent are part of the history of French contemporary art. . . . Picasso understood that the legendary immobility of his country could only oppose its powerful force of inertia to the development of his imagination." In reply they point indignantly to all that he had learnt in Spain, and to the Spanish blood in his veins that can never change its colour. But from a more detached angle it would seem probable that the magnetic force of Paris, composed of so many seductive elements equally attractive to a host of artists from all parts of the world, outweighed conclusively the provincial charms of the companions with whom Picasso had grown up at the 4 Gats. To this

[1] Maurice Raynal, *Picasso*, Cres, Paris, 1922, p. 37.

may be added the presentiment that the revolutionary trends his work was to take would never be tolerated in Spain. He later confided to Raynal his own opinion that "if Cézanne had worked in Spain he would have been burnt alive".

"A cure for life" was at the basis of what Picasso sought when he moved to Paris. Painting and life were inseparable. His life was lived daily through his eyes and he needed to see clearly in the deepest sense. Doubts assailed him as to where his vision with its growing discernment might lead him, and how the great talents which he knew he possessed could be used for its expression. The applause of his friends, and the pleasure that arose from the phenomenal ease with which he could communicate his ideas to others graphically, left him still dissatisfied and lonely. To quote Raynal again, "he felt the troubling solitude of nascent genius and the call to new horizons".[1]

But his return to Paris after more than a year of intense activity in Barcelona brought no immediate break in his work. The pitiable inhabitants of the streets of Barcelona appear to have accompanied him on his journey: the first images that haunted him on his arrival are closely similar. The hungry beggar watched eagerly by children eats the same bowl of soup in Paris, the madman in rags stirs the air with his fingers and mutters similar gibberish, and again the blind man crumpled and starving holds out an empty hand for alms. A universal population, irredeemable in its misery, continues to fill his work.

Two outstanding pictures dating from the summer of 1904 must be mentioned. One, a large gouache now in the Museum of Art, Toledo, Ohio, is known as *The Woman with the Crow*.[2] Its colour and the emaciated form of the woman with dreaming eyes, who bestows a kiss on the head of the bird, connect it inevitably with the Blue period, though the form is less sculptural than in many of the earlier pictures. The main emphasis lies in the long thin hand held vertically against the bird, which again recalls the mannerisms of El Greco.

Similar elongated hands appear in the other picture, a large etching known as *The Frugal Repast*, which I have already described. It is recorded that Ricardo Canals, a friend from Barcelona, had five years before encouraged Picasso to make copper-plate etchings, but only one example of this early work is known. It is a small etching of a picador standing with his legs apart, and holding a pike in his left hand. Picasso, as a beginner, had forgotten that the image would be reversed

[1] Maurice Raynal, *Picasso*, Skira, 1953, p. 18.
[2] See Zervos, *Picasso*, Vol. I, p. 107.

Picasso with Paul Eluard at Mougins, 1936.

Picasso holding a bull's skull on the beach at
Golfe Juan, summer, 1937.

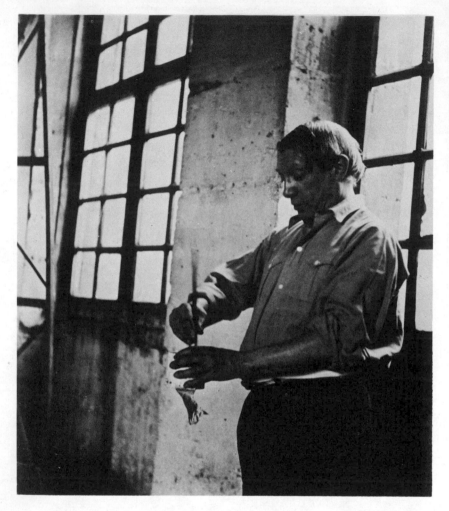

Picasso painting *Guernica*, 1937.

in printing, but he quickly covered his mistake by writing at the top, *El Zurdo* (the left-handed man).[1] At the feet of the picador, who appears to be posing for his portrait in an interior, is a small owl, the first appearance of this bird, which fifty years later was again to fascinate Picasso and became the subject of a great number of drawings and paintings.

The Frugal Repast is a mature work and masterly in execution, but as copper was too expensive, a zinc plate was used on which the traces of a landscape drawn by a former owner had not been entirely erased. Canals who had also come to live in Paris had acted as adviser, and according to Bernhard Geiser, the authority on Picasso's graphic work, "it was thanks to his guidance that Picasso became accomplished enough in the techniques of etching to be able to get the effects he wanted".[2]

Fernande Olivier

Soon after Picasso's arrival, while he was at work on this plate, he noticed in the dim corridors of the Bateau Lavoir a girl who came to fetch water from the one tap in the basement that supplied all the tenants. Her green almond-shaped eyes and regular features, crowned with the wild abundance of her auburn hair, could not be ignored. He spoke to her, and we know from her, as well as from many other sources, of the consequences of this chance meeting, which led to the first important attachment in his life. "La belle Fernande" was to become his companion, sharing his privations and the first fruits of his fame, during the next six years. Her version of their first meeting is that one hot summer afternoon she was sitting in the shade of the chestnut trees in the square with a girl friend, when a sudden storm made them run for shelter. In the passage was the young Spaniard whose black eyes she could not escape. He was holding a kitten in his arms and he laughed as he playfully barred her way. She remembers her astonishment, when she agreed to enter his studio, at the great blue pictures piled up against the wall and the family of white mice that he kept in a table drawer.

Even so Fernande did not yield to him at once. She had a secret which she did not dare to tell him. Six months younger than Picasso, she had been born in Paris of parents who ran a millinery business. At the death of her mother she was sent to live with an aunt whom she

[1] Bernhard Geiser, *Pablo Picasso, Fifty-five Years of His Graphic Work*, Thames and Hudson, London, 1955, Plate I.

[2] Ibid,, Preface.

hated with such violence that at the age of seventeen, to escape from her, she married a sculptor whom she scarcely knew. Shortly afterwards he went mad, and once more she had to flee. Continuing her story, she insisted that while they were living together it was she who refused Pablo's demands that she should marry him, without letting him know the reason. Even Don José, when they visited Barcelona together, could not believe that she could be so obstinate and advised his son to be more persistent.

Fernande Olivier speaks in her memoirs of the day-to-day joys and disappointments in the life of a couple whose combined ages added up to little more than forty. In her original way she also gives a lively picture from her point of view of the bohemian life that went on around them and the visits of penniless intellectuals and rich collectors of various nationalities.

The exuberant beauty of her youth, her healthy robust figure and her confidence, introduced a new element of optimism and delight which could not fail to affect the life and therefore the work of her lover. He expressed his love for her in innumerable drawings and portraits, and with the jealousy of a Spaniard confined her to his own attentions. She recalls how grateful she was for the piles of second-hand books that passed away the weeks when she could not leave the studio because she had no shoes. Picasso, the Andalusian, in his way treated her as an odalisque. She was never allowed to go out without him. He would sweep the floor himself and go out to buy food. In return, she says, "with some tea, some books, a couch, little housework to be done, I was happy, very happy".[1] For although Fernande had the reputation of luxuriating in laziness, she was a good cook and made excellent dishes on the small paraffin stove. With her sense of economy she managed to feed him and his friends on not more than two francs a day.

Fernande's memoirs contain a description of the impression he made on her which is worth quoting. "He had nothing very seductive about him if one did not know him, nevertheless his strange insistent regard demanded attention. Socially it was difficult to place him but this radiance, this internal fire that one felt in him generated a kind of magnetism, which I could not resist." Elsewhere she says, he was "small, black, thick-set, restless, disquieting, with eyes dark, profound, piercing, strange, almost staring. Awkward gestures, the hands of a woman, poorly dressed, badly groomed. A thick lock of hair, black and shining, slashed across his intelligent and obstinate forehead. Half

[1] Fernande Olivier, *Picasso et ses Amis*, Stock, Paris, p. 9.

bohemian, half workman in his dress, his long hair brushed the collar of his worn out jacket."[1] She remembers how in winter when they had run out of fuel it was warmer to stay in bed, until the neighbouring coal merchant generously delivered fuel without even asking for payment, because "my eyes pleased him". She tells how they devised ways of getting provisions without paying cash by asking a store to send them round. When the delivery boy arrived, Fernande would shout through the door: "Put them down, I can't open now; I'm naked." By this farce they gained a week in which to find the money. On another occasion their dog Frika returned home like a good Samaritan dragging a string of fresh sausages.

The Bateau Lavoir was dirty, uncomfortable and full of other people's noises. In winter ice formed in the tea cups and in summer the heat was intolerable. The neighbours, who included "painters, sculptors, writers, humorists, actors, washerwomen, dressmakers and hucksters" shared in the same medley. Picasso remembers the tragic scene when a man, slipping on the snow on one of the roofs, crashed to his death below; and the comedy of the oil stove thrown out of an upper window by its half-asphyxiated and furious owner. But poverty and discomfort were matched by vitality and companionship. This untidy bohemian community in the heart of Montmartre still retained the atmosphere of a village with its intimacy, gossip and passionate drama. The adventure that was being lived by the young Spaniard and his group of friends fitted in with the surroundings. They were accepted by all as an asset even though their neighbours were often incapable of understanding their strange talk and preoccupations.

Outside, under the trees in the square, Picasso would meet and talk with his friends, mingle with the neighbours or teach the children to trace in the dust with one continuous line the outlines of cocks and hens, rabbits, horses, birds or what you will.

La Bande Picasso

Among those who for diverse reasons had found their way from Barcelona to Paris were Paco Durio, sculptor and ceramist, formerly a friend of Gauguin; the gaunt Ramon Pichot; Zuloaga who already took the pose of a master; the engraver and painter Ricardo Canals, whose beautiful wife was Picasso's model for one of his most brilliant portraits; and the sculptor Manolo Hugué, who had a great appetite for jokes at the expense of any victim. Manolo was the son of a

[1] Fernande Olivier, *Picasso et ses Amis*, p. 25.

general and had been left to his own resources on the streets of Barcelona when his father went out to the war in Cuba. He soon learned to live by his wits. His inexhaustible fund of good humour compelled his friends to forgive even his most brazen and unscrupulous behaviour towards them. There are endless stories of his roguery, beginning with the time when his father ordered the police in Barcelona to bring Manolo to him. The general's speech to his son was so full of admonition and so moving that Manolo wept and asked for one favour only, which was to be allowed to embrace his father. The general was even more astonished when he discovered after his son's departure that his watch had gone too. Manolo would admit with a smile that apart from murder he had done everything. But he was a talented sculptor into the bargain, and his irresistible charm made him the most authentic and lovable of bohemians. Years later, when grave new of disorders in Barcelona reached Picasso, I remember his saying that if they tried to shoot Manolo, his executioners would be sure to miss because he would make them helpless with laughter.

The personality of Picasso as well as his talent won admiration and devotion among his friends. They were anxious to come to his help whenever their limited means allowed. Paco Durio, hearing once that Pablo had nothing left, tactfully put down outside his door "a tin of sardines, a loaf and a litre of wine". Manolo and de Soto, with Max Jacob's assistance, often set out with packets of drawings under their arms. In the hope of raising a few francs, which would be generously shared out among them, they made a tour of the dealers of the rue Lafitte; or if they failed there they tried bric-à-brac merchants such as the Père Soulier, a former wrestler and a great drinker. This picturesque tradesman kept a shop opposite the Cirque Medrano. Mixed in among the bedsteads and mattresses which were his stock-in-trade, a variety of pictures had accumulated, his choice having been guided by an instinctive love of painting. According to André Level, his flair had helped him to discover pictures by Renoir, the Douanier Rousseau and even Goya. He became indispensable to the artists who lived around, not because he made them rich by his purchases but because he often saved them from starvation. From him it was always possible to raise something to pay for immediate needs. But at what a price! Twenty francs for ten admirable drawings by Picasso was the exchange demanded by him over a drink in the café next door.

Other attempts elsewhere to raise a few francs also met with small reward. A series of fourteen etchings was made by Picasso with the help of a friend, Delatre, a former Communard, who owned a press and made prints on the rare occasions when they were in demand. The plates, varying in size, were remarkable for the precision of their line and the charm of their subject-matter, which consisted chiefly of harlequins and circus folk, or Salome dancing before a monstrously fat Herod.[1] They also included the earlier engraving, *The Frugal Repast*, which in this original edition, before the plates were bought by Vollard and re-edited in 1913, is now one of the rarest and most treasured of all Picasso's etchings. The edition was put on sale by a small but enthusiastic dealer, Clovis Sagot, of the rue Lafitte, but it brought no profit to be shared by the artist or anyone else.

Unlike most painters, who lose no opportunity of sending their work to exhibitions, Picasso refused consistently to show his paintings in public. To sell pictures was a necessity rather than a pleasure. He was miserable when they had gone and preferred to give them away rather than haggle with a dealer. In fact at this time he gave away more than he sold. His reluctance to exhibit may have been due in some degree to the disappointment of his early exhibitions, which he did not wish to risk again. More probably it came from a mixture of conviction of his own genius and doubt as to the reactions of others. As a result he preferred to remain proudly aloof rather than attempt to display his wares. Even Vollard did not as a rule show Picasso's work to strangers. He kept it hidden to be seen only by a chosen few.

Already in 1905 the names of Matisse, Braque, Vlaminck, Dufy, Friesz and Rouault could be found among the exhibitors in the Salon d'Automne or the more rebellious Salon des Indépendants. But Picasso saw no point in appearing in such mixed company. He had little interest in current theories and preferred to follow his own solitary and precarious path. To ease the pangs of hunger many artists helped themselves by drawing for the *Assiette au Beurre* and other illustrated reviews, but Picasso had neither the time nor the desire to follow their example, although on one occasion, it seems, he did contribute to the satirical review, *Frou-Frou*. Once also, he agreed to design a poster for a play, *Sainte Roulette*, by Jean Lorrain and his friend Gustave Coquiot. The poster being by an unknown artist was not a success and was turned down by the manager of the theatre, the Grand Guignol.

The First Patrons

Although he refused to make a gesture towards the public, visitors and collectors of various nationalities found their way to Picasso's

[1] Plate III, 2.

studio and began to buy from him the recent products of his untiring energy. Among those who discovered his retreat were Leo and Gertrude Stein, piloted there by a young author, Henri-Pierre Roché. The Steins were Americans who had recently settled in Paris. They were finding their way rapidly and with passionate excitement into the world of art and literature. Passing through London in 1902, Leo Stein bought his first modern painting, a Wilson Steer. Soon after, with the help of Bernard Berenson, he discovered the Cézannes at Vollard's gallery and bought a landscape. This led to further satisfaction when he added Van Gogh and Gauguin to his collection. At the Salon d'Automne of 1905, he was bold enough to buy, with his sister's approval, a "brilliant and powerful" portrait by Matisse. This picture had become the bull's eye for adverse criticisms aimed at a group of violently-coloured exhibits by those painters, Matisse, Derain, Vlaminck, Braque and others, who had become known as "Les Fauves", the wild beasts. Their method was a free and somewhat arbitrary use of pure colours which implied in consequence an even greater disregard for form than that of their predecessors, the neo-Impressionists. Their exuberance centred round the talented painter, the eldest in this youthful group, Henri Matisse, "le roi des Fauves".

The Steins were greatly impressed by the work and the personality of Picasso. The first purchase made by Leo from Clovis Sagot for 150 francs was however against Gertrude's wishes. It was a large upright canvas painted in 1905, predominantly blue in tone, of an adolescent girl holding a basket of red flowers.[1] On their first visit to Picasso's studio, they spent eight hundred francs buying paintings, an event without precedent.

The two enthusiastic explorers of uncouth appearance were not only courageous in their choice but also extremely hospitable. In her books Gertrude Stein has described the dinner parties at their apartment in the rue de Fleurus, where for years they brought together a remarkable assembly of creative talent. It would be true to say that nearly all the young poets, painters and musicians of the brilliant generation that came to Paris in the first decades of this century, from all parts of the world, visited their household sooner or later. But although they had been buying the work of both Matisse and Picasso for more than a year, it was not until the autumn of 1905 that the two painters met for the first time under their roof.

[1] See Zervos, *Picasso*, Vol. I, p. 113.

The Studio—Late Blue Period

Fernande remarks that before knowing Picasso she wondered how he could find any time to work during the day, so constant was the stream of his Spanish visitors, but she discovered that in spite of the total lack of gas or electricity he preferred to work by night. Most of his pictures before 1909 were painted by the light of an oil lamp, which he hung above his head while he squatted on the floor in front of his canvas. But often in the early days he could not afford to buy the oil, so he held a candle in his left hand while he worked with his right. André Salmon describes how on his first visit in company with Max Jacob, he found him painting in this way a "picture that was blue".

The weakness of the candlelight and its tendency to subdue yellow has been given as a possible reason for the overall bluish tone of this period, but that he should have miscalculated his effects is not credible. His sense of colour and familiarity with his materials were more than enough to compensate for the temporary distortions of artificial light. All such theories become nonsense beside his own words: "You are that which exists best in the world . . . the colour of all colours . . . the bluest of all blues." His preference for working by night frequently kept him up until six in the morning and for this reason early callers were not welcome. Happily the concierge, whose heart he had won, could be relied on to keep away all visitors except those she recognised as having a possible financial value. When Monsieur Olivier Sainsère, Conseiller d'Etat, arrived correctly dressed and with his top hat, the concierge would knock on the door shouting: "You must open, this time it's serious." At this Picasso would get up in his nightshirt and open for the distinguished collector while Fernande hid behind the canvases. Sainsère, looking round for a suitable place for his hat, would say urbanely to the young painter: "Please put on a pair of trousers, you will catch cold." He would then settle down to examine the newly painted canvases.

A visitor arriving at a more convenient hour, however, would find the door opened to him by Picasso with "the celebrated curl over a black-currant eye, dressed in blue, the blue jacket open on a white shirt held in at the waist by a poppy red flannel cummerbund with fringes. . . ."[1] The visitor was greeted by a strong smell of oil paint and paraffin, which Picasso used as a medium for painting as well as fuel for his lamp, mixed with the heavy smoke of black pipe tobacco. Once the stacks of paintings leaning against the walls had been passed,

[1] André Salmon, *Souvenirs sans Fin*, Gallimard, Paris, 1955.

he would find the canvas on which Picasso had been working propped up at the base of an easel in a clear space in the centre of the room. Picasso still likes to work leaning or squatting over the canvas at an odd angle, but he changes his position with the size of the canvas. On the floor to the right of the easel, paints, sable brushes and a vast collection of pots, rags and tins were spread out close at hand. In spite of the ample size of the studio and the almost complete lack of furniture, the room was overcrowded with objects. In that respect it resembled the attic in the boulevard de Clichy, and, in the future, the apartment in the rue la Boètie, the great rooms of the rue des Grands Augustins and the villa "La Californie"—in fact wherever Picasso has settled and gathered round him the material that is to feed his imagination and his work. Salmon gives us an inventory of what he remembers having seen on his first visit: "A paint cupboard made of boards, a small bourgeois round table bought from a junk merchant, an old couch used as a bed, an easel. Carved out of the original studio space, a little room containing a thing like a bed. This had become a retreat. Familiarly it was known as 'the maid's bedroom'. All kinds of buffoonery went on there behind our host's back and continued to do so until the arrival, not long delayed, of Fernande Olivier."[1]

As Salmon slowly became aware of the impact of the multitude of paintings that surrounded him, he says he was "bowled over by the revelation of a new universe".

Certain incongruities in the disorder attracted special attention. In the middle of the floor was a zinc bath-tub and in it were books by Paul Claudel and Felicien Fagus. In Fernande's little corner with its tottering floor-boards Picasso had placed on the wall, this time deliberately, an object by which she also was puzzled. In the first days after their meeting he had made a drawing of her, which he framed elaborately with a mount made from her blue chemise which he had asked her to give him. With the help of Max Jacob, who supplied two cerulean blue vases filled with artificial flowers, he set up the portrait as an altarpiece, half mocking and half in devotion to the girl he loved. Fernande could never decide whether this display was an echo of what she calls his 'mysticism' or just an elaborate joke placed above her bed to disquiet her.[2]

The arrival of Fernande did not disturb the friendship between Picasso and Max Jacob. In fact, the poet's genuine affection for her even outlasted her liaison with Picasso. Max's company was very

[1] André Salmon, *Souvenirs sans Fin*, p. 170.
[2] Fernande Olivier, *Picasso et ses Amis*, p. 53.

entertaining. There was great originality in his wit and he was an untiring entertainer. He would read his own poems with admirable conviction and enchant everyone with songs from comic opera. Of this Picasso never tired. But even with this unfailing flow of drollery and serious thought, as Salmon remarks, "too much friendship loses its value". The days of their closest intimacy were already over.

Au Rendez-vous des Poètes

Although Picasso has always demanded solitude for the hours in which he works, he has never been able to live without company. In Paris, as in Barcelona, his bias toward the literary world brought about some significant encounters that were to be of great importance both to him and to his new friends. André Salmon's first visit to the Bateau Lavoir resulted by chance in his first meeting with Max Jacob on Picasso's doorstep. Only a week before, Picasso himself had made the acquaintance, in a bar near the Gare St. Lazare, of an impetuous and brilliant poet of half Italian, half Polish origin, who had adopted France as his fatherland and exchanged his mother's name, Kostrowitzky, for that of Guillaume Apollinaire.

On the same evening the two young Frenchmen met at his door, Picasso took them to meet Apollinaire. The introduction was made in the same crowded bar, and has been described by Max Jacob in these words: "Without stopping a quiet but violent discourse on Nero and without looking at me, he absently extended his short strong hand (one thought of a tiger's paw). Having finished his speech he rose, swept us out into the night with great shouts of laughter and so began the most wonderful days of my life."[1] Not only was this a great event for Max Jacob, but it was this encounter which inaugurated the epoch when these friends, with other painters and poets, were to influence each other in close and fruitful collaboration.

Picasso's interest in the poets was liberally reciprocated by them, and as the circle grew his prestige increased among them. Before his death in 1907, Alfred Jarry became a friend, whose talent, wit and eccentric behaviour made a profound impression on Picasso, and his influence was remembered long after his death. Inventions such as Dr. Faustroll's Pataphysique and that monstrous, brutish character, the Père Ubu, corresponded to Picasso's growing desire to disrupt accepted appearances by any means he could find valid. Jarry's ability to handle dangerous weapons such as ridicule and obscenity was a stimulus to him, and although the Parisian wit of his plays was meat

[1] R. G. Cadoń, *Testament d'Apollinaire*, Debresse, Paris, 1945, p. 22.

too strong for French audiences, they whetted Picasso's Spanish
appetite for a riotous, full-blooded castigation of conventional ideas.

The young poets Pierre Reverdy and Maurice Raynal, as well as
Charles Vildrac, Georges Duhamel and Pierre MacOrlan all became
frequent visitors to Picasso's studio. He enjoyed their excited and
intelligent conversation and their appreciation of his work. This was
in many ways an attraction of opposites. Picasso usually remained silent
except for an occasional burst of enthusiasm which took the form of a
startling paradox or a monstrous joke. He seemed to be continually on
the watch, his eyes shifting rapidly among his companions, listening
to their remarks, and readily grasping their meaning. His friends, on
the other hand, were for the greater part extremely loquacious,
complicated and ebullient. They were attracted by the mysterious ways
in which he could control his own talent and youthful ardour with
apparent calm, the way in which he could express himself with such
originality in his words and such richness in his work. The increasing
frequency of their visits to his studio made one of them remark that
there should be a sign over the door, "Au Rendez-vous des Poètes".
The first visitors to arrive about midday were usually Apollinaire, Max
Jacob and Manolo. During the years spent at the Bateau Lavoir,
Fernande remembers very few meals with Picasso alone. She often
prepared food for the whole company on her paraffin stove, unless,
as sometimes happened, her admirer, the coal merchant, called in and
invited them all to come and taste his cabbage soup. "You should have
heard Apollinaire's grateful laugh," she told me, "as we trooped off
together."

The Rose Period

Salmon on his first visit had found Picasso painting in blue. The
"blue universe surrounded him". During the autumn and winter
of 1904 the sentiment and mannerisms of the Blue period still per-
sisted. A large painting in grey blues that departed little from monochrome had for its model a laundress who lived and worked in the
same building.[1] With the weight of her weariness she presses on her
iron. The accentuation of her long thin arms and the meanness of her
empty room suggest a sadness unrelieved except for the trace of a
smile on her pallid face. The angle of her shoulder raised above her
head conveys a melancholy, akin to that of the Old Guitarist. In
both cases, their antecedents lie in the expressive distortions of El
Greco and his medieval ancestors.

[1] See Zervos, Picasso, Vol. I, p. 111.

Another even larger painting, *The Actor*, is equally dramatic in its tension.[1] Again the model was a neighbour. With wasted arms and fingers writhing like dead branches in the wind, he gesticulates to his audience. His sinuous, elongated body, clothed in pink with blue trimmings, sways over the prompter's box on an empty stage. Whatever his rôle may have been, his attitude indicates clearly a state of exalted inner suffering and privation. In this picture the all-pervading blue has yielded to colours reminiscent of the paintings of the earlier days in Paris, though they are more subdued and more skilfully controlled. The form, again gothic in feeling, is built up without hard outlines, and the freedom of the brushwork has a more personal touch.

Unlike the *Old Guitarist* and the majority of the figures of the Blue period, *The Actor* seems to move within the three-dimensional space created by the depth of the background. For this reason, as well as the introduction of colours unusual in the previous paintings, it heralds new tendencies. For convenience the succession of styles that Picasso developed during the next two years has been labelled the Rose period. Alfred Barr more correctly divides the period chronologically into five short stages beginning with the Circus period of which this picture is the forerunner. Picasso was awakening from the cold blue world of his sublimated pitiable outcasts. He had found new company in Montmartre, and although the life of the circus ring and the stage was precarious, it was not in the same way wedded to despair. The clown and the actor belonged to a race of artists. Their skill and their courage in an atmosphere of uncertainty and danger had a similar appeal to that of the bullfight. They provided the climate in which his next inventions were to grow.

Harlequin

From the early days of the Blue period, taking his place somewhere between the blind beggars and the prostitutes, sharing with them the same café tables, another character makes his appearance. He is a youth disguised for a performance in which, to judge from his fragile looks, he is merely another victim, one of a troupe of players who impersonate the behaviour of a society from which they are outcasts. Whether comic or heartrending, his act is calculated to mislead because his particular drama lies less in his miming than in himself.

The image of Harlequin recurs intermittently throughout the work of Picasso.[2] Even during the Cubist period, shorn of literary allusions, the diamond pattern of his costume still betrays his presence. This

[1] Plate III, 1.   [2] Plate I, 7.

persistence has led Professor Jung to claim that the motive for his haunting reappearances is a subconscious desire in Picasso to portray himself in this disguise. The theory is strengthened by the frequency in early years with which we find Harlequin as Picasso's self-portrait. Let us not assume, however, that this is Picasso's only characterisation of himself. His love of disguises prompts him to imagine himself in many different rôles. It can be said that the bull, the horse, the minotaur, the owl, the dove, the meditating lover, the bearded artist and even the child holding a candle are also symbolic of Picasso himself.

The preference that Picasso shows, particularly in early life, for Harlequin suggests that analogies must exist between him and this legendary character. Picasso's Harlequin is not the elegant flirtatious entertainer loved by Watteau, nor Cézanne's proud youth in fancy dress, nor is he a buffoon. Though he may be a jester he speaks the truth, and though he may be wearing a disguise we detect him by his mercurial nature and his elusive ways. It would be legitimate to interpret this Harlequin, with his diamond coat of many colours, as the power to juggle with everything while remaining evasive and irresponsible. He is a thief who gratuitously steals up unperceived to take his prize, to prove himself capable of doing so and to test his luck. He can change his personality and slip into another's skin. His game is ambitious; it is a test of strength with the established order. During the nineteenth century Harlequin was out of favour among painters, but before it ended he made a brilliant reappearance in Cézanne's picture *Mardi Gras*. This painting which had been bought by Vollard was seen by Picasso in his gallery before it was purchased and taken to Russia by the collector Shchukine. Its subject was in consequence the first influence that Picasso acquired from Cézanne. This happened about six years before he was ready to absorb fully the great stylistic changes inherent in Cézanne's work.

Throughout the Circus period Harlequin dominates the scene. He is seen off stage, lithe and sensitive in physique, with his family and their attendant pets. In intimacy he nurses a baby while his wife stands nude arranging her hair. In the *Family of Acrobats with a Monkey* he watches the young mother with her child, in company with another important actor on Picasso's stage, the ape.[1] He appears at times as a small boy or wanders in open country with an acrobat and a dog, or again he stands in thought looking into the blind face of one of his companions.

Although these characters, like those of the previous period, are still

[1] Plate III, 7.

aloof, living in a world of their own, they have a serenity about them which seems to reflect the new sense of happiness which Picasso had found in his love of la belle Fernande. Two watercolours of the autumn of 1904 show a man, in one instance obviously himself, contemplating that one luxury attainable even in poverty, the naked beauty of a sleeping girl.[1] This is the first appearance of a theme which has recurred later with innumerable variations.

Throughout the Circus paintings the pervading solemnity of blue, transcendental and morose, was giving way to the warm caressing blush of rose pink. The old untouchables had yielded their place to the tangible presence of youth and affection. The circus folk are no longer solitary in their poverty, they appear surrounded by their companions. The pale emaciated forms of starving cripples are replaced by figures full of the grace of adolescence and often curiously androgynous in their physique.

Circus and Saltimbanques

Being a village within a city, Montmartre was almost self-contained. Within a small distance all the varied entertainments that could be desired were at hand. For some years the most popular place of entertainment among artists was the Cirque Medrano, which to this day still continues to enchant successive generations of Parisians. Its clowns, acrobats and horses had delighted Degas, Toulouse-Lautrec, Forain, Seurat and many others. There, behind the scenes and outside among the sideshows of the fair that traditionally occupies the whole boulevard during the winter, Picasso made friends with the harlequins, jugglers and strolling players. Without their being conscious of it, they became his models. With their families they camped beside the booths in which they performed under the warm glare of paraffin lamps. Their wives, their children, their trained pets, monkeys, goats and white ponies squatted among the props necessary for their acts. Detached from the everyday business of the great city they lived absorbed in rehearsing and giving displays of their agility.

There is an important picture, bought later by the Russian collector Morosov, and now in a Russian museum, of a little girl dressed in blue tights, balancing on a large ball.[2] In the foreground sits the massive figure of a wrestler in pink and blue, while in the distant treeless landscape, baked like the plains of Castile in summer, a woman with her child watches a white horse grazing. The two main figures, the little girl, fragile, ethereal, detached from the soil, and the young

[1] Plate III, 3.   [2] Plate IV, 2.

athlete, thick-set, muscular, seated squarely on a heavy stone block, are admirably contrasted. They form together a composition which is classical in its ordered simplicity and in which even the empty spaces unoccupied by the figures are still interesting and alive to the eye.

With the numerous paintings and studies that accumulated in the spring of 1905 Picasso had the intention of composing two large pictures, only one of which was achieved. Of the first, *The Circus Family*, only a large water colour,[1] now in the Baltimore Museum of Art, exists, though component parts appear in many other pictures. The scene is set in the open, Harlequin stands among his troupe watching a child practising on a ball, while the women are occupied with domestic tasks. Two features that recur in other sketches are the white horse and a ladder pointing towards the sky. The second painting, known as the *Family of Saltimbanques*,[2] is now in the National Gallery of Art, Washington. Measuring about seven feet square it was the largest so far painted by Picasso.

It is never necessarily true that a great composition into which an artist crowds all the efforts and discoveries of a period is the most moving and successful product of his work. In the case of *La Vie* painted two years earlier Picasso had allowed allegory and sentiment to cloud the aesthetic impact, and many smaller pictures of the Blue period give greater satisfaction. In the *Saltimbanques* there is no message, no allegory, and a balance between spontaneity and sensitive judgement relieves it of any suspicion of sentimentality. Picasso had assembled the studies of his circus friends and grouped them together under a blue sky with an empty, timeless landscape as their background.

In an early sketch the background was a racecourse scene reminiscent of Degas, with one of the riders taking a fall. All this is finally eliminated and there is in consequence a feeling of detachment among the figures who stand listlessly, apparently waiting for a command. The precarious balance of the composition, with five figures grouped to the left and a solitary figure of a girl seated in the right-hand corner, adds to an expectation of some unforeseen event. The evolution of each of the figures can be traced through the studies. The seated woman was formerly the subject of a painting where she wears a pointed hat covered with a veil such as was worn by the ladies of Majorca. Like a Tanagra statuette she balances it high on her hair. The little girl appeared in the first sketch without her flower-basket, caressing a dog. The elderly jester with a great paunch swelling his red tights, who seems to be the father of the troupe or the 'understander', has an

[1] See Raynal, *Picasso* (Skira), p. 31.   [2] Plate IV, 4.

extensive background of antecedents. Usually dressed in red and seated on a block, he has as a companion a slender youth. He is first cousin to the sybaritic Herod of the etching *Salome*, and wears the same mock crown as the bronze head of a jester modelled about the same time. He also reappears as the gargantuan king of a book-plate drawn for Apollinaire. But the tall figure of Harlequin on the extreme left of the painting is the most familiar. He stands hand in hand with the little girl facing the old jester. At the last moment Picasso gave him his own profile so as to indentify himself even more closely with his wandering companions. The six characters who seem otherwise aloof have a unity of purpose. Together they form a motley troupe. The freshness with which the picture is painted contributes to the mystery of their presence. This mystery haunted the poet Rainer Maria Rilke when in 1918 he asked if he might live in the same room with "the great Picasso", which then belonged to Hertha von Koenig in Munich. Sharing Picasso's fascination for the wandering circus folk of Paris, he was inspired to write the fifth of his *Duino Elegies* while living, he told a friend, "with the loveliest Picasso (the Saltimbanques) in which there is so much Paris that for moments I forget". In these lines he speaks of the wandering players he had beside him:

> "But tell me, who are they, these acrobats, even a little more fleeting than we ourselves. . . ."[1]

Life in Montmartre

"We all lived badly. The wonderful thing was all the same to live", wrote Max Jacob, who suffered more than anyone from an extreme poverty that his top hat, immaculate dress and exquisite manners failed to hide. His room in the rue Gabriel was so lacking in any comfort that Picasso presented him with a screen he had decorated to keep off the draught, though in the early years he was not much better off himself. The humiliating bargaining with the Père Soulier brought little satisfaction.

Restaurants where artists of all descriptions met to satisfy their hunger at the least possible expense abounded in the steep narrow streets that led up to the place du Tertre. Picasso and Fernande had picked one that suited them for various reasons—it was next door to the pawnbrokers, and the proprietor Monsieur Vernin was too soft-hearted ever to refuse credit. The "bande Picasso" was always to be

[1] Rainer Maria Rilke, *Duino Elegies*, translated by J. B. Leishman and Stephen Spender, Hogarth Press.

found there, as well as young actors and actresses. The animation and smell of cooking were both intense, but the final advantage of this bistro to Picasso was that he found the conversation so boring that it was an incentive to finish the meal fast and return home to work. Higher up the hill, the bearded Fredé, former owner of Le Zut, had recently opened a small café, Le Lapin Agile, which was later to become famous. It still exists, though it is only in its external appearance that it retains something of its former atmosphere. In its early days the Lapin Agile became one of the favourite haunts of the group of poets and artists which included Picasso. In the evenings they would congregate to exchange ideas and listen to recitals of Ronsard or Villon by Baur and Dullin, or the airs of the 'Caf-conc' sung by Francis Carco. In summer, on a little terrace under an old acacia they could get an excellent dinner for two francs including wine, and it became a custom to celebrate occasions such as the opening of an exhibition, or even the funeral of a friend, "chez Fredé". Inside the café, in the semi-darkness, could be seen the work of artists accepted by the *patron* as payment for their debts. There were pictures by Utrillo and Suzanne Valadon, with others by less-known names, and a highly-coloured Picasso in the gaudy yellows and reds of the Lautrec period was nailed to the wall. A tame crow belonging to Fredé's daughter Margot, who later married Pierre MacOrlan, hopped about among the guests. It was the same bird that appeared in Picasso's painting of 1904.[1]

Picasso enjoyed the usual café talk he found at the Lapin Agile, whether it was serious or rowdy, and chance meetings which might lead to new friendships. Certain people, however, he disliked because he felt they were wasting his time: those who insisted on asking questions in a pedestrian attempt to understand his work. He once made this unforgettably clear to three young Germans who came one evening to his studio. After standing a long time politely appreciating his paintings, at his suggestion they climbed the hill together to the Lapin Agile to have a look at the picture nailed to the wall. On the terrace they began earnestly to ask him to explain his theory of aesthetics, but Picasso's answer was as immediate as it was effective. Drawing from his pocket the revolver given him by Alfred Jarry and often used to express his high spirits, he fired several shots into the air. The three earnest Germans disappeared into the night and Picasso went in to explain to Salmon and his startled friends the reason for this outburst.

[1] See Zervos, *Picasso*, Vol. I, p. 107.

The same tactics were used one night when Manolo and Picasso were sharing a cab on the way home with a poet who had bored them considerably by insisting on reading his poems to them. This time the shots were fired through the roof, and the Spaniards slipped out of the fiacre on opposite sides. The bewildered poet, who again happened to be a German, was left to cope with the driver and the police, who locked him up for the night.

A Visit to Holland, and Sculpture

Among the many foreigners whom Picasso had met in Paris was a Dutch writer named Schilperoort, who in the summer of 1905 invited him to visit his home at Schooredam. For one month Picasso gazed in amazement at the flatness of the landscape and the opulent forms of the Dutch girls, head and shoulder taller than himself. At the end of that time he returned with several paintings of these girls, whose ample figures encouraged him to emphasise their sculptural and monumental qualities. In the painting known as *La Belle Hollandaise*, which shows a nude in a lace cap, he used a palette limited to pinks and greys.[1] It is prophetic of the colossal nude figures painted in the early 1920's, but it also had a more immediate influence in guiding Picasso to his first serious attempts at sculpture.

Thanks to Vollard, who some years later had the originals cast in bronze, there are in existence four sculptures of this period. These are the head of a jester with mock crown, pointed cap and equivocal smile;[2] a nude girl of gracious yet ample form, combing her hair;[3] a head of Fernande;[4] and the dynamic mask of a toreador with a broken nose. All these were modelled by Picasso shortly after his Dutch visit. They are all mature and masterly, though from previous years only one small seated woman of 1899 is known. His excitement was such that for a time it seemed that sculpture might take preference over painting; but with a few exceptions Picasso did not follow up this brilliant start until more than twenty years later. The jester, the most accomplished of these bronzes, has a rugged solidity due to its rough modelling, which catches the light and spreads it over the form. The face is sensitive and the jester's cap and crown spring from the head like a flower. It was begun late one evening after returning home from the circus with Max Jacob. The clay rapidly took on the appearance of his friend, but next day he continued to work on it and only the lower

[1] See Zervos, *Picasso*, Vol. I, p. 114. [2] Plate III, 4.
[3] See Zervos, *Picasso*, Vol. I, Plate 153. [4] Ibid., Vol. I, Plate 149.

part of the face retained the likeness. The jester's cap was added as the head changed its personality.

First Classical Period

It was during the months that succeeded the visit to Holland that the next stage of what is known as the Rose period arrived. The Blue period had already given place to the Circus period with its introspective but less morbid harlequins. They too were now to be forgotten in a more objective approach to the subject matter, in which aesthetic considerations were to grow in importance. The elongations and expressive distortions of Romanesque or Gothic origin were set aside, and Picasso's work began to show the influence of his study of Greek sculpture of the primitive and classical periods in the Louvre, and his continued interest in Egyptian art. There exists in the collection of Tristan Tzara a sheet covered with delightful sketches which indicate the widespread interests of Picasso at this time.[1] Over the figure of a girl acrobat in the centre of the paper is a woman in the Egyptian style drawn with bold unhesitating outline. Characteristically the eye, placed on the profile face, is seen as though full face. A mixed bag of objects and comic figures fills the rest of the sheet: men naked except for bathing slips and hats; a small elephant; a peacock and a hippopotamus showing both eyes on a head in profile; a vase of flowers; an ink blot transformed into the head of a negro; and in addition, a rough sketch of a gateway surmounted by an oriental dome. The sketches are slight but significant.

A classical tendency is clearly present in two of the earliest paintings of this period, *Woman with a Fan*[2] and *Woman in a Chemise*. (The latter is now in the Tate Gallery.) Both paintings have a serenity and a stylisation of gesture which suggest Egyptian art. In colour both recall the Blue period, but the simple well-rounded forms and elegant proportions herald a new epoch which was to last about a year during which all mannerist distortions were abandoned, and a search for simplified form took their place. There is an Arcadian atmosphere in the drawings and paintings of naked boys leading or riding bareback their well-disciplined horses.[3] A gouache known as *The Watering Place*[4] is a study of boys and horses for an important painting that Picasso was contemplating but which did not mature. It is a splendid composition on classical lines, the horses and their riders form an oval in the centre of the canvas, punctuating it with light and dark vertical forms.

[1] See Zervos, *Picasso*, Vol. VI, p. 85, No. 699.   [2] Plate IV, 6.
[3] Plate III, 9.   [4] See Zervos, *Picasso*, Vol. I, p. 118.

The studies in themselves, however, such as the *Boy leading a Horse*
in the Tate Gallery, are sufficient proof of Picasso's mastery of this
theme. As Alfred Barr writes, they have "an unpretentious, natural
nobility of order and gesture which makes the official guardians of
the 'Greek' tradition such as Ingres and Puvis de Chavannes seem vulgar
or pallid".[1]

The Portrait of Gertrude Stein

In the spring of 1906 Picasso surprised Gertrude Stein by asking her
if she would allow him to paint her portrait. She had by then become
an intimate friend. Although she may not have understood thoroughly
his saturnine nature and the many-sided significance of his work, she
had been captivated by his genius and the shining blackness of his
eyes. Of Leo Stein there are several drawings:[2] he had a bushy black
beard, gold-rimmed spectacles, awkward posture and intense pro-
fessorial look. Gertrude was unselfconsciously eccentric in appearance. Her squat and massive figure, regular features and intelligent
eyes, coupled with a masculine voice, were significant of a strong
personality. The proposal that she should sit for Picasso was surprising,
since at this time he found the actual presence of a model altogether
unnecessary. His circus folk lived nearby, but never were they asked
to come and pose for him in his studio. This practice singled him out
once more as an eccentric among painters, and the others accused him
of causing unemployment among the models.

When, as in this case, Picasso reverts to custom in order to make a
particularly careful portrait, he usually makes heavy demands on his
model. Gertrude Stein describes how she posed more than eighty
times for her portrait. "Picasso sat very tight on his chair and very
close to his canvas, and on a very small palette which was of uniform
brown grey colour, mixed some more brown grey and the painting
began." Fernande offered to amuse the sitter by reading aloud with
her beautiful diction stories from La Fontaine.[3]

Gertrude Stein could only account for his persistence by supposing
that a mystic attraction existed between Spaniards and Americans.
But although the likeness started to her satisfaction, it failed to please
him and little progress was made until "all of a sudden, one day,
Picasso painted out the whole head. 'I can't see you any longer when I
look,' he said irritably. And so the picture was left like that and he left

[1] Barr, *Picasso, Fifty Years of His Art*, p. 42.
[2] See Zervos, *Picasso*, Vol. VI, p. 82.
[3] *Autobiography of Alice B. Toklas*, John Lane The Bodley Head, p. 51.

for Spain."[1] This journey in the summer of 1906 lasted for some months. On his return in the autumn, he painted in the head without having seen his model again and presented the finished picture to Gertrude Stein.[2] She accepted it gratefully and declared she was satisfied. Others, shocked by the masklike severity of the face, were more critical. In reply to their disapproval Picasso remarked, "everybody thinks she is not at all like her portrait but never mind, in the end she will manage to look just like it". In proof of this Gertrude Stein kept the portrait beside her all her life and when she died bequeathed it to the Metropolitan Museum of Art, New York. By then it was acclaimed by all as an admirable likeness. It hangs there as an example of how Picasso can see more acutely and profoundly with the eyes of his imagination than when he is confronted with his subject.

There is only one other portrait of importance dating from this period. It is a self-portrait in a white singlet holding a small palette.[3] The head is treated in the same clear and determined way. From the wide-open eyes which are drawn with unhesitating precision comes a look of assurance and understanding not to be found in the earlier portraits.

Gosol

When the summer of 1906 arrived Picasso again felt an urge to return to Spain, an urge that existed in spite of the fact that Paris was rapidly becoming indispensable to him. His friends, and the recognition that he was beginning to receive from collectors and dealers, made life in the French capital not only more interesting but also financially less difficult. His means were still restricted; as soon as money came in it was spent at once on painting materials and food, or on some extravagance for Fernande. The pinch was becoming less acute, however, and after a sale more remunerative than usual it became possible to buy tickets for Barcelona for himself and Fernande.

Spain was still essential to Picasso. On crossing the frontier he became a very different character. Fernande remarks that in Paris "he seemed to be ill at ease, embarrassed, smothered in an atmosphere that could not be his", whereas in Spain he was "gay, less shy, more brilliant, animated, taking an interest in things with assurance and calm, in fact at ease. He gave out an air of happiness in contrast to his usual attitude and character."[4]

[1] *Autobiography of Alice B. Toklas*, p. 57.
[2] Plate IV, 1.   [3] Plate IV, 3.
[4] Fernande Olivier, *Picasso et ses Amis*, p. 115.

A minimum of time was spent on a duty call on his parents and friends in Barcelona before they set out for a remote village on the southern slopes of the Pyrenees. There once again Picasso could feel at home with the peasants whose company he had grown to enjoy on the Pallarès farm, and he could also enjoy at little expense the space and solitude he needed for work. The French landscape was unsatisfying to him in comparison with the wild ragged mountains of Catalonia. It stank of mushrooms, he said, whereas what he needed was the warm and bitter-sweet odour of thyme, rosemary, cypress and rancid olive oil.

They chose Gosol, a village near the frontier of Andorra, which could be reached only on mules. It consisted of a bare market-place surrounded by a dozen houses built of stone that became golden as it weathered in the sun, wind and snow. Above the purple earth of the orchards rose the snow-capped Mount Cadi, from which little clouds like boats set out across a sky of sparkling blue. Fernande speaks of the benefit both to body and spirit that this remote and lovely place gave Picasso; of the excursions made with smugglers into the forests; of the long stories of their adventures with the *carabineri*, to which Picasso would listen attentively. An understanding and mutual respect grew naturally between them.

The visit however ended abruptly. According to Fernande, typhoid broke out in the village and Picasso, showing his characteristic alarm when illness appears on the scene, insisted on crossing the mountains by mule track and reaching France and better sanitation with the shortest delay.

But before they left, in spite of days spent in exploring the mountain slopes, Picasso produced a prodigious quantity of paintings. As usual he chose as his subject-matter the people, the objects and the landscape round him. The square shapes of the houses with their small unglazed windows, the peasant women with long straight noses and scarves covering their heads, the weather-beaten faces of the old men, and Fernande in her serene beauty drawn with great tenderness, all these appear in his sketches. But there is also a series of nudes painted with classic purity and sensuous understanding. The warm earth colours of the mountain soil bathe their graceful bodies. A painting which shows the most complete mastery of the "Greek" idiom is the *Toilette*,[1] where two women, one nude looking into a mirror held by the other, stand against a bare background. They have lost all trace of the manner-isms of the *Old Guitarist* or the *Acrobat's Family*. This mood, of

[1] Albright Art Gallery, Buffalo. See Zervos, *Picasso*, Vol. I, p. 150.

which the *Woman with Loaves*[1] is again a splendid example of classical poise, continued its influence for a while after the return to Paris. The paintings of the autumn months repeated in their colour the happy glow of the summer, but a renewed insistence on form and a return to plastic distortions, significant of anxieties which were absent in the remote mountain air, again made their appearance.

A large vertical canvas, *Peasants and Oxen*,[2] is also related to the period though it is curiously unlike it in style. Here a man and a woman run barefoot together beside a pair of oxen. She carries a bunch of flowers while he lifts a basket overflowing with garlands above their heads. There are several reasons why this composition is unexpected and interesting. The proportions of the man with his minute head, great length of body and exaggerated forearms are unlike the elongations of limb that are to be found in the Blue period or the more conventional shapes of the Gosol nudes. The form throughout has angular rhythms that announce a first appearance of geometric shapes, and instead of the static, sculptural forms that had been evolving throughout the Rose period the figures are in agitated movement.

This composition was probably painted on Picasso's return to Paris. It seems symptomatic of the restlessness of his spirit and his constant discovery of new means of expression, often from ancient sources. Barr points out that at the time of his passage through Barcelona on his way to Gosol, his old friend Miguel Utrillo had just published the first Spanish monograph on El Greco. In this book, as well as in two magazines published in Paris that autumn, there were illustrations of El Greco's *St. Joseph with the child Jesus* which shows a clear affinity in composition with the *Peasants and Oxen*, though there are no oxen in the El Greco painting and a group of angels takes the place of the garland. The smallness of the saint's head in proportion to his body and the general feeling of the composition seem to bear out Barr's suggestion that after a lapse of some two years, Picasso again had El Greco in mind. There are also three preliminary drawings which help in an attempt to understand the origins of this picture, and Picasso's ability to blend ideas coming from very different directions. The first is a straightforward drawing of a peasant boy leading two oxen down the mountainside.[3] The second is a sketch of a blind man carrying a basket

[1] Philadelphia Museum of Art. See Zervos, *Picasso*, Vol. VI, p. 89, No. 735.
[2] Barnes Foundation, Merion, Pennsylvania. See Zervos, *Picasso*, Vol. I, p. 185.
[3] See Zervos, *Picasso*, Vol. I, p. 159.

of flowers on his shoulders and shouting his wares.[1] He is led by a child holding a bouquet; neither figure showing any marked distortion. There is little movement in the figures and the sketch has every appearance of being taken from life. The third, another of the same subject, shows a marked insistence on movement.[2] Both figures are launched in a wild forward rush in which they have lost the plodding realism of the former drawing, and both have greatly elongated bodies. In the step from this to the final painting, the two outstanding changes that have taken place are the addition of the oxen and the angular folds in the clothing. The change from the original drawing of the blind flower-seller to the bacchanalian peasants and oxen is complete in spirit as well as style. (It is moreover the last drawing in which the theme of blindness occurs until nearly thirty years had passed.) We can thus trace three different sources which played their part in the final composition: El Greco's *St. Joseph*, the peasant boy with the oxen, and the blind flower-seller, all seen by Picasso at different times and in different places.

The summer visit to Barcelona and Gosol was of marked importance in Picasso's development. He had again made contact with the Romanesque and Gothic art of Catalonia and had rekindled his passion for El Greco. But even more important to him was the discovery of the pre-Roman Iberian sculpture which had recently been shown in Paris. Bronzes found in excavations at Osuna, not far from Malaga, in 1903 had been acquired by the Louvre. Added to them was another exhibit, the polychrome portrait bust known as *The Lady of Elche*. In his eager search for new forms in art, these sculptures attracted him by their unorthodox formal style, their disregard for refinements, their rude barbaric strength and their closeness to his own origins. Their influence can be held responsible for the clearly defined sculptural features of the repainted head of Gertrude Stein, and the drawing of certain heads with large, heavily outlined eyes.[3] The tranquillity of classical proportions was already threatened by more primitive and vital influences.

But it is the transformation in the human form which is most striking. In female nudes of the Circus and the first Classical periods there is a tendency to idealise the long rounded thighs and exaggerate their length in proportion to the slender body surmounted by virginal breasts; but after Gosol the nudes, often composed as two figures facing each other, are statuesque in the simplicity of their heavy modelling and the suppression of any accidents or extraneous

[1] See Zervos, *Picasso*, Vol. I, p. 140.   [2] Ibid.   [3] Plate V, 3.

detail.[1] They have moved from the classical into a new atmosphere where preconceived rules of proportion are abandoned. It is these studies of the human form that foreshadow the great events that were about to occur and the birth of a new aesthetic conception—cubism.

[1] Plate IV, 5.

CHAPTER V

LES DEMOISELLES D'AVIGNON
(1906-1909)

New Tendencies and Matisse

THE PARIS Salon d'Automne had been founded in 1903 as a protest against the sterile academic control that was stifling the fashionable annual exhibitions. Its only rival was the anarchic, juryless Salon des Indépendants which held its exhibitions every spring. The opening was celebrated by the Nabis, a group of painters led by Maurice Denis, Bonnard, Vuillard and Sérusier, with a large memorial show of Gauguin, their first leader, who had died that year in the Marquesas Islands. The following year, for the first time a collection of thirty-two paintings by Cézanne was shown to the public, and in each of the two succeeding years ten more were exhibited. In 1907, the year after his death, the Master of Aix was honoured by his friends with a large retrospective exhibition of his work, though in general its significance was little understood.

Apart from these tardy recognitions of the older generation of pioneers, the Salon d'Automne became the stronghold of the Fauve group, who continued to astonish the critics and enrage the public with the wild brilliant colouring of their pictures. In the spring of 1906 their leader Matisse had anticipated the excitement of the autumn Salon by exhibiting with the Indépendants a large and revolutionary picture, *La Joie de Vivre*. The brilliant flat colours in which it was painted signified a break with his former style and alarmed the critics. His old friend Signac, a follower of Seurat's theories of pointillism and at that time the domineering Vice-President of the Indépendants, took it as a betrayal that he could never forgive. But in spite of his disapproval, the picture was bought at once by Leo and Gertrude Stein, and it was in their collection when Picasso saw it for the first time on his return from Gosol in the autumn. What is equally important, however, is that thanks to the Steins' hospitality Picasso met Matisse shortly after.

Fernande Olivier, who used to accompany Picasso on his visits, gives a spirited description of the meeting which gave birth to a long if spasmodic friendship. The French painter was then thirty-seven,

Picasso's senior by twelve years. "He was a sympathetic character", she writes, "the type of the great master, with his regular features and vigorous red beard. At the same time, behind his big spectacles, he seemed to mask the exact meaning of his expression. Whenever he began to talk he chose his words deliberately . . . very much master of himself at his meeting with Picasso who was always a bit sullen and restrained at such encounters. Matisse shone imposingly."[1]

In his orderly restraint, his careful planning and the ease of his brilliant conversation, Matisse was the antithesis of Picasso. He loved to exhibit his work whenever possible, he always wanted to learn from a comparison with other artists, whereas to Picasso, exhibitions were distasteful and his learning from others was a secret process. However, the attraction between the two painters was one which lasted, in spite of an intense rivalry and not always with the same degree of warmth, until the last days of Matisse's life. At his flat in Nice, where for some years before his death in 1954 Matisse lay bedridden, Picasso was one of his most constant visitors.

Recognition

Although exhibitions have no great interest for Picasso, he visits those of other painters out of curiosity. It is the act of creation that matters to him rather than the subsequent means of display. His first question on meeting a friend is "Have you been working?" and not "Are you having an exhibition?" or "What have you sold?" though this last question is not without interest to him.

In Montmartre his closest friends were all in some respect creative artists, but the demonstrations and theories expounded by groups of painters have never appeared to him relevant. Then as now he preferred the imaginative and witty speculations of his friends the poets.

By the end of 1906, Picasso, who was then twenty-five, had achieved a position which was unusual and enviable for so young a painter. This was particularly remarkable in that he had refused to compromise in his work in spite of severe hardship. Both Sagot and Vollard were now able to sell his pictures and the demand was increasing. The collection which had already become the most reputed in Paris, because of the audacious and discriminating choice of the Steins, contained many of his works. The undeniable mastery that he showed in the techniques of painting, sculpture, engraving and drawing in many different media convinced his admirers not only of his present genius but also of a brilliant career in store.

[1] Fernande Olivier, *Picasso et ses Amis*, p. 107.

Materially his life had become less precarious. He was better off than most of his friends, and he had as his mistress a spirited girl whose beauty never passed unnoticed. There would appear to have been every reason for him to consolidate his hard-won gains and continue to paint in a style that gained the admiration of his most sensitive and intelligent friends and patrons.

Conflicting Styles

But Picasso has always been assailed by the demon of perpetual doubt. His work on his return from the Arcadian summer months at Gosol showed signs of conflict. There were above all two tendencies that had not been resolved. One led towards a jubilant decorative conception. It had produced the tall picture of bacchanalian peasants running with their oxen: here form was sacrificed to the surface design of figures in movement. But the other trend, more static and severe, had as its first consideration a realisation of the existence of volume. In it there was an attempt to create the actual presence of an object on the canvas. In paintings done since his return from Spain the human form had become heavy and sculptural. The illusion of a third dimension on the flat surface of the canvas was made increasingly convincing by the conventional use of shading, but with a far greater freedom than academic standards would have allowed.

Many influences had been absorbed. Their traces were equally apparent in both tendencies. The early delight that Picasso had found in atmospheric appearances derived from the Impressionists and the debauched world of Toulouse-Lautrec had long ago been abandoned. It had been supplanted by a more plastic realisation of form during the Blue period. With the appearance of Harlequin and the circus folk, there was a partial return to atmospheric effects, particularly in the backgrounds of great pictures such as *The Acrobat with the Ball*. Later the intense study of Greek sculpture had borne its fruit in the athletic stature of the boys leading their horses and in the rich, fertile quality of the peasant women of Gosol. It had given fullness to their forms and grace to their proportions without a return to academic conceptions. That had never occurred to Picasso. Almost as soon as it had appeared, the classical calm gave way to more expressive means of representing the human form, which were not of the past but essentially of the modern age.

Picasso was alive not only to influences on his style in artistic expression, but to current trends of thought. The new ideas, theories and speculations of science, such as the fourth dimension and the exploration of the subconscious, were topical talk among intellectuals. From the material point of view the scope of civilised man had recently been enlarged by the use of electricity and petrol. There had also been discoveries in the history of the human spirit, such as the finding of the rock paintings at Altamira, and the adventures of men of imagination like Gauguin among primitive peoples, which were bringing about a revaluation of cultures formerly despised as barbaric. Works of art imported from Asia had had a superficial influence on European style since the first voyages of Vasco da Gama, and Japanese prints had caused a stir when they became popular in the nineteenth century, but it was not until the early years of the present century that the importation by missionaries and explorers of 'curiosities' made by the 'savages' of Africa and the South Seas gave rise to the view that art and beauty could have a meaning that had been suppressed by the canons of good taste.

Les Demoiselles d'Avignon

The problems that had kept Picasso in a turmoil of uncertainty, and forced him to exploit two almost opposite tendencies at the same time, found a solution in the spring of 1907. After months of work on drawings and studies, Picasso painted with determination and in the space of a few days a large picture measuring nearly eight feet square.[1] He took unusual care in the preparation of the canvas. The smooth type of canvas that he liked to paint on would not have been strong enough for so large a surface. He therefore had a fine canvas mounted on stronger material as a reinforcement and had a stretcher made to his specified unconventional dimensions. When he still considered the picture to be unfinished, his friends were allowed to see it, and from that moment he did not work on it any more. A new style, deliberate and powerful, met their astonished gaze.

At first glance this picture has the power of drawing the spectator to it by its atmosphere of sheer Arcadian delight. The flesh tones of five female nudes glow against the background of a curtain, the blueness of which seems to recall the intangible depths of the sky at Gosol, but he is checked in his initial enthusiasm when he finds himself in the forbidding presence of a group of hieratic women staring at him with black wide-open eyes.

Their presence is a surprise, and the small and tempting pile of fruit at their feet, poured out of a melon rind in the shape of a harlequin's hat upside down, seems irrelevant to the scene. The figure on the

[1] Plate V, 1.

extreme left holds back a red ochre curtain so as to display the angular forms of her sisters. Her appearance, particularly in the grave profile of her face, is unmistakably Egyptian, whereas the two figures she reveals in the centre of the picture, their tender pink flesh contrasting with the blue of the background, have more affinity to the medieval frescoes of Catalonia.

There is no movement in the three figures. Although singular and lacking in conventional grace, they are poised and serene, making a strong contrast with the two figures on the right, which, placed one above the other, complete the group. Their faces show such grotesque distortion that they appear to have intruded from another world. The figure above makes a niche for herself in the curtain, while the squatting figure below, opened out like a roast sucking pig, twists on her haunches from back to front, showing a face with staring blue eyes. Both have faces like masks which seem foreign to their naked bodies.

The opinions given by Picasso's friends were of bewildered yet categorical disapproval. No one could see any reason for this new departure. Among the surprised visitors trying to understand what had happened he could hear Leo Stein and Matisse discussing it together. The only explanation they could find amid their guffaws was that he was trying to create a fourth dimension. In reality, Matisse was angry. His immediate reaction was that the picture was an outrage, an attempt to ridicule the modern movement. He vowed he would find some means to 'sink' Picasso and make him sorry for his audacious hoax. Even Georges Braque, who had recently become a friend, was no more appreciative. All he could say as his first comment was, "It is as though we are supposed to exchange our usual diet for one of tow and paraffin," and the Russian collector, Shchukine, exclaimed in sorrow, "What a loss to French art!".

Even Apollinaire, who had shown such understanding in his first criticism a year before, could not manage at first to stomach such an incomprehensible change. He had already committed himself by writing in *Lettres Modernes* (1905): "It has been said of Picasso that his works reveal a premature disillusionment. I think quite differently. Everything enchants him and his undeniable talent seems to me to serve an imagination in which the delightful and the horrible, the low and the delicate, are proportionately mingled." Apollinaire now watched the revolution that was going on not only in the great painting but also in Picasso himself, with consternation. Picasso's disregard for the reputation he had won with such labour, was of no consequence beside the internal struggle that went on within him as he realised that he could no longer be an artist who accepts without a challenge the dictates of his muse. Artists of this kind, wrote Apollinaire, "are like prolongations of nature, and their works do not pass through the intellect". Picasso had become the other kind, who "must draw everything from within themselves . . . [and] live in solitude." It was after five years of pondering over the change that Apollinaire wrote this in his book *The Cubist Painters*. He finished his statement by saying, "Picasso was [formerly] the first type of artist. Never has there been so fantastic a spectacle as the metamorphosis he underwent in becoming an artist of the second type."[1]

Apollinaire, when he came to see the *Demoiselles d'Avignon*, brought with him the critic Félix Fénéon, who had a reputation for discovering talent among the young, but the only encouragement that he could offer was to advise Picasso to devote himself to caricature. Talking of this later, Picasso remarked that this was not so stupid since all good portraits are in some degree caricatures.

Picasso was not insensitive to the unanimous censure of his friends. It brought not only severe disappointment through the discovery that he had outstripped their capacity to understand him, but also the menace of renewed privations, since no one, not even Vollard, thought any more of buying his recent work. The solitude that his daring brought to Picasso was so great that Derain remarked to their new friend, Kahnweiler, "one day we shall find Pablo has hanged himself behind his great canvas".

Any man who fundamentally relied less on his own judgement or who was less conscious of the strength of his own individuality would undoubtedly have done something drastic, turned back or modified the direction of his advance, but criticism was a challenge to Picasso and he used it as a stimulus to further effort along the same lonely and exalted path.

The next months were spent on paintings that Barr classifies as 'postscripts' to his great work, and slowly his friends began to acclaim this picture that had so seriously disturbed them, not only as the turning point in Picasso's career but as the beginning of a new era in the modern movement. All, with the exception of Leo Stein—who could not stand the change and later condemned cubism as 'Godalmighty rubbish!'—sooner or later admitted its astonishing merits.

[1] Apollinaire, *The Cubist Painters*, 1913, (translation) Wittenborn, New York, 1944.

There were, however, two exceptions to the first general disapproval. Wilhelm Uhde, the German critic and collector, was at once enthusiastic in his admiration. In agreement with him was his young friend, Daniel-Henry Kahnweiler, to whom Uhde had described the picture in advance as a strange painting 'somewhat Assyrian' in style.

After his first acquaintance with the author of this revolutionary work, Kahnweiler became the lifelong friend of Picasso and the authoritative historian of cubism from its earliest years. At that time he had recently abandoned his prospects of a prosperous financial career in London and had arrived in Paris to try his hand as a picture dealer, attracted by the originality and force that he found among young painters such as Picasso, Derain, Vlaminck and Braque. They were chosen as the first to be exhibited in the gallery he opened in the rue Vignon.

Although there is some doubt about the origin of the title of the great picture, since Picasso himself never invents titles, it is probable that it was first named *Les Demoiselles d'Avignon* by André Salmon some years after it had been painted. The reason was partly the resemblance between these nude ladies showing their charms and scenes witnessed in a brothel in the Carrer d'Avinyó (Avignon Street) in Barcelona, and partly a ribald suggestion that Max Jacob's grandmother, a native of Avignon, was the model for one of the figures.

The idea of a large picture of female nudes began at Gosol, where many studies of groups and individual figures were made. The later sketches which led up to the composition itself are of great interest.[1] They show not only the stages of its formation but also the progressive elimination of any incidental story. In the first there are seven figures, two of which appear to be sailors visiting a brothel. One is seated holding a bouquet in the centre of the group of five nudes, while the other enters from behind a curtain holding an object which Picasso has said was intended to be a skull. It has been suggested that "Picasso originally conceived the picture as a kind of *memento mori* allegory"—the wages of sin, though it is unlikely that he had any "very fervid moral intent".[2] It corresponded most probably with his Spanish preoccupation with death.

In subsequent studies the composition begins to take its final shape and all anecdote vanishes. Sailors and flowers have gone, though the fruit remains in the foreground. The figures are backed by curtains which have no great depth. The scene appears limited to the small

[1] See Zervos, *Picasso*, Vol. II*, p. 12, Nos. 19 and 20, p. 13, Nos. 21 and 22.
[2] Alfred Barr, *Picasso, Fifty Years of His Art*, p. 57.

stage of a cabaret, but the strong accents in the rhythmic highlights on the folds of the curtains and their bluish colour have the same incalculable depth as El Greco's skies.

The figures on the left are painted with flat surfaces of pink with only a slight variation of tone. None of the conventional devices of shading or perspective is used to give them volume, but in spite of this their forms are not limp or empty. This remarkable effect has been achieved by the firm and sensitive way in which they are drawn. Volume is emphasised in a manner reminiscent of the Catalan primitives. Lines, dark or light, outline the essential shapes with great economy of means. The features of each face are drawn unequivocally: eyes, ears and noses are unmistakable. They are seen in full face or in profile irrespective of the position of the head to which they belong. They are not merely symbolic nor are they fleeting or accidental in appearance. They belong organically to each of the heads and give it life.

These methods could never have been tolerated by the Impressionists or their followers, the Fauves. It was their belief that the limitation of form by line was a falsehood. It imprisoned the form and isolated it from its surroundings. Objects, therefore, should not be drawn but painted with differences of tone and colour so that they bathe in atmospheric light. But Picasso thought otherwise. His appreciation of objects was passionate and clear like his native climate. By his use of line, colour and modulations of tone he established the presence of the object. He was willing to sacrifice all former rules and prejudices and by taking these risks he discovered new methods more appropriate to the expression of his sensibility.

In this sense the *Demoiselles d'Avignon* is a battlefield. The picture itself contains evidence of Picasso's internal struggle. It can be seen at a glance that the two right-hand figures are totally different in treatment from the others. Ghoulish and sinister, they make the already forbidding features of their companions appear dignified, almost gentle. The upper face is dominated by a wedge-shaped nose of enormous size. Heavy shading with green hatching spreads from its crest almost to the jaw. The structure of the face below depends on the strong sweeping curve of a monstrous snout which divides a terracotta coloured cheek from the heavy blue shadow on the side of the nose—a contrast which gives solidity to its flat surface. With astonishing economy and the use of revolutionary means the awful asymmetry of this mask-like face comes to life.

There has been much controversy about the impulses that combined to give birth to these two heads. Until recently it was supposed that

Picasso painted the whole picture after being greatly impressed by his discovery of African sculpture. This however is obviously untrue, for the three nudes to the left show no such tendencies. Their ancestry lies without doubt in the Iberian bronzes and Catalan murals, with which certain Egyptian influences have been assimilated. Further, Picasso has stated firmly that when he started the picture he was not conscious of any particular interest in negro art. The other two faces, so different in spirit, have, however, some generic resemblance to the barbaric simplicity of negro masks, and it also appears that they were painted in after the rest of the picture had already taken its present form in the spring of 1907.

It is well known that Vlaminck and Derain, a year or two before, had bought African masks, and Vlaminck is said to have discovered two negro statuettes among the bottles in a bar and brought them home under his arm as far back as 1904. Their enthusiasm for primitive sculpture was shared by Matisse, but Picasso was not struck by its significance until one day that spring while he was painting the *Demoiselles*. He paid a visit to the Museum of Historic Sculpture at the Trocadero, and found by chance that the ethnographical department contained a splendid collection of negro sculpture. Negro art in the Trocadero was esteemed only for its scientific value. There was then no attempt to present the objects as works of art, on the contrary they were piled into badly lit glass cases with complete disregard for those who might be interested in the startling originality of their form. This in some way made their discovery all the more exciting, and to this day Picasso remembers the emotion he felt at this first contact. It is significant that while the other painters who had already made this discovery continued to show no sign of its influence in their work, Picasso understood its importance and saw the profound implications that could be used to bring about a revolution in art. Shortly after this, he too began to buy from a dealer in the rue de Rennes. His first finds were not necessarily pieces of great value but they possessed vitality and a freedom from academic conventions that excited his imagination. With complete disregard for stylistic unity he completed his picture with two heads that sprang from his delight at his new discovery.

Like many of Picasso's most powerful works, this painting is an organised and wilful sum total of inconsistencies. It is as though a dramatic change in his attitude to art and its relation to beauty had taken place while he was at work. The commander had changed his tactics while the battle was in progress, but rather than suppress the evidence of conflict between two stages of his thought, he left it unfinished, allowing us to see clearly the evolution of ideas in his own mind. It is in fact our best clue in bridging the gulf that seems to separate the bewitching charm of the Rose period from the severity of the task on which he was about to embark. The barbarous appearance of the heads on the right and their disregard for all classical canons of beauty give the lie to statements such as "Beauty is truth, truth beauty", because no human face, and these must be recognised as human, could ever assume such monstrous proportions, and yet their powerful presence speaks profoundly and truthfully to our sensibility.

Picasso had finished working on the *Demoiselles* within a year of the appearance of Matisse's picture, *La Joie de Vivre*, to which it bears certain superficial resemblances. The subsequent history of the two pictures was however very different. Matisse according to his custom exhibited his canvas to the public almost before the paint was dry, and within a few weeks it had entered into an important collection where for many years it was constantly admired by a large international group of appreciative visitors. Picasso's painting remained in his studio almost unseen. It was never shown to the public until thirty years after it had been painted. For many years it lay rolled up on the floor in his studio and it was in this condition when it was bought without being seen beforehand by Jacques Doucet soon after 1920. Doucet, realising its importance, gave it a place of honour in his collection and although it was acclaimed by the Surrealists who reproduced it in *La Révolution Surréaliste* in 1925, giving it for the first time its present title, few people even knew of its existence until it was shown at the Petit Palais in 1937 and bought shortly afterwards by the Museum of Modern Art of New York. Lent by the trustees of this museum it has once been shown publicly in London, by the Institute of Contemporary Arts in 1949.

This history, as Barr points out, should be sufficient to refute those who have maliciously claimed that Picasso never acts without an eye to publicity.

Even during the early days of its seclusion, the influence of the picture on those who saw it was profound. Derain and Braque chose this moment to abandon Fauvism and turn their attention to a search for plastic values. As for Braque, after his first resentment, he quietly shook off his antagonism and became Picasso's close companion in the cubist adventure that was to follow. Even Matisse showed signs in his painting of the following year of a swing away from the flat colour patterns of *La Joie de Vivre* towards a realisation of form.

A vital reason for insisting on the importance of the *Demoiselles* is that in this picture Picasso for the first time became entirely himself. Out of the many influences that affected him he created with his intuitive deliberation a painting which combined discipline and vitality. Antecedents for the general scheme of the composition can be found in Cézanne's groups of female nudes which are organised into the great compositions of bathers. The central nude figure with its raised arm and drapery of his *Temptation of St. Anthony* may have provided a suggestion, and the idea of a closed interior bordered by curtains occurs in the *Olympia* of the same artist. But the economy of means, the strong decisive line, accentuated only where necessary, and the elimination of ornament, virtuosity and the picturesque give the *Demoiselles* a strength which is unparalleled in the work of any other artist of that period. There is a mastery of scale derived from the diminutive proportions of the fruit grouped in the foreground that gives a towering sense of authority to the figures standing above it. The control of colour which is based almost entirely on the contrasts of pinks and blues, the simplified, unmodelled shapes of the female form which are at the same time flat and voluminous, and the monstrous distortions of the two negroid heads, challenge our former conceptions of beauty and widen the horizons of our enjoyment.

Negro Period

There are many aspects of African sculpture that have intrigued Picasso. The simple blocked-out features of negro masks express with force the primeval terrors of the jungle, and their ferocious expressions or serene look of comprehension are frequently a reminder of the lost companionship between man and the animal kingdom. In more formal ways the able use of geometric shapes and patterns produces an abstract aesthetic delight in form. The simple basic shapes created by the circle and the straight line, the only unchanging features of beauty, are applied with startling aptitude. But above all it is the rich variety in which these elements exist and the vitality that radiates from negro art that brought Picasso a new breath of inspiration.

The paintings that followed the *Demoiselles* added to his discoveries. Many of them were direct 'postscripts' in which the sculptural appearance of the two wry heads was developed with a passionate fervour. A new architecture of the human form came to life in which classical proportions were a hindrance. Even the expressive distortions of El Greco and the Catalan primitives gave way to a more violent mode based on form that was essentially sculptural.

The head, that culminating feature of our human architecture, occupied Picasso's thoughts most profoundly during the spring and summer of 1907. Heads such as the upper one of the barbaric pair in the *Demoiselles*, which appear in several studies where the nose is heavily shaded with strong parallel lines coming down across the cheek, leaving a prominent cheekbone to catch the light, are held by most critics to be derived from the masks from the Ivory Coast. It is for this and other similar reasons that the period beginning with the *Demoiselles* has been labelled the Negro period. Negro influences are undoubtedly present at this stage and continue to show themselves in other more subtle ways throughout the cubist period, but the receptive sensibility of Picasso embraced many sources in addition.

Sympathy for the violent expression and primitive strength of negro sculpture came at a moment when Picasso was again preoccupied with the realisation of solid forms on a two-dimensional surface. His thoughts were inspired by sculpture, but it was not until two years later that he turned his hand again to modelling. Before this happened, though he thought as a sculptor, he acted as a painter. Even in a still-life such as *Flowers on a Table*,[1] the flowers are endowed with such solidity as to suggest the possibility of making a reconstruction in bronze. The planes, luminous with colour, are determined by strong outlines and heavy shading, a technique which suggests the fronds of a palm or the tattoed patterns on the naked bodies of negro statues. In the large *Nude with Drapery*[2] which is now in Russia, he combines his sculptural sense of form with a vigorous and exciting surface pattern accentuated by heavy hatching which gives the effect of light filtered by jungle vegetation.

These influences were assimilated and combined with the persistent love that Picasso had for archaic Iberian bronzes. Their resemblance can still be traced in paintings such as the *Woman in Yellow*.[3] To label all paintings of this period as "Negro" is in fact to oversimplify the problem of their origins and diminish their significance. Raynal suggests that it would be less misleading to call this period "prehistoric" or "prehellenistic", but if the period must have a label it would be more exact to use the term "proto-Cubist" invented by Barr, since all these tendencies led consistently to the birth of the new style.

Already by the end of 1907 the fireworks that form a surface pattern of the *Nude with Drapery* have died down, and more solid constructions take their place in paintings such as *Friendship*,[4] a composition of two nudes, now also in Russia.

[1] See Zervos, *Picasso*, Vol. II*, p. 17, No. 30.   [2] Plate V, 4.
[3] See Zervos, *Picasso*, Vol. II*, p. 23, No. 43.   [4] Plate V, 6.

This picture, painted in the spring of 1908, was again the result of a number of studies, large and small. It is painted with rich, warm earth colours and combines angular patterns with sculptural solidity almost as though the figures were constructed from wooden blocks. *Friendship* was one of fifty paintings by Picasso bought by the Russian merchant Shchukine, who paid frequent visits to Paris and established before 1914 the finest and most comprehensive collection of contemporary French painting in Europe. With magnificent examples of the work of Monet, Degas, Toulouse-Lautrec, Van Gogh and Gauguin already in his possession, he made the acquaintance of Matisse, from whom he bought freely. As a proof of his fundamental esteem for Picasso, Matisse had introduced him also to the Russian collector. From then until the war and the Russian Revolution put a stop to his coming and going, Shchukine was a frequent visitor to Picasso's studio, following his evolution with enthusiasm and buying many examples of his work. At an early date he recognised Matisse and Picasso as the greatest of their generation.

Literary Friends

The scandal caused by *Les Demoiselles* did not interfere with the visits of Max Jacob and Apollinaire to Picasso's studio. With the increasing necessity to see people by day and live more normal hours, he worked less frequently by night. In the morning he rose late and his ill humour was showered, as always, on anyone except his best friends or serious amateurs who inadvertently called too early. None the less he was always glad enough to receive visitors in the evenings when he was not working. Together they talked, sang and consumed large quantities of wine and spirits, as they explored together to the limits of their imagination, and tore to pieces anything or anybody they hated. Fernande tells of experiments with drugs, of nights when curiosity led them into the gentle dreams of opium. "Friendship", she says, "became more confident, more tender, all indulgent. The next day, on waking, having forgotten this communion we began again to snap at each other, for there has never been a circle of artists where mockery or malicious and wounding remarks were more honoured."

These soothing but dangerous expedients came to an end, however, when a young German painter, Wiegels, was found hanging in his studio as a result of excessive doses of ether. His funeral and his memory were celebrated in horrified remorse at the Lapin Agile. "Opium", says Picasso, "has the most intelligent of all odours", but it was not only the suicide of Wiegels that put a stop to its use. While under the influence of the drug Picasso found that his imagination and his vision became more acute but that his desire to paint what he saw diminished seriously. This threat of blissful sterility influenced him most.

. Although Montmartre was in itself almost self-sufficient, the brilliance of the literary group who gathered at the Closerie des Lilas tempted Picasso to cross the Seine and join its noisy discussions. Wrapped in a heavy shapeless overcoat that covered him to the ankles to keep out his enemy the cold, he would cross Paris on foot every Tuesday with Fernande. In spite of the distance she found that "it does good to walk when one carries youth on one's face and hope in one's heart".

Two poets, Paul Fort and André Salmon, were the organisers of these weekly reunions known as 'Vers et Prose'. Their friends who came regularly were poets, writers, painters, sculptors and musicians, young and old, boisterous and eccentric, but all talented. Picasso enjoyed breathing this air charged with intellectual fireworks. It was a delight to talk to poets such as Jean Moréas, who in spite of their lack of understanding of the problems that Picasso had at heart, provided a subtle commentary on a general human footing. He understood them, it mattered little if they misjudged him. In addition the circle included intimate friends: Apollinaire, Raynal, occasionally Braque, and, until his death, Alfred Jarry. The meetings were warmed by lavish drinking animated by passionate or witty discussions. Not infrequently they ended in protests from the *patron* of the café and the expulsion of the whole company.

Picasso's taste coincided in general with the literary extravagance of these reunions, but when it was a question of a closer understanding, no one among the poets could share his humours or his ideas more closely than Apollinaire. This man, whose origins were a matter of legend rather than knowledge, had travelled, and his knowledge of foreign languages and the more obscure and erotic paths of literature was vast. His love of the picturesque was tempered with a profound appreciation of reality and a desire to liberate man from hypocrisy and sterile, self-made limitations. "Picasso certainly possessed the same kind of sensibility, but Apollinaire helped him to become convinced of it himself. And it is in this way that by dint of listening to the dictates of his heart, Picasso perceived the emptiness of the absolute rules of Art."[1] In writing this, Maurice Raynal also quotes a saying that "man spends the first part of his life with the dead, the second with the living and the third with himself". Picasso's first years had been passed

[1] Maurice Raynal, *Picasso* (Crès), p. 39-40 (translation).

with the great examples that religion, history, literature and art presented in idealised form. He had aimed at a kind of ideal and conventional perfection, and this youthful dream continued until in a moment of clarity he perceived that it led rapidly back to the dead. He needed new and wider horizons, and these he found, not through the tiresome and confused arguments of painters, but by confidence in his own imagination, nourished by his understanding of poetry and his love of the shapes it took before his eyes.

The many books that littered his studio were of a variety that would baffle anyone who expected Picasso to make a coherent study of art and metaphysics. Mixed with volumes of the poetry of Verlaine, Rimbaud, and Mallarmé, and works by eighteenth-century philosophers such as Diderot and Rétif de la Bretonne, were adventure stories—Sherlock Holmes, Nick Carter and Buffalo Bill. On the other hand a type of book that was completely absent was the realistic or psychological novel. These books, shorn of imagination and drama, lacked all interest for him. They were an applied art rather than art itself.

The Douanier Rousseau

For some years the Salon des Indépendants, thanks to its policy of welcoming all who wished to exhibit, had shown the strange paintings of a humble little man, Henri Rousseau, a retired employee of the octroi or City Toll and in consequence nicknamed 'Le Douanier' by Apollinaire. He had had no training as a painter, although as far back as 1894 Jarry had made his acquaintance and admired his work. Jarry had even published a lithograph of a large painting of Rousseau called *La Guerre*. The naïve skill with which the little man painted, and the intensity of his imagination, brought him increasing popularity among the small group of young painters who were searching for an art unsullied by academic requirements. His sincerity was unquestionable and he enjoyed company. In his modest studio in the remote rue Perrel he entertained his friends with conversation and airs played on his violin. Up to his death in 1910 he lived in poverty, but the company that attended his soirées was by no means undistinguished.

The Autumn Salon of 1905 had accepted three paintings by the Douanier including an enormous jungle scene. Two years later Picasso discovered at the Père Soulier's shop an immense portrait of a woman. All he could see was the head, peering over stacks of grimy paintings. This was enough however to tell him that it was a most accomplished portrait in the great French tradition. He asked

Père Soulier if he could buy it for five francs, to which the dealer replied: "Certainly, it is by a painter called Rousseau but the canvas is good and you may be able to use it." As they pulled it out from the rubbish Picasso was delighted to find that it was a full-length portrait of a woman in a black dress with blue collar and belt, standing in front of an open window. Beside her hung a long striped curtain, and between the bars of a balustrade behind her was a landscape of flowers. When Picasso showed it to Rousseau later, the old man explained that it was the portrait of a Polish school teacher that he had painted years ago; the curtain had been put in to give the picture an oriental look and the landscape was the fortified zone round Paris which he knew well. Picasso had in fact found one of the Douanier's masterpieces. For years afterwards he kept it beside him and still says that it is one of the pictures he loves above all.

Partly in order to celebrate this discovery and the hanging of the picture in his studio, and also from a desire shared with his friends to honour the old painter, Picasso invited a large and brilliant company to a banquet given to pay homage to Rousseau. The 'Banquet Douanier' has become legendary. Three accounts by eye-witnesses describe the festive enthusiasm with which the little elf-like genius was welcomed and the ecstasy with which he received the rowdy, dis-organised compliments paid to him. But the events of the evening were so packed with riotous gaiety and confusion that there are many dis-crepancies between the various versions. Maurice Raynal, who was the first to record the evening, admits that "it was difficult to determine exactly how the party ended".[1] However, on the outstanding events and the memorable success of the banquet, Fernande Olivier and Gertrude Stein agree with him. The whole story is too long to tell here, but the following outline is based on their accounts and those of other eye-witnesses.

No ostentatious preparations had been made, but the studio was transformed with decorations that hid the untidy barnlike appearance of the room and gave the long trestle tables, laid for some thirty guests, a mysterious and festive air. A throne for the guest of honour, placed at one end, was surmounted by a banner with "Honneur à Rousseau" written across it, and his painting was displayed above, surrounded by flags and lanterns. Among the numerous surprises perhaps the most important was the failure on the part of the caterer to send the food, and the host's sudden remembrance that he had made a mistake and ordered it for the following day. This disaster acted as

[1] Maurice Raynal, *Picasso* (Crès), p. 52.

an encouragement to the guests to heighten their festive spirit by a liberal consumption of wine, which they made a substitute for food. Fortunately the prompt action of Fernande and some friends saved the situation by an improvised meal of sardines and a 'riz à la Valencienne' cooked by her in a friend's studio. Nobody regretted the absence of the dinner. On the contrary certain guests who had lost their way in the interminable corridors of the Bateau Lavoir were thankful for it when they arrived on the following day.

It had been arranged that Apollinaire should introduce the guest of honour when everyone was seated, and in spite of some preliminary mishaps, such as Marie Laurencin's fall, due to an overdose of aperitifs, into a tray full of jam tarts, this part of the ceremony was accomplished. The old man, clutching his violin and bewildered by the festive splendour of the scene, was overcome with emotion. His face lit up with joy as he mounted his throne, and all the evening his delight never diminished except for moments when, overcome by sleep, he dozed, his violin in his hand and a candle from a lantern above dripping unerringly on his bald head. Otherwise he sang his repertoire of popular songs including his favourite, "Aie, aie, aie, j'ai mal aux dents", and made the ladies dance to his music.

Among the guests of many nationalities were Spaniards, such as the tall gaunt Pichot who danced a ritual Spanish dance. There was also a strong contingent of poets, including André Salmon, who unexpectedly leapt on the table and recited an improvised ode to Rousseau, and Apollinaire, who found it a good moment to catch up with the arrears of his correspondence, and also wrote a spontaneous poem which he delivered in his impressive voice. The last verse ran:

> 'We are assembled to celebrate your glory.
> These wines which Picasso pours out in your honour
> Let us drink, since this is the hour to drink them,
> Shouting in chorus, Live! Long live Rousseau!'[1]

Through the thick clouds of smoke and the excited chatter of the guests there burst sudden explosions of violence, such as the incident caused by Salmon who began in his cups to hit out indiscriminately. His host however, aided by Braque, disentangled him from his neighbours and locked him away in a nearby studio. Good humour was quickly restored, and visits from local friends, including Fredé

---

[1] Maurice Raynal, *Picasso* (Crès), p. 50.

from the Lapin Agile with his donkey, added to the entertainment throughout the night.

The banquet was a tremendous success. Rousseau drank in, in every sense, the honours showered upon him with touching simplicity. His own vanity made him incapable of questioning the sincerity and whole-hearted admiration of all present, whereas a more sophisticated artist in a gathering composed partly of strangers might have feared a hidden element of playful mockery.

Picasso became deeply attached to this strange and lovable man, and Rousseau, who was incapable of discriminating between the senti-mental academic fantasies of Bougereau and work diametrically opposed to it in tendency, recognised none the less the genius of Picasso. This is clear from his famous remark: "Picasso, you and I are the greatest painters of our time, you in the Egyptian style, I in the Modern."

Picasso appreciated this admiration and reciprocated it. He keeps beside him permanently, wherever he is living, a small self-portrait of the Douanier and a companion portrait of his wife. The influences of his work keep on reappearing in unexpected ways at unexpected times, particularly in paintings of children and fishermen as late as 1936 to 1938.

Picasso is never slow in recognising originality of vision and talent even in unlikely places. With these qualities the portraits, jungle scenes and landscapes of Rousseau are strongly endowed. They also possess another quality which makes them essentially contempor-ary. Cocteau has commented on this quality in his preface to the catalogue of the Quinn Sale, in remarks about the Douanier's great painting, the *Sleeping Gypsy*. This picture, now in the New York Museum of Modern Art, was bought by the collector John Quinn on Picasso's recommendation nearly thirty years after it was painted in 1897. Cocteau wrote: "We have here the contrary of poetic painting, of anecdote. One is confronted rather by painted poetry, by a poetic object . . . by a miracle of intuitive knowledge and sincerity. . . . The gypsy . . . is the secret soul of poetry, an act of faith, a proof of love."[1] It is this conception of a picture being a 'poetic object' that was liberat-ing painting from the bonds that had required it to be a description of a scene. Painting could claim again its ancient right to exist as an object in itself, radiating its own associations and undiminished by being merely the reflection of something else.

[1] From Cocteau's introduction to the catalogue of the Quinn sale. *Masters of Modern Art*, ed. Barr, Mus. of Mod. Art, N.Y., 1954, p. 13.

A Duel

Perhaps on account of his own small but well-built physique, Picasso has always shown an admiration for the size and the well-developed muscular bodies of athletes. Apart from Apollinaire, whose proportions were not mean, three of Picasso's friends, Derain, Vlaminck and Braque, formed an imposing trio. All three were well built and proud of their strength. Braque especially, with his handsome features, was easily recognised by the cowboy-like swagger of his walk. In the early days of their friendship Picasso made comic drawings of an imaginary school for physical culture which they were to found.[1] Overwhelming two-legged monuments of muscle with ludicrously small heads were designed to advertise their venture. In reality Picasso limited his athletics to boxing, in which sport, as Fernande remarks, he preferred hitting to being hit. Even so, one lesson from Derain sufficed to complete his career in that form of sport.

There is a story of an event that took place a year before the banquet which would have caused serious anxiety had it not ended in inoffensive comedy rather than violence. Apollinaire, who believed himself insulted by three fairly harmless lines in an article by Max Daireaux, challenged the writer to a duel. Soon afterwards he appeared on Picasso's doorstep with a worried look, asking for advice. It was decided that he should choose as his seconds Jean de Mitty, a journalist and swordsman of repute, and Max Jacob. The place Ravignan for weeks apprehensively discussed the outcome of the encounter until at last Max Jacob, superbly dressed with a new top hat and monocle, called on the opponents. Negotiations took place between the opposing forces each installed in their favourite cafés, while Apollinaire waited in suspense in Picasso's studio. Finally, the literary ability of those concerned and a free exchange of aperitifs allowed them to draw up a document that was satisfactory to all concerned. Without loss of honour by either side the bloody encounter was avoided.

There was no lack of invitations for Picasso whenever he felt he wanted a change of air. Apollinaire was delighted to receive a visit from him and other friends at his mother's house in Le Vesinet, in spite of her disapproval of their unaccountable habits. On other occasions he invited them to his apartment in Paris. Here they were ceremoniously offered tea with a lavish accompaniment of wit. On Saturdays the Steins kept open house, and Picasso was a frequent visitor with Fernande in elegant and flowery hats. There were dinner

[1] See Zervos, *Picasso*, Vol. VI, p. 81.

parties given by Vollard in the cellar beneath his gallery. Distinguished artists of the older generation and collectors were often present to meet the young Spanish painter and eat the fiery rice dishes of colonial origin. The Germans also were pressing with their hospitality; a rich painter and friend of Uhde gave sumptuous feasts at which Picasso found himself surrounded by admirers.

In his domestic life, in spite of moments of violent disagreement, Picasso continued to cherish his companionship with Fernande. In common they enjoyed the close contact of their friends. Van Dongen, the Dutch painter whose portraits later became fashionable, had a little daughter for whom Picasso enjoyed drawing and making paper dolls. His love of children, like his love of animals, gives endless pleasure and refreshment to his imagination. There is an understand-ing between them that goes deeper than language. They provide that link with the primitive and the instinctive that becomes lost in a world based on reason and practical considerations.

The studio, already hopelessly overcrowded with paintings and objects that never ceased to accumulate, also became the home of various pets. Though it would have pleased Picasso to have had more exotic birds and beasts around him, he contented himself with cats, dogs, a tortoise and a monkey. These were among the many genera-tions of creatures that he has kept beside him, watching and fondling them with wonder and affection wherever he has lived. Max Jacob recounts how in his early days in Paris, Picasso paid frequent visits to the Jardin des Plantes by night, where one of his friends, the son of the curator, gave him access to the rarest and most fascinating animals.

The Beginning of Cubism

The spring in France and even more the summer have an irresistible tendency to draw painters away from Paris to the great varieties of landscape in the provinces. Early in 1908 both Braque and Derain left for the country with the troubling memory of Picasso's great picture, *Les Demoiselles*, and the two monstrous faces it contained. Braque, following in Cézanne's footsteps, went to l'Estaque near Marseilles and returned in the autumn with a number of landscapes, six of which he submitted to the Salon d'Automne. But the jury were upset by a tendency they had not seen in his work before. Colour, instead of being the supreme factor, had become subdued and there was an insistence on simplified geometrical forms. Matisse as a member of the jury pointed out to the critic Louis Vauxcelles, inventor of the term 'Fauve', the predominance of what he called "les petits cubes".

Two of the pictures were refused and Braque in annoyance at once withdrew the others. Happily, Kahnweiler was unperturbed by the new style and gave Braque a show in his gallery in November, which has rightly been claimed as the first cubist exhibition. Encouraged by this, Braque sent two more paintings to the Indépendants the following spring. The critics now had their full opportunity to show their scorn. Vauxcelles had already quoted Matisse's remark about 'les cubes' in his criticism of the show at Kahnweiler's gallery, and now in an unsympathetic review which would otherwise have been long ago forgotten, he followed it up and facetiously labelled the style 'Peruvian Cubism'. From then on the sadly inadequate title 'cubism' has been used as a label and was sanctioned by Apollinaire in his first articles in defence of the new style in 1913.

La Rue des Bois

During the same spring, Picasso, nervous and turbulent, stayed in Paris pushing his discoveries further. According to Fernande, he was still haunted by the death of Wiegels, the second suicide of a friend that had touched him closely and reawakened a sensation of the disquieting nearness of death. Rather than make a long journey to the south he decided, late in the summer of 1908, to overcome his prejudices and try the soothing influences of the French countryside. Having heard by chance from a friend of a vacant cottage on a farm situated between the forest of Hallatte and the river Oise, he set out with little knowledge of where he was going, accompanied by Fernande, a dog and a cat to cure his melancholy in the hamlet known as La Rue des Bois, some thirty miles north of Paris. Although their lodgings were primitive, with a farmyard at their doorstep, there was just enough room to work and to entertain friends from Paris for a few days at a time. Picasso was soon immersed in the refreshing influences of meadows and forest. For the first time since his early sketches at Corunna, and later at Horta de San Juan, he became interested in the subject-matter offered by the landscape on its own merits and not merely as a background for figures.

The verdant countryside of the Oise influenced his palette. Green became so predominant as to suggest to some that the work of these months should be called the Green period. In any case, with a violent thirst for wider horizons, a new experience had begun, and the paintings he produced at La Rue des Bois form a group to themselves.

In contemplating a landscape the eye has the ability to extend the sense of touch so that it seems possible to caress the surfaces spreading out into the distance. The walls of a house or the slope of a distant mountain can become as tangible to the imagination as a match-box held in the hand. The great landscape painters in the past had none the less neglected this sensation in favour of atmospheric effects. Strong contrasts of tone and colour were situated in the foreground while a blue haze was reserved for the furthest distance. A system of perspective in which the size of objects tailed off to vanishing points in the horizon completed the illusion of space. The image obtained according to these rules, however, made objects too intangible and indeterminate for Picasso. Just as he had taken liberties with the human form to enable the eye to embrace its shapes more completely, so now he began to treat landscape as sculptural form. All unnecessary detail was sacrificed so as to emphasise salient features, and the time-honoured rules of perspective were abandoned, together with any attempt to give an effect of immeasurable distance in the background. In fact, in the landscapes of La Rue des Bois,[1] background and foreground are merged together in a play of surfaces which seem to touch each other. The eye is invited to travel among them and enjoy the definite though subtle way in which it can be led into the depths of the picture, exploring paths as they disappear into recesses and returning over angular planes that push forward into the light. In the three-dimensional pattern made up of definite planes, the eye is never allowed to lose itself in awkward holes which could break the continuity of the surface of the picture and destroy the coherence of the composition. Trees, houses and paths belong to each other and invite the eye to feel and wander among them, enjoying their homely solidity. A house is without doubt a house, and a tree a tree. They present themselves as objects to be felt and to be loved.

The same objective spirit that affirms the presence of each object is not limited to landscapes. It appears in a series of still-lifes painted on Picasso's return to Paris.[2] They are composed in general of bowls and bottles set together on a table, and the presence of these simple utensils seems to be completely established. They exist as familiar objects and also as the component parts of a pattern in which nothing can be added or subtracted without destroying the effect of perfect balance.

Before leaving La Rue des Bois, Picasso amused himself by painting two pictures strongly reminiscent of the two painters upon whom he was meditating most at the time. In one, the central object placed on a crumpled patterned cloth with fruit in front of it, is the tall black hat so

<hr />

[1] Plate V, 5.   [2] See Zervos, *Picasso*, Vol. II*, p. 48.

characteristic of the later paintings of Cézanne.[1] The other is a flower piece[2] in which the central placing and simple formal shapes of blossoms and leaves are reminiscent of the style of the Douanier Rousseau, a spoon on one side is a characteristic sign of the more complicated sensibility of Picasso.

The same drastic elimination of detail and massing of form into sculptural units appear in several powerful studies of heads painted during the autumn. There is also a figure, 'ponderous and static', called *The Peasant Woman*,[3] in which, owing to a desire to emphasise the solid ample proportions of the figure, colour has again been reduced nearly to monochrome. The hieratic qualities of negro sculptures once more become apparent.

During the winter the tendency to keep colour subservient to form continued. Compositions of female nudes, aglow with an overall warmth of reddish brown, were acquired by Shchukine for his collection.

There is also a notable picture of a figure, *Nude on Beach*.[4] Flat angular shapes in this case are softened. Each part of the woman's body is modelled into curved shell-like volumes, linked together at their joints. The articulations, ornamented with flourishes that recall arabesques, resemble the knots between the trunk and branches of a tree. To increase the sensation of volume, back and front are shown simultaneously. Breasts and shoulder blades, belly and buttocks are together in view. The tall structure of the human form grows from large flattened feet planted on the sand. We are presented with a new architectural view in which the living units have been torn to pieces and built up again into a statuesque image. The limitations of a two-dimensional medium have been overcome by hiding from us neither front nor back but at the same time uniting both into a convincing whole.

Horta de San Juan, Summer 1909

By the time the next summer arrived it was impossible for Picasso to resist his desire to return to Spain. For a painter, travelling is difficult. He is in close contact with the material world which he contemplates, enjoys with his eyes and feels with the sensibility of his entire body, also he is to some extent impeded by paraphernalia needed

[1] See Zervos, *Picasso*, Vol. II*, p. 44, No. 84.
[2] Ibid., Vol. II*, p. 45, No. 88.   [3] Ibid., Vol. II*, p. 46, No. 91.
[4] Plate VI, I.

for his work. As he is so essentially influenced by his visual surroundings, concentration is easily dissipated if he moves too often from one
region to another. If he is to find time to penetrate the mysteries of the
objects that surround him and develop all the potentialities of his
talent, he will be unlikely to risk blurring his perception by frequent
kaleidoscopic changes in his surroundings. But by adopting a life of
comparative immobility, when he does travel he finds his reward in
the fresh impact and excitement of unaccustomed scenes.

Picasso has travelled very little outside the limits of his favourite
regions in France, which are confined to Paris and the Mediterranean
coast. In consequence each place keeps its associations intact and is
remembered for its own local population of beings both real and
imaginary. Recently, at Cannes, after finishing a bold and evocative
drawing of a bearded head, wearing horns like some ancient shepherd
king, beside whom was seated a faunlike creature piping to the stars,
Picasso said, "it is strange, in Paris I never draw fauns, centaurs
or mythical heroes like these, they always seem to live in these
parts".

A change often occurs in Picasso's style when he moves to new
surroundings and influences remain localised because of the intensity
of his perception and his capacity to differentiate clearly between
sensations.

It was ten years since he had visited his friend Pallarès in the remote
countryside of the province of Tarragona and made his first acquaintance with Spanish peasants, ten years since he had smelt the wild landscape that rises into the arid mountains of Teruel, whose angular
shapes close the distant horizon. On the way through Barcelona he
paid a brief visit to his family. Accompanied by Fernande he lunched
daily with his father and mother, but as soon as the meal was over he
preferred to go out with his friends in excursions to the heights of
Tibiado or places in the nearby mountains from where they could
look down on the great city below. These were passing pleasures:
as usual it was the remote calm of the countryside that was the object
of his journey, and soon, with Fernande, he was again installed in the
little village of Horta, in the blazing heat of midsummer.

As was to be expected after the experience of Paris and the immense
discoveries that had been made since his first visit, Picasso saw his
surroundings in a new light. If we turn back to the talented sketches of
ten years before, we find there the inquisitive delight of a youth
watching the life of the peasant folk and conscious of his ability to
seize its detail in rapid fragmentary descriptions of what he saw. But

during the ensuing years Picasso had learned to see with other eyes, and to demand from his work, not the mirrored image of ever-changing appearances, but the construction of a reality that he could now perceive more clearly in his imagination—an exteriorisation of his deepest feelings about the world in which he lived. With new insight he could now give a timeless quality to his work and endow each picture with a life of its own. This relationship between objective reality and the work of art was beginning to be resolved by the hazardous experiment of cubism. His interest still lay along the path that had been opened up to him the year before in the wooded slopes of the Ile de France. But the Oise had been exchanged for the Ebro, the northern forests with their dense green patterns reminiscent of the jungle scenes of Rousseau, for the feathery Mediterranean pines and olive trees dear to Cézanne. Pastures were replaced by terraced vine-yards and the close damp atmosphere of the north vanished in the hard light and the vast clear skies of Spain.

The first landscape to be completed shows the conical shape of an arid mountain.[1] It is sufficiently representational for us to be able to trace, above the roofs of the square stone houses, a path bordered by cypresses that leads up a granite slope to the Grotto of Beato Salvador. A severe analysis of the scene has however been made, and the forms are reconstructed with geometric simplicity. Picasso had taught himself to see beneath the bewildering detail of the surface. His intelligence had intervened and overruled his former pleasure in making copies of nature. He now deliberately stated the emotions conveyed to him by what he saw and what he knew. All liberties were permitted if they could help in this aim.

In the composition of this first landscape, the central position and shape of the mountain peak is in itself reminiscent of Cézanne's paint-ings of the Mont St. Victoire. The insistence on simple forms to the exclusion of all irrelevant detail is proof that Picasso was conscious of the views expressed by Cézanne in his frequently quoted letter to Emile Bernard: "You must see in nature the cylinder, the sphere, the cone." The underlying principles of form must be analysed, otherwise the confused surface detail of natural appearances will obscure its real nature.

A succession of six or more landscapes admirable in their clarity followed *The Mountain*, of which the best known are *The Factory*[2] and *The Reservoir*.[3] In the latter, the little town itself, set on a hill, is

[1] See Zervos, *Picasso*, Vol. II*, p. 76, No. 151.

[2] Ibid., Vol. II*, p. 78, No. 158.   [3] Plate VI, 6.

the focus of forms crystallised round a central tower. In others the houses unite with the angular solidity of the mountains or the spreading branches of palm trees whose regular rhythms are repeated in the sky. Picasso had found the landscape he required to verify what he had already begun to discover in his analysis of the human form. The shapes he saw in nature became the hard shimmering facets of an agglomeration of crystals or cut stones. The light is no longer cast upon them from one given arbitrary position but seems to radiate from beneath each surface. It is used not as a temporary illumination of the scene, but to accentuate the form of each object and become an integral part of its existence.

In these paintings, colour, which had been set aside as a problem which should not at this stage be allowed to interfere with the realisation of form, creeps in again. It is used to enhance the solidity of the form in the same way that Cézanne employed it, that is to say by shading one surface with a warm brownish colour and contrasting it with the adjoining surface shaded with a cool blue or green. The shading serves to accentuate the relief by making a strong edge between them. Cézanne still used colour for atmospheric effects, whereas Picasso's first consideration was to create the appearance of a reality in solid form.

During this time Picasso applied these principles in a remarkable series of heads.[1] They have the same monumental qualities as the landscapes but beneath their enduring rocklike appearance they are not lacking in expression. Emotion shines through the alternate rise and fall of the luminous planes with which they are constructed. The human face and human form are reorganised with a rich variety of invention. In some we seem to recognise the pointed vaults of Gothic cathedrals, in others the wooden features of a negro fetish chipped out by an adze. But formal considerations have not obliterated the human expression, which at times reappears with more intensity than at any other time during the cubist period. We are reminded of the anguished faces of Zurbaran. Spanish expressionism was still apparent in spite of new techniques.

It is not surprising that after these heads Picasso should have wanted to work out the relationship between the painted head and its three-dimensional counterpart in a first attempt at cubist sculpture. The bronze *Woman's Head*[2] was modelled after his return to Paris in the autumn. It follows closely the same conception of a surface broken into planes whose ridges catch the light.

[1] See Zervos, Vol. II*, p. 84.   [2] Plate, VI, 4.

Return to Paris

It was by a strange coincidence that Braque had returned from the Mediterranean in the autumn of 1908 with landscapes that were to be labelled 'cubist', and that Picasso coming from La Rue des Bois also brought with him paintings which, independently, showed a parallel tendency. From that time until they were separated in 1914 by the war there was a close association between the two painters. They watched each other's work and vied with each other in invention. The authorship of their paintings at the height of the cubist period is often difficult to determine, especially when they were working in close collaboration, though in Picasso's own words Braque, true to his origins in the Ile de France, "always has the cream", which a Spaniard would find too rich and unnecessary. It is impossible however to know which of them was the originator of each idea that created the new style. That in the formative stages they should independently achieve similar results suggests that a community of ideas was ripening in an atmosphere alive to the urgent need for a new form of expression. At the same time it must not be forgotten that the *Demoiselles d'Avignon* in 1907 was in advance of any other creative achievement.

The friendship between Picasso and Braque, though not without rivalry, was genuine and fruitful. Born the year after Picasso, Braque had come to live in a studio nearby in Montmartre, and he brought a methodical and questioning spirit into discussions on their new ideas. His first reactions had been of stubborn disapproval, but he had quietly abandoned the Fauve group, which was already in disruption, and alienated himself from them by paintings that met with the disapproval of Matisse and his old friends Dufy, Friesz and Marquet.

To Picasso, the company of Braque was stimulating. Together they shared not only their thoughts but their entertainments. In his generous moments Picasso is always anxious that his friends should share his own happiness, and in early days he thought it fitting that Braque should be found a suitable wife. The first choice was the daughter of the *patron* of a Montmartre cabaret, Le Néant, who happened to be a cousin of Max Jacob. One evening it was decided that Braque should be formally introduced to her, in company with Max and other willing friends. For the occasion they all hired the most splendid dress and set out complete with top hats, cloaks and elegant canes. The effect was overwhelming. Both the *patron* and his daughter were conquered at once by their distinguished guests, but it was difficult for their high spirits not to spoil the desired effect, and as night went by the atmosphere deteriorated seriously. When the time came for them to leave, the engagement was still not concluded and their presence was no longer desired. In the cloakroom they found that it was impossible to recognise their hired disguises, but adopting the easiest way out they all helped themselves to the hats and cloaks they fancied, an action which unfortunately made their return for further negotiations impossible. As it proved, this was just as well, for Picasso introduced Braque shortly afterwards to a girl of great charm who lived in the quarter, and who became his wife and lifelong companion. It is said also that Derain owed his marriage to Picasso's good services, and it was he who introduced Apollinaire to his wild and talented muse, Marie Laurencin. With unexpected concern he interested himself in the happiness of his friends.

CHAPTER VI

THE CREATION OF CUBISM
(1909-1914)

Move to Boulevard de Clichy

THE SUMMER MONTHS spent in the arid rocks and vineyards
of Spain had an excellent effect on Picasso. He returned to Paris with
a large number of paintings that showed a persistent development in
the new style. Vollard, having recovered from his earlier misgivings,
at once exhibited them in his gallery, and in spite of the hostility of the
critics and guffaws from the public, the small group of enlightened
admirers led by Gertrude Stein and Shchukine continued to buy.

Picasso at last found himself in a position to move from the squalor
and inconvenience of his old surroundings, and with Fernande and
their Siamese cat he installed himself in the same quarter in a studio
apartment at 11 boulevard de Clichy near the Place Pigalle. The
increasing volume of his work and his need for seclusion had already
induced him to spread into a second studio used exclusively for work
at the Bateau Lavoir, and this he kept as a store for several years until
Kahnweiler moved all his belongings for him to Montparnasse.

The contrast was so marked between the sordid surroundings in
which there was nothing that could be described as comfortable and
the bourgeois splendour of a great studio with a north light and its
adjoining apartment looking south over trees, that the men who
shifted their scant furniture and the heavy loads of canvases thought the
young couple must have drawn a lucky number in the National
Lottery.

Fernande says she felt misgivings about the new surroundings. She
thought that their new way of life, with a maid in apron and cap to
wait at table and the custom of Sunday afternoon receptions, which for
a while they adopted as a means of returning hospitality, could not
replace the spontaneous, disorganised enchantment of the early days of
their life together.

The furniture Picasso acquired was a mixture of any styles that
took his fancy. Among heavy oak pieces with simple lines, an immense
Louis-Philippe mahogany settee upholstered in plush, and a grand
piano, there stood a delicate piece in Italian marquetry, a present from

his father. To Picasso, 'good taste' and interior decoration are obstacles to his imagination, a stagnation of the spirit. On the walls of the dining-room he had hung as a joke chromo-lithographs framed in straw which Fernande says were more worthy of a concierge's parlour. In the studio, the fear that dust raised by a broom might get stuck to fresh paint forbade dusting and sweeping, and the usual splendid disorder was quickly established. It was added to daily by a collection of chosen pieces of junk such as glass, picked out because of the intensity of its blue, curiously shaped bottles, princely pieces of cut glass, fragments of old tapestries from Aubusson or Beauvais, musical instruments, old gilded frames, and above all, an ever-growing collection of African sculpture. Competition between him and other painters such as Braque, Derain and Matisse in the discovery of rare pieces and necklaces had reached a high pitch, and ivory bracelets from the same source made an exotic display on the arms of their girls.

Picasso continued to make the round of visits to his friends, always protesting to Fernande before they set out that it was a boring waste of time, always remaining taciturn while he was there, but nevertheless unable to live without these contacts which he enjoyed in his own way. The Saturday visit to the Steins at their studio in the rue de Fleurus was a regular event. There he always met Matisse to whom he invariably paid a visit on Fridays. At the Steins, they were both among the most honoured guests, Matisse with his brilliant flow of conversation and Picasso sardonic and reserved, inclined to look down on those who failed to understand him. He was particularly unhappy when asked for explanations of his work which he always tried to avoid, and which became all the more irksome in his broken French.

To Picasso the all-important activity was the continuous rhythm of his work. Locked into his new studio, he pursued every afternoon and again at night, the development of the new style that was steadily taking shape. The stage was now set for an unparalleled flow of invention and the establishment of a revolutionary movement in which he was without premeditation to become the prime mover.

The group which formed in Montmartre consisted in the first place of Picasso and Braque. Derain, a painter of great talent and an attractive personality, appeared at one time to be following the same path, but there are two other artists whose names are more closely linked with those of Picasso and Braque as creators of cubism. They are Juan Gris and Fernand Léger. Gris, a Spaniard from Madrid, lived in poverty in the Bateau Lavoir. He earned just enough to keep alive by drawing caricatures for illustrated reviews such as the *Assiette au*

Beurre. But his friendship with Picasso opened for him new horizons and he began to explore the possibilities of the cubist style as early as 1910. Fernand Léger had arrived in Paris a year before, coming from Normandy, and soon after his meeting with Picasso and Braque he began to invent his own cylindric simplifications of form which earned for themselves the nickname of 'tubism'.

Interest in cubism spread with astonishing speed from Paris to other countries. It was as though the new generation of painters had everywhere been waiting for an orientation. The simplification of form at the expense of representation was the fundamental step taken simultaneously by artists in countries as distant from each other as France and Russia, Italy and America.

Their motives were not necessarily the same. Painters such as the Russian, Malevich, and the Dutchman, Mondrian, after their first contact with cubism in Paris, pursued paths that led them to disregard all associations with objects in their desire to arrive at pure abstraction in colour and form. They sought for Platonic perfection based on the indisputable beauty of simple geometric shapes such as the circle and the rectangle. This road, which led to complete suppression of subject-matter and a search for absolutes, was foreign to the instincts of Picasso. Whatever merit their almost fanatical research may have had, it tended to narrow the rôle of painting to decorative and intellectual aspects. To deprive painting thus of all subject-matter and hence of all poetic allusions and symbols has always seemed to Picasso a form of castration. He is not concerned with purity except in relation to impurity. Perfection does not interest him because it implies a finality which is static and deprived of life. Art and life are inseparable to him and inspiration comes from the world in which he lives rather than from a theory of ideal beauty. However abstruse his work may appear it has always as its origin passionate observation and the love of a given object. It is never an abstract calculation.

Other painters, stimulated by the discoveries of cubism, formed groups, such as the Futurists dominated by Marinetti in Italy and the Vorticists in England. Amazed by the inventions of our age, they based their theories of aesthetics on the shape and movement of machines and the repetition of mechanical rhythms. In their desire to incorporate movement into the static art of painting, they showed the consecutive positions, for example, of the leg of a runner. But here they differed from the cubists, who by totally different and more subtle means managed also to introduce the fourth dimension, time, into the representation of an object.

Cubism, however, did not begin with theories. There was no question in Picasso's mind of creating a system any more than of founding a school. His urge was to make a break with the past, to substitute a living object for the fleeting sensual images of the impressionists —who, he said sarcastically, merely showed you what weather it was —and to render to the work of art its own internal life. To do this, new means had to be invented. The history of cubism reveals the discovery of these means.

The decade that followed the *Demoiselles d'Avignon* was to witness a revolution without precedent in the arts, the consequences of which are still not fully understood. No sooner had cubism made its appearance than its influence began to spread to other arts. It is true to say that the art of this century took its shape from the cubist paintings of Picasso and Braque, and that sculpture, architecture, the decorative arts, ballet, theatre design and to a lesser degree, literature, were all modified either profoundly or superficially by the cubist conception. The influence was bound to be far-reaching because cubism challenged fundamental assumptions concerning the rôle of the arts. It rescued art from idealism and from the belief that it should have as its purpose the creation of absolute beauty. It was not a campaign directed against any particular art form, but it had the effect of restoring to art its preoccupation with the complex nature of reality. Former movements of revolt such as impressionism had been limited to visual problems, but cubism pursued its enquiry into the very nature of the objective world and its relationship to us. It is for this reason that it can claim to be the most significant revolution in the history of art since the Renaissance, and that it continues to influence all branches of the arts in our time.

But there is no final solution in art, or rather in the words of Kant, art is a "finality without end". The artist can never completely visualise the final state of his production while he is at work on it, nor is he able to judge with certainty where his work will lead him. In order to succeed, he must make discoveries as he travels along the path he has chosen. This is the essential condition for his continuous inspiration. Picasso and Braque did not, as has been suggested, base their work on calculations as a guide to new laws of aesthetics. André Breton has stated that Picasso used measurements and mathematics to clarify his work.[1] Though this is far from the truth, the assertion may be derived from the friendship between Picasso and a mathematician, Princet, who frequented the cafés of Montmartre while earning his living as an

[1] See *Art of this Century*, New York, 1944, p. 15, and Barr, *Picasso*, p. 260.

actuary for an insurance company. Princet aroused the interest of Picasso and Braque by the exquisite way in which he laid out mathematical problems on paper, and he reciprocated their enthusiasm by theorising on the relationship between cubism and calculations developed from the golden section and current theories of the fourth dimension. But there is no doubt that his speculations were of little interest to Picasso or Braque and that they were subsequent to their inventions in painting. These speculations, however, inaugurated a spate of theorising, which was followed up by other mathematicians and by some of the more pedestrian followers of the cubist movement, such as Gleizes and Metzinger. Science inevitably arrives after the fait accompli to rationalise and elaborate the discoveries we owe to art.

Whatever calculations may have been made by others, Picasso himself jokes about his own complete inability to understand mathematics. His use of geometry is as instinctive as that of the first caveman who drew straight lines and circles long before the scientific faculties of man were sufficiently developed to make deductions and theories. But although mathematical calculations are absent, there is nothing haphazard about his work. It is prompted by an unerring sensibility and an intense desire to penetrate and understand reality in relation to human consciousness. It is in other words a search for truth. Art had been content to accept and enjoy appearances, but to the inquisitive spirit of Picasso this was not enough, and his dissatisfaction led him to enquire more deeply into the nature of our perception of the world around us. If superficial appearances were insufficient, the object had to suffer a dissection, an analysis which could enhance our understanding and appreciation of its presence.

The Cubist Portraits: Analytical Cubism

The first important canvas to be painted in the new studio, *La Femme Assise*,[1] still shows a formal structure reminiscent of the technique of Cézanne. The contrasted greens and reddish browns come from his Provençal landscapes. But particularly in the face of the seated woman there is a more severe analysis of form and a further restriction in the choice of colour. The rigours of the new discipline were in future work to limit the range of colour still further, until subtle passages from ochre to brown or grey were all that relieved it from monochrome. Even the greens of the Horta landscapes, which appear for the last time in this picture, were afterwards banished. It

[1] Plate VI, 5.

was necessary to create a clear conception of space before enhancing it with colour.

At the same time, while the processes of demolishing the object so that normal appearances became scarcely recognisable and abandoning the use of colour were at their height, Picasso produced some portraits for which paradoxically he demanded, as he had done for Gertrude Stein, the frequent presence of the sitter. The first of the series, to be exact, precedes the visit to Horta, when he painted a portrait of his friend Pallarès which has been kept jealously in Barcelona up to the present time. It was a portrait of Clovis Sagot,[1] and although cubist influences are apparent both in the form and the colour it is still an obvious descendant of Cézanne. The third, known as the portrait of Georges Braque,[2] was painted late in 1909. It is a lighthearted, almost grotesque caricature showing little concern for a likeness to its subject. This however is not the case with the three great portraits that followed in the next year. In them a resemblance to the sitter is one of the most surprising and easily recognised virtues, in spite of the dissection of the form and the angular rhythms with which it has been reconstructed.

The first of this sequence was the portrait of Ambroise Vollard,[3] painted in the winter of 1909-1910 and bought shortly afterwards by Shchukine. In spite of rigorous cubist treatment it is a remarkable likeness. Vollard himself relates that though many at the time failed to recognise him, the four-year-old son of a friend said without hesitation, on seeing the painting for the first time, "That's Vollard". The bulldog-like snout of the picture dealer and the high bald dome of his forehead detach themselves in warm tones from the grey monochrome and the continuous angular rhythms of the background. In spite of strong accents, there is nowhere an awkward interval or hole. The crystalline surface of the picture is unbroken.

The same qualities are present in the portrait of Wilhelm Uhde which followed.[4] There is a more austere consistency in the subdued colour, maintained here throughout with no concessions to flesh tones and a unity between the figure and its background, filled appropriately with a chimney-piece and books. The treatment is admirably fitting. It expresses with unexpected eloquence the dry, loyal personality of Picasso's scholarly friend. So true is the likeness that more than twenty-five years later, although I had never met Monsieur Uhde in my life, but knowing the picture well, I was able suddenly to recognise him sitting by chance in a crowded café.

[1] Plate VI, 3.   [2] See Zervos, *Picasso*, Vol. II*, p. 89, No. 177.
[3] Plate VI, 7.   [4] Plate VI, 8.

The style in the last of these three portraits has evolved still further. The patient sitter was Kahnweiler,[1] who well remembers the innumerable hours he had to pose. Here the analysis of form has been so uncompromising that although the features can be distinguished, the resemblance to the sitter is not so easily understood. The whole surface of the picture is organised as a pattern of small planes that recall the intricate honeycomb design of the Moorish vaulting in the Alhambra, though here they seem to float in the vertical plane of the picture. Each facet lends to its neighbour a continuous play of recession and intrusion like ripples on the surface of water. The eye wanders among them picking up here and there landmarks such as eyes, nose, well-combed hair, a watch-chain and folded hands, but in its passage it can continually enjoy moving over surfaces that are convincingly real, even though they are not intended to present an immediate resemblance to any given object. The imagination is confronted with a scene which though ambiguous appears undoubtedly to exist, and excited by the rhythmic life of this new reality, it devises with delight its own interpretations. The passage round the neck and shoulders can seem like a promenade among streets and houses glowing with light and clearly defined in their spatial relations to each other. Picasso is reported to have said: "In the paintings of Raphael, it is not possible to measure the exact distance from nose to mouth: I want to paint pictures in which this can be done." In this way his end has been achieved, there is a convincing precision in these three-dimensional recessions, though to the imagination they may suggest a depth of one inch or one hundred yards. The new sense of reality detached from representation creates a poetic ambiguity.

The portrait of Kahnweiler is one of the best examples of the style that has come to be known as analytical cubism. The desire to penetrate into the nature of form, to understand the space it occupies itself and the space in which it is situated, brought about a searching analysis in which the familiar contours of its surface have all simultaneously forfeited their customary opaqueness. The screen of outward appearances has been made to undergo a crystallisation which renders it more transparent. Each facet has been stood on edge so as to allow us to appreciate the volumes that lie beneath the surface. Instead of being invited to caress with a glance a smooth outer skin we are presented with a transparent honeycomb construction in which surface and depth are both visible.

Another picture which was painted earlier in 1910 and which has

[1] Plate VI, 9.

not evolved quite so far on the road of analytical cubism, *The Girl with a Mandolin*,[1] can in some ways also rank as a portrait. In this case also, contrary to an increasing tendency to paint with the eye of his understanding rather than direct from nature, Picasso demanded many sittings from his model. A girl named Fanny Tellier, who had posed for many of his friends, offered her services to him and came persistently to pose. He found her presence, to which he was unaccustomed, somewhat embarrassing, but did not let it interfere with prolonged concentration on his work, until finally it was the model who lost patience. After more sittings than she was in the habit of giving for a single painting she announced that she was indisposed and could not come the following day. "I realised that she meant not to come back at all," Picasso told me, "and consequently I decided that I must leave the picture unfinished. But who knows," he added, "it may be just as well I left it as it is."

If he had carried the painting further, it is reasonable to suppose that the process of elimination of resemblance to the outer appearance would have continued. As it is, there are signs everywhere of metamorphosis, although the upright figure of the girl holding her mandolin can be recognised without difficulty. Her head, her hands and her breasts have suffered the artist's wilful transformation, and there are arabesque flourishes that soften the hair that flows down her neck and find their echo in the detail of the frills of her dress and the ornamented frames against which she stands. Her right breast hangs like ripe fruit with a candour which appears both naked and clothed, while her head, which is partly merged into the background, evokes a different kind of ambiguity. It has been simplified into an undivided block with no features but the eye drawn as a sign on its surface, and it is extended by a rectangular shape which can be taken for the frontal surface of the face or a transparent shadow. That such ambiguity should be tolerated is an outrage to all classical standards of painting, but Picasso was discovering the importance of this mode which was to become one of the main assets of twentieth-century painting and pervade all manifestations of the new style. The simplification or elision of form in the head is repeated in the hands holding the musical instrument. But in spite of the economy in their shapes he has mysteriously managed to show their precise and sensitive activity as they play over the strings, merging into the discipline of his new conceptions a tender regard for female charm which is made apparent above all by the elegance of her poise. The picture is in fact such a

[1] Plate VII, 1.

bewildering combination of those qualities of elegant poise, classical proportions, selection of essential features, sober and subdued colours, that in spite of revolutionary treatment it has the serenity and inevitability of the architecture of the Greeks or the music of Bach. The human form has rarely been dissolved and recreated with more consummate skill.

Summer in Cadaqués

During the next eighteen months Picasso continued to push even further his analysis of form, sacrificing relentlessly the superficial appearances of objects but never losing touch with the origin of his inspiration. The summer of 1910 was spent at Cadaqués on the coast of Catalonia, in the company of Fernande and André Derain. His friend Pichot had asked him to share his house, and though Picasso found time for the pleasures of bathing and dancing the Sardana, he continued to organise his painting with the same severe discipline. Unlike his visit the year before to Horta, the landscape did not claim his attention, though as usual on arrival at a new place he acknowledged the change of scene with a few drawings, in this case of the black angular prows of fishing boats.[1] The work he produced was inspired in general by the human figure and the objects—musical instruments, fruit, glasses and bottles—that ornamented Pichot's interior.[2] He chose the most familiar forms, those close at hand, since they corresponded to his desire to touch as well as to see.

Derain, in spite of his close association with Picasso during these months, never felt tempted to carry out an analysis with the same rigour or to look so persistently behind the surface; but Braque, who had returned south to spend his summer at L'Estaque, continued at a distance to share Picasso's preoccupations, and independently he made important discoveries. The summer of 1910, according to Kahnweiler, was one of the richest in new developments for both painters. In the autumn Picasso, still doubting and dissatisfied with his achievements, returned from Spain with a large number of unfinished canvases.

However, it soon became apparent that a great step had been made towards establishing the new language of cubism. The change can be seen most clearly in a comparison of the portraits of Uhde and of Kahnweiler, one painted before and the other after the visit to Cadaqués. The former still plays with arrangements of the surface,

[1] See Zervos, *Picasso*, Vol. VI, p. 133, No. 1112.
[2] Ibid., Vol. II*, pp. 109, 110.

whereas the latter treats the sitter as a three-dimensional structure, existing as disrupted elements plotted in space in a transparent honey-comb, which is viewed from several angles and yet is welded together into a comprehensive whole. To quote Kahnweiler, "he had taken the great step, he had pierced the closed form".

The same development can be noticed from the *Seated Woman*[1] of early 1910, now in the Tate Gallery, to the tall *Nude Woman*[2] painted a few months later at Cadaqués. In the former, deep cavernous greens make a background to a figure which seems to be overlaid or loosely boarded up with shingles. It still presents a solid graceful mass, while the *Nude Woman* has disintegrated into a scaffolding built with powerful angular rhythms, recessions and transparencies, almost unrecognisable as the female form. Direct reference to outward anatomical appearance or to the play of light on swelling volumes of skin-covered flesh has entirely vanished. The remaining structure owes its reality to the invention of a new architecture which is beautifully human in its proportions and convincing as a three-dimensional 'ideographic' sign.

There is no doubt that the new system, though logical, was becoming progressively more difficult for the layman to understand. The danger of its becoming a hermetic exercise, an aesthetic delight for the few who cared for abstruse metaphysical problems, was felt by both Braque and Picasso. The obvious risk was that in analysing the object, all reference to its recognisable reality might vanish completely, and it was to avoid this that Braque, while at L'Estaque, had introduced into one of his pictures a nail painted with its cast shadow in a natural-istic way, as though it were pinning the canvas to the wall. Thus he brought together two different levels of reality, the nail functioning as an explanatory aside made by an actor or a footnote to a poem. Then, pleased with the effect of this shift from one level to the other, he began to introduce lettering. These elements from another sphere had their own reality and brought with them into a style, in which all other reference to reality had become difficult to interpret, wide associations which could enlarge the scale and the signification of the picture. The problem of retaining a line of communication with the objective world had been relatively easy when it was a question of dealing with the human form, in which associations are so strong that a slender resem-blance to an eye, a moustache, a breast or a hand is sufficient as a clue; but when less familiar objects are in question, a sign such as the tassel on the fringe of a tablecloth, the double curve of a guitar, the

[1] Plate VII, 3.   [2] See Zervos, *Picasso*, Vol. II*, p. 115, No. 233.

circular top and the cylindrical stem of a wine glass, the bowl of a pipe, the suit of a playing card or the first three letters in heavy type of the word 'journal', could be used to give the spectator an entry into the conception behind the picture.

There are many sequences of drawings by Picasso which start from an easily recognisable seated figure, and then proceed to eliminate appearances and to render shapes in simplified rectilinear planes, but always some clue remains as a symbolic link with the world in which the idea of the drawing originated.[1] However at this period, so great was the artist's desire to dissect form and recreate an object according to his own inspiration, that Kahnweiler was moved to plead that "cubist pictures should always be provided with descriptive titles, such as *Bottle and Glass*, *Playing Cards and Dice*, or *Still-Life with a Guitar*."[2] There should then be no danger of the paintings becoming merely an abstract decoration.

The Heroic Days of Cubism

When the summer spent in Cadaqués came to an end there was the usual long journey back to Paris. Talking recently of these repeated arrivals after months of absence, Picasso insisted that they were very unlike our present-day rapid returns to work after the holidays. He remembers that on one occasion at least it took him two days to get from the station to Montmartre. When the night train drew in at the Gare d'Orsay in the morning, friends were on the platform to meet him. The whole band then set off on a sort of triumphal progress through a series of bars, cafés, galleries and studios, exchanging items of news and gossip, and indulging in noisy arguments. Finally, exhausted more by his welcome than by the journey, Picasso unlocked the dusty silence of his own studio.

As soon as he was reinstalled, the flow of production and invention continued without check during the winter months. Braque was living nearby, and frequent visits to each other's studios kept them closely in touch, so much so that it was impossible in many cases to know who could claim to be the inventor of any given idea.

It would now be impertinent to attempt an exact chronology or to give credit exclusively to one or the other. Braque describes this fruitful collaboration in these words: "Closely linked with Picasso

[1] See Zervos, *Picasso*, Vol. VI, pp. 144, 145.
[2] Kahnweiler, *The Rise of Cubism*.

in spite of our widely different temperaments we were guided by a common idea. . . . Picasso is Spanish, I am French . . . but we said together during those years things that no one will ever say again . . . things that would be incomprehensible and that have given us so much pleasure. . . . It was rather like being roped mountaineers." The austere fervour with which they worked together was such that for a time neither signed his paintings, wishing rather to share anonymity, and "there was a moment", Braque has admitted, "when we had difficulty in recognising our own paintings."[1]

This should not lead us to imagine, however, that there was no difference in style between the two artists. Their divergent national characteristics, the subtle nuances of the French on the one hand and the dramatic precision of the Spanish on the other, help to give to each painting its identity. But both were searching along the same path, and both revolutionaries had in their blood the great traditions of European painting that they were seeking to revitalise. Both laid their new discoveries in the severe classical framework of a composition based on a central feature supported by receding planes. Closely woven into this foundation and contrasting with it are tilted parallel lines and curves placed with economy so as to give them their maximum significance. The dominating importance that the central figure acquires in pictures such as the *Jeune Fille à la Mandoline* is a reminder, coming when it might be least expected, of the composition of El Greco's *Expolio*. Braque found that the rectangular composition often became irksome towards the corners of the canvas and often enclosed his pictures as an oval. A rectangular composition within a rectangle was dull, it led nowhere; whereas placed in an oval—which as Picasso recently pointed out to me, can signify a circular plane seen in perspective—the whole picture gained a three-dimensional effect. One of Picasso's earliest oval pictures is a nude dating from 1910.[2] In it the total effect of the picture is almost spherical. "In the early days of cubism," he told me, "we made experiments, the squaring of the circle was a phrase that excited our ambitions . . . to make pictures was less important than to discover things all the time"—but he warned me again not to think it was ever a question of exact calculations. The aim was rather to create space in a convincing way and therefore a new reality. For this reason, he said, he had always hoped to make a painting that was literally spherical, and still keeps at hand some large

[1] Braque-Dora Vallier, 'La Peinture et nous', *Cahiers d'Art*, October 1954, XXIXᵉ Année, No. 1.
[2] See Zervos, *Picasso*, Vol. II*, p. 114, No. 228.

balls of clay with which to make experiments in three-dimensional and two-dimensional effects.

The Subject-matter in Cubism

Cubism, which appeared to many to be detached from reality, used as subject-matter the most common objects of everyday use—pipe, newspaper, bottle, glass, or the human form—and neither Picasso nor Braque was in any way detached from the daily events of the world around him, and which in turn influenced them both in their work. Just as the street and the circus had been the climate of the Blue and Rose periods, the world of science and mechanical invention was often in the background of cubism.

Two inventions in the early years of this century did a great deal to alter our relations with the force of gravity—the use of ferro-concrete in building, and the airplane. Both made it possible to carry heavy masses in the air without visible means of support, and both inventions were in consequence of interest to the cubists. By means of ferro-concrete the ancient conception that a building must be supported laboriously by columns and caryatids disappeared, thanks to a feat of engineering which could make great masses of concrete float in the air in a way hitherto impossible. At the same time a favourite slogan in the French press was "our future is in the air". Braque and Picasso were quick to see its importance. "We were very interested in the efforts of those who were making airplanes", says Picasso. "When one wing was not enough to keep them in the air they joined on another with strings and wire." In a letter to Braque we find him addressing his friend as "Mon cher Wilbur", a joke referring of course to Wilbur Wright.[1] In fact the resemblance between Monsieur Bleriot's flying machine and the overlapping facets and tenuous lines of an analytical cubist painting is not fortuitous. It is the result of observation and a discerning interest in the changing form of life, in particular in efforts to conquer another dimension in space.

In this connection also the superimposed planes of analytical cubism that often suggest the wings of a biplane or the overlapping wing-feathers of a bird give the effect of a recession in space. They are like the treads of a staircase seen from above and can create a sense of depth as convincing as the old methods of linear perspective.

[1] Kahnweiler is sceptical about the extent of the influence of the inventor of aircraft on cubism. He holds that the reason why Braque was nicknamed 'Wilbur' was simply that in their efforts to pronounce the name 'Wright' it took an unexpected resemblance to 'Braque'.

Céret

When summer came round again, instead of returning to Spain Picasso stopped short at Céret, a small town with great charm at the foot of the Pyrenees on the French side. It had been discovered by Manolo who continued to live there for many years, and before the outbreak of war in 1914 it became the spiritual home of cubism. Shaded by gigantic plane trees, its narrow streets are crowded with peasants from the mountains, leading mules whose bells echo as they pass by the fountains buried in moss and the crowded terraces of the cafés. In the luscious green of irrigated meadows, apricot groves and vineyards outside the town, a friend, Frank Havilland, had bought a small abandoned monastery where Manolo was already installed. It was a noble-looking eighteenth-century house surrounded by a large garden full of ancient trees and watered by a mountain torrent. Picasso took over the whole of the first floor and installed himself with Fernande. Four or five rooms of splendid proportions with a wide terrace overlooking the park gave ample scope for his work. Céret was close enough to the frontier for a frequent interchange between its population and the Spanish mountain folk, whose anarchist theories of justice and liberty were of the same fiery brand that Pablo had known in earlier days in Barcelona. On both sides of the mountain they were one race, Catalan, and Picasso could introduce his French friends, Braque and Max Jacob, who joined him there, to the people to whom he was closely akin. Max Jacob, though essentially fitted for Parisian elegance, was quickly acclimatised and began even to enjoy the perpetual choruses of frogs, toads, and nightingales that prevented him from sleeping. He managed to charm the elderly bourgeois whom he met in the café with his distinguished conversation and his horoscopes which earned him a few francs.

On the terrace of the Grand Café in the main street could be found most evenings the group of artists and poets who had come from Paris to pass the long pleasant days of summer in the company of their friend, whose dark piercing eyes seemed always to be discovering and absorbing new material for his work, and who was just as likely to be morose and reserved as witty and unexpectedly affectionate. They made a contrast with the local folk by the freedom of their dress, the gay colours worn by their stockingless girl friends and the variety of accents with which they spoke. The conversation rarely became dull. If there was any tendency in that direction, Picasso would remain silent and start drawing on the marble table top for the amusement of the girls or the wives of his friends. With one continuous line he drew animals, birds or portraits of people they knew. He could describe anyone he wished in this way, even upside down, so that the person sitting opposite was presented with a portrait the right way up. Even the most conservative among the inhabitants quickly grew to understand them and they were only mildly surprised when Picasso asked for such unusual things as the heavy red curtain from the butcher's shop for an ornament for his studio.

Picasso was the only one among the artist friends to have enough money, but this mattered little as living at that date, in the depths of the country, was cheap anywhere in France, and the *patron* of the hotel was a good friend of artists. During the three years before the war broke out, those who had adopted Céret, including Manolo and his wife Totote, were the composer Déodat de Severac, Braque, Max Jacob, Kisling, Pichot, Herbin, Juan Gris, Havilland and later Matisse. Picasso made several visits but it was only during the first that he was accompanied by Fernande. There was much that pleased him in these surroundings—the weather, the warm wrinkled faces of the old folk, the healthy, well-built girls, the mountain landscape and the variety of vegetation that surrounded the solid stone houses of the little town; and above all, ample space for work in a delightful setting, and the company, whenever he wanted it, of some of his most entertaining friends. There was no reason why Picasso should not have been happy except that pleasure is fundamentally of no interest to him and a prolonged state of undisturbed happiness is inconceivable.

Among the paintings produced at Céret during this first visit, landscapes are again very rare. There is one which is purely cubist in style although the broken shadows on the houses are painted with small short brush-strokes reminiscent of pointillist technique.[1] Characteristically there is a complete absence of colour, but without it this painting still evokes the deep shady streets of the little town. Otherwise there is no acknowledgement in any picture of the delights of the countryside. In company with Braque he was absorbed by further discoveries in the language of cubism. Two pictures, *The Bottle of Rum*[2] and *The Torero*,[3] are examples of how rigorous the new discipline had become. The disruption of the object is complete. In the three-dimensional pattern composed of its dismembered elements it is still recognisable, however, thanks to certain clues. In both cases, heavy capital letters forming parts of relevant words anchor the picture to its subject.

[1] See Zervos, *Picasso*, Vol. II*, p. 137, No. 281.
[2] Ibid., *Picasso*, Vol. II*, p. 132, No. 267.   [3] Plate VII, 2.

The Poet[1] and *The Accordionist*[2] are two large pictures painted at Céret. In both cases a single figure fills, in diamond fashion, the centre of the canvas. It is improbable that at the first glance the artist's intention will be understood, in fact it is said of the latter that its first owner in America enjoyed looking at it for years with the conviction that it was a landscape. There is no reason why a picture should not be enjoyed wrong way up, but if we wish to follow the artist's intentions, a cubist picture usually contains a clue. In this case on inspection the folds of the accordion are clearly visible near the centre of the picture, just where they would be expected. The armchair can be recognised by the spiral curls of the arms that protrude from behind a structure in the form of an obelisk which is the body of the musician. Pleasure can be found in a superficial excursion over these intricate broken surfaces whichever way up they may be placed, but there is additional satisfaction when the dignity and the convincing reality in space of this monumental figure is understood.

First Reactions to Cubism

While the stimulus of the cubist movement spread among painters, its vitality and the significance of its implications made themselves felt among poets. Its influence assisted in clearing the ground of the romantic fin de siècle nostalgia which was already half-strangled in its own pessimism. Although cubism was the invention of painters, and therefore difficult to define in literary terms, its form and many of the ideas that it contained tempted certain poets to make experiments on similar lines. Max Jacob and Apollinaire, captivated by the visionary assurance of Picasso, were the first to attempt to incorporate the influence of cubism into their literary style.

It is possible that Max Jacob was swayed by his deep affection for Picasso. Although his limited visual sense did not permit of a change of style in his attempts at painting, in his poetry the form of his imagery shifted away from symbolism to the complex and at the same time more factual style of Mallarmé, purged of all sentimentality. In his earlier days he had said: "In poetry interest will be born of the doubt between reality and imagination. . . . Doubt, that is art."[3] Doubt remained, but his mood, stimulated by the vitality of Picasso, had become more positive. In spite of his lack of understanding as a painter he was intrigued by cubism, and he was delighted when Kahnweiler as the publisher asked Picasso in 1910 to illustrate a poetic

[1] See Zervos, *Picasso*, Vol. II*, p. 139.
[2] Ibid., *Picasso*, Vol. II*, p. 135.   [3] Max Jacob, *Correspondance*, p. 31.

novel he had written entitled *Saint Matorel*.[1] Already in 1905 Picasso had made a drypoint sketch for a little book of poems by André Salmon, but *Saint Matorel* was honoured with four etchings. The announcement of the book was written by Max Jacob himself. From it Picasso's reputation would appear already to be widespread. "The authority of the name of Picasso dispenses with any necessity to present him to the public", he writes, but had it been intended for a cosmopolitan public such terms would at that date have appeared to be unjustified flattery.

The engravings were completed during the summer at Cadaquès. The cubist technique in painting found its equivalent without difficulty in etching, the short brush-strokes of analytical cubism being replaced by short lines or dots to shade certain planes and place them in relief.

This was the first of five books of poems by Max Jacob published during the next nine years to contain illustrations by Picasso. A second book, *Le Siège de Jérusalem*,[2] which appeared three years later, was also published by Kahnweiler. It was illustrated with three etchings and drypoints. The evolution of cubist painting is transferred to this medium: the introduction of lettering, wood-graining and paradoxically naturalistic detail presented no difficulty to Picasso.

The fascination of the cubist idiom spread later to other poets, in particular to Pierre Reverdy, who after the war became a close friend of Juan Gris; but it was Apollinaire, the first apologist of the new style, whose work as a poet was more affected than any by his close association with Picasso. Although his experimental revival in *Caligrammes* of the old conceit of constructing a poem in the shape of an image is an obvious link in technique between poetry and the new style in painting, the more profound influences must be looked for in the forms and structure of his poetry. He was essentially a visual poet who could use cubist methods in the multiple images that are conveyed in a poem such as 'Lundi rue Christine'. He delights in the ambiguity of dreams rather than a stark limited vision of reality.

Apollinaire was not only an excellent poet but also a great animator. He had been called by Picasso the Pope of cubism, and among the many caricatures there is one of Apollinaire seated as the Pope with triple crown and crozier and also pipe and wristwatch.[3] Anything that was modern and part of the movement which had as its intention the liberation of the human spirit was worthy of his enthusiasm. But this

[1] Max Jacob, *Correspondence*, p. 52.
[2] Ibid., *Le Siège de Jérusalem*, Kahnweiler, Paris, 1914.
[3] See Pascal Pia, *Apollinaire par lui-même*, Aux Editions du Seuil, Paris, p. 89.

quality, for which many had reason to be grateful, also led him into trouble with others who found him too eclectic and lacking in discrimination.

L'Affaire des Statues

In his search for new values Apollinaire was willing to take risks. His hope of finding talent in unexpected places, and his interest in rare and exotic forms of art, however, caused him temporarily considerable embarrassment in an incident that has come to be known as 'l'Affaire des Statues'. The painful events would have been unlikely to occur had they not happened to coincide with the spectacular theft from the Louvre in the summer of 1911 of La Gioconda. The story has been told on many occasions. The press has at one time or another given a variety of sensational versions, but an authentic account is presumably the one to be found in a letter written by Apollinaire in 1915 to his friend Madeleine Pagès. He explains that it all started with his employment as secretary, more from kindness of heart than for any practical sense, of a young Belgian adventurer called Géry-Pieret, who had a gift for entertaining people with extravagant stories. In 1907, it seems, Géry stole two Hispano-Roman statues from the Louvre, and with bombastic talk from which it was impossible to decipher the truth, he persuaded Picasso to buy them from him. Apollinaire, when he asked Picasso some years later to return them, was told enigmatically that he, Picasso, had "broken them up in order to discover the secrets of the art, both ancient and barbarian, from which they had sprung."[1] In 1911 the young Belgian again turned up penniless on Apollinaire's doorstep and to increase the poet's embarrassment, he had with him another statue from the Louvre. He had stolen this not only as a joke, he claimed, but also to show how badly guarded were the nation's treasures. There was indeed some reason to draw attention to this. Thefts of the despised exhibits of African art in the Trocadero by those who were becoming aware of their value were not infrequent. Apollinaire, again out of the warmth of his heart, did not turn him away but tried without success to get him to return the statue. A few days later, on 21 August, the incredible news was broken to Paris that the Gioconda was missing from its place in the Louvre.

Suspicion at once fell on the Belgian ne'er-do-well, though of this last crime he was in fact innocent. In panic he went to Paris-Journal, to which paper he managed to sell his story. He left the statue with the

---

[1] Apollinaire, Marcel Adéma, Heinemann, p. 144.

editor and then fled from Paris on the proceeds of his deal. As he crossed France he sent letters daily to the police from new addresses, boasting that it was he who had stolen the *Gioconda* as a job done to order.

Meanwhile Apollinaire, who was thoroughly aware of the danger of the situation, went to Picasso who had returned that very day from Céret, to warn him. After a search the two statues were unearthed at the bottom of a cupboard where they had been lying forgotten, and the two friends, scared and uncertain as to what they should do, wandered all night carrying with them this embarrassing treasure in a bag. They even contemplated washing their hands of the whole affair by dropping their incriminating load into the Seine. Finally they decided to follow Géry's example and take the statues to *Paris-Journal* so as to ensure their anonymous return. Unfortunately, however, before Géry fled from Paris he had returned at the last moment to beg for more money from Apollinaire, who as a last act of kindness and also as a means of getting rid of him had taken him to the Gare de Lyon and put him on a train. This gave the police sufficient evidence to suspect the poet, and on 7 September the papers announced the arrest of a thirty-year-old Polish writer, Kostrowitzky alias Guillaume Apollinaire, as the thief of Leonardo's masterpiece. A section of the press was quick to remember that he had been heard to declare at the *Closerie des Lilas* that "all museums should be destroyed because they paralysed the imagination", and that he had published new editions of erotic classics in order to make a little money. This was enough to convince the police that they had unearthed the leader of a dangerous international band.

Two days later Picasso, unaware of his friend's plight, was awoken at seven o'clock in the morning by a plain-clothes policeman who demanded his immediate presence before the judge for interrogation. The two friends were confronted with each other at the Prefecture. Both were untidy, unshaven and terribly shaken by the appalling consequences they believed might fall upon them—prison, exile, and every other form of disgrace. Their highly emotional behaviour seems to some extent to have baffled even the judge, who allowed Picasso to go free but bound him over to return if required as a witness, and sent the unhappy Apollinaire to prison. This happened in spite of their loyalty to each other, Apollinaire saying that Picasso did not know that the antiques he had bought came from the Louvre and Picasso declaring to the judge that he had before him "the greatest living poet".

Fortunately Géry, more mad than vicious, when he read in the papers of Apollinaire's arrest, sent a full and at last sincere confession to the police before fleeing the country. The affair came to an end with the release of Apollinaire after a week in prison, with a crowd of friends acclaiming him as he left La Santé. The story however though irrelevant to the creative work of both men was not easily forgotten. In spite of the doubtful distinction of being the only man to have been arrested in connection with the theft of *La Gioconda*, Apollinaire suffered greatly from the indignity he had undergone and was avoided by some of his more cautious friends. Picasso also was worried for many weeks. He was haunted by the feeling that there was trouble still in store and that he was being continually watched. As they were foreigners, their position in France might have become difficult and they could have been expelled, a prospect dreaded by both. As it was, Apollinaire's naturalisation as a Frenchman, when he tried to enlist on the outbreak of war, was retarded for many months because of the affair.

Changes at Home

It was about this time, though perhaps not as a direct result of his anxieties, that Picasso began to suffer from ill-health which obliged him to follow a strict diet without salt and pepper. Max Jacob remembers this as 'magnificent stoicism', but although Picasso delights in the pleasures of the table he is never greedy and always considers his health before his enjoyment. If normal food is likely to threaten his ability to consecrate every part of his being to his work he is happy enough to eat boiled macaroni and drink water rather than take a risk.

Though his work continued to evolve with undiminished strength, the winter brought other changes. Picasso's life with Fernande had not always gone smoothly. Intimate friends such as Gertrude Stein could read well enough the signs of temporary storms between them. Often Fernande would appear without her earrings owing to their absence at the pawnbroker's, and be glad to give French lessons to the Steins' American friends to earn a few francs. But although quarrels were mended countless times it seemed less probable as time went on that the liaison could be permanent, especially after the move to the boulevard de Clichy. Fernande's own wistful explanation is that having been the faithful companion of the years of misery, she had no idea how to be the same in prosperity. In six years her dishevelled penniless lover, whose insistent looks radiated fire, had become a painter whose reputation commanded the respect of all connoisseurs of the modern movement in France and whose fame was spreading across the world. But the fire in his eye was no longer meant for her alone. The jealousy with which he had held her to him in early days had given way to a freer attachment which in turn came to a sudden end when the confidence that had become established between them vanished before proofs of infidelity.

Picasso has always had a taste for an abrupt ending to an awkward situation. It happened in this case without recrimination and left the way open for him to form an association with a girl of a more tender and placid nature, who although lacking the impetuous beauty of Fernande had a quiet charm that suited his more contemplative mood.

The maiden name of Eva—Marcelle Humbert—was Gouel. Picasso enjoyed calling her Eva, an allusion to her becoming the first woman in his affection. In company with the Polish painter Marcoussis, her former lover, Fernande had met her at the Steins before realising that they were to exchange places in Picasso's favour. Since Eva entered his life at a time when naturalistic drawing had been abandoned for cubism, there are no portraits of her to which we can refer, though a few indifferent photos have been preserved. Her name however appears, perpetuating her memory, in many cubist pictures. "J'aime Eva" is a testimony of Picasso's love, written on the picture like a lover's inscription in the bark of a tree. With similar intent the title of a popular love song of the time, 'Ma Jolie', is often inscribed in paintings together with some notes or other musical signs.[1] This harping refrain had become familiar from visits to the nearby Cirque Medrano. The song, "O Manon, ma jolie, mon cœur te dit bonjour", became an obsession. It makes its reappearance in many different forms, incorporated into drawings and paintings as a tribute to the newly kindled passion for Eva.

During the winter of 1911-12, before this new attachment, Picasso had made a habit of frequenting with his friends, particularly Kahnweiler, the many more or less sordid night clubs whose signs illuminated the streets of Montmartre outside the seclusion of his studio. The attempt to squeeze more entertainment from an atmosphere which had already become too familiar, and his liaison with Fernande that had grown stale, came to an end in the spring. With the arrival of Eva a change became imperative. New surroundings and solitude were again necessary in order to enjoy his newly-found love and combine this delight with his inner compulsion to pursue the discoveries of cubism.

Already in May he decided to leave Paris. Avignon was the first

[1] Plate VII, 5.

destination, but soon the charm of Céret drew him back to the Pyrenean countryside in spite of its recent associations with Fernande. The break had been sudden, and the escape to these remote surroundings would have been a guarantee against recriminations had not his old friends the Pichots, whom he found at Céret, raised a storm by tactless references to his rupture with the girl whom they admired and who by chance was staying with them. Picasso packed his bags and returned with Eva and an enormous Pyrenean dog to Avignon.

But in this city he could find nowhere to stay, and with his usual disregard for local charm or any other consideration apart from adequate space for work, he took the train to Sorgues, a small nondescript town in the fertile plains six miles north of Avignon. This place on the main road towards Orange and Paris would no longer be likely to attract artists or lovers who wished to find solitude, but in those days, before the roar of heavy traffic had disturbed the shade of the avenues of plane trees, and before the swift flow of the irrigation channels had become contaminated by factories, Sorgues-sur-l'Ouvèze was a quiet place to which to retire, and the Villa les Clochettes that Picasso rented for the sum of ninety francs a month an appropriate though charmless dwelling. They were joined by Braque and his wife Marcelle, who rented part of the Villa Bel Air on the outskirts of the town, and in the bleak shelter of their hired villas they lived in close proximity for one of the most brilliant and productive epochs of cubism.

With his health restored and the seclusion he needed, Picasso's energy was again fabulous. His newly-formed ideas took shape with innumerable variations but with a dominant reference to Eva, "Ma Jolie". On 12 June he wrote to Kahnweiler, ". . . I love her very much and I shall write her name on my pictures".[1]

As so often happens in the midi, the bare whitewashed walls of hired rooms tempted him to use them for sketches. On one occasion in later years when this happened, a furious and short-sighted landlord made him pay fifty francs for a new coat of paint. "What a fool," said Picasso referring to this years later. "He could have sold the whole wall for a fortune if he had only had the sense to leave it." But at Les Clochettes the story was different. Picasso had painted on the wall an oval picture which he did not want to abandon when he returned to Paris in the autumn. The only way to avoid doing so was to demolish the wall with great care and send the whole piece intact to Paris. This was carried out on Kahnweiler's orders and later the painting was remounted on a wooden panel by experts. Sabartès has managed

[1] Picasso, Catalogue, Musée des Arts Décoratifs, Paris, 1955.

recently to find the man who actually packed the piece of wall with the painting, and who remembered that he noticed in it a mandolin, a sheet of music with "Ma Jolie" as its title and a bottle of Pernod. The picture still exists as a proof that a simple artisan was capable of reading the hermetic signs of cubism at the time it was painted.

Psychological implications

The Beginning of Collage

When Braque first came to Paris, he had been sent there by his father, a house painter and decorator, to learn the technique of making trompe l'œil surfaces of marble or grained wood. He had abandoned this to become a landscape painter and later he evolved through fauvism to cubism, but his skill in the craft of the painter-decorator never left him. At the height of analytical cubism, soon after he and Picasso had begun to add lettering to their paintings, he started to introduce trompe l'œil surfaces into his pictures, using the combs and varnishes that he had learned to employ in his early training. His purpose was the same, again he wanted to introduce elements which would identify themselves easily with reality.

Picasso at once saw the possibilities in this innovation, and the use of graining combs appears in a picture called *The Poet*,[1] painted in the spring of 1912. In this case the combs are used to make a formalised representation of hair and moustaches. But even before, in an oval still-life, there appeared a use of trompe l'œil which was still more revolutionary. Short-cutting Braque's painted imitations of wood and marble, and remembering his father's habit of pinning cut-out pieces of paintings on to his canvases to try out new ideas, he took a piece of oilcloth on which the pattern of chair-caning was very realistically reproduced, cut it to the shape he required and stuck it on the canvas. This recollection of his father's technique must not be allowed to imply that Picasso had the same ephemeral effects in mind. On the contrary, he has affirmed that the papiers collés which followed "were always intended to be what they are: pictures in their own right".[2]

By sticking on pieces of oilcloth or paper, Picasso violated one of the canons of aesthetics which for centuries had required a homogeneity in the surface of the picture. Cézanne had scandalised the critics by leaving bare patches uncovered by paint in his canvases. They had argued that the paint should cover the entire area of the picture, and

[1] See Zervos, *Picasso*, Vol. II*, p. 152, No. 313.
[2] Barr, *Picasso: Fifty Years of His Art*, p. 260.

indeed since the earliest days of the Renaissance, when painters
abandoned the embossed and gilded crowns and haloes dear to the
Middle Ages, no break in the continuity of the painted surface had been
tolerated.

The process of combining two different versions of reality which
had begun with Braque's painted nail now became more involved.
The *Still-life with Chair-caning*,[1] a small oval picture dated winter
1911-12, is rich in inconsistencies which have been organised so
that they form a unity. On the right there is an analytical version of a
glass goblet and a sliced lemon, while on the left a clearly discernible
pipe stem protrudes through the letters 'JOU' of the word '*Journal*'.
Though the first letter, J, lies flat on the paper to which it belongs, the
U appears to peel off in an independent movement. Below, pasted to
the canvas, is a piece of oilcloth realistically patterned with chair-
caning. Its edges are camouflaged and it is partly over-painted with
shadows and stripes so that at the bottom of the picture it does not
appear to lie all in the same plane. This curious mixture of techniques
however holds convincingly together within an oval frame made of
a coil of good hemp rope. If we consider the implication in this picture
and "stop to think which is the most 'real' we find ourselves moving
from aesthetic to metaphysical speculation".[2] The chair-caning which
looks real is false. The letters copied from a newspaper are given a
different and independent meaning; instead of being informative
their purpose is aesthetic and symbolic; while the pipe, the glass
and the lemon become real in their own right because of their lack of
imitation.

In all painting the artist requires us to become the willing dupes of
our eyes, to enjoy for aesthetic reasons without question the reality of
the object or the image offered to us. Here, Picasso wilfully disturbs us
by combining within the same frame various degrees of deception
which at different times and in different places we have already
accepted, but put together in this way, they set up a play of contradictory or complementary meanings. In addition he presents us with a
picture which by its composition, its self-contained light and its sober
colour is a delight to the eye whether its deeper implications are
understood or not.

It is an object with a reality of its own that lightheartedly poses
disturbing questions about reality itself—a metaphysical pun. The
austere aesthetic research of analytical cubism is grinning at its former
sobriety, "adding insolence to paradox".

[1] Plate VII, 9.   [2] Barr, *Picasso: Fifty Years of His Art*, p. 79.

Papier Collé and the Return of Colour

During the short visit to Céret in the spring of 1912 Picasso made a series of charcoal line drawings in which he used patches cut out from the coloured patterns of nineteenth-century wallpapers and pieces of newspaper to enrich the content of his picture. Braque at the same time was at work on a similar trend, and from then onwards the technique of papier collé began a career which spread into many different spheres, ranging from the poetic collage of superimposed images invented by Max Ernst and the surrealists, to commercial advertising.

The cut-out piece of paper as used by Picasso and Braque imposed a new discipline and enabled them to reintroduce, at first with great economy, colour.

The flat definite shape of a piece of coloured paper could be used as a unit in the design. It could play its part as a patch of shadow or a change of texture, or, if it had words printed on it, like a visiting card or a label from a packet of tobacco, it could enrich the picture with these associations, becoming an ideogram, or a visual joke or metaphor.[1] Deflected from its original meaning and made to describe something different, a piece of newspaper could be the shadow or the body of a guitar. By juggling with our conceptions and our symbols of reality, cubism transposes abstract ideas into the plane of the plastic arts.

Colour now came back in its own right as an abstract value, not as something that belonged to an object and hence the victim of form and light. To quote Braque, "colour acts independently of form . . . colour could give sensations that upset space and that is why I had abandoned it. . . . The impressionists . . . had sought to express atmosphere, the Fauves, light and the cubists, space. . . . It was therefore necessary to bring back colour into space. . . . The adaptation of colour came with the papier collé. . . . There it became possible to dissociate colour clearly from form and see its independence in relation to form. . . . Colour acts simultaneously with form but has nothing to do with it."[2] As later in abstract painting, colour was to be enjoyed for itself, but it was also to act simultaneously with the form of objects as their complement.

[1] See Zervos, *Picasso*, Vol. II**, p. 226, No. 490.
[2] Braque-Dora Vallier, 'La Peinture et nous', *Cahiers d'Art*, October 1954, XXIXᵉ Année, No. 1.

The Widening Influences of Cubism

From Sorgues Picasso wrote to Kahnweiler asking him to move all his belongings from the studio flat in the boulevard de Clichy, as well as what remained at the Bateau Lavoir, to a studio he had taken in the boulevard Raspail, Montparnasse. His new life with Eva was to be marked by a break with all the habits he had formed in Montmartre. He was exchanging the bohemian charm of La Butte for the more banal surroundings of Montparnasse, which was however a quarter newly discovered by artists from all parts of the world. Intellectuals of all sorts were to be found at the Closerie des Lilas, as well as at the two famous cafés, La Rotonde and Le Dôme, where political exiles such as Trotsky joined in passionate discussion with poets and painters. The new address, 242 boulevard Raspail, was however temporary. A year later Picasso moved again to a dreary though well-lit studio in a modern block of flats at 5 bis rue Schoelcher, overlooking the trees and tombs of the Montparnasse cemetery.

Cubism had by now become the most important and controversial topic in all discussion of the arts, but Picasso remained remote from all manifestations that savoured of group activity, though many were ready to acclaim him as the leader of the new movement. Such an idea was entirely foreign to him, and he began to give rude answers to trite questions about the importance of negro sculpture in the cubist revolution, and continued to refuse to exhibit in the Salons. In the summer of 1911 his absence was already conspicuous in the first great manifestation of cubism at the Salon des Indépendants, which included Delaunay, Gleizes, La Fresnaye, Léger, Metzinger, Picabia, Le Fauconnier, Archipenko, Marie Laurencin and Marcel Duchamp. But neither that, nor the Salon de la Section d'Or organised by the Groupe de Puteaux who met in the studio of Jacques Villon, held any attraction for him.

The critics who attacked this show as well as the Salon d'Automne of the same year, which included many of the same painters, could not however forget the absent originator of the new style. Gabriel Mourey wrote in *Le Journal*: "May I be permitted to avow that I do not believe in the future of cubism, no more in the cubism of its inventor Picasso than of . . . his imitators. Cubism, integral or not, has already had its last word." Only Apollinaire in *L'Intransigeant* and Salmon in *Paris Journal* continued to defend the movement.

In foreign countries, thanks to isolated enthusiasts, Picasso was slowly becoming known. The Thannhauser Gallery in Munich, where a first exhibition had been held in 1909, showed his works again in 1911. In the winter of 1910-11, thanks to the disinterested enthusiasm of Roger Fry, two Picassos were included in an exhibition entitled "Manet and the Post-Impressionists" at the Grafton Galleries in London. The pictures chosen were Gertrude Stein's *Nude Girl with Basket of Flowers*[1] of 1905 and the pre-cubist *Portrait of Sagot*.[2] Even these pictures which would now appear simple for anyone to understand raised a storm of abuse and were bitterly parodied in an exhibition at the Chelsea Arts Club put on in haste to demolish the foreigners by ridicule. A certain wit signing François Rotton sent in a caricature of the portrait of Sagot entitled *Portrait of the Artist (painted with his left hand)*.

In his second Post-Impressionist Exhibition in 1912 however, Fry included thirteen paintings and three drawings by Picasso, among which were a number of important analytical cubist pictures. In the same year the Stafford Gallery held an exhibition of drawings, mostly of the Blue and Pink periods, with prices ranging from £22 to £2 10s. But in spite of his courageous showing of the cubism of Picasso and Braque in London at an early date, Roger Fry failed to follow the significance of their work. This can be judged from the preface to the catalogue, in which he says: "The logical extreme of such a method would undoubtedly be the attempt to give up all resemblance to natural form—a visual music; and the later work of Picasso (e.g. c. 1911-12) shows this clearly enough. . . ."[3] With the advantage of knowing what followed we can now see that this was never Picasso's illogical aim.

Although the first appearance of the painting of Picasso across the Atlantic was in 1911 at the Photo Secession Gallery of New York, it was not until the great Armory Show, long remembered for the scandal it caused, that cubism made its impact on the United States, first in New York and later in Boston and Chicago. In these exhibitions, the work of Picasso was dispersed among that of other painters, Braque, Duchamp, Gleizes, Marie Laurencin and Picabia, but all the same it did not fail to make an unforgettable impression.

Collectors from abroad continued to buy Picasso's painting. His reputation was steadily increasing and in the future he was never again to feel anxiety about how he was to make enough money. Little by little the problem changed to how to use it and how to deal with the

[1] See Zervos, *Picasso*, Vol. I, p. 113.   [2] Plate VI, 3.
[3] See Benedict Nicolson, 'Post-Impressionism and Roger Fry', *Burlington Magazine*, January 1951, p. 11.

incessant demands of his less fortunate friends. A second Russian collector, Morosov, began to buy paintings with admirable discrimination, but confined himself to pre-cubist work, and Shchukine, never having been seriously affected by the shock that according to Gertrude Stein he had suffered from the *Demoiselles d'Avignon*, continued to take back with him to Russia after his frequent visits some of the finest examples of cubism. Even in Spain, though Madrid showed no interest at all, the Dalman Gallery in Barcelona organised an exhibition of cubist art which seriously upset those friends of Picasso who had considered themselves pioneers of the modern movement at the time of the 4 Gats. They were frightened by the incomprehensible inventions of the man they had formerly considered a genius.

It was not until 1913 that the first book to defend cubism against the scorn of the critics and the indignation of the public was published in Paris, although in Munich Max Raphael had spoken favourably of cubism in the book *Von Monet bis Picasso*. Guillaume Apollinaire, the untiring champion of the modern movement, however, was more thorough. In *Les Peintres Cubistes* he wrote lyrical passages which continue to arouse the enthusiasm of all who are sensitive to poetic criticism. "The modern school of painting", he says, "seems to me the most audacious that has ever appeared. It has posed the question in itself of what is beautiful." In his eagerness to include all who are young and active he praises the work of painters of minor talent as well as the great creators of the movement, yet we owe to him the famous observation that Picasso "studies an object as a surgeon dissects a corpse", and his profound admiration for his friend appears in a sentence such as "his insistence on the pursuit of beauty has since changed everything in art".[1]

Synthetic Cubism

I have already mentioned that the papier collé was the source of the next development in cubism. The large coloured surfaces cut out of paper reintroduced colour in the form of a coloured patch rather than a painterly suggestion of colour created by the touch of a paintbrush. Colour had been kept in reserve, its relative scarcity during the analytical period had made the subtle nuances of tone all the more important, but now it was to return, not to describe the lighting or the relief of an object but as a delight in the sensation, colour, itself.

[1] Apollinaire, *The Cubist Painters*, 1913, English translation, Wittenborn and Co., New York, 1944.

In a large picture, the *Card Player*,[1] painted in the winter of 1913-14, the old techniques of analytical cubism have taken a new breadth, the breaking up of surfaces is now handled by means of large flat coloured areas each given a relationship in space to its neighbours and fitted securely into a three-dimensional pattern. The arabesques of decorative designs borrowed from wallpaper are here painted trompe l'œil imitations.

But the spirit of the papier collé, the desire to return to the object itself, and incorporate it into the picture, so as to witness with enjoyment the metamorphosis that it could be made to suffer, had other consequences. To quote Cocteau: "He [Picasso] and Georges Braque, his companion in miracles, debauched these humble objects . . . that one finds on the slopes of Montmartre, the models which were the origin of their harmonies; ready-made ties from the drapers, imitation marbles and woods from bar counters, advertisements for absinthe and Bass, soot and paper from houses that are being demolished, chalked curbstones, the emblems of the tobacco shops where two Gambier pipes are naïvely held together by a sky-blue ribbon."[2] With a preference for the humblest, all materials were now to be pressed into the service of these alchemists. The silk purse must be made from a sow's ear. The magic lies in giving value to that which is usually despised. What virtue can there be in making a gold nugget out of gold?

But the transition from analytical to synthetic cubism was not abrupt. As early as 1912 the papier collés of Céret show a preference for large flat surfaces, but at the same time they often incorporate objects treated analytically. Throughout the following year there are many pictures in which the two styles exist side by side.

At the same time there is an increasing appreciation of the sensuous pleasure of surface textures. The use of sand stuck to the canvas offered an invitation to touch the rough coloured surfaces and enjoy their existence quite apart from any representational meaning. Also the way in which rough surfaces catch the light made them a lively ground for colour lightly brushed on.

Cubist Constructions

In the late autumn of 1913 Apollinaire became editor of a monthly review, *Les Soirées de Paris*. In his first number[3] he published five

---

[1] Plate VIII, 7.   [2] Jean Cocteau, *Picasso*, Stock, 1923, p. 12.
[3] *Les soirées de Paris*, No. 18, 15 November 1913.

reproductions of cubist constructions made by Picasso.[1] Their appearance caused such disapproval among its forty subscribers that all but one of them cancelled their subscriptions. The constructions were made out of the most unconventional and humble materials, built up so as to form a bas relief. The materials consisted mostly of wood, tin, wire, scraps of cardboard and paper, with or without patterns, images and colours. The theme in most cases centred round the guitar. None were made with much regard for permanence. They were fragile and very little remains of them all except their photos. It is possible to detect in them influences derived from negro sculpture that assert themselves here more obviously than in painting. There are certain African masks from the Ivory Coast in which the eyes are made as cylinders sticking out ferociously from the face, and an echo of this exchange of a dark hole for a protruding circle, negative for positive, is introduced into some of the constructions, when for instance the hole in the centre of the guitar is transformed into a projecting cylinder.

Picasso was here making a statement which challenged the nature of existence. The conception of substituting negative for positive became a diverting exercise which appealed to the imagination of his friend Apollinaire. It was a favourite habit of the poet to give special names to his friends. For Picasso he had found one suggested by a bronze bird from Benin that he had discovered. This strange creature held a butterfly in its beak and was attended by two rampant snakes. Picasso's name henceforth became the 'Oiseau de Bénin' or the 'Ucello noir'. In *Le Poète Assassiné*, a poetic tale published in 1916, Apollinaire describes how after the poet's death, his friend the painter, "dressed in blue linen and bare feet" whom he names "l'Oiseau de Bénin", builds a monument in honour of the dead hero. The government having refused to grant a site he chooses a spot in an opening in the forest where he hollows out of the ground an exact likeness of the poet "so perfectly that the hole was full of his phantom—a profound statue in nothing, like poetry and like glory." Again in a poem entitled 'Pablo Picasso' published in *Sic*[2] the author of *Caligrammes* arranged the typography of the page so as to leave spaces in the form of the objects that appear in Picasso's cubist still-lifes, framed by the words of the poem.

The constructions have none of the meticulous care with which certain artists, fascinated by the abstract beauty of geometric forms in space, have realised their ideas in metal and plastic materials in more

---

[1] See also Zervos, *Picasso*, Vol. II**, pp. 356, 357, 361, 362, 363 and 387.
[2] *Sic*, No. 17, May 1917.

recent years. They were roughly put together. The materials were chosen with a feeling for their texture. Here and there a few boldly painted lines or circles enhance the strength and the sensuality of this composite object and add a reminder of the plastic strength of primitive sculpture. The simultaneous multiple image is at the basis of each construction. Each object within it is invariably seen from more than one viewpoint. In order to understand the roundness, flatness, fulness or hollowness of the object, as well as what goes on in space around it and behind it, every liberty is taken.

The first constructions were built up in deep relief on a background. From them Picasso evolved a remarkable example of polychrome cubist sculpture in the round known as the *Glass of Absinthe*.[1] Using cubist and collage techniques he again established a play, a joke between varying degrees of reality, by placing on the glass which was modelled out of wax, a real absinthe spoon and an exact replica of a lump of sugar. The glass, scooped out so as to show the surface of the liquid within, is poised on its saucer and the whole, with the exception of the spoon, is cast in bronze and painted. The painted patterns and the elegant poise of the little object give it a gay and vaporous look which brings to mind the top-heavy slanting hats and the tight-fitting lace chokers of the ladies of those times.

The Woman in a Chemise

During the winter of 1913-14 Picasso produced one of those works which in later years stand out among other paintings of the period as being prophetic of trends of development. It is a large canvas in which ochre and purple tones have been allowed to invade the restrained palette of analytical cubism. The picture has had several titles but is usually known as the *Woman in a Chemise*.[2] I once had the good fortune to have it lent to me for some months after it had been acclaimed by the surrealists and shown in their exhibition in London in 1936 as a splendid and powerful example of fantastic art. It was in fact so powerful that a friend to whom I had let my house for a month during its visit complained that it gave her nightmares and endangered the future of her expected child. I also was deeply moved by it. The references to reality are direct and highly sensual. In describing this picture after he had known it for twenty years, Paul Eluard wrote: "The enormous sculptured mass of the woman in her chair, the head big like that of the Sphinx, the breasts nailed to her chest, contrast wonderfully . . . with the fine measure in the features of the face, the

---

[1] Plate VIII, 5.   [2] Plate VIII, 3.

waving hair, the delicious armpit, the lean ribs, the vaporous petti-coat, the soft and comfortable chair, the daily paper."[1] New and dis-quieting relationships between abstraction and sensuality, between the sublime and the banal, between stark geometric shapes and allusions to organic reactions are brought into being. I have not only been moved by the familiar flesh pinks, greys and purples of this great female nude, by the enveloping arms of the chair which embrace and protect the seated figure, not only loved the cavernous depths that surround the strong central pillar round which is built the enveloping egg-like, womb-like aura of her body and its culmination in the cascade of dark hair which seems at times to transform the upper part of the picture into a landscape by the sea, but also I have been haunted by those pegged-on breasts hanging like the teeth of a sperm whale strung on the necklace of a Fijian king, germinating sensations of tenderness, admiration and cruelty.

With masterly authority of line and composition, the erotic content of this picture, which is almost unbearable in the complete-ness of its implications, becomes laden with poetic metaphor. The act of creation is situated in one symbolic seated figure surrounded by the newspaper, the armchair and the linen of our everyday existence. The dream and reality meet in the same monumental statement.

Avignon

Picasso again spent the summer of 1913 in the exhilarating company of his friends and the relaxing heat of Céret. Again a prodigious amount of work was produced, but in addition, the nearness of Spain tempted him to cross the frontier with Max Jacob so as to see a bullfight. In a letter to Apollinaire dated 2 May Max Jacob mentions this, and also says that they were all deeply upset by the news of the death of Pablo's father in Barcelona and adds that Eva's health was not good. How-ever they found entertainment in a small travelling circus where they made friends with the girl performers and the moustachioed clowns "who seemed to have been painted up as a cubist studio joke".

The following year it was again Provence that attracted Picasso. With Eva he went to stay for several months at Avignon, and was joined by Derain as well as Braque. Again he worked with his usual untiring vigour. A flow of paintings and papiers collés of increasing brilliance was the product of this visit, but before the summer ended

[1] Paul Eluard, *A Pablo Picasso*, Trois Collines, Genève-Paris, 1944, p. 36.

the situation had changed. On 2 August 1914 war was declared, and Picasso said goodbye at the station to Braque and Derain, who both left hurriedly to join their regiments. The break had come at the moment when cubism was in full development, when its creative impetus backed by the sensibility of Braque, Gris, Léger and many others gave promise of a great future. There appeared to be no limit to the consequences of its challenge in the spheres of poetry and philosophy as well as art.

Picasso stayed on at Avignon with Eva, sad, worried and solitary. It was not his war. Even when surrounded by friends he had always been alone, taking refuge in his work. Now he was more isolated than ever. Though he did not realise it at once, the farewell he took of his friends was to be final, for although they returned from the war, he has himself said that after their parting on the station at Avignon he never found Braque or Derain again.

The pictures of these summer months however contain a gaiety of colour and an exuberance of form that have tempted critics to label them 'Rococo Cubism'. There is a still-life called *Vive la France*[1] because one of the goblets standing on a table, among vases of flowers, playing cards, fruit and bottles, has written on it the words 'Vive la' above crossed French flags. The background is an ornate flowered wallpaper. Here, as in the large green canvas *Woman seated in an Armchair in front of the fireplace*,[2] the technique of the papier collé is imitated in painting. Even the edges of certain areas are given trompe l'œil shadows to give the impression that they are actually or partly stuck to the surface. Picasso obviously enjoyed the joke and he has enhanced some patches with bright coloured dots giving a pointillist effect like the texture of sand. Both pictures, typical of this period, betray a lively, almost frivolous mood. Gentle curves describe the forms and the elaborate patterning covers large areas of the pictures, adding to their exuberant charm.

This mood extended to constructions made of the most varied materials and to drawings of a wildly grotesque nature in which realist details are introduced into a cubist structure. In the drawings, features in themselves recognisable as part of the human form, such as eyes, breasts, hair, hands and feet, are the clues in an orgy of distortions which surpass all liberties formerly taken with anatomy. Yet in spite of the outrageous proportions and grotesque expressions which could suggest that they are no more than a joke, a communication is established. The drawings become clear to a sense which bypasses all logic

[1] Plate VIII, 4.   [2] Plate VIII, 2.

and belongs to the world of dreams.[1] In this way they can be said to be prophetic of the discoveries of the surrealists, Max Ernst and Miró, ten years later. They are a truthful account of the reality of the subconscious. "Surprise laughs savagely in the purity of light."[2]

[1] See Zervos, *Picasso*, Vol. II**, p. 358.
[2] Apollinaire, *The Cubist Painters*.

CHAPTER VII

FIRST WORLD WAR—PARIS AND ROME
(1914-1918)

Cubism at the outbreak of the War

SINCE THE APPEARANCE of the *Demoiselles d'Avignon* the new style had had only seven years to evolve, but the pace of its development had been vertiginous. Its influence had spread in all directions. Even painters of established repute, such as Matisse who could not endorse its discoveries, found themselves adopting certain of its principles, until it could be said that no artist sensitive to the problems of painting could escape being influenced to some degree. At the same time the storm of anger that cubism had aroused among academicians and Philistines was equally significant. No one in fact who professed an interest in the arts could ignore it. A new conception of the rôle of painting and the relationship between art and life had come into being.

The accumulation of ideas that had found expression in cubism and in consequence enlarged the sphere of the arts is too vast in all its implications to be described in a few pages and has not yet been fully understood, but I shall try to make clear some of the most important factors. A primary condition was the disregard for the photographic image of objects. Art was no longer required to copy nature or even to interpret it. Instead it was made to intensify our emotions and associate us more profoundly with nature by endowing the work of art with new powers. These powers however are not the fruit of intellectual speculation; they are closely akin to the primeval heritage of art that had become overlaid with convention and forgotten.

Cubism though revolutionary was not a rupture with the past. It was a positive creation which again brought into the field of our sensibility values well known to primitive man. The insistence on the objective power of the work of art in its own right has its distant echoes in the wonderful and formidable appearance of negro masks and fetishes, as well as the ritual images and sculptures of the cave-dwellers. Picasso enjoys making the claim that "some day we shall paint pictures that can cure a man of toothache", a claim which was also made for the icon and the miraculous images of saints, though other forces considered by us as foreign to the arts such as faith or superstition had to come to their aid. In this case the arts made their appeal independently of religion, forfeiting the advantages and despising the charlatanism of such combinations.

Every aspect of painting had undergone an inquisitorial revision. Form, colour, light, space, surface textures, signs, symbols and the meaning of reality had all been stripped of their former conventions and reinstated and developed with fresh significance.

Under the rigorous dissection of analytical cubism objects had lost their momentary superficial appearance; they had been made to reveal their existence as entities plotted in time and space. The new sense of objects conceived in three or even four dimensions seen from many angles had surpassed the narrow convention which required the single viewpoint of Vitruvian perspective. The limited view of an object seen from one given place was inadequate and the new conception introduced two factors of interest; movement on the part of the spectator rather than the object and knowledge of the object based on more than a limited glance.

Following the ascetic intensity of the analytical period which owed much of its passionate seriousness to Cézanne's long contemplation of nature, the introduction of the papier collé came with a disconcerting burst of light-heartedness. Two different conceptions of reality were brought together in the same picture, and just as words can change their meaning according to the context in which they are used, so objects were made to vary in significance, playing more than one rôle in the manner of a visual pun. I have already mentioned the visiting card or the piece of newspaper which when pasted on to a painted still-life played its part in the composition as an area of colour, light or shade but also retained its own identity. Similarly a piece of black paper cut in the shape of the shadow of a guitar could give the illusion of substance to the guitar itself. The Cézannian endeavour, which dominated analytical cubism to give to an object a plastic form, led in synthetic cubism to the form's becoming an object. Form began to dominate for its own sake and its appearances and implications were examined so as to emphasise its greatest significance; optical effects were exploited; concave forms could be made to become convex; positive and negative were interchangeable. To live in the imagination forms had to achieve a metamorphosis and attain a new reality of their own.

But in spite of its revolutionary trends, cubism retained an instinctive attachment to classical tradition in more than one aspect. With his love of things as entities in themselves, Picasso was never tempted to mutilate an object by cutting it off mercilessly at the edge of the canvas, a habit often exploited by Degas and the painters of atmosphere to whom the plasticity of an object was less important. With the desire of a sculptor to handle things and feel all round them Picasso, however much he may distort, never makes an arbitrary cut which would leave an object incomplete. Even when it is partly hidden by something else in the picture we are made aware of its presence by transparency or linear implication. In addition to this, whatever it may be, head, figure, guitar, pipe or glass, the object is an entity bathed in the aura of its own reality. The composition of cubist pictures owes throughout another important debt to tradition. They are invariably built round a central mass in a manner which recalls the Byzantine icon or such pictures as the *Expolio* of El Greco. The characteristic recurrence of egg-shaped compositions is also reminiscent of the ancient symbol of the universe and the germ of life, the almond-shaped vesica piscis which frames the figure of God in Byzantine art.

The far-reaching discoveries of cubism become a coherent style thanks to the fundamental simplicity of their conception. Geometric simplifications adopted instinctively by the artist allowed him to create new harmonies with the same precision whereby crystals form with the frost.

That the creation of the cubist style is due to the genius of Picasso working in close collaboration with Braque is beyond question, but as Salmon points out "the founders of schools, if really they are masters surpass the framework of the school itself. Picasso had, already in 1908, a right to say he knew nothing and wanted to know nothing of Cubism. He playfully asserted that imitators did much better than inventors."[1] Regardless of the theorising and stylisation inflicted on cubism by minor followers the work of its originators remains as a source which will continue to fertilise the arts and a volcano which will inflame the minds of many generations to come.

At the outbreak of war in 1914, however, the great majority of critics on all levels were hostile. A few writers such as Rémy de Gourmont and Anatole France admitted that the cubists were serious and resolute, even though the public imagined them to be purely frivolous and interested only in the scandal they caused. Even so Jules Romains, after years of reflection, thought that "the activity of Picasso was no more than a perpetual imposture and that his cubism roused our illusions".[2]

[1] Andrew Salmon, *Souvenirs sans Fin*, Vol. I, Gallimard, 1955.
[2] See Zervos, *Picasso*, Vol. II (Preface), 1942.

In spite of incomprehension and violent opposition, cubism took root. Although in literature its influence was indirect and interior, it changed the face of the modern world by the power it exercised over painting, sculpture, architecture and the applied arts. Interior decoration, advertising and commercial design imitated its geometric rhythms. But the further it flowed from its source the less was it understood and the more adulterated it became. Feeble imitations of its angular patterns appeared like a shadow of modernism which spread over textiles, furniture and even female fashions. Though cubism remained in itself incomprehensible to the public its ghost became fashionable. In another respect, its origins in African sculpture linked cubism inevitably with negro spirituals and jazz. Two very different sources, one the dark primitive communities of the jungle and the other the highly developed society of our civilised cities joined together to produce a new musical style with cubism as an unexpected link.

At an early date during the war the influence of cubism entered into the public domain in another way. Gertrude Stein tells the story of how she was walking one cold autumn evening in the boulevard Raspail with Picasso. A convoy of heavy guns on their way to the front passed them, and they noticed to their astonishment that the guns had been painted with zig-zag patterns to camouflage their outlines. "We invented that" exclaimed Picasso, surprised to see that his discoveries in the breaking up of forms should have been pressed so rapidly into military service. Realising the possibilities of using cubist technique to make recognition of an object less easy in warfare, he said later during the war to Cocteau: "If they want to make an army invisible at a distance they have only to dress their men as harlequins." Harlequin, cubism and military camouflage had joined hands. The point they had in common was the disruption of their exterior form in a desire to change their too easily recognised identity.

Paris goes to War

Mobilisation and war brought with them inevitable confusion and the dismemberment of the various groups of intellectuals who contributed to the modern movement. It struck a blow that threatened to paralyse the movement for ever leaving irrefutable evidence only in the achievements of the cubists that a new style had come to life. The disruption and desolation of the next four years were such that it is surprising that all was not lost. As it happened, it was the older and more traditional habits of society that suffered most. The younger generation was able to regroup its energies. The survivors, once freed from the army and reinforced by new blood, became more than ever determined to change the old order which had been responsible for such a disaster.

In common with all Frenchmen of military age, the artists found themselves mobilised and many foreigners who had settled in Paris volunteered in the Foreign Legion. Braque, Derain and Léger were drafted at an early date to the front. To escape internment, Kahnweiler and his German compatriots fled to neutral countries, while others such as Gris found themselves stranded and almost penniless in France. Apollinaire, however, wishing to prove his love of France and to share to the full the ordeal of his friends, applied for French nationality. Having finally overcome bureaucratic objections arising from 'l'affaire des statues' he was accepted in the. artillery. The same zeal he had shown for the arts and the same loyalty to his friends were now transmitted into the comradeship and the ordeal of battle.

Picasso returned, accompanied by Eva, to his studio in the rue Schoelcher. He found Paris a changed city, robbed of its gaiety and anxiously watching the approach of the German armies. The life as he had known it a few months before was almost eclipsed by the brutal and immediate exigencies of war. To him, whose preoccupation had always been his work, the present upheaval was a heartbreaking display of human stupidity, but he did not, like Apollinaire, feel it to be his responsibility to take an active part in the quarrel. His idea of war was that it was a business for soldiers.

Max Jacob and the Death of Eva

Among the few friends who had not been forced for one reason or another to leave Paris was Max Jacob, whose health made him ineligible for military service. Emotional and delicate, he continued to live a life of passionate disequilibrium. He related to his friends how some years before, while he was in a state of trance in his squalid lodgings in Montmartre, a vision of Christ had appeared to him. As time passed his exalted sense of guilt increased his desire to withdraw into monastic life. As a Jew he could not do this until he had been baptised.

Picasso showed no surprise at his friend's intention but neither was he able to associate himself with the increasing fervour that led Max to his conversion. During the first winter of the war Max had discovered in Montparnasse a priest who was willing to baptise him, and not long after in the presence of Pablo Ruiz Picasso whom he had chosen as godfather, he was admitted into the Christian faith. He received the name of Cyprien, one of the many saints who are to be found in the birth certificate of his Malaguenian friend. Much to the distress of the new convert, Picasso had wanted him to be baptised 'Fiacre' after the patron saint of gardeners, but he was quite willing to give up his joke in favour of this closer and more conventional link. At the ceremony he gave his godson a neatly bound copy of *L'Imitation de Jésus-Christ* in which he wrote "To my brother Cyprien Max Jacob, Souvenir of his Baptism, Thursday, 18 February 1915, Pablo".[1]

A letter received by Max Jacob a few months later proves that although Picasso did not take his rôle of godfather seriously he did not mock either. He wrote: "My dear godson Max, I am sending you the money you ask for and I shall be very happy to see you again soon. I am deep in house-moving and you will arrive just right to give me a hand such as you have always offered as a friend. You know how little I ask on these occasions: only your moral support, encouragements, in short the friendly hand of Max Jacob. Meanwhile, here is mine, your old friend Picasso."[2]

There is no certainty that the money referred to in this letter was for Max Jacob himself. The war was causing great hardship to many artists, and about the same time as this undated letter, Max wrote to Salmon asking him to subscribe to a fund he was trying to raise for the cubist painter Severini who was in danger of dying from hunger and tuberculosis.

In the winter of the same year tragedy came nearer. Eva, "small and perfect", finally wasted away and died after a short and terrible illness.

In a letter written in November to Gertrude Stein, who was at that time in Spain, Picasso speaks of spending half his time in the metro on his way to and from the nursing-home. Even so he had found time to paint a harlequin and he ends the letter by saying, ". . . in short my life is very crowded and as usual I never stop".[3] When the end came a month later a very small group of friends accompanied Picasso to the cemetery. Juan Gris who was among them said in a letter to Raynal at the front: "There were 7 or 8 friends at the funeral, which was a very sad affair except, of course, for Max's witticisms, which merely emphasised the horror." He adds coldly, probably referring to the jokes: "Picasso is rather upset by it."[4] We find Picasso

[1] See Penrose, *Portrait of Picasso*, p. 41.
[2] Max Jacob, *Correspondance*, Ed. de Paris, 1953.
[3] Elisabeth Sprigge, *Gertrude Stein*, Hamish Hamilton, London, 1957, p. 110 (Yale Collection letters).
[4] *Letters of Juan Gris*, collected by D. H. Kahnweiler; translated by Douglas Cooper. Privately printed, London, 1956, p. 34.

writing to Gertrude Stein on 8 January 1916: "My poor Eva is dead . . . a great sorrow to me . . . she has always been so good to me." He continues, "I would also be very happy to see you since we have been separated for so long. I would be very happy to talk to a friend like you." Gertrude Stein, the determined, egocentric materialist pagan seemed a possible source of comfort. She was connected with his past and his nostalgic memories of Montmartre, and was at the same time a refreshing influence on account of her liberty of thought and vigour in action.

Neither the conversion of Max nor the untimely death of his mistress did anything to change Picasso's attitude to religion. He remained detached from its problems and avoided its rites just as he kept aloof from the war which surrounded him but was not his war. There is however a drawing of Christ on the Cross, dated 1915, which is an isolated but very careful study rather in the style of El Greco, which we may choose to associate with his personal feelings at this time.

The Crystal Period

It was impossible for the atmosphere of pessimism shared by so many of his friends not to affect Picasso's work. The exuberance that had crowned pre-war days and at the last moment produced the rococo pictures painted at Avignon was past, doubt once more penetrated his spirit and made it impossible for him to continue in the same vein. Deprived of the company of Braque, Picasso found no other painter with whom he could share in such intimacy the excitement of new discoveries. Matisse spent most of the period of the war in his apartment on the Quai St. Michel, but though they met frequently the war did nothing to soften the old rivalry. Minor cubist painters who followed in Picasso's wake, such as Gleizes, Metzinger, Severini and many others, had developed nothing which could be of interest to him out of their theoretical approach.

The crisis that arose was not due only to the war. The exclusivity of the new style demanded that it should either be pushed even further towards the abstract and the decorative or that it should yield, and combine with other modes of expression. The theorists claimed that any return to a more representational art was reactionary and a sign of defeat. Picasso however, refusing as usual to hedge himself in with rules, continued on the one hand to paint pictures with even greater severity and geometric precision, and on the other to surprise and anger the more consistent but less talented artists by making drawings which were almost photographic in their naturalism.

During the first autumn and winter of the war there was no abrupt change, only a tendency towards a more rigid structure. Space and form began to spread into larger simpler shapes bounded more often by straight lines. Curves became all the more emphatic owing to their rarity. Large rectangular shapes were filled with flat colour or illuminated with dots, often lined up in rows like a pattern on a fabric. In most cases the compositions were based on a central object which could be a man, a guitar, a woman seated in a chair, or a still-life group on a table. The identity of figures and objects was often merged in playful ambiguity.

There are photographs that show the young painter in his studio in the rue Schoelcher, standing in front of some large canvases on which he had been at work for some months, constantly repainting and changing their appearance. In one he wears his working clothes—old patched trousers rolled up at the ankle, a creased jacket and a conventional English cap. His expression is relaxed except for his penetrating stare and in his right hand he clasps firmly that constant companion of those days, his pipe. Another photograph shows him in shorts stripped to the waist. His costume and his well-built, muscular physique would suggest a boxer were it not obvious from the background that the ring in which he fights is his world of canvas and paint, his only antagonist being doubt in his own mind as to how to express his passionate imaginings.

Before the spring of 1916 a few large pictures were painted of which the *Man with his elbow on a table*[1] and the *Guitar Player*[2] are the most important. They are imposing in their size as well as in the angular strength of their design. The *Guitar Player* is remarkable for a new dramatic organisation of light. The simplified rectangular head illuminated by a small circular eye stands out fiercely in front of a light background. Below, the dark mass of the body gains a sense of towering height from tall rectangles which seem to be lit up with spots like the windows of skyscrapers at night. At their base in a horizontal patch of light is a hand holding a guitar. But to realise the complete detachment from atmospheric painting that the new style had attained we must look at pictures such as the *Harlequin*[3] painted in 1915, now in the Museum of Modern Art, New York. The clear flat colours are bounded almost entirely by straight lines making contrasts which would be intolerably harsh were not their relations to each other in tone and their proportionate sizes so miraculously balanced. The nervous touches of the brush of the analytical period have been entirely

[1] Zervos, *Picasso*, Vol. II**, p. 255, No. 550.   [2] Plate VIII, 9.   [3] Plate VIII, 8.

eliminated, as have all other concessions to impressionist technique. The *Girl with the Mandolin* of 1910 appears almost sentimental when compared with the calculated severity of this canvas.

It is these qualities, developed with even greater precision in the still-life paintings of the following years, that suggested to Raynal the name 'Crystal' for this period. Such pictures reach their culmination in the two versions of the great composition *Three Musicians*,[1] painted in 1921, which I shall discuss later. It was at this moment, however, during the early years of the war, when Picasso had reached a high degree of purity in his style, that he produced a new surprise for his friends.

'Back to Ingres'

It has often been said, not without malice, that Picasso steals anything from anyone if it intrigues him sufficiently. There are those who claim that during his close collaboration with Braque he would hurry home after a visit to his friend's studio to exploit ideas suggested by the work he had just seen. These rumours spread to such a degree, says Cocteau (who is himself not averse from the habit of borrowing, especially from Picasso), that minor cubist painters would hide their latest pet inventions when he paid them a visit from fear that he would carry off some trivial idea on which they had staked their hopes of fame. It is not the theft however that is important—the world of ideas should have no frontiers—it is what is made of it afterwards. A worse practice which can lead to complete sterility is indicated by Picasso when he says: "To copy others is necessary but to copy oneself is pathetic."

During the years when Picasso was discovering cubism his faculties were fully occupied; he was completely dedicated to his new-found invention, and allowed himself no deviations. At the same time he was conscious of other modes of vision. His admiration for the work of great masters such as Ingres, and his careful study of their painting in the Louvre during his early years in Paris, may at first sight appear incongruous with his cubist discoveries. But even during the most hermetic period of cubism he shared with all great artists a desire to keep in close touch with reality, and knew that there has been more than one way of doing so.

To the surprise of those who were not intimate with Picasso's ways of thinking and working, he again revealed his extraordinary ability as a conventional draftsman by an increasing number of

[1] Plate X, 4, and Zervos, *Picasso*, Vol. IV, p. 127.

naturalistic drawings. The subjects were varied; sometimes apples or
a bowl of fruit, sometimes a man seated in a chair or a couple dancing.
In the summer of 1915 he once more astonished his friends with a
careful and exquisite pencil drawing of his old dealer Vollard[1] in which
the outline and shaded forms produce an almost photographic likeness, making an extraordinary contrast with the cubist portrait
painted five years before. It is a masterly portrait, irreproachable by
academic standards. The line is so sensitive and precise that critics
immediately drew a comparison with Ingres.

It is certain that Picasso has always had a great admiration for the
master of Montauban, but it was not only the faithful likeness of the
model traced with sensitive strokes of a pencil that enchanted him.
Ingres with his horror of anatomy had been content to think of the
curved surfaces of his models without regard for the inner structure.
He elongated their limbs and rounded their joints in ways that earned
him the censure of contemporary critics. His eroticism and his understanding of the female form urged him to include more surfaces of
flesh than can be seen from one point of view. It is in fact surprising
that this painter who, unlike the cubists, had a horror of penetrating
beneath the surface was close to them in the need he found for distortion, and in his tendency towards a multiple view of the same
object. In another way also he anticipated them. His use of colour, in
which he denied himself atmospheric effects and used flat unmixed
colour, was closer to Picasso's taste and more comparable to the
Harlequin of 1915 than was the complicated mixing of colour practised
by Delacroix and the impressionists.[2]

Several other pencil drawings of friends were to follow the portrait
of Vollard. In the summer of 1915, Max Jacob wrote to Apollinaire
who was at that time a sergeant in the artillery at the front: "I pose at
Pablo's and in front of him. He has a portrait of me in pencil which is
very much the old peasant, it looks at the same time like my grandfather, an old Catalan peasant, and my mother."[3] Yet if it offended
the vanity of the poet it was acclaimed by all who had not become too
fanatically cubist, as an admirable likeness and a masterly drawing.[4] A
year later it was Apollinaire's turn to sit for Picasso. After accepting a
commission in the artillery he had returned to Paris with a serious
head wound, for which he was trepanned. Picasso did several drawings

[1] See Zervos, *Picasso*, Vol. II, p. 384.

[2] See J. T. Soby, *Modern Art and the New Past*, University of Oklahoma
Press, 1957.

[3] Max Jacob, *Correspondance*, Vol. I, Ed. de Paris.   [4] Plate IX, 1.

Picasso presides at the bullfight at Vallauris. On his right, Jacqueline Roque, behind her his daughters Paloma and Maïa. On his left his son Claude and Jean Cocteau. 1955.

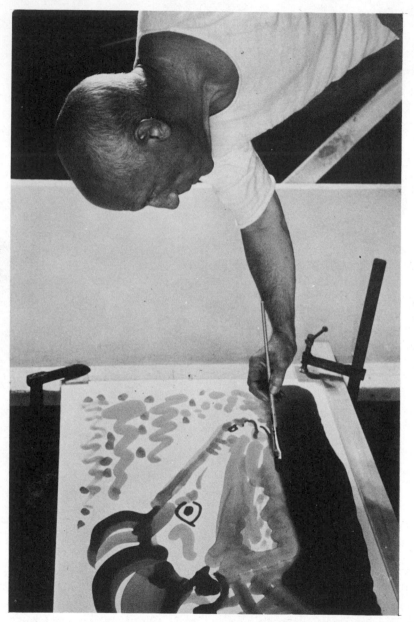

Picasso painting, 1956

of him. One in particular[1] shows him seated, dressed in his uniform, the Croix de Guerre pinned to his breast and his forage cap crowning his head bandaged as a result of his wounds from which he was eventually to succumb. The criticism of the more bigoted followers of cubism failed to affect Picasso. He continued to go his own way, working at the same time on conventionally realistic drawings and developing in painting an even more rigorous cubist technique.

Life during the War

The perilous military situation which had brought the front line close to Paris had at least one compensation for those who were suffering the infernal misery of the trenches. They could escape when on leave and find themselves quickly in a very different atmosphere. Montparnasse had by this time superseded Montmartre as the centre for intellectual life, and artists and poets returning from the battlefield gathered where they were certain to meet their friends. The café terraces which were only a short walk from the studio apartment of Picasso in the rue Schoelcher were thronged with those who had arrived unexpectedly from the front. The company was widely international, those in uniform such as Léger, Raynal, Braque, Derain, Apollinaire and many others mixed again with painters, sculptors and writers such as Modigliani, Kisling, Severini, Soffici, Chirico, Lipchitz, Archipenko, Brancusi, Cendrars, Reverdy, Salmon, Dalize. There was no lack of talent among them and such encounters were a welcome contrast to the ceaseless roar of cannon and the stench of death not more than fifty miles from the gates of Paris. The dominating mood was one of careless bravado, few while on leave troubled themselves with political or social issues. With death so close their reaction was to joke. Gertrude Stein quotes Picasso as having said cynically: "Will it not be awful when Braque and Derain and all the rest of them put their wooden legs up on a chair and tell about the fighting."[2]

Apollinaire with his talent for story telling, mixing fact with fantasy, describes this atmosphere in *La Femme Assise*. "To-day", he writes, "Paris solicits me, here is Montparnasse which has become for painters and poets what Montmartre was fifteen years ago, the refuge for their simplicity." Among his characters in this book is one, Pablo Canouris, "the painter with blue hands", who has the eyes of a bird and speaks "French in Spanish". Attributing to him both charm and

[1] Plate IX, 2.
[2] Gertrude Stein, *Everybody's Autobiography*, Random House, New York, 1937, and Heinemann, London, 1938.

great talent comparable to Picasso's, he leaves the reader in doubt as to what is legend and what is truth. But Picasso did not enjoy the description of a passionate and frustrated love affair with Elvire, a young woman painter, which appears to be a caricature of one of the ephemeral attachments formed by him in the two years that followed the death of Eva.[1]

Among those who remained in Paris and continued to entertain their friends were Roch Grey (Baronne d'Oettingen) and Serge Férat, who had formerly vigorously supported the review *Les Soirées de Paris* and who continued to participate in its successor, *Sic*. A record of their conviviality is preserved in a drawing made by Giorgio di Chirico which shows, seated at table around a frugal meal, the painter Léopold Survage, Roch Grey, Picasso and Serge Férat, while on the wall above them hangs Rousseau's full-length portrait of himself.[2] Chirico's view of Picasso in this as in other drawings is not flattering. He insists on his short stature and his tough impertinent look, but above all he cannot resist exaggerating the blackness of his eyes which he draws as enormous excrescences ready to drop out of their sockets. It is observation rather than love that emerges from these sketches.

The departure of Kahnweiler from France owing to the war brought several young painters into serious financial difficulties. He had been their friend and a sincere advocate of their work. Fortunately for them a Parisian dealer, Leonce Rosenberg, a convinced supporter of the modern movement, became the wartime centre for their sales. Picasso transferred to him the care of all such transactions until 1918 when his brother, Paul Rosenberg, with whom he had formed a new friendship, became his official dealer, an arrangement which lasted for many years.

In the spring of 1916 Picasso was seized with a desire to move into a house of his own, which he could now well afford. The gloomy atmosphere of the rue Schoelcher with its view over a sea of tombs had continued for long enough, and he decided to move to a small suburban house with a garden in Montrouge. He soon discovered the rashness of this change, for although he was waited on by a faithful servant and there was little to interrupt him in his work, he still needed contact with his friends. In consequence he found that he was scarcely ever at home. Owing to the war, all forms of transport were slow and rare. Whenever he visited his friends in Montparnasse their conversations continued until late in the night, so that a long walk home through dark deserted streets became almost a nightly event.

[1] See Gertrude Stein, *Autobiography of Alice B. Toklas*, p. 183.
[2] See Penrose, *Portrait of Picasso*, p. 42.

These nocturnal wanderings were in fact an old habit. Picasso enjoyed the sensation of being conscious when others were asleep; it felt like a triumph over death. The absence of noise and movement left more room for his own imagination. He enjoyed the loneliness of the night with its sparse and ghostlike population. It seemed like an echo of his own loneliness, the solitude of genius. But these solitary thoughts were at this time often willingly sacrificed for the company of another mind of great originality. Erik Satie, the composer, lived at Arceuil, in the same direction as Montrouge, but even further from Paris. His wit, and the highly imaginative and inventive turn of his thought, made him an excellent companion with whom Picasso could enjoy his long trek from the café back to bed.

The Russian Ballet

While he lived in the rue Schoelcher Picasso had often received the visits of an agitated and brilliant young poet who, on leave from the front, would dash up the stairs when he came to call with his eyes closed so as to avoid seeing the large plaster moulds of the Parthenon frieze that were its permanent decoration. He plunged eagerly into the unfamiliar atmosphere of Picasso's studio, where again, but for different reasons, he felt uneasy among the negro masks and strange objects that hung haphazard on the walls. Jean Cocteau, the elegant and talented youth who had already become known for his precocious association with the Russian Ballet, rapidly perceived that even if he could not understand the full significance of Picasso's enormous paintings and the bizarre collection of objects that littered the studio, he had yet some astonishing things to learn. "Picasso's admiration", he wrote, "favours much more what he can use than beautiful accomplishments. It is due to him that I lose less time in gaping contemplation at what cannot be of use to me and I understand that a street song listened to from this egoistical angle is worth 'The Twilight of the Gods'."[1]

Cocteau had been working for some months on his second project for a ballet. The first, *Le Dieu Bleu*, had been presented in Paris in 1912, and in London a year later, by Serge Diaghilev, the impresario and producer of the Russian Ballet. It was neither good nor successful but during the early years of the war, in spite of the exigencies of military service, Cocteau had evolved rapidly. With the intention of becoming ultra-modern, he made the acquaintance of Erik Satie and obtained his promise to write the music for a ballet which was to astonish the whole world by its originality. The plot was well advanced

[1] Jean Cocteau, *Picasso*, Stock.

when he invited Picasso, in the spring of 1917, not only to design the costumes and scenery but also to come with him to Rome, whither the ballet company had returned from America for rehearsals, and there to meet Diaghilev.

Picasso's aversion from travelling and the fact that the ballet, though reputed for its high standard in dancing, had little connection with the modern movement in the arts, seemed to make it hopeless for Cocteau to succeed in dragging Picasso away from Paris. However to the astonishment of all and with the insistent disapproval of serious-minded cubists, Picasso accepted. In February he started for Italy on a journey which was to have lasting consequences for him and for the future of the ballet.

Since the first season of the Russian Ballet in Paris in 1907, Diaghilev had entertained his audiences with displays of oriental grandeur in the costumes and scenery of Bakst, whose taste for lascivious opulence had a savour of the romanticism of the nineties. Diaghilev however, with admirable judgement, realised that the unrivalled talent of his dancers and musicians must be brought into contact with the contemporary movement in western European painting. This was to become all the more important when the return to its native land of the ballet loved by the Czar became impossible owing to the Revolution. The acceptance of Cocteau's project, in which two such revolutionary figures as Picasso and Satie were to take part, was an adventurous step for Diaghilev, the first which later was to classify his ballet in every way as the spearhead of the avant garde. It opened the way for many other productions which were to make it one of the most important manifestations of the modern movement for the next ten years.

Cocteau had devised a theme which was eminently suitable to Picasso. Its title *Parade* at once conjured up ideas of the circus and the music hall with their glamour, their illusions and their garish entertainment. Formerly in Montmartre and Barcelona Picasso had watched theatrical performances with keen eyes from the auditorium or the wings. His paintings of the lean Harlequins were comments on life behind the scenes, but on this occasion he had been asked to join the company and work with them. All these circumstances added to the enthusiasm with which he set to work in Rome. There he at once made the acquaintance of Diaghilev and those who surrounded him. These included two brilliant young Russians who were to become close friends of Picasso, Stravinsky and Massine.

"We made *Parade* in a cellar in Rome where the troupe rehearsed . . . we walked by moonlight with the dancers, we visited Naples and

Pompeii. We got to know the gay futurists", wrote Cocteau. Picasso had in fact met Marinetti in Paris as early as 1909. The leader of the futurists and his disciples had watched keenly every new development in cubism and had worked out their divergent ideas of painting. Futurism differed from cubism fundamentally in the way it stressed the importance of movement and the machine. Picasso, as we have seen, had not neglected the idea of movement in painting, but the methods he favoured were more subtle and indirect. He did not despise their efforts, but the only painter among them whose talent he really admired was Boccioni, who was killed on the Italian front. Differences of opinion, however, did not interfere with their friendship, and the Italian painters were willing to lend a hand in the making of the framework of some of the more extravagant costumes and in helping Picasso to paint the enormous drop curtain.

The visit to Italy was quickly over. After a month in Rome and a few days in Florence and Milan, Picasso was back in Montrouge. Work between the trio, Cocteau, Satie and Picasso did not always continue smoothly. On several occasions the patient Satie was on the point of abandoning the project. Had it not been for his admiration for Picasso, to whom at one time he wished to dedicate his music, it is unlikely that *Parade* would ever have been produced. In a letter to his talented young friend Valentine Gross (afterwards Valentine Hugo) Satie unburdened himself. "If you only knew how sad I am", he wrote, "*Parade* is changing, for the better, *behind* Cocteau! Picasso has ideas that please me better than those of our Jean! And Cocteau doesn't know it! What can be done! Picasso tells me to continue with Jean's text, and he, Picasso, will work on another text, *his own*—which is astounding! Prodigious!

"I am getting frantic and sad! What can be done! Knowing the wonderful ideas of Picasso, I am heartbroken to be obliged to compose according to those of the good Jean, less wonderful—oh! Yes! less wonderful! What can be done! What can be done! Write and advise me. I am frantic. . . ."

Fortunately the crisis passed and a week later Satie wrote again from Paris: "It's settled. Cocteau knows all. He and Picasso have come to understand each other. What luck!"

The first performance of *Parade* was fixed for 17 May 1917 at the Théatre du Châtelet where in spite of the war the Russian Ballet was to give its first wartime season. At the appearance of the great drop curtain[1] accompanied by Satie's sombre music for the overture there

[1] Plate IX, 4.

was a sigh of pleasure and relief. The audience who were expecting to be outraged, instead found themselves bewildered by the fact that the inventor of cubism should present them with something that they could understand. The curtain was a delightful composition in a style which was only indirectly cubist; it owed its inspiration rather to the popular art of the circus poster. Its subject resembled a back-stage party among the harlequins and circus folk of pre-cubist days in a happy tranquil mood. A large white mare with wings attached by a girth quietly licks her foal while it nuzzles up under her for milk. A ballerina with budding wings standing on her back reaches up to play with a monkey above on a brightly painted ladder. In the foreground are familiar circus objects such as an acrobat's ball and a drum lying near a sleeping dog, while in the distance behind the folds of the tent can be seen a romantic landscape of ruined arches. The colours, mostly greens and reds, are reminiscent of the tender melancholy light in which the saltimbanques appeared ten years before. In their reappearance they seemed less soulful, having gained new vitality in a style strengthened by the disciplines and inventions of cubism.

The delightful hopes offered by the drop curtain were however to be shattered as the curtain rose. The music changed; sounds "like an inspired village band" accompanied by the noises of dynamos, sirens, express trains, airplanes, typewriters and other outrageous dins broke on the ears of the startled audience. The technique of collage and the visual puns of cubism suggested to Cocteau the name of "ear deceivers" for these noises. They announced, together with rhythmic stamping like "an organised accident", the entry of the gigantic ten-foot figures of the 'managers'. Only the legs of the performers showed beneath towering structures built up of angular cubist agglomerations. The French manager carried at the end of a grotesquely long arm a long white pipe, while his other, real arm, pounded the stage with a heavy stick.[1] The American manager, crowned with a top hat, carried a megaphone and a poster showing the word 'Parade'.[2] Both were decked out with forms in silhouette appropriate to their native scenery; the back of the Frenchman was outlined with shapes suggesting the trees of the boulevards and the figure of the American towered up like a skyscraper. The third manager was a horse. Its head held high on a long wrinkled neck had the fierceness of an African mask. Two dancers hidden inside its body pranced about the stage with perfect realism. It was not by violent colour that the audience was shocked. The backcloth was in monochrome, it represented houses in

[1] See Zervos, *Picasso*, Vol. II**, pp. 404, 405.   [2] Ibid., Vol. II**, p. 406.

perspective with a rectangular opening like an empty frame in the centre. The costumes of the managers, including the horse, were also sombre. Among the other dancers the dazzling Chinese conjuror, with his angular movements, seemed like some brilliant insect.

In addition to the managers there were only four dancers. The Chinese conjuror, danced by Massine, wore a costume of brilliant yellow, orange, white and black with bold patterns symbolising a rising sun eclipsed in wreaths of smoke; his headdress in the same colours looked like flames or petals of a flower. Cocteau's directions for his miming were: "He takes an egg out of his pigtail, eats it, finds it again on the end of his shoe, spits out fire, burns himself, stamps on the sparks, etc." With the conjuror appeared a little girl who "runs a race, rides a bicycle, quivers like the early movies, imitates Charlie Chaplin, chases a thief with a revolver, boxes, dances a ragtime, goes to sleep, gets shipwrecked, rolls on the grass on an April morning, takes a Kodak, etc." The other two dancers were acrobats, their tight-fitting costumes were decorated in blue and white with bold volutes and stars, "simpleton, agile and poor . . . clothed in the melancholy of a Sunday evening circus" they danced a parody of a pas de deux.[1]

The managers fulfilled the function of scenery. Their size reduced the dancers whom they introduced, to the unreal proportions of puppets. As they stumped about the stage they complained to each other in their formidable language that the crowd were mistaking the preliminary parade of the actors for the real show which was to go on inside their theatre, and for which no one had turned up. Finally their fruitless efforts brought them to a state of exhaustion and they collapsed on the stage, where they were found by the actors, who in turn also failed to entice an imaginary crowd inside for their performance.

The plot was simple and inoffensive enough but Cocteau managed to mystify and outrage the audience by calling it a 'ballet realiste'. To them the deliberate confusion of real and unreal was inadmissible in a ballet just as it was incomprehensible in cubist paintings. The same conception had penetrated Satie's music. He had formerly annoyed an audience by calling some of his compositions for the piano "petits morceaux en forme de poire"; and in this case, to explain the strange mixture of sounds, he said modestly, "I composed a ground for certain noises that Cocteau found indispensable to determine the atmosphere of his characters".

As the ballet came to an end the mounting anger of the audience expressed itself in an uproar. The Parisian intelligentsia were incensed,

[1] Cocteau, *Le Coq et l'Arlequin*, p. 74.

believing that they had been made the victim of a farce produced to make them look ridiculous for having sat through it. Cries of "Sales Boches" (the worst possible insult in the wartime atmosphere of Paris) were shouted at the company. The audience rose to their feet in an ugly mood menacing the producer as well as Picasso and his friends. The situation was saved however by the presence of Apollinaire. The black bandage on his head and his Croix de Guerre commanded respect. Patriotism and sentimentality finally prevailed over the audience's conviction that they had been insulted.

Parade was an event of importance in the growth of the new spirit in the arts. Apollinaire had written an introduction in the programme with the title 'Parade et l'esprit nouveau'. It described the ballet with enthusiasm and spoke of its significance in the dawn of a new era. There was hope that the modern movement, which was proving that it could survive the disruption caused by the war, would soon blossom into new wonders. He claimed that the fusion of the designs of Picasso and the choreography of Massine produced a kind of super realism (surréalisme) which heralded the New Spirit. It was to him "the starting point of a series of manifestations . . . which should completely alter both arts and manners". He added that the spectators "will certainly be surprised, but in the most agreeable way, and charmed, they will learn to understand all the grace of the modern movement of which they have no idea". Apollinaire was right. In spite of the uproar at the first performance, Diaghilev produced *Parade* again. With each production it won more respect but the total number of its performances was not great. It remained a ballet for the élite and a victory in the campaign of the avant garde.

Picasso stepped into his new rôle as theatrical designer with the same assurance that had won for him his entrance to the academies of Barcelona and Madrid. Léon Bakst, who had until then been the most popular stage designer for the ballet, wrote a generous introductory note for *Parade*. In it he praised the way in which Picasso had discovered a new branch of his art, and showed how the collaboration of the great painter with Massine had led to a new choreography and a new form of truth.

Picasso had influenced the ballet, but the ballet was also to have its influence on him. Not only did it give him a chance to paint on a larger scale than had been possible hitherto, and to see his costumes and constructions realised, and moving in space and light, but also it brought him into close relationship with the human form. Since 1906 his constant interest in the natural beauty of the figure had been overlaid by the stylistic problems of cubism, in which the still-life composed of a quota of domestic objects had furnished the greater part of the subject-matter. But humanity is the inexhaustible source of Picasso's inspiration, and the ballet accelerated his return to a less exclusive repertoire.

Rome, and the exhilaration of a troupe of dancers of amazing talent, provided the first stimulus which was to dissolve the melancholy of the early war years and the loss of Eva. Unable to live without the company of women, Picasso had indulged in a few passing flirtations since her death; but it was not until he set eyes on Olga Koklova, one of Diaghilev's dancers, in Rome that a new influence of lasting importance came into his life. During the war he had introduced several of his temporary mistresses to Gertrude Stein at her apartment in the rue de Fleurus—all of them girls of intelligence, beauty and often of talent, but none managed to win his heart.

The dancer Olga Koklova who attracted his attention among so many was not a great ballerina. She had taken her part in the corps de ballet, and as one of the four girls in *The Good-Humoured Ladies*, in which she made her first star appearance in 1917, she had reached the high standard demanded by the tyrannical Diaghilev. Olga Koklova was the daughter of a Russian general, it was in her tradition to be associated with fame, and the ballet, which she had joined against her father's wish, was her first step on this path. She was captivated by its glamour. Even when she had ceased to be part of the troupe she kept in close touch with her Russian friends and continued to practise her dancing. But with the arrival of Picasso in Rome her career as a professional ballerina came rapidly to an end.

A Visit to Barcelona

When after the Paris season Diaghilev took his ballet to Madrid and then to Barcelona, Picasso went with him. In the Catalan capital it was received with enthusiasm, though experiments such as *Parade*, considered too advanced for a more provincial Spanish audience, were omitted. Joan Miró, who was then a student at the Art Academy of the Cercle di San-Luc, remembers how he watched every performance from the gallery, and, what was even more important, how he met Picasso for the first time.

On his return to his home, Picasso was welcomed by his old friends. They once more gave him a generous reception and entertained him at the music halls of the Parallelo during long nights with flamenco dancing and parties given in his honour. A photo taken in the studio of a friend shows him surrounded by his admirers, such as Miguel Utrillo, Iturrino—the painter with whom he had shared Vollard's gallery in 1901—Angel de Soto, Ricardo Canals and more than a dozen others.

It was five years since Picasso had been in Barcelona; during that time his father had died and his mother had gone to live with her daughter Lola who had recently married a doctor, Don Juan Vilato Gomez. Though he did not neglect his family, Picasso preferred to escape from their admiration and affection. He stayed in a hotel near the harbour. From the window he painted a landscape with the monument to Columbus which stands at the end of the Ramblas as its central feature.[1] The picture is the forerunner of a series of variations on the theme of a window looking into the brilliant light of the Mediterranean, flanked by shutters, with a table loaded with objects and backed by the silhouette of the ironwork balcony. In this case, however, the central feature, the table, is missing.

There is also a portrait of a girl with a mantilla,[2] painted in pointillist technique, which is both the first realistic portrait in oils for many years and one of the last examples of a systematic use by Picasso of Seurat's methods. These with a dozen other paintings he left with his mother when he returned to Paris. When she settled in her daughter's home she had taken with her the large crumpled canvases of his youth. *Science and Charity* and *The First Communion* covered the walls on which they remain to this day, guarded jealously since the death of Señora Ruiz Picasso by Señora Vilato and her sons and daughter.

It is perhaps of some significance that during this short stay in Barcelona, those paintings which are the more traditional in style are the more accomplished. Cubism had relaxed its rigour and given way to a manner which, although less exciting to the intellect, was more readily a vehicle of his present emotions. This can be seen in the still-life and figure paintings, which though cubist in style, contain a flow of curves or an angular movement not unlike the stylised gestures of marionettes.[3] It is still more evident in the realistic painting of a harlequin,[4] now in the Modern Art Museum of Barcelona. The picture in which he seems to have concentrated the maximum of his emotion, however, is a painting of Olga wearing a mantilla.[5] This portrait, the first of Olga, is painted with conventional consideration for the beauty of his young love. It presents her with great tenderness and a realism which surpasses even that of the pencil drawings of Max Jacob and

---

[1] See Zervos, *Picasso*, Vol. III, p. 19, No. 47.   [2] Ibid., Vol. III, p. 17.
[3] Ibid., Vol. III, pp. 18, 20.   [4] Ibid., Vol. III, p. 11.   [5] Plate IX, 5.

Vollard. Those who see in Picasso the enemy of classical beauty are here obliged to admire his power to master the conventional idiom in its most human and unambiguous form. Yet beneath the smooth oval of the young and sensitive face we can divine a temperament already formed and unwilling to compromise. The dark discerning eyes appear to have settled on the object of their adoration with a possessive intent, and the straight delicate mouth set firmly above a well-developed chin hides its resolution behind a faint smile. Picasso gave the portrait to his mother, who treasured it for many years.

In addition to this evidence of a strong amorous preoccupation there exists a series of drawings of the bullfight, made during these same summer months.[1] Among the varied and significant events of the corrida it was the battle between the bull and the victim of its outrageous bestial courage, the horse, which interested Picasso. Plunging its horns deep into the horse's belly the bull holds its dying prey disembowelled and pinned to the ground. The agony of the horse, its neck stiffened in a final ejaculation, can be taken to be symbolic of the supreme act of love and of death. Its towering phallic head searching for a release from its mortal destiny is a symbol which recurs later in the painting of Picasso. It finds its most dramatic expression nearly twenty years later in the studies for *Guernica*.

The image of the horse gored by the bull is too complex for a simple sexual interpretation. It cannot be dismissed merely as a sign of brutish domination. It is rather the uncontrollable escape of the spirit, symbolised in the death throes of the horse, its neck stretched as though in a final orgasm. It is the gesture of the victim, analogous in Picasso's memory with the aweful appearance of his friend the German painter who was found hanged from the rafters of the Bateau Lavoir. Was this similarity between the act of creation and the giving up of the ghost a meaningless coincidence?

Marriage and the Move into Paris

When the Russian Ballet left Barcelona on a tour of South America, Olga Koklova stayed on with Picasso. The attachment between the Russian ballerina and her Spanish lover had grown rapidly. She spoke French fluently and enjoyed the long fantastic stories that he told her in his thick Spanish accent. In the autumn of 1917 they returned together to his suburban villa at Montrouge, where she settled in with the faithful servant, the dogs, the caged birds and the thousand and one objects that had followed Picasso from one abode to the next in ever-

[1] Plate IX, 6.

increasing numbers. But this temporary solution satisfied neither Olga nor Picasso himself. Montrouge had been useful as a retreat. He had worked there spasmodically and often at night, sometimes kept awake against his will by bombardments. On one occasion, finding the din too great, he searched the house for a canvas on which to work, and finding none he picked on a painting by Modigliani which he had acquired. Setting to work on it with thick paint which allowed nothing to show through, he produced a still-life with a guitar and a bottle of port.

On 12 July 1918 Picasso married Olga Koklova. Those who came to the wedding were his friends rather than hers. In compensation, the civil wedding at the Mairie of the 7th Arrondissement was followed by the long rites of the orthodox Russian ceremony. Apollinaire, Max Jacob and Cocteau were the witnesses. Only two months before, Picasso had similarly paid his respects to Apollinaire at his wedding which had taken place at the church of St. Thomas Aquinas, near where the poet lived in the boulevard St. Germain.

The wedding was soon followed by a move towards the centre of Paris. The rue la Boètie is a busy thoroughfare in a fashionable quarter with shops dealing in carpets and expensive semi-antique furniture. About this time art dealers such as Paul Guillaume, one of the first to collect African sculpture, were moving into this neighbourhood. In his gallery in the Faubourg St. Honoré he held, early in 1918, a joint exhibition of Matisse and Picasso. The public were again mystified, as they had been by the drop curtain of *Parade*, to see among work they still failed to understand a few paintings showing a return to realism. In the catalogue Apollinaire explained almost apologetically: "He changes direction, comes back on his tracks, starts off again with firmer step, always becoming greater, fortifying himself by contact with unexplored nature or by the test of comparison with his peers from the past."

Close to this new gallery Picasso took a two-story apartment that had been found for him by his new friend, Paul Rosenberg, whose brother Leonce had opened a gallery in a neighbouring street. Paul Rosenberg had dealt chiefly in the old masters. He quickly recognised, however, the genius of the creator of cubism, although he had no use for his brother's idealism in shepherding the whole cubist flock. In the rue la Boètie he opened his own gallery next door to Picasso, who now became surrounded by dealers as formerly he had been by artists. But Paris is a concentrated city and the move away from the bohemian cafés of Montmartre and Montparnasse did not mean that he was cut off from his friends, though one of them wrote, "Picasso now frequents 'les beaux quartiers'."

Olga took an active part in seeing that the new drawing-room on the street and dining-room giving on to a garden were furnished according to her taste, and that there were sufficient goodlooking chairs to seat the numerous visitors whom she intended to entertain in correct style. Picasso made his studio on the floor above, taking with him his hoard of objects that had found their way into his life by choice or by chance. The pictures by Rousseau, Matisse, Renoir, Cézanne and others were hung haphazard or propped against the walls, recreating the favourable atmosphere of disorder.

Guillaume Apollinaire

After months of treatment in hospital, Apollinaire had recovered from his wounds sufficiently to take up his literary activities again. New books and articles from his pen once more appeared in the avant garde publications of Paris, while an exchange of ideas went on between him and writers who had taken refuge in Switzerland and America. *Les Mamelles de Tiresias*, a light-hearted drama, had its single stormy performance soon after the scandal caused by *Parade*. Apollinaire had called it a 'surrealist' drama, but a critic referred to it as a 'Cubist play'. This annoyed the more purist followers of the movement he had formerly championed. They sent to the press a letter of protestation against Apollinaire claiming that he had made them look ridiculous.

At the moment of Apollinaire's wedding in the summer of 1918 there was a feeling of optimism, which proved to be short-lived, that his health was improving. The severity of his wound had reduced his vitality and in the autumn of the same year he fell a victim to the virulent epidemic of Spanish influenza that accompanied the Armistice. He died just at the moment when the streets of Paris were decked with flags and the crowds beneath his window were shouting "Hang Guillaume!" Hearing the cry from his deathbed he had to be reassured by his wife that the 'Guillaume' they were out for was the German emperor.

The same day Picasso remembers walking at dusk along the windswept arcades of the rue de Rivoli. As he passed in the crowd, the crêpe veil of a war widow blew across his face, wrapping his head so that momentarily he was blinded. This was the prologue to the news which he learned by telephone shortly after, that Apollinaire whom he loved had just died. The call came while he was drawing a portrait of himself in the mirror, a portrait which marks the end of an epoch for two reasons. A great friend had gone and Picasso, with this drawing, abandoned his habit of making frequent lifelike self-portraits. With the death of Apollinaire Picasso lost the most under-standing of his youthful friends. He was overcome with grief. The suddenness with which the end had come paralysed his thoughts. At his request Cocteau wrote to Salmon saying: "Poor Apollinaire is dead—Picasso is too sad to write—he has asked me to do so and deal with the notices to the press." For the large circle of devoted friends and those others who admired Apollinaire for his courage and patriot-ism, the frenzied rejoicing at the victory of the allies was eclipsed by their sorrow.

Three years later a committee of the friends of Apollinaire asked Picasso to design a monument to be set up on the grave of the first champion of cubism. Sufficient funds were finally raised, but for reasons which remain obscure the monument has never been erected. Certain writers claim that Picasso never made a suitable design,[1] but in spite of his aversion from producing anything to order, Picasso did make a series of drawings and small sculptures in 1927-28 which he showed to the committee. His ideas varied from a monument of massive anthropomorphic shape[2] to elegant linear sculptures made of metal rods[3] which drew in space three-dimensional outlines based on the human form. Picasso told me recently that the committee turned all these down as unsuitable. "But what did they expect," he added. "I can't make a muse holding a torch just to please them." Although a partial solution was found in the monolith designed by Serge Férat which now marks Apollinaire's grave in the Père Lachaise cemetery there is still a feeling that some day a sculpture by Picasso should com-memorate the greatness of his friend. Recently a gigantic bronze head, a portrait of Dora Maar dating from 1941,[4] has been offered with the proposal that it should be set up near the church of St. Germain des Prés. Whether or not this bust which was not designed for the pur-pose would be an appropriate memorial is still being debated.

The Armistice

With the end of the war Paris at once regained its position as the centre of attraction for artists, poets and philosophers throughout the world. It was largely the prestige of the modern movement and the widespread influence of cubism that drew to it again the younger

[1] Marcel Adéma, *Apollinaire*, p. 271.
[2] Plate XII, 4.   [3] Plate XII, 6.   [4] Plate XX, 3.

generation, now disillusioned and angry at the madness to which life had been reduced during the past four years. They blamed society for its blindness and violently opposed the pious hopes that there should be a return to tradition and pre-war values both in art and life. The war, it had been claimed, was to end war, with the result that victory became an excuse for self-complacency.

In reaction to these tendencies small groups had sprung up during the war in Switzerland, Germany, England and the U.S.A. Although the difficulty of communication hampered their contact with each other they showed remarkable affinities in their ideas. In Switzerland, sheltered by neutrality, a group led by Tristan Tzara and Jean (Hans) Arp came into being. There was a close similarity between their contempt for the rules that should supposedly govern art and the ideas making themselves felt in New York in the work of Marcel Duchamp, Picabia and Man Ray, and later in the more political attitude of Richard Huelsenbeck in Berlin.

The first sign of the new movement in Europe was the opening of the Cabaret Voltaire in Zürich in May 1916. Hugo Ball, its founder, was a pacifist and a poet, fanatically devoted to the movement in which the names of Picasso and Apollinaire stood out as the main sources of inspiration. He inaugurated his premises as a place to exhibit the work of contemporary artists and hold debates. The catalogue of his first exhibition contained poems and other contributions by Apollinaire, Arp, Cendrars, Kandinsky, Marinetti, Modigliani, and Tzara. The exhibition contained four etchings and one drawing by Picasso. This was followed in July 1917 by the first number of the review which took the name of the new movement, *Dada*. In its desire for a clean sweep of the hypocrisy of the past, Dada wished to destroy everything, even that which had so recently been considered admirable. To the Dadaists "Cubism, marvellous in certain aspects . . . was drifting towards an odious estheticism".[1] A new more violent attack was to gather force in Paris as soon as the way became open.

The outcry of the Dadaists had however no immediate effect on Picasso. That they should attack his less inspired followers who were attempting to create a 'school' from their superficial understanding of his inventions did not trouble him, any more than did the tendency towards abstraction of painters such as Arp and Kandinsky, and the more distant theories of the Russian constructivists. He had already

[1] Georges Hugnet, 'Dada and Surrealism', *Bulletin of the M.O.M.A.*, New York, November-December 1936.

sown the seed of many conflicting tendencies. Two such opposite styles as the pure design in line and colour of Mondrian on the one hand and the poetic imagery of Max Ernst on the other both owed much to his work. With his perpetual curiosity he watched the new movements and continued on his own course.

Biarritz

For the first time since he had said goodbye to Braque and Derain at Avignon at the outbreak of war, Picasso returned to the south of France in the late summer of 1918. This time it was in response to the invitation of a rich Chilean lady, Madame Errazuriz, who had taken a villa at Biarritz as a refuge in the early days of the war. It was in her salon in Paris that Picasso had begun to work on *Parade* with Satie and Cocteau in the autumn of 1916. Now, with a feeling of relief that the war was coming to an end, he and his young bride spent several weeks enjoying the luxury of the villa, and revelling in the sea which from his childhood in Malaga and Corunna had always been one of his loves.

The ocean beaches and new company provided a relief from the noise and dust of Paris still at war. Picasso showed a sociable interest in his holiday surroundings by drawing portraits of his friends and their children. It was here that he met Paul Rosenberg, who lived with his family nearby, and one picture he found time to paint was a portrait of Madame Rosenberg seated in a decorative chair with her child on her knee;[1] another is a small painting of girl bathers with the Biarritz lighthouse in the background.[2] The artificial poses of the girls relate them more closely to the 'mannerist' pictures of 1902 to 1904 than to cubism, but the standing figure that dominates the composition is twisted in such a way that both her front and back are visible, a liberty in distortion which does not occur at that early date. More important than this painting is a drawing of girls on the beach.[3] The delicacy of the line, and the ease with which subtle distortions in the manner of Ingres can be accepted, puts this drawing among the highest classical achievements of graphic art. The movements of the girls are so balanced and the space so organised that the fifteen nude figures that enter into the composition are nowhere crowded by each other. Several other complex drawings of figures were done during these weeks, the main theme being the serenade. Picasso clothed his guitarists in the costumes of the commedia del'arte, which had impressed him in Rome. Accompanied by cherubs and barking dogs,

[1] See Zervos, *Picasso*, Vol. III, p. 85.   [2] Ibid., Vol. III, p. 83.   [3] Plate X, 1.

they perform to reclining odalisques in a series of charming studies.[1]

Besides these idyllic drawings Picasso found time to paint murals on the whitewashed walls appropriate to his amorous mood.[2] In a space between two nude female figures, over a drawing of a vase of flowers, he wrote a verse from 'Les Saisons' of Apollinaire:

> "C'était un temps béni nous étions sur les plages
> Va-t'en de bon matin pieds nus et sans chapeau
> Et vite comme va la langue d'un crapaud
> L'amour blessait au cœur les fous comme les sages."

On hearing of this, Apollinaire, who was living at that time in Paris, wrote back, just two months before he died, to Picasso, "I hope your wife is well. . . . I am very happy that you have decorated the Biarritz villa in this way and proud that my verses should be there." He then continued by describing a new trend in his thought which coincided with Picasso's return to classical realism. "The poems I am writing now will enter more easily into your present preoccupations. I try to renew poetic style but in a classical rhythm. . . . On the other hand, I do not want to slip backwards and make a pastiche." He then explains his intentions further by making a contrast between authors: "Is there today anyone more fresh, more modern, more exact, more laden with richness than Pascal? You appreciate him I believe and rightly. He is a man we can love. He is closer to us than a Claudel who only dilutes with some good romantic lyricism vulgar theological generalities and political or social truisms."[3] Apollinaire was referring to conversations he had had lately with Picasso in which they had both agreed that thought and intuition could be more illuminating than obedience to reason. But this was as far as Picasso went in his appreciation of Pascal. Neither then nor at any other time has he shared the religious convictions of the philosopher of Port Royal. Firmly and persistently he repeats, "Il n'y a pas de bon Dieu".

[1] See Zervos, *Picasso*, Vol. III, pp. 72, 73.
[2] Ibid., Vol. III, p. 80, Nos. 229, 230.
[3] Lettre inédite d'Apollinaire à Picasso, 11 September 1918, *Cahiers d'Art*, 1947, p. 142-3.

CHAPTER VIII

'BEAUTY MUST BE CONVULSIVE'
(1918-1930)

The Ballet in London

IN SEPTEMBER 1918 the Russian Ballet arrived in London and stayed there for nearly a year, ending with a season more brilliant than ever before. Diaghilev again sought the co-operation of Picasso. During the season in July at the Alhambra Theatre in Leicester Square he risked a second production of *Parade*, and put on a new ballet, *The Three-cornered Hat*, for which Picasso had designed the costumes and scenery.[1] The music was by De Falla and the theme a Spanish tale, in which an old grandee tries to use his authority to seduce the fiancée of a young miller and fails lamentably, much to the delight of the village folk and the audience. Nothing of the revolutionary nature of *Parade* was involved, but the theme gave Picasso admirable scope to utilise and enjoy the atmosphere of his native country in the costumes and scenery.

Another new production during the London season was *La Boutique Fantasque*, for which Derain had been asked for the first time to design the costumes and scenery. He accomplished this with admirable charm, contributing a ballet as French as Picasso's was Spanish to Diaghilev's repertoire. Picasso was once more persuaded to leave Paris. Both he and Derain came to London to supervise the painting of the scenery, which was done skilfully by Vladimir Polunin and his English wife Elizabeth.

The Three-cornered Hat proved to be a most popular ballet from the start. The simple outlines and dry colour of the back-cloth, with its gigantic pink and ochre archway against a pale blue sky filled with stars, showed little trace of cubism except in the organisation of the angular walls of the houses. Like De Falla's music, it was saturated with the warmth and excitement of the Spanish night. The rhythms of flamenco dancing, which Massine had learnt during his visit to the Peninsula, were given a masterly interpretation by the cast dressed in costumes admirably adapted to the action. In his designs, Picasso

[1] See Zervos, *Picasso*, Vol. III, pp. 107, 109, 110 and 111.

had instinctively drawn on the curves and zigzags characteristic of the flourishes and patterns used by Spanish peasants as decorations for their wagons and mule-harness, rhythms that probably descend from the calligraphic arabesques of the Moors. The acid contrasts of greens, pinks, scarlet and black were equally evocative of Spain. "All the costumes are, without exception, full of warmth and strength but tempered with a taste for dignity which is very Andalusian", wrote the critic Jean Bernier. The drop curtain for which many sketches are in existence had also been greeted with applause. In the foreground a man and a group of women in Spanish costumes look over a balcony into the arena at the end of a fight from which the dead bull is being dragged off by mules, but here again the technique of cubism was not in evidence and the audience were put to no strain in their enjoyment.

It was now nearly twenty years since Picasso had originally dreamt of crossing the channel to the city that had inspired him in his youth. But since the day he had left Barcelona as a hungry youth in search of a country of bold, beautiful and emancipated women and a society in which the aristocrats were eccentric poets and the beggars wore top hats, much had happened to modify his hopes. He arrived instead as an artist already famous, and with Olga at his side, he chose to stay at the Savoy Hotel where the Ballet Company had made their headquarters.

As was to be expected, Picasso worked hard on the last-minute preparations of the *Three-cornered Hat*, supervising the painting of the scenery and adding final touches to the costumes at rehearsals. He even appeared in the wings on the opening night with paint and brushes to put his final touches to the costumes on the dancers before they appeared on the stage. The dancers themselves were enchanted with the results. Karsavina, who danced the rôle of the Miller's wife opposite Massine, said afterwards that the costume he finally evolved for her "was a supreme masterpiece of pink silk and black lace of the simplest shape; a symbol more than an ethnographic reproduction".

The arrival in London of the Russian Ballet came at the moment after the war when it had suddenly become fashionable to take an interest in the arts, and in particular those which could be styled avant garde. The ballet provided a combination of the prestige of great dancers and the scandal caused by young revolutionary artists, which both pleased the snobs, and on another plane, attracted the attention of the intellectuals. The painstaking work of Roger Fry, seconded by Clive Bell, had persuaded the élite of Bloomsbury to open an eye towards modern painting. With rare exceptions these pioneers failed to arouse a genuine appreciation of the modern movement in art even in their own circle. The general admiration for the perfection of the ballet, with its music and its dancing, helped them however to bring to the attention of an otherwise unreceptive public the work of painters such as Picasso, Derain and later Matisse. It was a roundabout way of convincing London, which in those days was always ten years late in its appreciation of the modern movement, of their importance; but it bore its fruits when three years later the first important exhibition of over seventy of the works of Picasso was held at the Leicester Galleries with a preface to the catalogue by Clive Bell.

The social life that accompanied the success of the ballet drew Picasso and his wife into a round of rich parties. Olga was delighted at these attentions and Picasso, unlike Derain who took his applause in a plain blue serge suit and sought more bohemian society, ordered himself suits at the best tailors and appeared at fashionable receptions immaculately dressed in a dinner jacket.

Clive Bell describes a party given in honour of the two visiting painters by Maynard Keynes in the house they shared in Gordon Square. They had invited, he says, to meet Picasso a few unfashionable friends. Other guests from the ballet were Ansermet, the conductor whose famous beard is well known from the drawing Picasso made of him in Barcelona, and Lydia Lopokova, a friend of Olga's, whose dancing had won the hearts of many Londoners and in particular of Keynes himself whom she was later to marry. Waggishly the hosts placed Ansermet at the head of one table with Lytton Strachey to match with his beard at the head of a second. To meet the distinguished guests they invited "some forty young or youngish painters, writers and students—male and female".[1]

The compliment was returned by Picasso more than once in the rue la Boètie where Clive Bell was invited to call on him whenever he felt inclined, and on one occasion after lunch Picasso lined up his guests, who were, according to Clive Bell, Derain, Cocteau and Satie, on a row of chairs and drew their portraits as a conversation piece.[2] The drawing has been reproduced more than once but in it the place attributed to Derain is occupied by Olga. Although frequently there were guests to lunch and invitations to excellent meals at gourmet restaurants, Picasso was in fact seeing less of his old friends since his move to 'les beaux quartiers'. Braque, on his return from the war with

[1] Clive Bell, *Old Friends*, Chatto and Windus, London, 1956.
[2] See Penrose, *Portrait of Picasso*, p. 50.

a serious head wound, had been precariously ill and in a difficult mood. All thoughts of a renewal of the pre-war relationship between him and his former friend and collaborator vanished. He disapproved of Picasso's new manner of living and despised the way he appeared fashionably dressed at the theatre. In his work, after a few strictly cubist paintings, he abandoned the rigours of his former style for a more fluid, perhaps more personal, mode, from which however the influence of Picasso never entirely faded. Years later Picasso used to say, with affection of his own brand, "Braque is the wife who loved me most".

Pulcinella and Cuadro Flamenco

In 1920 and 1921 Diaghilev produced two more ballets with Picasso's designs. The idea for the first had been broached as early as 1917 when Picasso was in Rome. From a newly-discovered manuscript of 1700 Diaghilev had evolved the idea of a ballet inspired by an episode from the commedia del'arte called *The Four Polichinelles Who Look Alike*. Picasso with his early love of Harlequin at once found this hook-nosed companion a suitable character for his attention, and in the many drawings done during the next three years he had the idea of adaptations for the new ballet in mind. In the sketches of naked odalisques serenaded by Pierrot and Harlequin done at Biarritz the masked face of Pulcinella first appears, though it is not until January 1920 that we find the projects for the stage-sets.[1] The first ideas for the backdrop were based on the baroque decorations of the Italian theatre. It was composed of a false proscenium opening on to a false stage with a chandelier and richly decorated pilasters and ceiling. In the centre was a further false opening with a long perspective flanked by arcades which opened on to a harbour with ships, somewhat reminiscent of the silent piazzas of Chirico. Though the forced perspective and asymmetric angular trompe l'œil showed its cubist origins, the whole effect was of "unabashed romanticism". But in the final version these complicated extravagances were suppressed, and the form was highly simplified. The perspective giving on to the night sky between houses, with a large full moon above a boat in the harbour, was treated in a rigorously cubist style. The romanticism had been boiled down, the baroque décor had vanished and only these symbols of the Neapolitan scene remained, strengthened and made more monumental in scale. The white costumes and shiny black masks of the pulcinellas and the simple white bodice, apron and short red skirt

[1] See Zervos, *Picasso*, Vol. IV, pp. 6-9.

of Pimpinella stood out clearly in the moonlight and gave full scope
to Massine's immense talent for mime.

There was trouble during the rehearsals of this ballet. Diaghilev
criticised the designs and was discontented with the music of Stravinsky.
The composer had looked forward to this collaboration with Picasso,
who had recently designed the cover for the piano score of his *Ragtime*,[1]
but it seemed to be resulting in failure, although Stravinsky had said:
"The prospect of working with Picasso, who would do the décor
and costumes and whose art was infinitely precious and suited to me,
the memory of our walks and our many impressions of Naples . . .
all this succeeded in conquering my hesitation."[2] There had been
some muddle about dates and insufficient liaison between Picasso and
Massine. In spite of all this, the first production was a success. Stravinsky's fears were allayed. He says: "*Pulcinella* is one of those spectacles
—and they are very rare—where everything holds together and where
all elements, subject, music, choreography and decorative scheme form
a coherent and homogeneous whole. . . . As for Picasso he performed
a miracle and it is difficult for me to say what enchanted me most,
his colour, his plastic expression or the astonishing theatrical sense of
this extraordinary man." Cocteau also was full of praise. "Think of
the mysteries of childhood", he writes, "the landscape it discovers in
a blot, Vesuvius at night seen through a stereoscope, Christmas chimneys, rooms seen through a keyhole, and you will feel the soul of
this décor."

The next ballet for which Diaghilev again demanded Picasso's help
was the *Cuadro Flamenco*. In a letter to Kahnweiler in April 1921 Gris,
who had been invited to go to see Diaghilev in Monte Carlo, com-
plains that he was originally asked to design the décor and that "Picasso
had stepped in and taken it for himself".[3] As a Spaniard Gris was
an equally appropriate choice. But the idea had been born, four
years earlier when Picasso was in Spain with the Ballet. However,
we learn from Gertrude Stein that there was a coldness between
Gris and Picasso at this time, which had not thawed when Gris died
in 1927.

With his flair for recognising talent and his immediate enthusiasm

[1] See Zervos, *Picasso*, Vol. VI, p. 160, No. 1344.

[2] William S. Lieberman, *Dance Index*, Dance Index Ballet Caravan Inc.,
130 W. 56th Street, New York, Vol. V, No. 11, 12. November-December
1946.

[3] *Letters of Juan Gris*, collected by D. H. Kahnweiler; translated by Douglas
Cooper. Privately printed, London, 1956.

for flamenco dancing, Diaghilev had found a troupe of gypsy dancers during his visit to Seville. It included girls of unusual beauty and passionate matrons who danced and sang as though they were possessed. Among the male dancers was an old toreador, who having lost his legs below the knee, danced with additional fury on his stumps until the more squeamish London public demanded his withdrawal. Their orchestra consisted of two guitarists. On the stage the troupe sat in the conventional way in a semi-circle in front of a drop curtain that had been designed by Picasso.[1] He was able to use here the idea which he had abandoned for *Pulcinella* of a curtain that showed not only the proscenium with gay rococo ornament but also the adjoining boxes filled with dandyish couples watching the performance. The romantic effect of the surroundings, rich in Spanish bravado, gave without effort the perfect atmosphere for this type of performance.

Mercure

The last ballet in which Picasso took part was not originally produced by Diaghilev—the last, that is, if we except *Train Bleu*, for which an enlargement of a small painting by him, of two colossal partially draped women striding across a beach, was used as a drop curtain. Massine had parted company from his former impresario to produce a ballet for Comte Etienne de Beaumont in a series of private entertainments known as Les Soirées de Paris in the summer of 1924. With the collaboration of Satie and Picasso the strangest ballet and the most original since *Parade* was put together. Between them "they composed a short work in three tableaux crowded with mythological incident and spiced with mundane fantasy. The ballet was in part deliberately scatological. It attempted to shock as well as to amuse."[2] The theme, which was a skit on the stories of the Greek gods, was the least interesting feature. But Picasso used the occasion to realise some new and interesting ideas.[3] The drop curtain in subdued browns and greys had as its theme two musicians. In its atmospheric softness of tone the striking feature, which was repeated in the costume designs, stage effects and backcloths, was the use of line. From childhood, as I have already said, Picasso had enjoyed accomplishing the feat of drawing a figure or an animal with one continuous line. His ability

[1] See Zervos, *Picasso*, Vol. IV, pp. 87-9.
[2] William S. Liebrman, *Picasso and the Ballet*, Dance Index, N.Y., Vol. V, Nos. 11-12, 1946.
[3] See Zervos, *Picasso*, Vol. V, pp. 92-103.

to make a line twist itself into the illusion of a solid being without taking pen from paper, had become an amazing act of virtuosity and a delight to watch. The costume drawings for *Mercure* are a masterly example of this kind of calligraphic drawing. With characteristic inventiveness, he had foreseen how they could be carried out on the stage. Remembering the success of the Managers in *Parade* he devised with Massine a variety of constructions. The chariot for the rape of Persephone in which Pluto rides with his prize, and the horse he drives, were drawn in iron wire set on large simplified white shapes. The result in terms of form and movement achieved with such simple means was a triumph. But somehow the ballet was not a great success, either at its first appearance or later in 1927 when Diaghilev took it over. The critic Cyril Beaumont thought that the "whole thing appeared incredibly stupid, vulgar and pointless", and if it had not been for the music of Satie and Picasso's innovations in the décor it would soon have been forgotten. In the great retrospective exhibition of Picasso in Paris in 1955, however, the drop curtain was exhibited as one of his major works. Though lacking in intensity in an exhibition consisting mainly of easel pictures, it provided an important example of his style in the early twenties.

Portraits and Drawings

The Russian Ballet with its circle of musicians, dancers and painters had inspired Picasso with the desire to make drawings of his friends from life. A series of line portraits drawn with a fine lead pencil show boldly and faithfully the features of Stravinsky,[1] Satie, De Falla, Diaghilev, Bakst and Derain.[2] There are more complicated shaded drawings of Cocteau, Ansermet and Massine. All of them recall the perfection of Ingres. However, they also contain a touch of caricature in the features, emphasised particularly in the hands, which makes it impossible to attribute them to anyone but Picasso. With discernment he recognised the essential features and acted on that counsel of Van Gogh's in a letter to Theo, "exaggerate the essential".

The portraits of friends connected with the ballet began in Rome, where Picasso made rapid and humorous sketches of Diaghilev, Massine, Bakst and Cocteau paying him visits in his studio. Later in London he made drawings during rehearsals of groups of dancers in various poses. The tendency towards the sentimental in the sketches of these sylphs is held in check again by a slight well-judged dose of caricature. The tenderness of their gestures is made gently ridiculous

[1] Plate IX, 3.   [2] See Penrose, *Portrait of Picasso*, p. 47.

by the enormous size of their hands placed delicately against their cheeks. In one drawing the sense of arrested movement of Lopokova poised on Massine's knee while dancing in *La Boutique Fantasque* becomes the major consideration.[1]

As a result of Picasso's desire to use his talent in this way we have a magnificent portrait gallery which extends beyond the circle of the ballet in the early twenties. Poets often came to him asking for a frontispiece for a book of poems they were publishing. His willingness to comply is evident from the long list of those whose portraits he made between 1920 and 1925. It includes Aragon, Huidobro, Salmon, Valéry, Parnak, Reverdy, Breton, Max Jacob, Cocteau, and Radiguet.

Picasso's renewed interest in realistic drawings led him often to make copies of photographs and picture-postcards that he picked up by chance. A postcard of a young couple in Tyrolean national costume was transformed into a large and splendid pencil drawing which is no slavish copy, but rather a noble and inspired study, drawn with such vitality and freshness that the original photo would look a travesty of reality beside it.[2] There is similarly a well-known drawing of Diaghilev and Selisbourg taken from a photograph for which they had dressed themselves with the greatest care.[3] In this case the photograph still exists. In comparison with the direct simplicity of the drawing, in which all superfluous detail is eliminated and only a pure unhesitating line remains to describe their features, the photograph is a poor, insufficient likeness of the two men. Just as Picasso had delighted in showing even as a child that he could rival the masters, here it gave him great satisfaction to show that he could beat the camera. The handsome swagger of Diaghilev with his top hat perched at a slight angle and a debauched twinkle in his left eye exists with an extraordinary economy of line. Beside him the figure of his portly seated companion attains more volume by the perfect placing of a few lines than by all the detail of modulated tones from which line is absent in the photograph.

Another example of the same process of translation from a photograph is a portrait of Renoir[4]—a painter who is not readily associated with Picasso, though a large and very fine painting of a nude by Renoir hung for years in the dining-room at the rue la Boètie.

The interest in line drawings, so well demonstrated in the portraits, continued in many compositions of nude bathers. The sensitivity with

[1] See Zervos, *Picasso*, Vol. III, pp. 114–15.   [2] Ibid., Vol. III, p. 143.
[3] Plate IX, 7.   [4] See Zervos, *Picasso*, Vol. III, p. 137, No. 413.

which Picasso controls line can be a prolonged source of delight to those who care to enjoy its subtlety. It varies from a certain deliberate coarseness, as in parts of the portrait of Stravinsky,[1] drawn soon after the first night of *Pulcinella*, which is "curiously modest, without inflection or accent, as prosaic and casual as the sack suit which it describes",[2] to graceful perfection in the exquisite composition of *The Bathers* drawn in 1918 at Biarritz. In all cases the miraculous effect brought about is that the form enclosed or suggested by the line is convincingly present, whether it is in the strong nervous interlocked hands of the musician or the full and tender shapes of naked girls. By implication the eye sees what is not there, the white paper is transformed into living flesh.

Le Midi

After his visit to Biarritz in the late summer of 1918 Picasso has scarcely ever spent a summer without visiting the sea, either on the Brittany coast or more often his native Mediterranean. These places, not yet overcrowded with the holiday makers who now besiege the coast everywhere during the summer months, were a refuge from the fashionable life into which he was being drawn in Paris. Though such contacts pleased and flattered the worldly side of his nature, a nostalgia for a freer, more bohemian life such as he had known and in which his imagination had thrived before the war remained. Even the Côte d'Azur was still unfashionable in summer. The beaches were almost deserted and he could fully enjoy the refreshing influences of the sea, and the tranquillity of the company of his young wife and the son she bore him in the summer of 1921. He could benefit from this atmosphere to devote most of his time and thought to his work.

The first visit after the war was to St. Raphael in the summer of 1919. Picasso installed himself in a large hotel looking out to sea. In his room he painted several versions of a theme he had begun at Barcelona.[3] Just as Matisse had been doing in Nice, he used the window with its shutters and balcony as the background for objects seen against the light outside. But unlike Matisse, instead of evoking the atmosphere of the harem with odalisques reclining in cool shadows, he placed against the light a table piled up with familiar objects, guitars, bottles and fruit, using the open window as the proscenium of a stage.

He continued to elaborate these cubist still-lifes after his return to the rue la Boètie. They differed from pre-war compositions chiefly in the

---

[1] Plate IX, 3.   [2] Barr, *Picasso: Fifty Years of His Art*, p. 110.
[3] Plate X, 2.

treatment of light, which now invaded them and illuminated the still-life, so that it belonged both to the brightly coloured objects and to the limitless depth of their background. Also the strict observance during the analytic period of the picture plane as a continuous shallow surface, which had already been abandoned in synthetic cubism, now gave way to the introduction of a realistic background of the sea or the sky line of Parisian roofs. This renunciation of a homogeneous cubist style for the still-life and its background, implied that cubist and realistic treatment of objects was not incompatible.

Monumental Nudes

In addition to the still-lifes Picasso continued to develop his interest in the female form. The summer had produced many studies of girls running, dancing and swimming, with a clear expanse of sea and sky as their background. They are the prologue to paintings covering a great variety of moods, sometimes idyllic and sometimes sinister, which were to follow during several years. In these early days there appear for the first time figures from classical mythology, such as the centaur and the satyr, who in a gouache of 1920 are seen fighting together for a naked girl held in the centaur's arms.[1] Here again, just as in line draw-ings, it is the plastic solidity of the form that is emphasised. In spite of the overpowering light of the Mediterranean sun, form has not been allowed to dissolve into atmospheric effects. Picasso's instinct has urged him towards a more tactile sensation of the human form and a feeling for the physical weight of bodies and limbs. To the dismay of those who had begun to look to him for a renaissance of graceful classical discipline founded on the influences of the paintings he had seen at Pompeii and the voluptuous smoothness of flesh in Raphael and Ingres, his preoccupations led him to a new and disquieting version of female nudity. These conventional influences were too sweet to confine his turbulent spirit. Distortion was again in demand as an emotional necessity. This time it was not the elongated, emaciated, El Greco-like distortion of the Blue period but that of a more earthy, ponderous conception that emerged.

The appearance of the robust and fleshy type of female, reminiscent of the Dutch girls of 1905, came as a surprise. As usual when there is an abrupt change in Picasso's work we are tempted to look for some enlightenment close at hand. That the series should have begun at the time of his wife's pregnancy seems not without importance. The fertile promise of her distended form and his recognition of his own intimate

[1] See Zervos, *Picasso*, Vol. IV, pp. 62, 63.

part in the creative process must have awakened his wonder. Another
association linked with his childhood can also be brought into account.
Picasso once told me how, when very young, he used to crawl under
the dinner table to look in awe at the monstrously swollen legs that
appeared from under the skirts of one of his aunts. This childish fascination by elephantine proportions impresses him still. Such exaggeration
seems both frightening and supernatural and both sensations were
recaptured by him in these paintings. The first of these monumental
figures, such as the *Two Female Nudes* of 1920, often lean their heads
together sentimentally.[1] Patient and statuesque, they seem to dream or
a coming ordeal. Their fleshy bodies, their growing breasts, their
strong enveloping hands and heavy feet firmly rooted to the ground
are preparing for the future tasks of maternity.

The Three Musicians

At the same time, Picasso true to his nature did not pursue exclusively one particular trend. Concurrently with the colossal women he
painted cubist pictures of increasing purity—still-lifes and harlequins
whose simplicity in form and economy in colour provided the appropriate material. They culminated in the summer of 1921 in a great
composition known as the *Three Musicians*,[2] of which there are two
versions painted both at the same time. The more resolved of the two,
now in the Museum of Modern Art, New York, is one of Picasso's
major achievements. In describing it Maurice Raynal says: "Rather
like a magnificent shop window of cubist inventions and discoveries,
the *Three Musicians* is a masterpiece of wit and poetry. With it Picasso
summed up his long series of figures from the Italian Comedy, which
he had treated in increasingly abstract fashion, reaching the limit here."[3]

A composition of three figures in the rigorous technique of synthetic
cubism was a feat Picasso had not attempted before. The flat coloured
shapes, simple and rectilinear in form, are arranged so that everywhere
their significance is legible. Each shape becomes an ideogram, a
significant 'sign' of reality. But it is the hieratic appearance of the
masked figures, apparent even in a small reproduction, which is
astonishing. Their monumental scale is wittily created not only by the
construction of their masses but by comparison with the tiny spiderlike
hands with which the musicians play their instruments. We have
noticed Picasso's preoccupation with hands before. At this particular
period, remembering his father's saying "it is in the hands that one

[1] See Zervos, *Picasso*, Vol. IV, p. 16, No. 56.   [2] Plate X, 4.
[3] Maurice Raynal, *Picasso*, Skira.

sees the hand", he made a great number of drawings of his own hands seen from all angles, and also of the plump graceful hands with fruit-like fingers of his wife. In portraits such as that of Stravinsky he had usually been tempted to exaggerate the size of the hands. They become ponderous and expressive of their tactile sense, but in the *Three Musicians* on the contrary the hand is reduced so as to become the smallest unit, thus giving a key to the gigantic size of the figures.

Fontainebleau: Mother and Child

After the birth of his son Paul (known as Paulo) in February 1921, instead of returning to the sea, Picasso rented a large and comfortable villa at Fontainebleau. From the point of view of the health of his wife and son it was a considerate action to forgo the delights of the coast for a bourgeois residence within a reasonable distance of Paris. But Picasso was not entirely happy about his new rôle as paterfamilias. Although the size of the villa allowed him to keep aloof from the exigencies of the nursery, and although his love of Olga is evident in the drawings he made of her suckling her child or playing the piano among the genteel furniture, he remarked to friends who visited him that he was thinking of ordering a Parisian street lamp and a pissotière to relieve the neat respectability of the lawn.

It was during this summer that he painted the two versions of the *Three Musicians*; the *Three Women at the Fountain*,[1] a large composition in his neo-classic style; landscapes of the nearby lanes; the gate of his villa; still-lifes; and in addition made pencil sketches of the villa both inside and out and of his wife and child. The variety of subject was only equalled by the variety of his style.

But stressing that Picasso is mainly interested in the reality of the life that goes on round him, the major theme that he developed at this time and which, with the sole exception of the portrait of Madame Rosenberg and her daughter, he had neglected since the Blue period, was the 'mother and child'. There are a number of variations of paintings of a mother playing with her naked infant on her knees, in which the neo-classical figures and the colossal females of the previous months reveal a new look of contentment, a sense of fulfilment.[2] The sentimentality which he had allowed to filter into his youthful pictures of maternity was eliminated by a severe sculptural simplification of form which has as its basis a sense of banality rather than of idealism. Refinement and grace is banished, with the result that a splendid image faces us, a vital picture of human life.

[1] See Zervos, *Picasso*, Vol. IV, p. 119.   [2] Plate X, 3.

More gigantic nudes with placid expressions appeared during the same year.[1] They are painted with the same brutal sense of realism which seems to be inspired by the naïve retouching and tinting seen in the enlargements of cheap photographers, combined with the simplifications of late classical sculpture. The twilight colours of the Blue period had given way to the broad prosaic light, the grisaille of an overcast midday. The pose taken up by the nude figure is often made all the more formal by the addition of a cornice to support the elbow.[2] Picasso has taken a perverse pleasure it seems in taking subjects of voluptuous delight and in denying himself any of the aids he had formerly used to evoke sympathy and emotion. They confront us in their stark banality, and yet these females seem to carry about them the timelessness of goddesses, indestructible and reassuring as an eternal symbol of the female form. In this instance the sublime owes its life to the commonplace.

Exhibitions

Picasso's friendship with Paul Rosenberg was increased by the dealer's usefulness as a protector of his interests and the organiser of exhibitions in his fashionable gallery. In October 1919 Picasso decorated the invitation card which announced an exhibition of drawings and watercolours with the first lithograph he had ever made, and added a second drawing of Olga as a cover to the catalogue.[3] During the following two years exhibitions were held in Rosenberg's gallery, and in 1921, as has already been mentioned, London saw for the first time an important collection of the work of Picasso: twenty-four oil paintings and forty-eight drawings, watercolours, and etchings dating from 1902 to 1919 were shown at the Leicester Galleries. The picture that dominated and greatly impressed Londoners was the *Woman in a Chemise*, and there were other fine examples of cubism. The catalogue had as its preface a reprint of an article by Clive Bell, in *The Athenaeum*, in which he compares the talents of the two painters who had emerged as the leaders of the modern school: Matisse and Picasso, and analyses "why the latter" and not Matisse, "is master of the modern movement". His argument is that "besides being extraordinarily inventive, Picasso is what they call 'an intellectual artist'." This needed some explanation since the word intellectual can imply something very foreign to the creative artist. "An intellectual artist is

[1] Plate X, 5.   [2] See Zervos, *Picasso*, Vol. IV, p. 122-3.
[3] Ibid., Vol. VI, p. 163, Nos. 1371, 1373.

one who feels first . . . and goes on to think", he says, and continues later: "Matisse is an artist; Picasso is an artist and something more—an involuntary teacher if you like." Clive Bell, like many others, was struck by the power that Picasso possesses to feel and to analyse his emotion. Though he tends to separate dangerously the emotional and the intellectual processes, Clive Bell is undoubtedly right when he draws attention to the the vast influence that Picasso in spite of himself already in the early twenties had on other artists. To this day no one can claim to be the pupil of Picasso, he has never had the time or the patience to teach systematically, but such is his capacity to set others thinking by his work, by his chance remarks in conversation, by his writings and by his way of living, that he has become one of the greatest teachers of our time.

Although the prices asked for these pictures seem now absurdly low they represented at the time a high level for a painter who was just reaching his fortieth year. Picasso was in fact becoming rich with the proceeds of what he sold and could afford all the comforts he and his family wanted. He was not much perturbed when owing to the law that gave the French Government the right to take possession of all property belonging to enemy aliens the two great collections of Uhde and Kahnweiler were put up for sale by auction. The Kahnweiler sale was held in four sections spread over the years 1921 to 1923. Apart from a mass of less valuable drawings, collages and objects, it offered to the public 381 cubist paintings by Picasso, Braque, Gris and Léger of which 132 were by Picasso. The three other painters were nervous about the effect of having such a large part of their former work put up for public auction. Braque even appeared at the first sale and protested loudly at the ineptitude of exposing the work of French painters, Léger and himself, to such unnecessary risk supposedly in the interests of the French State. He felt so strongly about it that seeing Léonce Rosenberg, one of the organisers of the sale, he walked up to him and slapped him in the face.

In the light of the subsequent appreciation in value of these works the prices they fetched seem trivial. Very few foreign buyers were attracted, and it was chiefly those collectors such as Roger Dutilleul and André Lefèvre, who had already bought paintings from the cubists before the war, joined by Alphonse Kann and the Belgian collector René Gaffé, who were able to add judiciously to their possessions. Kahnweiler, who had returned from Switzerland, bought back what he could of his former stock. The expected setback in the value of cubist and post-cubist painting however owing to this glut on the market was only temporary. It did not seriously affect Picasso's sales of his current work which were being ably handled by Paul Rosenberg.

The Dinard Still-lifes

After one of his lengthy summer absences from Paris, Picasso returned to find as he opened the cupboard where his winter suits used to hang that the moths had been hard at work. Nothing of his best suit remained except the framework of its seams and the buckram linings, through which could be seen, as in an X-ray, the contents of his pockets—keys, pipe, matchboxes and the other things that had resisted the attack of the insects. The sight delighted him and still made him chuckle when he told me the story years later. Transparency had been a problem since the·early days of cubism when the desire to see behind the visible surface of objects had led him to dissect their form. Here nature had given a demonstration of how it could be done by other means.

In 1922 Picasso went for the summer not to the Mediterranean but to Brittany. The nature of the coast with estuaries and rocky headlands jutting out into the ocean was reminiscent of the windswept beaches of Corunna where he had made his first independent discoveries in the cold, stormy light of the Atlantic. Just as he had sketched the over-dressed Galicians on the beaches and the Torre de Hercules thirty years before, so now he made contact with his new surroundings by making line drawings in pen and ink of Dinard, where he rented a villa for his wife and child, and of St. Malo as it appeared across the water.[1] But the paintings which characterise this visit to the ocean are still-lifes, cubist in tendency. They rely on a new use of heavy straight lines or stripes superimposed on clearly defined patches of bright colour. This method of introducing light into the picture appeared first two years before in a composition of a guitar set on a table. The stripes give an inter-locking transparency like a net or ribbed glass to the solid shapes that they imply.[2] Fish lying on torn sheets of Le Journal, bottles of wine, fruit dishes, glasses and an occasional guitar are the basis of a number of fascinating transparent pictures which suggest light filtered by slatted shutters or the ripples chasing each other across the estuary. The paintings vibrate with a luminous joie-de-vivre, but this well-being ended abruptly when Olga was taken seriously ill and Picasso was obliged to rush her to Paris, nursing her with ice-packs on the journey,

[1] See Zervos, Picasso, Vol. IV, pp. 152, 153.
[2] Plate XI, 1; and see Zervos, Picasso, Vol. IV, pp. 166-78.

while little Paulo was violently car-sick all the way. An operation followed and Olga's health was restored.

Varied Styles

In a statement made to Marius de Zayas, Picasso said: "The several manners I have used in my art must not be considered as evolution, or as steps toward an unknown idea of painting."[1] He did not change his style in the hope of finding an ultimate solution, changes happened because of his urgent desire to cope with the flood of ideas that were continually being born within him. "I have never made trials or experiments", he continued. "Whenever I had something to say I have said it in the manner in which I have felt it ought to be said. Different motives invariably require different methods of expression." So we find in the rapid changes from one style to another which from this time on became characteristic of Picasso's work, the signature of his personality.

For the next two years the neo-classical trend continued simultaneously with purely cubist still-lifes. In these there is a brilliance of colour, expressive of an enjoyment of life, which had never appeared formerly in such an unrestrained manner. Surface textures made with sand, which had begun some ten years earlier, were now exploited with a sensuous delight in the contrast between rough and smooth which gave a variety of tactile sensations to the whole canvas.

After the unhappy ending of the visit to Dinard the next five summers were spent on the Mediterranean. The visit to Juan-les-Pins in 1924[2] is particularly memorable for forty pages of sketchbook drawings.[3] These were done in addition to gay, almost frivolous landscapes in which the mock-gothic towers of the Villa la Vigie, in which he was staying, appear in the foreground. The drawings were afterwards used to embellish Balzac's story *Le Chef d' Œuvre Inconnu* which Vollard published in 1931, illustrated with thirteen full-page etchings. At first sight they appear to be abstract doodles made up of lines which form

[1] Published in *The Arts*, New York, May 1923; quoted by Barr, *Picasso: Fifty Years of His Art*, p. 270.

[2] Barr attributes these drawings to Juan-les-Pins, 1926, Zervos to 1924, Boeck 1924 and 1926. Evidence comes from the publication of some of the drawings in No. 2 of the *Révolution Surréaliste* of 15 January 1925 and the fact that Picasso spent the summer of 1924 at Juan-les-Pins, but did not return in 1925.

[3] Plate XI, 5; and see Zervos, *Picasso*, Vol. V, pp. 130, 132, 134, 136, 138, 142, 144-6.

dots like the knots in a net wherever they cross, making clever concave or convex patterns. But as I have insisted before, abstraction, that
is insistence on form for its own sake without reference to any associations, is completely foreign to Picasso. If we compare these arabesques,
which resemble diagrams of constellations of black stars, with the still-
lifes of the same period, we find that they are mostly variations on
the same themes. The original subject-matter of most of the drawings
reveals itself as the shapes of musical instruments, while others, evoking the resemblance between the guitar and the human form, are
more anthropomorphic. In some of the most complicated kind a large
black circle is made to suggest both the head of a female figure holding a guitar and a black sun spreading light over the sea. With such
simple means cubism had been coaxed into an evocative mood, prophetic of further developments. It had happened unexpectedly, in the
manner of the genius who could say: "In my opinion to search means
nothing in painting. To find, is the thing."[1]

The Great Still-lifes

Throughout these years of changing styles the still-life remained
a constant theme to which Picasso could return. The subject-matter
remained much the same, and in general they were variations on a
theme which gave scope each time for new subtleties. They served
as a touchstone with which he could sort out, as Raynal puts it, "his
ideas and technical finds".[2] But Picasso with his profound interest
does not easily exhaust a theme, on the contrary the deeper he goes
the more he finds. So in the years 1924-25 the still-life took new proportions in his hands. The brilliancy of colour and the masterly compositions of these paintings give them great distinction in the whole
panorama of his work.[3] He also found ways of extending the subject-
matter beyond the usual cubist repertoire. He included classical plaster
casts of heads, or the clenched fist holding a scroll which has an air
prophetic of the more tragic setting of *Guernica*. In the great composition *The Studio* of 1925 other less conventional material was
introduced.[4] The picture became a synthesis of classical motives: the
bearded head, the open book and the clenched fist, together with an
architectural landscape reminiscent of the scenery for *Pulcinella* which
had its origin in a toy theatre he had made to amuse his son.

[1] 'Picasso Speaks' (statement made to de Zayas), *The Arts*, New York, 1923;
quoted by Barr, *Picasso: Fifty Years of His Art*, p. 270.

[2] Maurice Raynal, *Picasso*, Skira.   [3] Plate XI, 4.   [4] Plate XI, 3.

Surrealism

Although Picasso had been living aloof from the bohemian world since his marriage, he was not unaware of the many divergent movements that were making Paris once more the centre of the arts. The war had had various influences; in some it brought about, as a reaction to the violence of movements such as cubism, futurism and expressionism, a longing for a return to a more orderly way of living and thinking, a reasoned return to tradition. "Back to Raphael, Poussin, Ingres and Seurat", seemed in this light a cry of hope, echoed in Apollinaire's wish to "renew poetic style but in a classical rhythm", a cry to which Picasso had responded in his neo-classical painting. The proof of his conversion seemed convincing when he helped to design the scenery for Cocteau's adaptation of *Antigone* when it was performed at the Théâtre de l'Atelier only five years after the scandal that had been caused by *Parade*.

But Picasso recognised other influences that were closer to his nature. He had never denied his discoveries and had continued to paint cubist pictures side by side with others in the neo-classical style. There was no question of antagonism between the two. When after the war the Dadaists assembled from the various countries in which they had begun their activities, Picasso was eager to see what would ensue, and while remaining aloof he frequently attended their rowdy manifestations.

Paris owed much of its esteem among the younger generation in France and abroad to its revolutionary traditions. In addition it had the prestige of having been adopted as their home by those such as Apollinaire and Picasso who already had a world-wide influence. As an example of Picasso's magnetic appeal, I mention that as far back as 1911, the first sight of his work in an exhibition in Cologne induced Max Ernst, then only twenty, to forsake the conventional means of earning a living for which he was being trained and to become a painter. Among many of his generation, hope for the future (for which Picasso was the symbol) did not lie in a return to the past. On the contrary, the violent protests of Dada coincided closely with what Ernst had learned in his youth from Picasso and later from the war. As soon as possible after the armistice he left Germany for good and settled in Paris under the roof of the poet Paul Eluard.

In company with André Breton, Philippe Soupault, Louis Aragon and Eluard, Max Ernst linked his activities as a painter with the group of young poets who had begun to publish their work in a review of

Dadaist tendency, *Littérature*. The group was joined by Tzara and Arp on their arrival from Zürich and by Picabia, Duchamp and Man Ray when they reached Paris from America. The Dadaists were soon in a position to express themselves. They edited reviews, held exhibitions and gave performances calculated to insult and enrage the public, who in revenge always crowded to see them, because Dada was all the talk of the day and because they were completely mystified about its aims. The scandal more than once caused an uproar which brought in the police. The Dadaists were uncompromising in their violence not only against the bourgeoisie but also against the futurists, and the members of the Section d'Or, a group supported by those who hoped to steer cubism on to rational lines.

Before long, however, factions in the heart of the movement itself began to give trouble. The nihilism of Dada could not continue, and it so happened that the last of its manifestations was attended by Picasso. This was a performance that Tzara, the most uncompromising among them, put on at the Théâtre St. Michel in 1922, called the *Soirée du Cœur à barbe*. At the beginning of the performance hostile demonstrators from the newly formed surrealist group, led by Breton and Eluard, leapt on to the stage, and in the riot that followed Picasso was heard shouting from his box, "Tzara, no police here". In the confusion the sound of the word "police" linked with the name of Tzara made Breton jump to the conclusion that the arrival of the gendarmes in the theatre which happened immediately afterwards, was the deliberate and unpardonable act of Tzara, engineered against him and his friends. Tzara in consequence claims that Picasso was the unwitting cause of his prolonged estrangement from the Surrealists, whose ideas in reality were not far from his own. But it is clear that Picasso did not intend to be drawn in on one side or the other. He returned to the rue la Boètie, to his wife and his work, intrigued by ideas but uninterested in quarrels.

Having shaken off the purely destructive influence of Dada, Breton and his friends began the work of forming a group which would interpret the thought of the modern movement. The slogan: "A new declaration of the rights of man must be made", appeared printed on the cover of their new review *La Révolution Surréaliste*. It contained declarations of policy, surrealist 'textes' by Eluard, Péret, Aragon, Reverdy and others, and among the illustrations was a reproduction of one of Picasso's 1914 constructions, photographed by Man Ray. In the following number two pages of the previous summer's drawings from Picasso's sketchbook of Juan-les-Pins were given, and in the

fourth published on 15 July 1925 the *Demoiselles d'Avignon* was reproduced for the first time, eighteen years after it was painted. It was in
fact due to Breton that the painting was unearthed where it lay rolled
up in Picasso's studio, and set up in a place of honour in the Paris
house of Jacques Doucet who bought it for his collection.

The brilliant and turbulent poets and painters who formed the
surrealist group had in common a desire to probe the origins of the
creative process in art; an investigation which had begun on the one
hand with poets such as Rimbaud and Mallarmé and on the other
with Freud's examination of the subconscious. When the term 'surrealist' invented by Apollinaire was adopted as the name of the new
movement, Breton wrote in explanation: "This word . . . is employed by us with a precise meaning. We have agreed to refer by
it to a certain psychic automatism, which more or less corresponds
to the dream-state."[1] An appreciation of the importance of the subconscious was essential to the surrealists. In the work of Picasso they
stressed its influence at the expense of aesthetic considerations. "Picasso",
they claimed, "is surrealist in cubism", but they had a horror of tendencies that led to abstraction even greater than his.

Picasso was in general more attracted by the activities of the poets
of the surrealist group than by those of the painters. He still asserts
that of all that was going on during the twenties their activities were
the most interesting. Though he never allowed himself to be drawn
into their deliberations he let them reproduce his work in the *Révolution
Surréaliste*; and for the first time his antipathy to exhibiting in a group
exhibition was overcome when paintings of his were hung, with his
permission, in the first Surrealist Exhibition at the Galerie Pierre in
1925. This however was a very different matter from the professional
scramble, characteristic of all 'salon' exhibitions. The Surrealist movement owed its strength to an alliance between poets and painters and
an attitude towards human conduct which transcended purely artistic
considerations. Picasso had found again, in association with the poets,
the climate he had known before the war.

In the fourth number of the *Révolution Surréaliste*, Breton published
a long illustrated article on Picasso in which he analysed his reasons
for his great admiration. Reality, he claimed (speaking of what is
understood vulgarly as real), is not just what is seen, and the painter
should in consequence refer to a model which is purely interior. He
realised that this had been the achievement of Picasso in cubism, and

[1] *Littérature*, No. 6, Second Series, November 1922. Trans. D. Gascoyne,
Surrealism, Cobden-Sanderson, 1935.

praising his clairvoyance and courage he wrote: "That the position held by us now could have been delayed or lost depended only on a failure in the determination of this man."[1]

The surrealists were severe in their condemnation of fashionable society and included ballet in their censure. When Max Ernst and Miró accepted the proposal made to them by Diaghilev at the instigation of Picasso that they should design the décor and scenery for the ballet *Romeo and Juliet*, Breton and Aragon protested and attempted to exclude them from the group for their collaboration with "the international aristocracy". This was surprising since only a year before, Breton had praised Picasso's designs for *Mercure*. The row, which was smoothed out by Eluard, was typical of the attempts on the part of Breton to enforce a purist discipline on other members of the group. In his aloofness Picasso held a position of unassailable authority which he used generously as in this case for the benefit of younger artists who had impressed him by their talent.

Beauty must be Convulsive

The association with the surrealists had the effect of bringing out in a sudden burst a new and disquieting manifestation of the underlying restlessness of Picasso's mind, which had been for a while partially overlaid by domestic happiness. Breton's dictum that "beauty must be convulsive or cease to be" coincided with Picasso's desire to return to a more dynamic form of painting. In the spring of 1925 he joined Diaghilev and Massine for a while at Monte Carlo, and it is no coincidence that the great picture he painted early that year was of three figures dancing together; but the mood of *Three Dancers*[2] is very unlike that of the graceful costumes and poses with the touch of picaresque good humour that had its origins in the commedia del'arte. It is a wild and frenzied performance in which two abandoned females joining hands with their companion perform lascivious contortions. Livid pinks, reds and blues suggest the coloured projectors of a night club, though the background is in reality a window looking out over the sea. It is above all in the decomposition of the most frenzied of the women that a new spirit makes itself felt. It is as though Picasso presents this figure, chaotic in structure and ecstatic in gesture, as a mirror of the absurd and monstrous which is only too common in life. The necessity to express his rage could no longer be contained.

[1] André Breton, 'Le Surréalisme et la Peinture': *La Révolution Surréaliste*, No. 4, 15 July 1925.

[2] Plate XI, 2.

The encouragement around him to give freer vent to the subconscious inaugurated a new epoch in which the monster was to become a major character on his stage.

Social Contacts

Picasso's mood was changing. The routine of the smart set in which he had become involved began to pall. His appearance with Olga at first nights, made conspicuous not only by the unmistakable fire in his black eyes but by the bullfighter's cummerbund worn beneath his well-cut dinner jacket, had become familiar to the snob society who frequented the sumptuous parties and performances of the Paris season. For a ball given by Comte Etienne de Beaumont, Picasso with his delight in disguises had found a magnificent suit of a matador, and on more than 'one occasion he was asked to design decorations for the festivities. Like the majority of Spaniards he has an insatiable appetite for good entertainment and good company. The night is never long enough to tire him. He has no need of the stimulus of alcohol. When he is in a festive mood his reserve at moments breaks down. The unexpected comments interjected into conversations, the apt stories told in an eager voice finishing with an enquiring "n'est-ce pas?" and a high-pitched resounding chuckle, make his company both delightful and disturbing.

During his long visits to the Mediterranean the sources of his inspiration were varied and often unconventional. André Level speaks of seeing him in the market at Cannes suddenly seduced by a cardboard plate on which some fruit he had bought was handed to him. After enjoying the feel of its texture, he quickly made a sketch on it of fruit, squeezing the juice out of flower petals to colour it. Having signed it he exchanged the decorated plate for a pile of empties with which he returned home, delighted at his find. Alive to his surroundings, he absorbs the colours of the landscape, the light reflected from the sea and the athletic movement of the bathers who play on the beaches. He can be equally enthralled by such chance discoveries as a strangely-shaped piece of driftwood, a bit of rusty iron or bamboo roots which have been modelled into grotesque shapes by the waves.

Visitors to France, including Hemingway, were among the friends with whom he spent the hours when he was not working, in conversation by the sea or at table. There are photos of beach parties where instead of sunbathing the guests diverted themselves by dressing in strange costumes. One of these shows the Comte and Comtesse de Beaumont in gay disguises, with Olga dressed as a ballerina. Among the party is Picasso's mother, who was paying her son a visit, sitting on the edge of a canoe with a strange hat fringed with beads. The only one in the group who is not disguised is Picasso himself who sits in the centre in a conventional felt hat and white shirt buttoned up to the neck.

Renewed Violence

Enjoyment of such pleasures was only a part of Picasso's life. In the world of his thought he was still isolated and lonely. At the same time, though he never seems to despise those around him for not being able to follow his meaning, a desire to mystify the public in general is not foreign to him. The outrageous joke of making a collage out of his own unlaundered shirt tails was both an intentional insult and at the same time a miraculous feat in transforming so mean a thing into an object that gave pleasure to the eyes. Another example of his 'malicious art' is the large collage of the same year, 1926, called *Guitar*,[1] in which the main element is a coarse dishcloth perforated by nails whose points stick out viciously from the picture. Picasso told me that he had thought of embedding razor blades in the edges of the picture so that whoever went to lift it would cut their hands. There are no decorative curves to soften the cruel impact of the picture and there is no charm of colour. It is an aggressive and powerful expression of anger in a language which makes it painfully plain. Though it was shown in the great exhibition in Paris of 1955, Picasso has kept this picture to this day in his studio like a curse which he allowed to explode for his own satisfaction. Other paintings of the years that follow show the growing violence of his mood in more elaborate form.

Monstrous Distortion

The liberties that Picasso now chose to take with the human form seem unbounded. Even the most daring reassortment of features and revision of proportions did not however prevent the recognition of the human head and human form. The cubist method of describing an object simultaneously from more than one viewpoint had induced Picasso as early as 1913 to inscribe a profile on a head seen full-face.[2] But in 1926 the same idea was carried further in paintings of violently distorted heads, in which the recognisable features—eyes, mouth, teeth, tongue, ears, nose and nostrils—are distributed about the face in every position, with the bold line of a profile making a central division of the head. In some cases both eyes appear on the same side of the

[1] Plate XI, 6.   [2] Plate XI, 7.

face, in others the mouth takes the place of an eye—every imaginable permutation is tried but miraculously the human head survives as a unit powerfully expressive of emotion. In this process of reassortment the spherical mass of the head itself begins to disintegrate and token hairs are made to sprout from anywhere they may be required by the artist. Nothing remained unviolated, but the power of this sign language lies in the discovery that the association these vestiges of resemblance to our own features hold for us is so strong, and it gives a new and strange fascination to find that we can reconstruct our own image from such complete and improbable distortions.

The human body was subjected to the same wanton rearrangement of its form. In Cannes during the summer of 1927, Picasso suddenly broke away from the flat patterning derived from synthetic cubism of the pictures such as the *Three Dancers* and began to draw fantastic reconstructions of the human form, with heavy modelling. The bathers he saw every day on the beach passed through a metamorphosis into elephantine sculptural shapes, skipping lightly across the beach or attentively turning the key of a bathing hut.[1] The anatomy of these females is extremely droll. Their swollen forms have no immediate resemblance to anything in nature, but they are still convincingly organic, and bear out Picasso's remark that: "Nature and art are two different things. Through art we express our conception of what nature is not."[2] But if they are not recognisable as conventional human forms, the habits on the beach of these massive creatures are touchingly human; especially those who finger the tiny key set in the lock of a hut they are trying to open. A sexual metaphor can have many interpretations: the locked hut is in the first place a symbol of privacy which in this case seems in danger of being invaded by powerful female or hermaphrodite monsters of Picasso's own creation.

This series of charcoal drawings, together with pen sketches and a maquette for a monument in similar terms made at Dinard the following summer, were among the suggestions that Picasso showed to the committee for the Apollinaire memorial without gaining their approval.

Picasso returned to Dinard for two successive summers. It was a retreat from the places where he could be too easily interrupted by his increasingly numerous friends. The large, ugly art nouveau villa with a garden that he rented was close to the quay where the ferry from St. Malo landed its passengers. From his window he could hail the

[1] Plate XII, 1. See also Zervos, *Picasso*, Vol. VII, pp. 38-47.
[2] 'Picasso Speaks', quoted, Barr, *Picasso: Fifty Years of His Art*, p. 270.

arrival of the young poet Georges Hugnet who lived across the water, and with whom, after announcing to his wife that he was going out, he would spend long hours wandering on the crowded beaches. He was glad to escape from the family, the English governess who had been engaged to give Paulo a good orthodox education and the villa whose only attraction was the space that it afforded for the creative disorder that surrounded his work. In addition to pen and ink drawings which were more elegant versions of the anthropomorphic forms of the previous summer, the pictures he painted were mostly scenes of bathers tossing a ball.[1] Again the liberties taken with the human frame were extraordinary. Their limbs and bodies, flattened out like broken matchboxes and clothed sometimes in striped bathing costumes, are in violent, concerted movement in front of a brilliantly coloured background of sea and rocks.

During the first of these visits to Dinard, colour and agitated movement were the main preoccupation, but in Paris Picasso worked with stricter discipline on large compositions with a rigid construction of flat coloured surfaces with straight black lines giving an architectural feeling of space. Pictures such as the *Studio*[2] and the *Painter and his Model*[3] make a sober contrast with the dynamic exuberance of the summer months. Though capable of a restraint which can be seen in other simple sculptural images of serene metamorphoses of the human form, he also had visions of more diabolical changes for the female body. A woman seated in a chair could resemble the convulsed tentacles of an octopus,[4] and another seen against the sea could look like a bloodless monument made of bones and driftwood, her hollow frame composed of pieces balancing precariously on each other.[5] In many of these inventions there is a striking contrast between the vicious bonelike structure of the head, with a vertical jaw, its teeth opposing each other like a trap for vermin, and the ethereal pale blue sky against which it is seen. These excursions into realms formerly forbidden by a canonical respect for beauty were more profoundly disturbing than the attacks made by cubism on academic conceptions of painting. They upset man's vision of himself which had sprung from classical tradition. In future we were to discover, thanks to Picasso's violent awakening, that the image of man that did not reside only in an ideal conception but that in its nature it should be organic and alive.

During this period the image of one person for whom his tenderness remained unaffected was not submitted to such violent disruption.

---

[1] Plate XII, 2.   [2] See Zervos, *Picasso*, Vol. VII, p. 64, No. 142.
[3] Plate XII, 8.   [4] Plate XIII, 1.   [5] Plate XIII, 3.

From the day his son was born Picasso often enjoyed the pleasure of drawing portraits of him, and during these years, among pictures of monsters, we find several delightful portraits of Paulo in fancy dress. In one he is Pierrot, in another Harlequin holding a wand and a bunch of flowers, and in a third he wears the gold-braided suit of a toreador.[1]

At the same time there appears in another picture violent in colour a profile easily recognisable as a self-portrait, set in juxtaposition to a sharp red-tongued monster. A bright green stripe runs down the front of its long neck as though it lived by drinking poison.[2] For more than ten years Picasso had ceased to make the portraits and drawings of himself that were so frequent in his early life. In several paintings of 1929 however we find the same profile. Here it is disconcerting to find it in such close association with this powerful and aggressive head, an obvious symbol of the emotional stress which was leading him towards a crisis. Whatever the cause of the stress may have been it resulted in great activity and powerful images.

A Crucifixion

Emotional strain is again evident in some drawings made the same year which resulted in a small painting of the Crucifixion.[3] Some of the studies, particularly those of Mary Magdalene, emit an agonising sense of despair which is more intense than the resulting picture.[4] Picasso submits this figure to the convulsive torments of her grief with distortions that might seem grotesque were they not drawn with such calm deliberation. Nude and arched backwards so far that the head and buttocks seem to touch, she becomes a terrifying emblem of anguish. Other sheets of drawings are crowded with the symbols of the crucifixion translated into Picasso's idiom. Grotesque profiles of the crowd of onlookers are marshalled by a figure wearing a helmet; a horse grazes while a long muscular arm places a ladder against the cross. Anguished female forms in turmoil, their bosoms dovetailed together, lie writhing at the feet of Christ.

Following Picasso's habit of noting the date of each drawing, sometimes even the hour, they are dated from 25 May to 17 June 1929, but it was not until 7 February 1930 that he produced the small painting that still belongs to him and is unique in his work, not only in its subject-matter but also in the fierce contrasts of its yellows, reds and blues and the disconcerting changes in scale throughout the picture.

---

[1] Plate XI, 9.   [2] Plate XII, 3.   [3] Plate XII, 7.
[4] See Zervos, *Picasso*, Vol. VII, pp. 114-16 and 130.

It is not an easy picture to interpret, though the symbols such as the three crosses, the soldiers casting dice, the centurion with his lance, in this case on horseback like a picador, the ladder, the sponge and the upraised arms of the Magdalene can all be distinguished.

This calvary appears to have no other relation to religion than its iconography, and by all conventional standards it must be considered blasphemous. But blasphemy by its very nature is an acknowledgment of the power of religion, especially when it attains great violence. Religious subjects, if we exclude the *Choir Boy* and the *Burial of Casagemas*, had never in the past developed beyond sketchbook notes. In this case the preliminary drawings and the use of certain elements taken from recent metamorphic bone figures indicate that this painting was a sketch for a more important work. That it was abandoned was perhaps due to a shift in Picasso's thought, when he became interested two years later in the Isenheim altarpiece of Matthias Grünewald. Working from reproductions of this deeply-moving masterpiece, he made a remarkable series of studies which translate Grünewald's crucifixion into a composition constructed with Picasso's expressive bonelike forms. The drawings make an appeal which is aesthetic rather than religious. Both they, and even more the *Crucifixion*, are of great importance as being the forerunners of *Guernica*,[1] painted seven years later, because they contain suggestions of its composition and some of the same ideas, especially the weeping women.

The transcendental qualities of the *Crucifixion* are obvious. The conventional symbols seem to have been submitted to the ferment of the subconscious. They reappear with new and spontaneous significance related to Picasso himself. The figure of Christ has superimposed on its breast a draped head with two small eyes and an angry open jaw showing its sharp gnawing teeth. The picture is too violent to evoke pity for any of the victims, their frenzied gestures deny all tenderness, but the anguish of life in which misunderstanding can lead to hate and murderous violence is present like flames in a furnace.

Sculpture

Just as in 1906 when Picasso's desire for a fuller representation of form had resulted in modelled heads and figures carved in wood, so after a lapse of over twenty years he began again in 1928 to realise in three dimensions the sculptural forms of his drawings. Except for the *Glass of Absinthe*, none of the cubist constructions had been sculptures in the round. They were intended to be viewed like a picture from in

[1] Plate XVII, 1.

front only. In painting during the twenties Picasso had alternated
between representing form by modelling or by line. To use modelling
when it came to solid three-dimensional sculpture would appear to be
the normal solution, and in fact that was the method he first adopted
when early in 1928 he began again to make what was virtually a copy
of his charcoal drawings in solid form.[1] But the inventive genius of
Picasso was not long to see that three-dimensional figures could also
be drawn in other ways. In the autumn he made a construction in iron
wire which was related to the big architectural still-lifes painted the
same year, and also to line drawings.[2] It was like a simplified diagram
of the strange sketchbook drawings reproduced later in the *Chef
d'Œuvre Inconnu*. The idea of diagrams in space may be traced back to
the Russian constructivists ten years earlier, but Picasso managed to
evoke in his new linear sculpture a lyrical sense of the human form
which was his original invention and one which has been exploited
widely since the war by young sculptors.

Other sculptures followed, always linked with his painting and
sometimes themselves painted in black and white. There was no
separation between the two activities which are usually classified as
different arts. With Picasso they were both his children and like the
hen and the egg, who could tell which came first? There are sculptures
which seem to originate from elements in a painting, like the *Head*
of October 1928[3] which stands on a tripod and resembles closely the
figure of the artist in the painting of the same year called *The Painter
and his Model*. On the other hand, it is a common practice with Picasso
to construct a sculpture out of material he picks up around him, and
soon after to paint a picture in which the shapes of his sculpture
appear. Again, after that he often paints the sculpture with new ideas
that have been discovered while making his picture. This continual
interchange of ideas from one medium to another gives the work of
Picasso a homogenity that echoes from one method and one style
to another.

[1] Plate XII, 4.   [2] Plate XII, 6.
[3] See Barr, *Picasso: Fifty Years of His Art*, p. 157.

CHAPTER IX

BOISGELOUP: SCULPTURE AND THE
MINOTAUR
(1930–1936)

Le Chef d'Œuvre Inconnu and Ovid's Metamorphoses

"THERE ENDS OUR art on earth," solemnly exclaimed the friend
of the old mad painter in Balzac's story *Le Chef d'Œuvre Inconnu*.
He and the young Poussin were looking for the first time at the picture on which the aged artist had been working for over ten years.
In his attempt to arrive at the perfect image of his imaginary model
he had hidden all resemblance to reality beneath endless improvements. To him the confused daubs of colour and the multitude of
bizarre lines which formed a thick wall of paint was a masterpiece,
more alive and more beautiful than the woman it was supposed to
represent. Balzac's story raises the problem of comparative realities
which had occupied Picasso since the early days of cubism. When
confronted with the living model, the work of art is not in competition. It is a fiction, "a lie that makes us realise truth, at least the
truth that is given us to understand", to quote Picasso's own statement. The fiction becomes valuable when its power is sufficient to
compel us to see in it a new vision of reality.

It was this story that Vollard chose for Picasso's illustrations when
in 1931 he published a volume which puzzled book collectors by its
diversity of styles.[1] Vollard used as an introduction sixteen pages from
the enigmatic Juan-les-Pins sketchbook, which I have already described, executed as wood engravings by Aubert. Besides these cryptic
inventions he inserted in the text over sixty engraved drawings and
thirteen etchings which have the clarity and the sensitivity of line
drawings by Ingres. The opposition of two such different styles was
well chosen. Apart from the visual excitement it produces, it reaffirms
the necessity for multiple reactions between art and reality. Here, just
as in the cubist *Still-life with Chair-caning*, the drawings that imitate
nothing, those of Juan-les-Pins, exist with an autonomous reality of
their own and in this way outshine the seductive charm of those that

[1] Plates XI, 8, and XI, 5.

have a clear resemblance to a subject. A second book, Ovid's *Metamorphoses*,[1] was published in Lausanne by Albert Skira the same year, illustrated with thirty etchings. In this book there was no inconsistency of style. The astonishing perfection of line in the drawings that describe the struggles of the naked heroes and heroines continues in the same classical manner throughout.

The *Chef d'Œuvre Inconnu* started Picasso on a series of etchings known as the 'Vollard suite' which is one of the greatest triumphs of his graphic art. A few years earlier Vollard had introduced Picasso to an engraver, Louis Fort, who was an expert in the preparation of copper plates and who owned a stock of "wonderful old Japanese paper whose mellow pulp inevitably excited his [Picasso's] taste".[2] The incentive of working with an expert craftsman has often led Picasso into new paths, and was the means on this occasion of bringing him back to engraving in a way which proved more fertile than ever before.

Boisgeloup: New Activities

Outside Paris in the direction of Rouen, two miles from the little town of Gisors, Picasso found in 1931 a small seventeenth-century château lying at the edge of a village named Boisgeloup. At the gateway, leading into a spacious courtyard, stands an elegant little Gothic chapel. The grey stone château with its well-proportioned slate roof and windows is backed by the luxuriant growth of great trees. The long row of stables which faces the main building across the courtyard affords ample space for studios of every description. Louis Fort's press for etchings was brought there and installed and the more spacious coach-houses were transformed into sculpture studios, for this acquisition coincided conveniently with a new urge to make large sculptures for which there had been no space in the apartment studio in Paris.

Just as the meeting with Fort had facilitated the return to engraving, so a renewed contact with Picasso's old friend, the sculptor Gonzalez, opened the way to a period of activity in plastic creation which has continued with varying intensity to this day. One of the virtues of Gonzalez was that he was an excellent craftsman in metal, and as well as being an accomplished artist himself, he was quick to appreciate the ways in which he could put his talent at Picasso's disposal. He realised that sculpture was the nerve-centre of Picasso's work. His friend had told him that in early cubist paintings "it would have

[1] Ovid, *Les Métamorphoses*, Lausanne, Skira, 1931.
[2] André Level, *Picasso*, Crès, Paris, 1928.

sufficed to cut them up—the colours after all being no more than
indications of differences in perspective, of planes inclined one way
or the other—and then assemble them according to the indications
given by the colour, in order to be confronted with a 'sculpture' ".
Picasso was referring here to the paintings of 1908 and the bronze
Woman's Head[1] of the following year which had been modelled by
him in Gonzalez' studio. He had succeeded there in translating the
portraits of Fernande painted at Horta into a three-dimensional head.
Gonzalez said of Picasso in 1931 that "he must be conscious of a true
sculptor's temperament since . . . I have often heard him repeat 'I find
myself once more as happy as I was in 1908' ".[2] The result of this
recaptured delight was the appearance of a number of pieces of
sculpture, some of them six feet or more high, made of pieces of iron
welded together. Sometimes they were painted and most of them
were later cast in bronze.[3]

Ideas for sculpture had appeared at frequent intervals, and from
time to time in later years Picasso had made cubist constructions
similar to those of 1913. In the summer spent at Juan-les-Pins in 1930
he took advantage of a heterogeneous collection of objects picked up
on the beach to make designs in low relief which were glued to the
back of a canvas and unified by means of sand stuck to the surface.
The fortuitous encounters of objects normally unrelated to each other,
of which the surrealists were at that time exploring the advantages,
suited Picasso's taste for metamorphoses. "The chance meeting on a
dissecting-table of a sewing-machine and an umbrella", praised for
its strange poetic consequences by Lautréamont, was at the source of
these bas-reliefs which contained anything from an old glove and a
child's toy to fragments of roots or palm branches. In addition to the
effect of the bizarre encounter there were masterly qualities of composition and touches of humour.[4]

These objects of intimate charm were at one end of the scale. Other
projects for sculpture in the round, such as the monument to Apollinaire, were emerging simultaneously, though, like the idea he had at
one time of monumental constructions to be placed along La Croisette,
the sea-front at Cannes, many of them never materialised. "I have

[1] Plate VI, 4.
[2] J. Gonzalez, 'Picasso sculpteur', *Cahiers d'Art*, 11, Nos. 6-7, p. 189-91,
Paris, 1936.
[3] Plate XIII, 2.
[4] Plate XIII, 9. See also Kahnweiler-Brassaï, *The Sculptures of Picasso*, Nos.
79-83.

to paint them," he told Kahnweiler, "because nobody's ready to commission one from me." There is for instance a painting of a monument,[1] the scale of which can be judged from the figures standing beside it. The severe box-like outlines suggest a skyscraper whose walls have been decorated by a geometric construction like a gigantic woman's head from which spring three long strands of hair. In the centre is a long mouth placed vertically and showing two rows of sharp teeth. It is a powerful image which inspires fear rather than love, analogous to the 'malanggans' from New Ireland, possibly like those strange ceremonial carvings that are reputed to cause instant death to any woman who sees them.

At Boisgeloup with Gonzalez beside him and the necessary facilities, sculpture in iron began to show new possibilities. The cubist collage had already revealed the unexpected things that could happen by using actual objects as the raw materials and combining them in a new entity. Pieces of scrap iron, springs, saucepan-lids, sieves, bolts and screws, picked out with discernment from the rubbish heap, could mysteriously take their place in these constructions, wittily and convincingly coming to life with a new personality. The vestiges of their origins remained visible as witnesses of the transformation that the magician had brought about, a challenge to the identity of anything and everything.

In a different mood Picasso took a penknife and whittled out of long slender pieces of wood human figures which later he had cast in bronze.[2] With his ability to give volume and monumental scale to an object of trivial size, he gave these figures dignity and vitality. The most impressive sculptures of the Boisgeloup period, however, are the great heads with protruding noses and eyes that were modelled in clay and plaster. They date from a year or two after his arrival.[3]

At Boisgeloup Picasso found a retreat where he could work with concentration amounting to frenzy, a condition which is essential to him if he is to find prolonged happiness. Gonzalez was astonished at the excitement and pleasure that he took in his work. The rare visits from friends were a delight to him. These included Braque, whose friendship had been rekindled through the overwhelming passion they both had for painting and an underlying warmth of affection; also Kahnweiler and his brother-in-law the poet Michel Leiris, with their wives. These companions provided moments when it was possible to enjoy the shade of the great trees and examine at length Picasso's various creations. There are a number of delightful landscapes painted from

[1] Plate XII, 5.   [2] Plate XIV, 2.   [3] Plate XIV, 4.

the windows, in which the little church and the adjoining houses appear in sun or rain.[1] The grey walls and fine masonry of the house pleased Picasso's sense of the monumental, which was also evident in things with which he surrounded himself, such as the St. Bernard dog of which he was very fond, the skull of a hippopotamus that was placed in the hall, and a very fine example of Baga sculpture of majestic proportions from French Guinea. This piece, with an exaggerated arched nose and a head almost detached from the neck, found its echo in the monumental plaster heads in the stables across the courtyard.

Still-lifes

There are still-lifes painted in 1931 which depend on colour and transparency for their effect rather than an insistence on form. Shapes are indicated with an arabesque of heavy lines giving rather the effect of a stained glass window.[2] The decorative leaves of the philodendron are a characteristic of many paintings of this period, and also appear on some of the iron sculptures. Picasso had been impressed by the overwhelming vitality of this plant. He once left one that had been given him in Paris in the only place where it would be sure to have plenty of water while he was away in the south. On his return he found that it had completely filled the little room with luxuriant growth and also completely blocked the drain with its roots.

Anatomy Reshaped

The liberties that Picasso had taken with the human form might be held to be a sacrilege. The distortions had surpassed what could be considered as a legitimate means of expression. They had gone beyond the not uncommon device of exaggerating the gestures by which emotion becomes manifest, and had become a declaration of rage against humanity itself, a vengeance in which the victim was hanged, drawn and quartered. But the contrasts in Picasso's work and in his nature are such that while perpetrating this violence he found it neces-sary to present us with a new anatomy of his own invention, con-structed with ingenuity, grace and humour.[3] In sheets of drawings set out like a catalogue he offers a great variety of solutions. He replaces limbs, breasts, bellies, heads, eyes, noses, ears and mouths with forms of varied qualities: some are rigid and elegant, some soft and bloated, some tenuous and fragile, some massive and tough: pieced together

[1] See Zervos, *Picasso*, Vol. VII, pp. 141-2.
[2] Plate XIII, 7, and Zervos, *Picasso*, Vol. VII, p. 133, No. 326.
[3] Plate XIII, 8. See also *Minotaure*, No. 1, Albert Skira, Paris, 1933.

these elements make new creatures that have each an individuality and a droll resemblance to the infinity of shapes that healthy or deformed humanity, stripped naked, can present.

With precision and without repetition Picasso devised a great number of plausible solutions in paintings as well as in the sheets of drawings. In two-dimensional art, figures could be balanced according to any whim, but in sculpture the problem was different, the laws of gravity imposed their restrictions. In spite of this, Picasso found the means of converting the ideas of his invented anatomies into plaster and succeeded in constructing heads in which the various elements hold together as though by magnetism.

Moonlike Heads: a New Model

In the spring of 1932, with another of his periodic bursts of energy, Picasso produced a series of large canvases, some of which were exhibited that summer in the great retrospective exhibition at the Galerie Georges Petit. He had discovered a new highly sensuous version of the female nude.[1] Most of these figures painted with flowing curves lie sleeping, their arms folded round their heads. In several paintings the boisterous philodendron sprouts up in the background.[2] The sleeper's breasts are round and fruitlike and her hands finish like the blades of summer grass. The profile of the face, usually with closed eyes, is drawn with one bold curve uniting forehead and nose above thick sensuous lips. Its outline, easily recognisable, recurs in all the nudes and gives a clue to their origin.

Picasso's new model whose voluptuous influence is so strongly marked in these canvases, mostly of large dimensions, was Marie-Thérèse Walter, a young girl whom he had met by chance some while before and who attracted him by her firm, healthy figure, her blond nordic looks and her strange aloofness. She always behaved according to her own inclination, changing her mind or her manner of living in an inconsequential way as though controlled by the influence of the moon or by some even less calculable force. She had a robust coarseness and an unconventionality about her which formed a complete contrast to Olga and the world into which she had drawn him, a world which curtailed his freedom and attempted to inflict on him a life which he found boring and fundamentally despised. The massive plaster heads made at Boisgeloup were also inspired by Marie-Thérèse.[3] Set high on a long tapering neck they seem to be detached from the earth and float like the moon racing through clouds. The eyes are

[1] Plate XIII, 4.   [2] Plate XIII, 6.   [3] Plate XIV, 1 and 4.

sometimes drawn on the surface with a deep incision or in other cases modelled like a ball and added to the cheek like a satellite.

Talking to me one day, Picasso said he was sorry that in working on these heads he once spoilt his original intention. Working at night in the studio at Boisgeloup he had first built up a very complicated construction of wire which looked quite incomprehensible except when a light projected its shadow on the wall. At that moment the shadow became a lifelike profile of Marie-Thérèse. He was delighted at this projection from an otherwise indecipherable mass. But he said, "I went on, added plaster and gave it its present form." The secret image was lost but a more durable and splendid version, visible to all, had been evolved. And he added: "When you work you don't know what is going to come out of it. It is not indecision, the fact is it changes while you are at work."

Widespread Recognition

Barr lists fifty important exhibitions of the work of Picasso held in various countries between 1930 and the outbreak of war in 1939. The vast number of paintings he had produced were becoming scattered all over the world. Besides those in the great collections of Shchukine and Morosov in Russia, many had found their way into collections in Germany until that country under Hitler's régime became like Russia, hostile to modern art. At the same time Picasso's reputation grew steadily in America, Switzerland and England as well as in France. An exhibition entitled 'Abstractions of Picasso' held in New York in January 1931 was followed by a retrospective collection of thirty-seven paintings at the Reid and Lefevre Gallery in London, which was hailed as one of the main events of the summer season. Pictures from the Blue period, such as *La Vie*, hung on the walls, with recent still-lifes and invented anatomies. In New York two other exhibitions were held the same year. But the most important exhibition of this period was the great retrospective held at the Galerie Georges Petit in Paris in June–July 1932. Among the 225 paintings, 7 sculptures and 6 illustrated books that were shown were many important early works, as well as the *Crucifixion* and the most recent paintings of the sleeping nudes. There were many remarkable pictures, including the *Burial of Casagemas*, of which the public knew nothing. The choice of the exhibits was made with the help of Picasso himself.

To coincide with this manifestation, Christian Zervos published a number of his review *Les Cahiers d'Art* almost entirely dedicated to Picasso, containing many reproductions and articles in French, English,

German and Italian by a long list of distinguished poets, painters, musicians, and critics.

'The Sculptor's Studio'

Picasso's brilliant career of discovery in the arts was not accompanied by the same success in his family life. He found in himself strong desires for a tender relationship with a woman who would remain at his side as the inspiration of erotic pleasure and the traditional pillar of his household. In his youth Fernande's bohemian nonchalance had failed to bring this about, and Eva, patient and perhaps too well-ordered, had died. With Olga there was no lack of a possessive urge to found a family but it soon became obvious that the Spanish desire to observe custom was not strong enough in Picasso to conquer his mercurial nature. The many exquisite portraits of Olga and Paulo, alone or at play together, speak eloquently of Picasso's devotion in early years. The conflict between them was due to Picasso's instinctive horror of being trapped and forced to act in ways that interfered with the flow of his creative work. His success in wooing her, resulting in the birth of their son, was the only creative side to their marriage. Once that was accomplished the incongruity of their ambitions led slowly to the situation in which she became a menace to the liberty of spirit that he could not live without.

Olga was beautiful, passionate and insistent. She was tenacious but she did not covet the wealth that was now theirs, nor was she annoyed that the possibilities of enjoying it in conventional ways left Picasso indifferent. His tastes remained simple. Though he had enjoyed complying with Olga's choice in buying the most expensive clothes, he himself usually wore the same threadbare suit. The large range of silk ties bought in Bond Street remained at the bottom of a trunk. He was more in the habit of spending money on unusual objects that excited his fancy or of giving unobtrusively and generously to his less fortunate friends. But to Olga, it was necessary to be respected and well thought of in high society, and to her the recognised methods by which this should be attained were inflexible. Years later when Picasso was asked why he could not share the same life, he replied with simplicity, "she asked too much of me".

The growing estrangement between Picasso and his wife lay upon him heavily. There is more than one indication in his activities during the years from 1932 to 1936 that he was seeking ways that would liberate him. It has been said in a way that is misleading that for a while he even gave up painting. Indeed it is true that the canvases dated 1933 are less numerous than usual. This may be taken as an indication of the emotional agony through which he was passing, but Picasso's work is his life, and as usual in moments of crisis his resourcefulness allowed him to discover new methods of expression.

In the summer of 1933, after a short visit to Cannes, he returned for a few weeks to Barcelona, and the following year he made a longer journey to San Sebastian and Madrid, whence he again visited Toledo and the Escurial. He came back to Paris from the second journey stimulated once more by the atmosphere of his native country, and as had happened before after his visit in 1918, the bullfight became again the theme of a series of paintings more full of movement, colour and violent significance than ever before.

Although there were moments when he could not find in him his habitual urge to paint, Picasso never ceased to draw. Over a period beginning in 1927, Vollard had commissioned him to make a series of etchings which numbered finally in 1937 a hundred plates.[1] They began with the illustrations of the *Chef d'Œuvre Inconnu*, but it was in 1933 that Picasso arrived at his most fertile production. Between 20 March and 5 May he engraved forty etchings on a theme which had been close to him since he had been at Boisgeloup, *The Sculptor's Studio*. The set was completed the following spring with six more.

An early watercolour painted by Picasso in 1904 shows a pale young man poorly dressed in contemplation of a girl asleep on a bed in their mean lodging.[2] As was not unusual then, the profile of the man is recognisable as a self-portrait. The subject is one in which Picasso has felt himself involved throughout his life, and one to which he has given an extraordinary variety of interpretations beginning with this emotional watercolour. In the late twenties the theme reappears as a formal cubist composition divested of all trace of emotional weakness. The direct amorous relationship between two lovers has been complicated by the girl's becoming the artist's model, and still greater changes have taken place in the manner of their presentation. The subject is hidden beneath the scaffolding of a severe geometric composition, and the emotion it conveys is based on a less obvious appeal. It no longer tells a tender and easily interpreted story, on the contrary with rigid machine-like forms, the couple face each other imbued with

[1] The 'Vollard Suite' consists, apart from 27 miscellaneous plates, of the following groups: (i) *L'Atelier du Sculpteur*, 46 plates; (ii) *Le Viol*, 5 plates; (iii) *Le Minotaure*, 11 plates; (iv) *Rembrandt*, 4 plates; (v) *Le Minotaure aveugle*, 4 plates.
[2] Plate III, 3.

a passion which amounts almost to hatred. Strangely enough, however, in the version dated 1928, between the geometric shapes of the two antagonists, active and passive, a conventionally realistic profile is drawn on a canvas on which the artist is at work.[1] Picasso has gone beyond formal considerations and, not without wit, places this reminder of the comparative realities of nature and art reversing their accepted relationship a degree further than had happened in Balzac's story.

In the series of etchings known as *The Sculptor's Studio* this same riddle is the main theme, treated with a richness of variety. Drawn in the neo-classical style with an unhesitating line, the bearded sculptor is intent on his work which stands enthroned before him. At his side is his lovely companion who shares his passions and his anxiety. Their anxious looks are directed towards a third presence; the work that she has inspired and he has created. In this situation, unlike that which occurs in family life, the artist is sole master of his own creation. His eye watches with astonishment the life and movement that has come into his marble children, crowning the results of his conscious labour, while in his arms he holds tenderly the soft white body of his muse. In almost every image we find the drama of the lovers between whom a third presence has appeared, breaking into their unity like a nightmare as they lie together. In the plate dated 3 April the sculptor lies beside his companion, his hand on a window which looks out on an Arcadian landscape, and raises himself to contemplate the apparition that he has made.[2] Standing on its base at the edge of their couch is the statue of two young horses struggling together in amorous play. It is their life and movement that fills the gaze of their creator. Lying immobile, his bald head crowned with ivy, his thoughts are far from the girl beside him. With limp fingers he caresses her as she lies asleep, gloriously naked to his touch, her wreath of flowers tangled in her hair.

Other images show them both awake, but still their glances never meet. It may be that the violence of the sculptured group of a bull attacking two horses, or the bacchanalian abandon of a naked girl entangled in garlands, led in by a youth who has thrown her over the back of a young bull, engrosses too completely their attention;[3] they sit or lie, their bodies entwined together but their thoughts apart.

The Horned God

Picasso had found a way in the Vollard suite of revealing his sense of drama in the form of a new mythology, which enriched by its

[1] Plate XII, 8.　　[2] Plate XIV, 6.
[3] See *Picasso: Suite Vollard*, Editions Parallèles, Paris, 1956, No. 56.

references to the classics was at the same time the mirror of our daily thoughts. For as he has said, "there is no past or future in art".

As early as 1913, at a time when cubist discoveries were an all-absorbing interest, Apollinaire spoke of Picasso's "hybrid beasts who have the consciousness of the demi gods of Egypt". But it is not always possible to trace the origins of the actors on Picasso's stage, several of whom have followed him through his life, reappearing in different circumstances but always keeping their personality. We can watch Harlequin from the days when he appeared as a self-portrait of the half-starved artist, disguised in carnival dress, to his robust, self-confident look as he carouses with his companions of the commedia del'arte; or we can remember the innocent child holding a dove of the Blue period, her reappearance in the troupe of the Saltimbanques, and again as a mock angel standing on the back of the winged mare in the drop curtain of *Parade*. Now in the Vollard suite she makes a new entry fearlessly leading a terrifying character, the Minotaur stricken with blindness, his arms searching his darkness, his muzzle bellowing to the sky and his eyes white and dead.[1]

The bull-headed man had made his entry in the arena of Picasso's imagination at the time when the female form was being submitted to the most monstrous distortion. There is a small painting, *Composition*, dated 1927,[2] of a nude seated in an armchair with a body which has suffered such distortions that it is not easy to decipher. The head tossed back convulsively has a distinctly bovine form and on either side in patches of light on the figured wallpaper appear two realistic human profiles, one made of shadow, the other of light. Although this appearance of the human beast may be fortuitous, for it is rarely combined elsewhere with the female form, he is drawn with complete clarity in a collage dated 1 January 1927,[3] which nine years later was made into a Gobelin tapestry. Here in an abbreviation of the whole figure the bull's head runs nimbly mounted on a pair of human legs.

But in the etchings of the Vollard suite we are introduced to the Minotaur as a powerful and well-defined character who revels with the sculptor and his lascivious models.[4] He takes his place in their orgies as one of the guests. He drinks with them and enjoys caressing their tender flesh. There is an innocent gentleness in his eye that is belied by the strength of his muscles and the horns that crown his head. The human beast or horned god, in spite of his excesses, is accepted as one

[1] Plate XV, 7.   [2] See Zervos, *Picasso*, Vol. VII, p. 34, No. 78.
[3] Ibid., Vol. VII, p. 58, No. 134.   [4] Plate XIV, 8.

of the family. The patriarchal head of the artist becomes interchangeable with that of the demigod, as if they both wore masks. But treachery, violence and lust are hidden beneath his ingenuous mien, forming an essential part of his bestial destiny.

The strange fellowship between Picasso and animals is astonishingly clear. As we have already seen, he is never without their company. They take their place in his household as familiar spirits, their animal nature is a symbol of lovable and hateful qualities shared by human beings. The Minotaur joins the family with the same intimacy as the canine dynasty that has always reigned under his table, and Picasso admits that in drawing the head of the bull he has more than once had in mind the head of his favourite Airedale, Elft.

There are two etchings of the Minotaur dying in the arena before the gaze of awestruck spectators,[1] in which the mystery and anguish of the death of the brute is powerfully present, but none are more troubling than those of the blind Minotaur.[2] As he strides along by the boats leaning on his staff he spreads terror among the fishermen. Only children are without fear. The little girl clutching a dove to her breast leads him with confidence. The blind beggars that impressed Picasso so profoundly in his youth and seemed to him the symbol of that which is the most appalling state of man, and at the same time the condition which could give birth to a new form of vision, are closely akin to the more complex image of the stricken Minotaur. Blinded like the goldfinches of Picasso's own parable, so that he shall sing better his lament, he proclaims like Oedipus the crimes that are his fate.

Picasso the Poet

For years it had been Picasso's habit to leave Paris during the summer, usually for the Mediterranean, but the summer of 1935 was an exception. He stayed at home. He was in no humour to return to places where he would be surrounded by the frivolous holiday atmosphere of fashionable acquaintances. In a letter to his old friend Sabartès, who had returned to Spain after many years in America, he wrote significantly, "I am alone in the house. You can imagine what has happened and what is waiting for me. . . ."[3] To add to the sordid complications which were bound to follow his break with Olga, one consolation had arrived which was also not without difficult consequences. Marie-Thérèse gave birth to a daughter whom they named Maria Concepcion, or, as an abbreviation, Maïa.

[1] Plate XIV, 9.   [2] Plate XV, 7.   [3] Sabartès, *Documents Iconographiques*, p. 28.

Confronted by these two events Picasso took the course, always distasteful to him, of consulting lawyers. The solution that appealed to him then was to divorce Olga and try to realise once more his desire for a family, this time with Marie-Thêrèse. But legal procedure proved to be so complicated, owing to Picasso's Spanish nationality which he had no desire to forfeit, that after long exasperating consultations the idea was abandoned. For months he was plagued by these abortive proceedings, so much so that for a while he could not bear to go upstairs to his studio where everything reminded him vividly of the past and the ways in which he had sublimated his melancholy.

In the autumn he escaped from Paris to the seclusion of Boisgeloup where he could work without interruption on his sculpture, paint, and draw without the same weight of past memories to depress him, and above all indulge secretly in a form of expression which brought new satisfaction to the days when he had not the heart for his usual work. Some months later the news that Picasso was exploring yet another path reached his mother, whom he had visited in Barcelona both in 1933 and the following year, but to whom he rarely sent more than verbal greetings by friends. ". . . They tell me that you write. I can believe anything of you", she said with her usual confidence in him in one of her letters. "If one day they tell me that you say mass, I shall believe it just the same."[1] But for many months Picasso let no one know what he was jotting down in the little notebooks that he hid as soon as anyone came into the room.

Slowly the desire to communicate his thoughts to others induced him to read scraps of his writings to a few close friends. He had been haunted in the past and still is to this day by substituting one art for another, writing pictures and painting poems, and in some of his first attempts, which have never been published, made at Boisgeloup, he had used blobs of colour to represent objects in his poems. Abandoning this idea he started to write again, stressing visual images in words and using his own form of punctuation which consisted of dashes of varying length to separate the phrases, but this concession to the rules of grammar soon seemed to him too conventional. As he explained to Braque who had come to lunch one day at the rue la Boètie, he found that "punctuation is a cache-sexe which hides the private parts of literature".[2] In consequence he suppressed all forms of punctuation so as to let the words stand by themselves, fitted together like stones in a dry wall.

[1] Sabartès, *Portraits*, p. 19.   [2] Ibid., p. 125.

Picasso's reticence in showing his poems was due partly to the fact that he had no pretensions about the quality of his poetry. He therefore suffered to an even higher degree from the same bashfulness that he still has, after more than sixty years, in showing anything on which he has just been working, largely because he hates to admit that it is finished and resents having anyone see what he is doing while he is still at work. Another difficulty was that his poems could not be understood by the majority of his friends because they were in Spanish. It was fortunate therefore that in November 1935 Sabartès should have been free to accept the invitation of his companion of the 4 Gats to come to Paris and join him in the half-deserted apartment. His old friend could understand better than anyone not only the poems but also the circumstances that had driven him to explore this new medium of expression. Soon after his arrival Picasso began to read out loud his private meditations to a few Spanish friends and then to translate them word for word to others. Among the first who came eagerly to hear them were the surrealist poets among whom this kind of poetry, spontaneous and free in form, was highly appreciated. Sabartès had typed the poems out clearly but Picasso had rapidly made each sheet his own again by covering it with corrections made with pencils of various colours.

One of the first to acclaim the poems with enthusiasm was André Breton, whose admiration for Picasso's work in other media was already known. The result was that several of them were published a few months later in a special number of *Cahiers d'Art*, with a preface in Breton's most eloquent style. He draws attention to Picasso's eagerness "to represent all that belongs to music" in his work as a painter. "We learn from this", he says, "the necessity of a total expression by which he is possessed and which compels him to remedy in its essence the relative insufficiency of one art in relation to another."[1]

Sabartès tells, similarly, how one morning while he was unobtrusively laying the table for their bachelors' lunch Picasso appeared from the next room saying "Look! Here is your portrait." But on this occasion, unlike the earlier portraits it was painted with words.

To Picasso the new discovery was not a sideline or a hobby. It was a means of translating into words his intimate visual life. Like the relationship he had created between painting and sculpture, it was in close liaison with his varied means of expression. The poems are like monolithic slabs made up of words, each sparkling with meaning

[1] A. Breton, *Cahiers d'Art*, 10th Year, 7-10, Paris, 1935, p. 186.

like separate crystals: "Poetry that cannot help being plastic to the same degree that [his] painting is poetic."[1]

Again we can see through the brilliant kaleidoscopic flow of images how close Picasso is to his surroundings. "The point of departure", Breton writes, "is immediate reality". In the torrent of words there is continual play between the object at hand and its poetic image. Their paradoxical behaviour comes to life in proverbs such as "the knife that bounds with pleasure has no other resource than to die of pleasure". Colour plays an important rôle with violence or tenderness. From the following fragment we can judge how words have been applied as a painter uses colour from his brush:

"listen in your childhood to the hour that white in the blue memory borders white in her very blue eyes and piece of indigo of sky of silver the white glances run cobalt through the white paper that the blue ink tears away blueish its ultramarine sinks so that white enjoys blue rest agitated in the dark green wall green that writes its pleasure pale green rain that swims yellow green in the pale forgetfulness at the edge of its green foot the sand earth song sand of the earth after noon sand earth"[2]

Hermetic and personal in that Picasso does not stop to explain his images, they are a direct transcription of his thoughts, inspired equally by the sensations gathered from his immediate surroundings and memories often going far back into the past and traceable in some cases to events in his childhood. His memory is long, but it is the automatic flow of sensation from the subconscious freely transmitted in words which is even more important.

Mingling with unpremeditated imagery are echoes of his lasting dissatisfaction with society in general. In a language of authority which seems prophetic of what was shortly to come he starts a poem with these words: "give wrench twist and kill I make my way set alight and burn caress and lick embrace and watch I ring at full peal the bells until they bleed terrify the pigeons and make them fly about the dovecote until they fall to the ground already dead from fatigue I shall block up all the windows and doors with earth and with your hair I shall catch all birds that sing and cut all the flowers I shall rock in my arms the lamb and give him my breast to devour I shall wash him with my tears of joy and sorrow and I shall send him to sleep with the song of my solitude by *soleares*"[3]

---

[1] A. Breton, *Cahiers d'Art*, 10th Year, 7.10, Paris, 1935, p. 186.
[2] Ibid., p. 187.   [3] *Cahiers d'Art*, 7.10, 1935, p. 190.

The Return of Jaime Sabartès

The solitude of Picasso had become more than the inevitable solitude of genius. To escape the fashionable world into which he had been drawn during the past ten years he had hidden himself away with his work as the only possible solace. Friendship to him is an indispensable asset to life and it was his memory for those who had shared his thoughts and affection in the past that had prompted him to write to Sabartès asking him to come to Paris and help him with the growing menace of unanswered letters and official chores. Sabartès describes with shrewdness and affection Picasso's welcome at the station and their arrival at the half-deserted flat in the rue la Boètie. "Since that day", he writes, "my life follows in the wake of his"[1]— for Sabartès has remained ever since Picasso's closest confidant and devoted friend. Author of books written with modesty and the authority of one who has shared intimately the anxieties and the joys of his great compatriot, he remarks to those who come to him asking enthusiastically for further information: "Ah! you also, I see, have caught the virus."

The discomfort and disorder of the apartment had been increased by the fact that for days together Picasso shunned the idea of going up to his studio on the floor above. The two friends camped among indescribable piles of objects, paintings, documents and unanswered letters which had accumulated like geological strata. The process had gone on for years, because of Picasso's intense dislike of tidying things up and his conviction that some precious object would be lost if this should be attempted. For hours they talked. Late into the night Picasso would keep his companion awake discussing people and life in cynical terms or talking amiable nonsense rather than letting him fall asleep. The dry humour and picturesque originality of Sabartès' remarks, his complacent pessimism and his quiet enthusiasm for Picasso's genius, his unobtrusive competence and complete devotion made him the best possible medicine for his friend's troubled spirit.

As he had done in the past, Picasso found endless ways of teasing him. In the mornings he would lie in bed as long as possible and annoy Sabartès by continually asking him the time, sometimes repeating the question before Sabartès had finished his answer. "Wouldn't it be better for you to get up?" Sabartès would say. "Why?" asks Picasso. "Mon vieux, if only to get this obsession out of your head",

[1] Sabartès, *Portraits*, p. 110.

and Picasso would go on, "Let's talk of something else. . . . What time is it?"[1]

Paul Eluard

Picasso's affinity to surrealism had brought him in touch with Paul Eluard soon after the young poet had returned to Paris from the war and recovered from the illness brought on by a gas attack on the western front, but there had been no intimacy between them until more than ten years later. At this time Eluard like Picasso had gone through the misery of a separation from his wife, Gala, who by a coincidence was also Russian.

One of the first things that marked the beginning of a friendship which was to be long and full of consequence was a portrait drawn in pencil and dated by Picasso 'ce soir le 8 janvier xxxvi'.[2] Six months later it was used as a frontispiece to the first translations of Eluard's poems to be printed in London and at the same time Picasso agreed to illustrate *La Barre d'Appui*, a book of poems that Eluard was about to publish with Zervos in Paris.[3] With Eluard watching he took a copper plate and divided it equally into four parts. Three of them he filled with etchings. In the first he drew the head of Nusch, the beautiful fragile girl whom Eluard had just married; next to her in heavily patterned arabesques he made a birdlike woman watching the flaming edge of the sun as it literally burst through a wall. Below in the third quarter was the sleeping head of Marie-Thérèse merged into a landscape of houses and the sea, and to complete the four quarters Picasso printed the impression of his right hand on the plate.

Eluard delighted in his new intimacy with Picasso. He said at the time with candour that he was happy to be alive in this troubled century above all because he had met Picasso. On the other hand the poetry of Eluard, lyrical, passionate and rich in images was of the kind that Picasso admired most in surrealist literature. Eluard loved painting with an understanding rare among writers. He had collected round him far more pictures and objects than he could ever hang on the restricted wall space in his apartment. They were acquired in the same way that he lived, with vision and enthusiasm. Max Ernst, Miró, Dali and other surrealist painters were then among his closest friends, and of all the poets that Picasso had known it was Eluard who had the most complete appreciation of his work. A poem dedicated 'To Pablo Picasso' dated 15 May 1936 begins:

[1] Sabartès, *Portraits*, p. 115.　　[2] Plate XV, 5.
[3] See Barr, *Picasso: Fifty Years of His Art*, p. 194.

'What a fine day when I saw again the man I can't forget
Whom I shall never forget
And fleeting women whose eyes
Made me a hedge of honour
Wrapped themselves in their smiles'

and finishes:

'What a fine day a day begun in melancholy
Black beneath green trees
But which steeped suddenly in dawn
Entered my heart by surprise.'[1]

Touched by Eluard's insight and sympathy Picasso found it easy to collaborate with him. In the early days of their friendship Eluard had completed a book of poems, *Les Yeux Fertiles*, which gave Picasso the idea that one of the poems, 'Grand Air',[2] should be engraved on a plate and illustrated by him. It was possible by means of a process invented by Lacourière for Eluard to write his text on the plate and for Picasso then to illuminate it with drawings. The clear bold hand in which the poem is written does not betray for a moment the disability from which Eluard suffered since his war wounds, which made his hand tremble violently as though with some deep emotion until his pen actually touched the paper. Under the signature of Eluard is the date 3.6.36, 3 heures 15 while in the opposite corner Picasso dated his 4 Juin xxxvi. The finished plate is a testimony to the sensitive and confident understanding that had sprung up between poet and painter. The text and its illuminations combine with consideration of each other's meaning. Picasso surrounded a poem of lyrical optimism with an atmosphere of high-spirited, amorous enjoyment.

Picasso Acclaimed in Spain and Paris

In the spring of 1936 Eluard accepted the invitation of a group of young Spanish artists and poets to go to Barcelona and make a speech at the opening of a retrospective exhibition of Picasso's work that was to be held there, and later to travel to Bilbao and Madrid. Members of the ADLAN[3] group had been to Paris, and thanks to their youth and enthusiasm they had managed to get Picasso's cooperation in

[1] Paul Eluard, *Selected Writings*, trans. Lloyd Alexander, London, Routledge and Kegan Paul, 1952.
[2] Plate XV, 6.   [3] Amigos de las Artes Nuevas.

assembling what was to be the first exhibition of his work in Spain since 1902. The demands for photographs, values for insurance and other ancillary scraps of information which inevitably accompany such activities bore Picasso and often put him in bad humour. He is likely to put off making the decisions which his visitors need by saying anything—"perhaps", "we shall see", "come tomorrow" or even "yes" in order to get rid of them. But he is inclined to be well-disposed towards his own compatriots, especially when they are young and genuinely interested in his work.

In Barcelona Eluard arrived for the opening and speeches were made by him and others on the radio. "I speak of that which helps me to live, of that which is good", were the opening words of his address. "Picasso wants the truth", he continued. "Not that fictitious truth which will leave Galatea inert and lifeless, but a total truth which joins the imagination to nature, which considers everything as real and which going ceaselessly from the particular to the universal and from the universal to the particular comes to terms with all variety of existence, of change, provided that they are new, that they are fecund."[1]

As it travelled through the three Spanish cities, the exhibition was hailed by the younger generation with enthusiasm. In Barcelona Ramon Gomez de la Serna gave a recital of Picasso's poems. Later when it opened in Madrid, Guillermo de Torre wrote a preface to the well-documented catalogue, in which he proclaimed that "Picasso is without doubt the supreme contemporary example of . . . an inventive spirit in continuous eruption". But Picasso, true to his habit of keeping away from such manifestations, did not follow his exhibition to Spain.

In Paris also the fame of Picasso was once more established by three exhibitions of recent work. Zervos showed his sculpture and the Renou and Colle Gallery held an exhibition of drawings, while Paul Rosenberg, in his gallery next door to Picasso's apartment, filled the great room and the entrance with the splendid canvases that he had painted intermittently during the last two years. The two main themes that were visible in the brilliantly coloured pictures made a strong contrast. One series was of girls either reading, their eyes demurely lowered in concentration, or asleep, their heads resting on their folded arms.[2] The reds, purples, greens and yellows that shone in these great canvases had the quality of stained glass heavily outlined with sweeping black

[1] Eluard, 'Je parle de ce qui est bien', *Cahiers d'Art*, 7.10, 1935.
[2] Plate XIV, 5 and 7.

curves. They radiated a warm luscious tranquillity unlike the wildly distorted females of the preceding years. The other theme dated from Picasso's return from Spain in 1934 where he had once more renewed his contact with the drama of the bullfight. As in the other paintings the colours were generally brilliant, but here there was violent move-ment and fury and agony reigned among the dying animals.[1]

In the apartment next door to the gallery Sabartès found it difficult to keep well-meaning friends from annoying Picasso with their effusions. Those who attended the private view had been overawed by the strength of the new work. Picasso had again taken them by surprise. The twenty-eight paintings and eight gouaches spread their light and their emotion throughout the gallery like "windows through which could be seen images of flame and crystal".[2] At the opening "le tout Paris" was there breathless with excitement, only Picasso himself was not to be seen among the crowd. Such enthusiasm was taken by him at its just value. When later he went to see the exhibition and received extravagant congratulations from a friend, he explained afterwards to Sabartès that this same man had visited him at Boisgeloup and on seeing the paintings there had told him, Picasso, in private that "he was scandalised and found himself obliged to give him some friendly advice: the paintings were decadent and unhealthy, his style revealed exhaustion, which was deplorable".[3]

Fame had always been suspect, "hollow like glory" in Apollinaire's phrase. Even the prize awarded him by the Carnegie Institute in 1930 for the portrait of Madame. Picasso painted in 1918 had not im-pressed him. When the French Government sent representatives to choose one of his paintings about the same time, he described the visit to his friend the dealer Pierre Loeb in these words: "Four of them came; when I saw them, with their striped trousers, their stiff collars, their looks at the same time timid and distant, I thought again of my youth which was so tough. I thought that those people could have been of more help in the past with a few hundred francs than today with some hundreds of thousands. I began to show them some paint-ings, my best paintings, but I felt they wanted the Blue period. We arranged vaguely another rendezvous to which I shall not go."[4]

Secret Visit to Juan-les-Pins

After the acclamations of the early spring Picasso became more restless. The constant stream of well-wishers interfered with his

[1] Plate XIV, 3.   [2] Sabartès, Portraits, p. 129.   [3] Ibid., p. 133.
[4] Pierre Loeb, Voyages à Travers la Peinture, Bordas, Paris, 1945, p. 54.

thoughts and his work and on 25 March he disappeared to Juan-les-Pins, taking with him Marie-Thérèse. Sabartès describes putting him on the train and receiving instructions that his mail should be forwarded to him addressed to Pablo Ruiz as soon as he had found where he wanted to stay. For six weeks Sabartès received regularly letters of varying humour. On 22 April things went well, "I work, I paint, I write and I begin to go to bed later . . ." but the next day it was different: "I write to you at once to announce that from this evening, I am giving up painting, sculpture, engraving and poetry so as to consecrate myself entirely to singing. A handshake 'from your most devoted friend and admirer—Picasso"; but again by 27th things had changed for the better. "I continue to work in spite of singing and all. Your faithful servant who kisses your hands. Your friend—Picasso".[1]

Such frequent letter-writing in itself was so unusual as to be disquieting, and a certain sign of restlessness. Sabartès' misgivings were therefore justified when little more than a fortnight later he received a telegram announcing Picasso's return. He brought with him more drawings of extraordinary scenes in which the main characters were the Minotaur and naked girls who watch or motivate his actions, illustrations of new unwritten stories that he had been inventing in his Mediterranean retreat. Among them was a pen drawing of the Minotaur moving house, in which the innocent smile of the monster makes him almost lovable, in spite of his crimes.[2] He marches along briskly dragging a cart into which he has piled his furniture, consisting of nothing but a mare and her foals disembowelled by his own hands. In other drawings the monster lies on the grass gleefully watching the dance of a distracted nymph, or in agony he falls to the ground transfixed with a spear while the maidens with detachment watch him die.

To another drawing dated 27 April xxxvi he gave the title *Two old men looking at themselves in a mirror*.[3] Their fat bodies and hairy toothless faces are convulsed with laughter as they sit together naked looking straight into the mirror which, in this case, can be nothing other than the eye of whoever looks at the drawing, a disconcerting and significant way of involving himself and all concerned in the ribald grimace of old age.

Summer in Paris

Almost at once after his return, Picasso began work on a commission from Vollard that he had shelved for an unknown period, the

---

[1] Sabartès, *Portraits*, p. 135.
[2] See Zervos, *Picasso*, Vol. VIII, p. 130, No. 276.   [3] Ibid., p. 130, No. 277.

illustrations for the *Natural History* of Buffon.[1] To do so he went to the studio of Roger Lacourière, high up on the slopes of Montmartre, where many painters have worked, helped by the excellent equipment and the skill of the master-printer and his craftsmen. Picasso enjoyed working once more with technicians who welcomed the inventive way in which all processes were questioned by him, and frequently new and startling results were obtained. He worked with great freedom, choosing from the animal kingdom those that interested him for the illustrations and producing a set of aquatints which are surprising in the gentle fluency of their treatment and their profound likeness to birds and beasts that were nowhere to be seen in Montmartre. Though the thirty-one illustrations were completed at the rate of one a day, the book was not published until 1942, three years after Vollard's death.

Other activities crowded in on Picasso as well as the aquatints for the Buffon, illustrations for Eluard and drawings for the poet René Char. Friends persuaded him to design a drop curtain for a play by Romain Rolland with which they intended to celebrate the 14 July in 1936 on the great stage of the Alhambra.[2] As usual time went by and the maquette was still not done. Indeed it is very unlikely that the curtain would ever have materialised had it not been possible to find in the abundance of Picasso's production a recent watercolour of the Minotaur series which fitted as though it had been specially designed for the purpose.

Picasso was in a more sociable mood since his return, and could be found almost every evening at one of the cafés at St. Germain-des-Prés, where he spent long hours talking with his friends and usually leaving untouched his glass of mineral water. Paul Eluard and the elegant and charming Nusch, with her irresistible laugh, joined often by Zervos and his wife, were constant companions.

The surrealist group had extended its activities into many different countries, and in the summer of this year the first international exhibition was opened in London by Breton and attended by Eluard, as well as a number of painters and poets from Paris. It was thanks to the intimacy which had grown up between them that Eluard was able to persuade Picasso to allow nine of his works to be shown, including some of the large canvases which had appeared at the Rosenberg gallery earlier in the year. Other companions who frequented the same cafés were the Braques, Man Ray, Laurens the sculptor, Pierre

[1] Buffon, *Histoire Naturelle*, Fabiani, Paris, 1942.
[2] See Zervos, *Picasso*, Vol. VIII, p. 136, No. 287.

Loeb, Michel and Zette Leiris, and the faithful Sabartès. Paulo, now old enough to be included in adult company, was astonished at his father's ability to see so many friends. Going from one café to another until well after midnight he would not infrequently walk home. Sometimes he stopped, alone or with friends, to visit the Gare St. Lazare to watch the night trains leaving, before finally going to bed.

At St. Germain-des-Prés early in the year, Paul Eluard had introduced to Picasso a young girl with black hair and dark and beautiful eyes who was a friend of his and of the poet Georges Bataille. Her quick decisive speech and low-pitched voice were an immediate indication of character and intelligence. She was a painter and an experienced photographer and had found her way into surrealist circles because of her interest in their work and their revolutionary attitude to life. Thus there were many reasons why Picasso should pay special attention to Dora Maar, among the numbers of attractive young women who were always seeking to make his acquaintance. Although she had been brought up in France, her father was a well-to-do Yugoslav who had lived for many years in the Argentine. His real name, Markovitch, had been abbreviated by his daughter. Owing to her South American connections, she had the advantage of being able to talk to Picasso in his own language as well as in French.

Civil War in Spain

About the same time that Picasso was planning to leave with Eluard for the south of France, news reached Paris of the military uprising under General Franco in Spain. In surrealist circles with their strong left-wing bias and their insistence that the artist should not seek refuge in an ivory tower but rather take a militant part in social revolution, there was no doubt from the first on which side their sympathies lay. Those like Maurice Raynal who could remember Picasso's "bitter outspoken indignation in 1909, early in the reign of Alfonso xiii, when Ferrer, one of the socialist leaders of an uprising in Barcelona, was hailed before a military court and summarily executed",[1] were not surprised to see him share the same view as his more politically conscious friends, a view that became more definite as time went on. On their side the Spanish Republican Government, urged by the group of young intellectuals who had so recently planned the exhibitions in Spain, were not slow to appreciate the importance of Picasso's world-wide reputation, and as a gesture of recognition he

[1] Raynal, *Picasso*, Skira, p. 99.

was made Director of the Prado Museum in Madrid by the Republican Government.

Summer at Mougins

The departure for Mougins, a little hilltop village a few miles inland from Cannes, took place in early August. Picasso went alone in his spacious Hispano-Suiza in which he could transport all the material he needed and have room on the return journey for the many objects —pebbles, shells, bones, driftwood, pottery or frames—that had taken his fancy on the beaches or in the shops during the summer. He preferred to travel by night but never had any inclination to drive. As he once remarked, "I prefer the carrier pigeon to the compass". His chauffeur, Marcel, in consequence had to be prepared to pack everything into the car and start at once as soon as the final decision to leave had been made. The road was covered at great speed and dawn broke on a landscape of white rocks, cypresses and olive trees. By midday he had exchanged the grey streets of Paris for the brilliant sunlight of the Mediterranean.

This time the village that Picasso chose for the summer was suggested by Paul Eluard, who had taken the apartment of a friend in the ramparts of the old town of Mougins close to an unpretentious hotel with the exalted and well-justified name, 'Le Vaste Horizon'. Here he was met by Zervos and his wife and shortly afterwards others arrived, the summer visitors including Man Ray, Paul Rosenberg and René Char, and others who stayed for periods varying in length from one meal to several weeks. On the terrace shaded by vines and cypress trees the tables were joined at every meal to seat a large company of friends.

The morning bathe was a daily ritual. Picasso usually went with Eluard and others to the beach, returning refreshed from the sea to a late lunch which was always enlivened and prolonged by unfailing wit and enthusiasm, engendered by the contact of poet and painter. During these meals, which rarely passed without some anxious comments on the news from Spain, Picasso's humour was a series of contrasts. Dressed in a striped sailor's vest and shorts, at times he would enchant the whole table with boisterous clowning. Holding a black toothbrush to his upper lip and raising his right arm he would give them an imitation of Hitler's ranting, or he would enjoy telling of the grotesque adventures of Manolo whose safety in the present crisis was on his mind. At other times, using whatever material was at hand such as burnt matches, lipstick, mustard, wine or colour squeezed from flowers and leaves, he would quietly draw portraits on the tablecloth taking quick glances at the youthful smiling face of Nusch or at Eluard's daughter, Cécile, with eyes that seemed to devour what they saw. At other times his restless fingers would fold the paper napkins and with delightful skill, tear all sorts of creatures out of them. Bulls, horses and men in paper, wire or cork roamed between the wine glasses and were swept away when the three dark-eyed daughters of the house came finally to clear the table.

Returning by the main road from Cannes one day at noon under a scorching sun, Picasso was the victim of an accident which he describes with its consequences in letters to Sabartès. The Ford in which he was sitting in the back was driven by me. At a bend we collided with a car that was coming towards us on the wrong side of the road. The shock was sufficiently violent to shake up everyone in the car without doing them serious damage, but Picasso was thrown against the body-work and bruised in the chest so badly that it took him several weeks to recover completely. However, his tact was such that in spite of my anxiety and frequent enquiries I never discovered how much he had been hurt until I read the letters to Sabartès published over ten years later. He wrote: "A secret . . . the other day, coming from Cannes by car with an Englishman, I had an accident which left me bruised all over almost incapable of movement, broken and reduced to dust. I thought at first that I had some ribs broken, but yesterday I had an X ray taken and it seems that it is nothing; but I am still stiff at least for some days. Don't be frightened. . . ." Four days later, 3 September, he wrote reassuringly, "I am all right". It took considerably longer, however, for the effects of shock and bruising to wear off completely.

Some days before the accident an expedition along the coast to St. Tropez had been arranged to visit the writer Madame Lise Deharme, who was spending the summer in a farmhouse close to the sea. Picasso had learned that Dora Maar was one of her guests. After lunch they disappeared together for a walk along the beach. He talked to her with candour, telling her of the complications in his life and of the existence of his small daughter Maïa. He also asked her to accompany him back to Mougins. In a drawing dated 1 August xxxvi Dora Maar, dressed as though for a journey, can be seen opening a door, on the other side of which she finds a bearded patriarch sitting with a staff in one hand and a dog on his knee, a comment on Picasso's sense of his advancing years in contrast to Dora's youth.[1]

[1] See Zervos, *Picasso*, Vol. VIII, p. 139, No. 295.

Throughout this summer painting was not in great favour with Picasso. It seemed as if he were remaking his contacts with a world from which he had been excluded, now opened to him again by the casual enjoyment of the healing atmosphere of the Mediterranean and the lyrical company of his friends. Together with Eluard and Nusch he enjoyed making trips by car to the villages along the coast or in the mountains behind. One of these expeditions took them by chance to the little town of Vallauris, whose main industry since the time. of the Romans has been ceramics. Leaving the Hispano by the roadside, they wandered into one of the many potteries where vessels of many kinds were being thrown on the wheel in traditional style. The ease with which the craftsman could make the clay obey his manipulations delighted them both. Picasso understood at once that he had come across a new field to explore, but he did not begin there and then. The hope that was born that day was in fact to be realised, but not until ten years later. On their return to Mougins the same evening, Eluard added the following verse to the poem 'à Pablo Picasso' on which he was at work:

> "Show me this eternal man always so gentle
> Who said fingers make the earth rise higher
> The knotted rainbow the coiling serpent
> Mirror of flesh in which a child is pearled
> And these peaceful hands that go their way
> Naked obedient reducing space
> Charged with desires and images
> One following the other hands of the same clock"[1]

Other new ideas were to interest Picasso on his return to Paris in the autumn. The example of Man Ray's discoveries in making photographic prints from shadows thrown on the sensitised paper by objects or textiles, combined with the technical skill and understanding of these processes by Dora Maar, offered Picasso the chance of mastering yet another art. Again the wilful defiance of rules combined with a sense of what after all was possible produced some fascinating prints made from a combination of shadow printing and drawing on the photographic plate.[2]

New friends, new thoughts and new techniques reinforced Picasso's

[1] Paul Eluard, 'à Pablo Picasso', *Les Yeux Fertiles*, selected writings; trans. Lloyd Alexander, Routledge and Kegan Paul, London, 1952.
[2] *Cahiers d'Art*, Vol. XII, 1937.

energy. Never before had he been in possession of such power. Talent, knowledge and experience combined to nourish him during these months of relative idleness which however, by the standards of other artists, must still be counted as fertile. But as Picasso's morale improved the political situation in which as a Spaniard he was involved became daily more threatening.

CHAPTER X

GUERNICA
(1936–1939)

Le Tremblay

IN THE LATE autumn of 1936, Vollard told Picasso that he had been seduced by the rustic masonry of an old farmhouse at Le Tremblay-sur-Mauldre, not far from Versailles, and that he had bought it with the intention of offering it to Rouault so that he could paint in the country. Unhappily Rouault disliked the place and refused to use it, in spite of the fact that there was a fine barn which could serve as a studio, with a large window looking on to the garden. Picasso on the contrary at once appreciated the possibilities of this new retreat which was free from the associations with his separation from Olga, which haunted Boisgeloup. It would enable him to spend a few days each week in seclusion, far enough from the inquisitive attentions of his friends in Paris. He accepted Vollard's invitation and began to work during his visits here on a series of still-lifes.[1] These paintings are characterised by brilliant colour and by the charm of homely objects, such as jugs, plates, saucepans, cutlery, fish, fruit and flowers, among which we find the not infrequent intrusion of the head of the horned god or the bull.[2] Several are night scenes, lit by the flame of a candle or by stars that have found their way in through the window.

These pictures breathing an atmosphere of rural charm are, according to Sabartès—one of the few to have seen them all—"the refrain of a marvellous period in Picasso's pictorial production and even in the history of art".[3] Since few of Picasso's friends were invited to Le Tremblay, more than half of the paintings he made there during the next two years remain unknown even in reproduction, though in 1939 thirty-three of them were exhibited at Paul Rosenberg's gallery.[4]

Among those that have been seen by the public are some large paintings of nudes on the sea-shore.[5] Constructed with Picasso's invented anatomy, they are not unlike the bonelike *Seated Bather* of 1929 except that they are purged of its threatening looks, and flesh completely hides their bones. The swelling forms of these females

---

[1] Plate XVI, 2.   [2] Plate XVI, 3.
[3] Sabartès, *Portraits*, p. 150.
[4] See Zervos, *Picasso*, Vol. VIII, pp. 166–71.   [5] Plate XV, 1.

resemble ripe fruit. They sit on the sand absorbed in a book, or in the extraction of a thorn from the foot. Others enveloped in the blue haze of a calm sea play together with a toy boat, while from behind the horizon rises the immense head of a companion, like an inquisitive cloud covering the sun, to spy on them. There are also some revealing drawings of Marie-Thérèse with Maïa on her knee, and a portrait of Marie-Thérèse seated in a chair reading, wearing a red hat and a gay striped dress.[1]

Dream and Lie of Franco

At Le Tremblay Picasso was happily detached from the disquieting preoccupations of Paris. His short visits gave him the opportunity to enjoy a replica of family life; but on returning to Paris he again became involved in the growing anxieties of his friends. The news from Spain was bad, and as in all civil wars, where even brothers can be divided against each other, the situation was vexed by mixed loyalties, suspicion and hate. His mother in Barcelona sent news of the burning of a convent within a few yards of the apartment in which she lived with her widowed daughter and five grandchildren. For weeks the rooms had reeked with the stench, and her keen black eyes, the model of her son's, ran with tears from the smoke.

To the group of young poets, painters and architects who had recently organised the exhibitions of his work, the defence of democratic liberty had become a matter of life and death. Many had hastily taken up arms and departed for the front. Others, disproving fascist propaganda, which claimed that the art treasures of Spain were being pillaged and burnt by unruly mobs of anarchists, set to work on surveys of neglected ancient monuments and the organisation of new museums. In Paris also there was a remarkable unity among intellectuals in support of Republican Spain, which, as Soby suggests, was unparalleled since the days of the war of Greek independence, a hundred years earlier.[2]

It was this year that had been chosen by the French Government for a great International Exhibition, and it was of great importance to the Spanish Republicans that their Government should be well represented. A young architect, formerly an active member of the ADLAN group, José Luis Sert, had been charged with the propaganda service. With Luis Lacasa he was asked to design the Spanish Pavilion. Picasso

[1] Plate XVI, 1; also 5.
[2] See James Thrall Soby, *Modern Art and the New Past*. University of Oklahoma Press.

had already consented to produce some manifestation which would make his sympathies clear to the world, and there was much speculation as to what form it would take.

Already in January he had begun to engrave two large plates divided into nine spaces, each the size of a postcard.[1] It was originally intended that the prints should be sold separately for the benefit of Spaniards in distress. When the work was finished, however, on 7 June, the sheets of etchings shaded with aquatint were so impressive as a whole that it was decided to sell them intact with an additional sheet which was the facsimile of Picasso's manuscript of a long violent poem. To these three sheets were added French and English translations and a cover designed by Picasso giving the folder the title *Sueño y Mentira de Franco* (Dream and Lie of Franco).

The story of violence and misery inflicted by the arrogant leader of the military rising reads from picture to picture like a strip cartoon or the popular Spanish 'Alleluias' Picasso had known as a child. To personify the dictator he invented a grotesque and loathsome figure crowned with headdresses symbolic of his pretensions as the hero of Christianity, the saviour of Spanish tradition and the friend of the Moors. He carries a banner in which the Blessed Virgin takes the shape of a louse. He attacks the noble profile of a classical bust with an axe. He kneels protected by a barbed-wire fence in front of a monstrance in which is displayed 1 Duro. Riding a pig he tilts at the sun. The horse he mounts with pomp drags its entrails on the ground and later, slaughtered by his own hand, lies writhing at his feet. Women lie stretched out dead in the fields, flee with their children from their burning houses or raise their arms in gestures of despair. Only one creature can hold evil at bay, the bull who in its innocent strength disembowels the monster with its horns.

". . . cries of children cries of women cries of birds cries of flowers cries of timbers and of stones cries of bricks cries of furniture of beds of chairs of curtains of pots of cats and of papers cries of odours which claw at one another cries of smoke pricking the shoulder of the cries which stew in the cauldron and of the rain of birds which inundates the sea which gnaws the bone and breaks its teeth biting the cotton wool which the sun mops up from the plate which the purse and the pocket hide in the print which the foot leaves in the rock"—with this torrent of verbal images Picasso finishes his poem, the preface to his visual account of the calamity of which Franco was the originator.

The Spanish war had made itself felt so acutely to Picasso that he

[1] Plate XVI, 7; see also Larrea, *Guernica*, Plates 24 and 25.

could not avoid becoming personally involved. The loathsome shape he had invented for Franco came from a personal image of a monster which he understood as lurking within himself. Not long after he had finished the series, I asked him to sign a copy I had bought.[1] He did so, but when he had written my name beginning with a small P, I was astonished to see that the capital letter with which he commenced his own signature had fundamentally the same form as the twisted grotesque head that he had invented for the man he hated most. The strength he gave to the image borrowed subconsciously from so intimate a source was an indication of the degree to which he felt himself involved. The desire to implicate himself by means of his own initial could not be more convincing. Just as formerly he had often based the image of the hero, Harlequin, on an idealised self-portrait, here in reverse the subconscious origin of the shape he gave to the man he most hated was equally personal.

A Mural for the Spanish Pavilion

When in the first winter of the civil war Picasso promised to make an important contribution to the Spanish Pavilion, it became obvious that it would be necessary to find a studio which would give him sufficient scope. By good fortune Dora Maar knew of a large empty room which had been used by the poet Georges Bataille for the lectures and discussions of a group he had founded named 'Contre-attaque'. It was on the second floor of a seventeenth-century building which before the Revolution had been the residence of the Dukes of Savoy. By a coincidence it was situated in the rue des Grands Augustins near the river, the same street in which Balzac had set the scene of his story of the mad painter.

The spring passed, however, without any sign that Picasso had discovered what form his contribution to the Spanish Pavilion should take. The problems that arose were complex and their solution greatly intrigued those who looked to him for a valid expression of the feelings of thousands of people outraged by the civil war. Since the painting was to be used as the main feature in one of the pavilions in an international exhibition which would be visited by a public from all over the world, it was hoped that its appeal would be couched in a style which would deeply affect the masses. Was it possible that the inventor of cubism and strange distortions, styles which the public in general considered abstract or even demented, could make an appeal to ordinary people? The Spanish Government had asked Picasso

[1] Plate XVI, 7 and 8.

to take on this task, knowing that his reputation was in itself an attraction; but of those responsible it was only his younger and more ardent admirers such as Sert and the writer Juan Larrea (then in charge of the Information Office in Paris), who had complete confidence in the results. As usual Picasso decided to tackle the problem in his own way. Trusting his inspiration, when the time came he painted a picture whose strength could be ignored by no one. Its impact on the thousands of visitors to the exhibition came as a shock even to those who could not fathom its meaning. But as later the public grew slowly more familiar with its idiom, it came to be recognised as a lasting protest against war, surpassing the limitations of partisan propaganda and remaining valid even after the cause for which it had been painted had met with defeat.

Premonitions

The preparation for the great mural had come about unperceived. In the spring of 1935, soon after he had drawn a series of engravings of the Minotaur, Picasso produced an etching which has since become famous not only for its unusual size and splendid quality but also because of suggestions in it which now seem prophetic of the catastrophes which were soon to follow.[1] The engraving is dominated by the sinister entry from the seashore of the Minotaur, his eyes reflecting the light of a candle held by a fragile little girl who, greeting him with a bunch of flowers, fearlessly halts his advance. His right arm stretches forward in a menacing gesture, while beneath it, slipping from a horse which has become hysterical with fear, lies the figure of a dying woman dressed as a matador, her sword helpless in her hand and her white breasts stripped and defenceless. From a window above, two women with their tame doves contemplate the scene, while at the extreme edge of the picture a naked man mounts a ladder in an attempt to escape.

Other etchings of the preceding months are also based on the theme of the horse and his lovely rider who, decked out in the borrowed finery of the matador, becomes herself the victim of the bull's onslaught. In a sudden violent encounter the monster triumphantly exposes her exquisite and ill-disguised weakness.[2]

Taken as a series, these scenes often show ambiguity about the intentions of the beast. In some cases, in a paroxysm of anger and with irresistible force, the bull blindly rapes innocence and destroys virtue.

[1] Plate XVII, 4.
[2] See *Picasso: Suite Vollard*, Editions Parallèles, Paris, 1956. No. 22.

At other times, though always characterised as a creature of over-whelming strength, the monster is innocent of such crimes. Elsewhere, in some earlier versions, the bull is more playful. Rather than destroy the fair amazon he wrests her from his rival, the horse, and with fire in his eyes, seeks her lips with his bovine muzzle.

In his use of mythical and symbolic creatures Picasso could indulge his predilection for ambiguity, as a means of approaching truth. There are certain animals and birds whose behaviour and appearance make them appropriate symbols of human passions, but in his desire to use this vital and universal link with antiquity, Picasso did not limit him-self to over-simplified conventional interpretations, nor did he arbit-rarily draw parallels between their actions and moral issues in the manner of La Fontaine. By encouraging a sense of ambiguity he left the spectator the liberty of choosing his own interpretation.

Picasso Furioso

On 29 April 1937 news reached Paris that German bombers in Franco's pay had wiped out the small market town of Guernica, the ancient capital of the Basques. This gratuitous outrage, perpetrated at an hour when the streets were thronged with people, roused Picasso from melancholy to anger. Acting as a catalyst to the anxiety and indignation mingled within him, it gave him the theme he had been seeking. He had at hand the factors necessary for his task, and his recent work, more than ever a mirror of the Spanish scene, was an appropriate prologue. His exceptionally visual memory, which kept fresh the observations and discoveries he had made throughout his life, nourished his imagination. The experience gained from the many styles he had used gave him technical assurance. The more recent introduction into his work of the myths born in the Mediterranean and revitalised by him gave a new plane on which he could present this drama. Finally the atmosphere around him of friends who shared his thoughts, and his own unparalleled energy intensified by the horror of the war, armed him with great strength and the vision of genius.

The first characters to appear on his stage in hasty sketches were the horse, the bull, and a woman stretching out from a window with a lamp in her hand to throw light on the calamity in which they were all suddenly involved.[1] In successive versions, some drawn rapidly in pencil, numbered and dated, and others painted on canvas, the per-sonalities of the actors began to evolve, while at the same time they

[1] *Cahiers d'Art*, 1937, No. 4-5.

appeared together in compositions. From the beginning Picasso chose
the stricken horse as a central feature.

Ten days after the first sketch, a canvas eleven and a half feet high
and nearly twenty-six feet long had been set up at one end of the room
in the rue des Grands Augustins.[1] It was stretched from wall to wall,
and from the tiled floor below to the massive oak beams supporting
the rafters. The room, though it seemed vast, was not quite high
enough for the width of the canvas, and it could only be fitted in by
sloping it backwards, which meant that the upper part had to be
reached with a long brush from the top of a ladder. In spite of having
often to climb to this perilous position Picasso worked fast, and the
outline of the first version was sketched in almost as soon as the canvas
was up.

Thanks to the presence of Dora Maar a continual photographic
record of the development of the painting was kept.[2] It is a unique and
vivid account of the changes in the composition as it evolved. "It
would be highly interesting," Picasso commented, "to fix photo-
graphically, not the successive stages of a painting but its successive
changes. In this way one might perhaps understand the mental process
leading to the embodiment of the artist's dream."[3] As had always
been his practice, Picasso lived with his work and allowed his ideas to
evolve with it as though it were in itself alive. "At the inception of
each picture someone is working with me", he has said, referring to
this secret dialogue between the artist and his creation. But he continued: "Toward the end I have a feeling of having worked all by
myself and without collaborator."[4]

Simultaneously with the great canvas, a large number of studies,
very moving in their intensity and often carried as far as a finished
picture, formed part of an output which continued daily, except when
with great regularity he paid his weekly visit to Le Tremblay. There
for a while his fury lay dormant and he continued with equal energy
to paint the series of still-lifes and portraits of Marie-Thérèse and
Maïa, saying, "you see, I am not only occupied with gloom".

As the painting developed it was possible to watch the balance that
Picasso kept between the misery caused by war, seen in the anguish
of the women, the pain of the wounded horse or the pitiful remains of
the dead warrior; and the defiant hope of an ultimate victory. Many

[1] Plate XVII, 1.
[2] *Cahiers d'Art*, 1937, Nos. 4-5.
[3] Quoted by Larrea, *Guernica*, p. 13.
[4] ibid., pp. 52, 53.

writers have tried to interpret Picasso's symbolism and often they have committed the error of over-simplification. Juan Larrea, in an extensive and otherwise authoritative study of *Guernica*, states surprisingly that the horse transfixed with a pike represents Nationalist Spain.[1] To others the horse and its rider are the heroic victims of a brutal attack from the bull; but on examination we find, particularly in the early versions, nothing to suggest that the bull is in this case the villain. On the contrary he appears to be searching the horizon for the enemy, who is in fact not present in the scene at all. His enemy is the common enemy of all mankind, too vile and too universal to be contained in a single image. What we see in the painting is the effect of his enormity: the dead child, the house in flames, lacerated bodies, hysterical cries of agony and looks of astonishment that such things are possible.[2] The omission of the evil spirit that has caused this disaster is a more effective insult than its introduction, as in *Dream and Lie of Franco*, in the shape of a loathsome monster. Also it makes prophetic reference to the impersonality of modern warfare which allows the victims increasingly little chance of knowing who is their aggressor.

Symbols of hope come and go at various stages during the progress of the work, as though Picasso were debating how to give them undeniable authenticity. In the first version, across the centre of the picture the dying man raises high his clenched fist, the challenge given by anti-fascist fighters. Soon after, we find him holding a handful of corn in front of the round disc of the sun while his other hand still grasps a broken sword. Later the warrior is again transformed and arrives at his final position. Now the head lies where his feet were before. His defiant arm is obliterated and only the hand grasping the sword remains unchanged. In the same process the disc of the sun has been contracted into an oval shape like an eye without a pupil. The vesica piscis, which was used in Byzantine art to make a transcendental frame round the image of God, is rolled over on its side, empty. The bull also, which dominated the left half of the painting, watching the horizon as though ready to attack intruders, becomes reversed in position and looks over his shoulder in a more bewildered attitude. Only the lamp with its welcome light, the light of truth shed on a

[1] Larrea, *Guernica*, p. 34.

[2] Jerome Seckler who interviewed Picasso in 1945 reports him to have said: "The bull is not fascism, but it is brutality and darkness . . . the horse represents the people . . . the *Guernica* mural is symbolic . . . allegoric. That's the reason I used the horse, the bull and so on. The mural is for the definite expression and solution of a problem and that is why I used symbolism." 'Picasso Explains', *New Masses*, 13 March 1945.

scene of havoc, which had been present in every drawing, held by the outstretched arm of the woman at the window, remains. The other symbols of hope have one by one disappeared. Even the sun is finally degraded and its source of light made artificial by its centre being filled with an electric light bulb. To compensate for the warrior, now torn to pieces, the distraction of the bull and the insult to the sun, a bird perched inconspicuously on a table in the background flaps its wings and with open beak shrieks to the sky. The introduction of the table, with its domestic reference, into what was formerly an entirely outdoor scene, adds to the universality of the image.[1]

The evolution of the horse to its final state, in which it dominates the centre of the composition, is also of interest. There are many sketches, sometimes of the head only, reaching upwards with gnashing teeth and a tongue thrust out of the deep cavity of the mouth like a dagger, at other times of the animal writhing on the ground with outstretched neck reminiscent of the bullfight drawings of 1917. An early drawing dated 2 May (1937) shows the dying horse with the bull, the woman with the lamp and a prostrate figure with a Greek helmet. From a wound in its belly springs a small winged horse, which might be taken as an allusion to an after life of the soul, and recalls the *Burial of Casagemas*. This simple optimism however does not anywhere

---

[1] In an article entitled 'Soleil Pourri', published in a special number of *Documents—Hommage à Picasso*—in 1930, Georges Bataille drew attention to ambiguities inherent in the sun as a symbol. He points out that the midday sun which is too bright for the eyes is beautiful but that when obstinately looked at it becomes "horribly ugly". "If . . . in spite of all it is observed with enough concentration this supposes a kind of madness and the notion changes its meaning because in light, it is no longer the production which is apparent but the waste, that is to say the combustion, expressed well enough, psychologically, by the horror which is seen in an incandescent arc lamp." He goes on to describe the Mithraic rite in which "the initiate was spattered with the blood of a slaughtered bull". The bull itself is also in this case an image of the sun but only when slaughtered. It is the same as the cock, "of which the horrible cry, particularly solar, is always close to the cry of a creature whose throat is being cut". It is of interest that Picasso's image of the degradation of the sun shows some analogy and that it was painted in the same room in which previously Bataille had held his discussions with the group 'Contre-attaque'. The references to the mythological significance of the bull and the cock are also particularly important when it is remembered that before 1930 there are few references to these creatures in Picasso's painting. The first appearance of the minotaur in his work, as we have noted, dates from 1928, but the idea did not blossom into the great series of drawings for the Vollard suite until five years later. Once more the interchange of ideas between Picasso and his friends the poets is apparent.

reappear. In the early stages of the painting the animal in its death throes lies curled up on itself as though returning to the womb. As the composition suddenly reached its final shape early in June, the horse's head was raised high in the centre of the picture, rivalling in importance the sun and the arm holding the lamp. Instead of reaching upwards in a final ejaculation towards the sky, the open mouth spits defiance like the last salvo from a fortress that will not surrender: a gesture which echoes the cry of the defenders of Madrid: "They shall not pass."

The most moving figures in the picture are very naturally the four women. Their attitudes and expressions are significant of astonishment, fear, and the agony of overwhelming grief. The success with which Picasso conveys these emotions is clearly due to his long experience in the distortion of the human form. The distortions are skilfully controlled so as to accentuate gestures and movements which reveal tense emotion. The stretching upwards of the arms and neck of the woman falling from the burning house convinces us of the reality of her plight and accelerates the speed with which she will crash to the ground. The feet of her terrified companion below are eloquent of their need to cling to the earth as she runs out half-dressed and crouching from the danger that threatens from the sky. By looking again at the drawings we can see how carefully Picasso had studied the anatomy of grief and the primitive animal-like movements that come to the surface under the influence of uncontrollable fear. Many of the drawings go beyond what he needed for the final composition and date from after its completion. The richness of Picasso's invention overflows the limits of any single painting however great its proportions. The decomposition caused by sorrow in these figures and heads can hardly be surpassed. Each feature is interpreted with astonishing freedom. Both nostrils, both eyes and ears are crowded on to the same profile so that their testimony shall not be lost, and yet it is not the distortion that surprises us, nor the tears that stream across the cheeks, it is rather the fact that we can read so plainly the intention of the signs he makes and accept with such conviction the reality of the emotion he describes.

The discoveries of cubism, the purity of line of the neo classical period and the unbridled distortions of the later nudes had all united to give Picasso powers which permitted him in the summer months of this year to create this "monument to disillusion, to despair, to destruction".[1] As he worked on it not only was he discovering new ways of expression, he also never ceased to question the validity of what he had

[1] Herbert Read, 'Picasso's Guernica', *London Bulletin*, No. 6, October 1938.

already done. Returning to his opinion in the early days of cubism he felt that colour would distract him in his aim. From the start, although he treated the composition itself in monochrome, in the studies he used combinations of colour—greens, purples, pinks and yellows—which added to their emotional quality. They contain an acrid bitterness in their contrasts which recall Spanish images of saints.

During the weeks in which the great painting evolved through such startling changes, Picasso at times reverted to his former practice of pinning pieces of patterned wallpaper to the canvas so as to introduce colour and the presence of another kind of reality. When visitors arrived he discussed with them the movements of the figures as though the painting were alive. Once when the picture was nearly finished I called with Henry Moore. The discussion between us turned on the old problem of how to link reality with the fiction of painting. Picasso silently disappeared and returned with a long piece of toilet paper, which he pinned to the hand of the woman on the right of the composition, who runs into the scene terrified and yet curious to know what is happening. As though she had been disturbed at a critical moment her bottom is bare and her alarm too great to notice it. "There," said Picasso, "that leaves no doubt about the commonest and most primitive effect of fear."

Universality of Meaning

It is the simplicity of *Guernica* that makes it a picture which can be readily understood. The forms are divested of all complications which would distract from their meaning. The flames that rise from the burning house and flicker on the dress of the falling woman are described by signs as unmistakable as those used by primitive artists. The nail-studded hoof, the hand with deeply-furrowed palm, and the sun illuminated with an electric light bulb, are drawn with a child-like simplicity, startling in its directness. In this canvas Picasso had rediscovered a candour of expression which had been lost, or overlaid for centuries with the refinements of artistic skill. He had proved such excellencies to be unnecessary, even a hindrance to an understanding of reality. When visiting an exhibition of children's drawings, some years later, he remarked: "When I was their age I could draw like Raphael, but it took me a lifetime to learn to draw like them."[1] It was only this profound humility which could open to him the secret of instilling life into myths and symbols.

Again in his choice of symbolism he had realised the strength of

[1] Herbert Read, letter to *The Times*, 26 October, 1956.

simplicity. Herbert Read points out: "His symbols are banal, like the symbols of Homer, Dante, Cervantes. For it is only when the widest commonplace is inspired with the intensest passion that a great work of art, transcending all schools and categories, is born; and being born lives immortally."[1]

In his eagerness to press on rapidly in his work and concentrate only on essentials, he allowed the wet paint to run down the canvas here and there, and as though by a secret agreement, such accidents as the trails of white that run like saliva from the teeth of the horse, appear to be carefully premeditated effects. Again when he altered the position of the bull's head, he did not trouble to paint out entirely a redundant eye, with the result that the animal has now three eyes with which to scan the horizon even more effectively.

The structure Picasso chose for his composition can be seen traced on the canvas in the first of Dora Maar's photos. Its main feature is a triangle, the apex of which goes beyond the top of the picture, leaving space for a vertical column in the centre which originally contained the vertical arm with its clenched fist and later the sun and the horse's head. There is nothing revolutionary in basing a composition on a triangle, it recalls Cézanne's great composition *The Bathers* or, as Barr suggests, the pediment of a Greek temple; but as we have already noted, Picasso often uses the simplest and most traditional forms as a frame for the most revolutionary inventions, beneath which the firm basic structure tends to disappear. In the case of *Guernica* the sharp angular patterning and strong contrasts of light and shade purposely suggest rather the calamity and chaos brought about by an explosion than a well-balanced composition.

The Public and Picasso

Before two months from the day Picasso made his first sketch had elapsed, the great canvas *Guernica* was ready to take its place in the Spanish Pavilion at the Paris Exhibition. Economies enforced by the war had required their plans to be modest, but the architects had reserved a place of honour for it, and nearby they set up two of the large statues made four years earlier at Boisgeloup. In the courtyard in front was a mercury fountain designed by Alexander Calder, and Joan Miró also contributed a mural which was placed at the head of a stairway leading to a gallery above.

The immediate reactions of the public were confused, and the press was divided on political grounds. The less numerous critics of the

[1] Herbert Read, 'Picasso's Guernica', *London Bulletin*, No. 6, October 1938.

right wing had no hesitation in condemning it for its intention as well as its appearance, while the left wing supported it, though the less enlightened among them would have preferred a painting which was an obvious call to arms. Others with an equally grave misconception of the poetic nature of the painting hailed it as a form of social art or 'social realism' with a predominant political purpose. Those who appreciated its true nature at once were the intellectuals from many countries, who recognised in it a great work of art and a crystallisation of their feelings about the horrors of war and Fascism, which for them had become almost synonymous.

Zervos produced a number of the *Cahiers d'Art* almost entirely devoted to the painting, and including Dora Maar's admirable photos of its progress, as well as the preliminary studies and small canvases.[1] It contained articles by Zervos himself, Jean Cassou, Georges Duthuit, Pierre Mabille, Michel Leiris, a poem by Paul Eluard and an important contribution by the Spanish Catholic poet José Bergamin. Throughout, their praise for Picasso, who had put on record with such majesty the calamity of Guernica, is tempered with a sense of foreboding. "In a rectangle black and white such as that in which ancient tragedy appeared to us, Picasso sends us our announcement of our mourning: all that we love is going to die, and that is why it was necessary to this degree that all that we love should embody itself, like the effusions of a last farewell, in something unforgettably beautiful." These words of Michel Leiris reveal the gratitude felt towards Picasso for expressing the despair of those who knew themselves and their hopes to be menaced, realising that they were incapable of extricating society from its approaching doom. He had interpreted their forebodings and so made their anxiety more bearable.

Guernica has been compared with other great works such as *The Massacre at Chios* by Delacroix, Gericault's *Raft of the Medusa* and Goya's *Madrid 2 May*. In the scale of its monumental appeal it has much in common with these paintings, but whereas they all used the recognised idiom of their time to portray catastrophes that had occurred, in *Guernica* Picasso found a more universal means of conveying the emotion centred round a given event, and in consequence arrived at a timeless and transcendental image. In addition, the symbolic use of the familiar and humble enabled him to present disaster in an emotional way without overstatement. It is not the horror of an actual occurrence with which we are presented; it is a universal tragedy made vivid to us by the myth he has reinvented and the

[1] *Cahiers d'Art*, 1937, Nos. 4-5.

revolutionary directness with which it is presented. The power of
Guernica will grow.

Return to Mougins

With *Guernica* finished Picasso closed his studio and set out once
more to join Paul and Nusch Eluard at the Hôtel Vaste Horizon at
Mougins, taking Dora Maar with him. A third passenger in the
Hispano was Kasbec, an Afghan hound Picasso had acquired not long
before. The drowsy oriental dignity or sudden alertness of this slender
animal earned him a considerable amount of attention. He never left
his master's side, and his profile with its sharp sensitive nose became
traceable for several years among the human heads that Picasso invented. In fact Picasso has told me jokingly that his two most important
models in these years before and during the Second World War were
Kasbec and Dora Maar.

An early appearance of the beautiful and distinguished features of
Dora Maar in drawings by Picasso was a pen and ink sketch which
has the inscription "Mougins 11 Septembre xxxvi fait par cœur".[1]
His memory did not fail him. It is easily recognisable and has captured
a vision of her fresh intelligent looks, her dark eyes and boyish windswept hair. Many other highly realistic sketches followed, including
an early one in which the lifelike appearance of her head grows
majestically from a body half human, half bird;[2] and in the spring of
1937 her profile becomes recognisable in a drawing of mermaids
peering from the sea at the Minotaur as he loads on to his boat the
body of a girl, nude and limp.[3]

Not long after this, Picasso painted a portrait which glows with
rich and appetising colour.[4] Dora Maar is seated and holds her right
hand to her cheek. The painted fingernails prod gently into the flesh
and hold back her hair, the blackness of which glistens with blues and
greens. There is a smiling expression of relaxed happiness in her face
and her eyes sparkle with animation. So natural does the likeness
seem that it comes as a surprise to realise that the two eyes, one of
which is red and the other blue, are painted both on the same side of
a face which is drawn in profile. They swim together in reds, pinks,
greens, yellows and mauves; colours which are far too brilliant to
be thought of usually as flesh tones but which joyously convey the
radiance of her youth. It is interesting to compare this portrait with
that earlier version of the lover's homage, the portrait of Olga painted

---

[1] See Zervos, *Picasso*, Vol. VIII, p. 137, No. 289.   [2] Ibid., p. 140, No. 297.
[3] Plate XV, 8.   [4] Plate XV, 2.

twenty years before. The new idiom, in which colour and form are charged with poetic associations, surpassing the mere fact that it is also a remarkable likeness, adds qualities which are lacking in the masterful but conventional technique of the earlier painting. Even in his desire for a literal expression, Picasso had found the means of using the discoveries of cubism to great advantage.

During the next weeks at Mougins Picasso's energy, in no way sapped by the ordeal of *Guernica*, expressed itself not only in his physical enjoyment of the unfailing sunshine but also in the constant invention of his mind. Unlike the previous visit, when he had been content to make drawings in a small room with no more than the strict essentials, he installed himself in the only room with a balcony in the hotel. When he emerged on to the terrace for meals he would tell his friends, who were then occupying the entire hotel, what he had been doing. Sometimes he had painted a landscape of the little town with its towers and houses grouped against the sky, but more often he would announce that he had made a portrait. As a reaction to his recent preoccupation with tragedy, he was seized with a diabolical playfulness. The 'portraits' were most frequently of Dora Maar, but at other times he would announce that his model was Eluard or Nusch or Lee Miller.[1] The paintings were strangely like their models but distorted and disguised by surprising inventions. Eluard first appeared in the traditional costume of an Arlesienne, and a few days later, in a second painting, he was dressed as a peasant woman suckling a cat.[2] Nusch had been given the hat of a Niçoise and her eyes, so often half closed with laughter, had become bright-coloured Mediterranean fish. In each case, beneath the buffoonery, there was a masterly handling of colour and form as well as a likeness, the reasons for which were almost impossible to define. The profile of Lee Miller seemed all the more recognisable when combined with large liquid eyes that had been allowed to run with wet paint and an enormous smile from a pair of bright green lips. It was by a combination of characteristics set out in hieroglyphic shorthand that the person in question became ludicrously recognisable.

Picasso was again happy in the unpretentious surroundings of Mougins. He was able to enjoy at his leisure the warmth of affection and animation which Eluard infused among his friends. "The poet is he who inspires far more than he who is inspired" was Eluard's favourite way of describing that uncalculating generosity of spirit of which he himself was an example. Again the association between two

[1] Plate XVI, 6.   [2] Plate XVI, 4.

characters, poet and painter, who each had so much to give was fertile, and it was reinforced by Eluard's contempt for the ivory tower and his interest in the cause which Picasso had particularly at heart.

Though Picasso enjoys company he also needs independence and solitude. Not infrequently he would disappear. Sometimes Marcel the chauffeur would take him to Nice to pay a call on Matisse, and sometimes he would wander all night with Dora Maar along the deserted promenades of Antibes or Juan-les-Pins.

In the morning the beaches provided the main attraction. Sunbathing with the party of friends from Mougins and frequent dips in the sea would be the prelude to searches along the beach for pebbles, shells and roots or anything that had been transformed by the action of the waves. The small neat well-built physique of Picasso was at home in these surroundings. His well-bronzed skin, his agile controlled movement, his athletic figure and small shapely hands and feet seemed to belong to the Mediterranean scene as though he were the reincarnation of the hero of an ancient myth. During one of his wanderings with Dora they found among the rocks, not far from an old refuse dump, the bleached skull of an ox which had been scoured by the sea. With his usual delight in disguises Picasso, closing his eyes, posed for Dora to take his photograph, holding in one hand the skull and in the other a staff such as he had put into the hand of the blind Minotaur.

On another occasion Picasso returned to the hotel with a monkey, which for a while became such an absorbing companion that Dora finally grew jealous. The animal had joined them as one of the family and was taken everywhere with them until one day it became extremely nervous in company with Kasbec on the beach and bit Picasso's finger. By a coincidence it was reported the same day in the local paper that the king of some small state had died of poisoning from a monkey's bite. With his usual prudence in face of a threat to his health and in deference to Dora Maar, he promptly returned the monkey to the shop it had come from.

Picasso's love of monkeys has been permanent. Watching these animals one day in the Jardin des Plantes in Paris, Dora Maar remarked to him that she thought she saw a connection between their looks and the distortions of the Blue period, such as the elongated limbs and fingers, the crossed arms and the attitude of crouching in fear. "Oh yes!" he replied, "so you have noticed that!" Certainly among the Harlequins of the Circus period, the ape appears as one of the family and later reappears climbing the ladder in the drop curtain for *Parade*.

To Picasso it is not only the appearance and the anatomy of monkeys that counts, he enjoys them as caricatures of human beings. When he finds himself in company with friends, after the first polite formalities have been exchanged he says sometimes, half in joke, "so here we are in the monkey cage". Again he does not spare himself in this comparison: in a lithograph of 1954 of the *Artist and his Model* the painter has become a monkey.[1] Man Ray tells how one day he was present when a Swiss psychiatrist asked Picasso what he thought was the relationship between the drawings, which he had brought, of some of his patients and modern tendencies in art. The reaction of Picasso was to say nothing. Turning his back he proceeded to mime with convincing realism the gestures of a long-armed ape, and with a crayon he produced a meaningless scribble which he thrust at the professor with a chuckle.

The Autumn in Paris

Finally, late in September the modest room which had served as bedroom and studio was emptied of the accumulation which had piled up during the summer. This consisted of painting materials, easels, a great number of canvases including portraits and landscapes, drawings and sketches, pebbles and shells carved or engraved with a penknife, and strange objects of many kinds, including the skull of the ox. All these were packed carefully into the Hispano and the return trip to Paris began more reluctantly than the journey south. The day before, Paul Rosenberg who had also been staying on the coast had called, and was shown the brilliant canvases from which he had the right to take first choice. He reserved a large number without hesitation.

The relaxation of Mougins had not deadened Picasso's anxieties nor had it made him forget the train of thought that had developed during the painting of *Guernica*. Before going south but after the picture was finished he had made a large etching and some drawings of the head of a woman weeping, with tears streaming across her cheeks and a handkerchief stuffed between her teeth. On his return he took up the same theme again. As had happened at the time of the *Demoiselles d'Avignon*, he continued for some months to add postscripts to his major work. On 26 October he finished the last version of the theme of the woman weeping.[2] In colour it is very different from the studies made before going to Mougins. The lurid acid effects had been exchanged for brilliant contrasts—red, blue, green and yellow. The result of using colour in a manner so totally unassociated with grief, for

[1] Plate XXIII, 4.   [2] Plate XVII, 2.

a face in which sorrow is evident in every line, is highly disconcerting. As though the tragedy had arrived with no warning, the red and blue hat is decked with a blue flower. The white handkerchief pressed to her face hides nothing of the agonised grimace on her lips: it serves merely to bleach her cheeks with the colour of death. Her fumbling hands knotted with the pain of her emotion join the teardrops that pour from her eyes. Simultaneously they are her fingers, her hand-kerchief and the tears that fall like a curtain of rain heralding the storm. Her eyes like those of Dora Maar are rimmed with black lashes; they nestle in shapes like small boats that have capsized in the tempest, emptying out a river of tears. As the stream follows across the contour of her cheek it passes her ear, the form of which is not unlike a bee come to distil honey from the salt of despair. Finally as we look into the eyes themselves we recognise the reflection of the man-made vul-ture which has changed her delight into unbearable pain. This small picture contains some highly complex images. Its intensity is due again to the clarity with which each statement is made and to the strength and pertinacity of contrasts. Picasso sometimes obtains a dramatic effect by reversing the order to which we are accustomed, as he has done in the centre of the woman's face. Here above the handkerchief there is a jagged black hole between the eyes where we would expect to find them divided by the bridge of the nose. Instead of a ridge he makes a cavity. The breach that he has made in such a vulnerable spot, torn open as though by some projectile, makes a formidable contrast in a face which, though tortured in its expression, shows every sign of vitality.

Paul Eluard and the Spanish War

In Picasso's varied moods, saturnine despondency or sullen rage are most often dispersed by the arrival of a friend. Paul Eluard had been the most frequent visitor throughout the painting of *Guernica* and his ideas, more defiant towards the gathering storm than those of most other poets, were a continual stimulus. To the poem he wrote in the summer of 1937, which has become an almost inseparable companion to Picasso's painting, he gave the title 'The Victory of Guernica'. This was meant ironically and also as a sign of stubborn optimism in the final outcome of a struggle in which, Eluard was convinced, human rights and human love would finally triumph.

To contradict the errors, often deliberate, that were being circu-lated in the press both in Europe and America, Picasso made a state-ment in May 1937. It was issued at the time of an exhibition of Spanish

Republican posters in New York, where it had previously been reported that he was pro-Franco. It began: "The Spanish struggle is the fight of reaction against the people, against freedom. My whole life as an artist has been nothing more than a continuous struggle against reaction and the death of art. . . . In the panel on which I am working and which I shall call *Guernica*, and in all my recent works of art, I clearly express my abhorrence of the military caste which has sunk Spain in an ocean of pain and death. . . . Everyone is acquainted with the barbarous bombardment of the Prado Museum by rebel airplanes and everyone also knows how the militiamen succeeded in saving the art treasures at the risk of their lives. There are no doubts possible here. . . . In Salamanca, Milan Astray cries out, 'Death to Intelligence'. In Granada Garcia Lorca is assassinated. . . ."[1]

Six months later a second statement addressed to the American Artists' Congress was published in the *New York Times*. The last paragraph contained this even more definite confession of faith: "It is my wish at this time to remind you that I have always believed and still believe, that artists who live and work with spiritual values cannot and should not remain indifferent to a conflict in which the highest values of humanity and civilisation are at stake." These words were borne out by Picasso's generosity towards his less fortunate compatriots. He gave large sums for Spanish relief and often sold pictures specially with this aim.

Visits from Paul Eluard and Nusch were a pleasure to Picasso. As a proof of friendship he frequently drew or painted the exquisite charm of Nusch. The drawings were often done while sitting together on the terrace at Mougins. Sometimes in the paintings he would playfully elaborate the portrait, adding allusions to things they had noticed together. These portraits, like many made in the intimacy of his family and those closest to him, are often kept by Picasso to remind him of moments of happiness. With her usual taste for originality and elegance, Nusch one day appeared at the rue des Grands Augustins in a new black dress and hat. On the lapels were two gilt cherubs and the top of the hat was ornamented by a horseshoe. The pale fragile face of Nusch, with her combination of ethereal charm and simple candid high spirits, looked all the more enchanting in the severity of these clothes. Picasso remarked that the hat was shaped like an anvil with the horseshoe in position to be hammered into shape. In the portrait he painted as soon as she had gone he traced the base of the anvil in transparent shadows vertically across the oval shape of the face.[2] The

[1] Quoted by Barr, *op. cit.*, pp. 202 and 264.   [2] Plate XV, 3.

gilt cherubs appeared on the lapels and her dark hair surrounded her head with the movement of clouds.

Visit to Paul Klee

In the autumn of 1937 an unforeseen event made it necessary for Picasso to pay a short visit to Switzerland. As he found himself in the neighbourhood of Paul Klee, he called on him with his friend Bernhard Geiser. After the closing of the Bauhaus, Klee had taken refuge from Nazi tyranny and was living in a suburb of Berne. Although he had watched Picasso's extraordinary career and appreciated the growing influence of his work for many years, the two men had never met. Klee was so modest and retiring in temperament that when he had visited Paris in 1912, attracted by the inventions of the cubists, he had not dared to call on either Braque or Picasso though he greatly admired their achievements. Picasso's talent in particular affected him so deeply that he tended to avoid seeing too much of his work from fear of being caught in its spell.

Living in exile and harassed by political events, Klee's health had already begun to suffer, but he greeted Picasso with great warmth. "He was magnificent, very dignified and worthy of respect for his attitude and his work," Picasso told me. The studio was pleasant and, unlike his own, very tidy and meticulously arranged, in fact to Picasso it was more like a laboratory than a studio. Frau Klee entertained them by playing Bach, and the two painters parted with their mutual esteem greater than ever.

Picasso's description of Klee as "Pascal-Napoleon" which has been reported[1] is not, as might be thought, a cryptic reference to the character or achievements of either of these great men, but, he assured me recently, rather a comment on his looks which reminded him of them both. He also denied having made to Klee the trite remark which has been attributed to him: "You are the master of the small size, I am the master of the large."

Mougins, 1938

In the summer of 1938, with the Eluards, Picasso again sought the secluded hospitality of Mougins. He painted portraits of Nusch, sometimes producing more than one in the same day.[2] The now familiar arrangement of two eyes in the same profile was applied with tenderness and respect for the beauty of her features. At the same time he

[1] See W. Grohmann, *Klee*, Lund Humphries.
[2] See *Cahiers d'Art*, 1938, Nos. 3-10, pp. 180-3.

made portraits of the three dark-eyed daughters of the house, the youngest of whom, Ines,[1] accompanied Picasso to Paris and has remained at the rue des Grands Augustins with her husband to this day as his housekeeper. In addition, he showed unceasing interest in the features of Dora Maar, which he saw with untiring freshness of vision, giving them a rich variety of interpretation. The portraits he made of her ranged from lifelike drawings in the classic style to distortions based always on observation of the ever-changing light and expression in her face.

Picasso was also impressed by the bucolic look of the village youths who sat in the cool shadow of the plane trees in the village square. It was they who inspired a series of grotesque heads of men sucking lollipops.[2] Always enjoying the absurdity of such contrasts which corresponded to the underlying uneasiness in his thoughts, he accentuated the uncouth coarseness of their features and the greediness with which they took their childish pleasures.

This uneasiness became most apparent in a large picture completed in February of the same year. The *Girl with a Cock*,[3] painted in vivid blues, pinks and greens, is a striking though indirect reflection of the violence of the Spanish war, which was then going from bad to worse. To quote Barr: "Through the power of Picasso's imagery what might seem perverse and minor sadism takes on the character of hieratic ritual, perhaps even symbolic in significance."[4] The moronic ruthlessness of this female holding on her knees a trussed cock she is about to slaughter is highly disquieting. There is no feature in the picture to attenuate the brutality of the scene, yet surprisingly, as Meyer Schapiro has pointed out, there is something in the outline of the girl's face and the straight black hair that perhaps suggests Picasso's own profile, in which case this is another, though less convincing, example of the subconscious process of identification that we have already noticed in the monster of *Dream and Lie of Franco*.

During 1938, a year of great activity, Picasso began to decorate forms with small lines that suggest basketwork. In certain drawings the whole surface of the paper is covered with tracery which gives angular crystalline shapes to the figures and their surroundings. As in the earlier "anatomies" the human form is dislocated and pieced together again with great freedom. Often the breasts of the women are

---

[1] See *Cahiers d'Art*, 1938, Nos. 3-10, p. 187.
[2] Plate XVIII, 3; see also *Cahiers d'Art*, 1938, Nos. 3-10, pp. 163-6.
[3] Plate XVII, 5.
[4] Barr, *Picasso: Fifty Years of his Art*, p. 212.

accentuated by spirals which recall Picasso's predilection as a child for drawing these curves which resembled his favourite form of cake.[1] Among shapes that are mostly rectangular the spirals attract the eye and gain a significance in addition to their association with food.

Guernica *Travels*

After the close of the Paris exhibition *Guernica* was shown in Norway in the summer of 1938. On its return an exhibition was planned in London, sponsored by a strong committee of left-wing politicians, scientists, artists and poets. When the moment arrived for the painting to be shipped to London with sixty-seven of the preparatory paintings, sketches and studies, the political situation, culminating in Chamberlain's visit to Munich, looked so sinister that I telegraphed to ask Picasso what he wished us to do. His reply was immediate and definite. I was to continue with the arrangements. The purpose of the picture was to draw attention to the horrors of war and it must take its chance. The exhibition opened at the date planned, announcing itself as under the auspices of the National Joint Committee for Spanish Relief.

For the first time those who were not endowed with an understanding of his work joined enthusiastically with others who had been convinced for years of the greatness of Picasso and who admired this monumental proof of his genius. In general the studies made a more direct appeal than did the picture itself, which demanded a greater effort to be understood. Yet the people who came to see the exhibition in large numbers were deeply impressed, very few went away without something of its emotional power making itself felt to them. When it closed in the West End, a second exhibition, this time opened by Major (now Earl) Attlee, was held in the Whitechapel Art Gallery. Here the workers of the East End had their first chance of seeing original works by Picasso, and for this reason as well as their interest in the cause of Spain the gallery was constantly crowded.

The New Burlington Galleries, where the picture was shown in the West End, had two large adjoining halls. By coincidence the larger of the two, which had not been available for *Guernica*, turned out to have been booked by Franco's supporters for an exhibition of a large painting by Zuluaga who by then had become the champion of academic art in Spain. A large, dull and conventional composition, whose purpose was to exalt the military prowess of Franco, hung at the end of the room, its subject was the defenders of the Alcazar of Toledo.

[1] Plate XVIII, 1.

Flags, guns, uniforms and religious images, adding arrogance to incompetent painting, made a contrast with the lack of any such bombast in the room next door where the naked tragedy of war revealed itself through women and children. It was gratifying to the promoters of the *Guernica* exhibition that the rival show remained nearly empty throughout.

After two additional exhibitions in Leeds and in Liverpool the great picture left for New York, where it was shown in the most complete retrospective exhibition of Picasso's work that had till then been collected together, at the Museum of Modern Art. Here it joined that other great picture painted thirty years before, *Les Demoiselles d'Avignon*, which had been bought by the same museum a few years earlier. As the outbreak of the European war made it impossible to return the painting to Europe, Picasso was glad to leave it where it could be seen and appreciated. It remained in America on loan until it was brought back to Europe for the great exhibition at the Pavillon de Marsan in Paris in 1955. After a tour of European cities it has now returned to New York.

Illness and Recovery

Sabartès gives an intimate account of the weeks of misery spent by Picasso in the icy winter of 1938, when a prolonged attack of sciatica kept him immobilised in bed in great pain. Sabartès described Picasso's restlessness, his sleepless nights, the procession of visitors who all knew of some certain cure, and finally the appearance of a doctor who managed almost miraculously to cure him instantaneously by the cauterisation of a nerve.

A few days before the attack, he painted two still-lifes. These are similar in subject-matter, except that the first contains two sources of light: a candle, and a version of the sun resembling the white rectangle of a paper kite with a fringe of black rays. The other objects are the same in both; on a table which fills the lower part of the picture, a palette and brushes lie on an open book, and beside on a pedestal stands the head of a bull. In the first version the head is black with lines scratched into the paint to define its eyes and snout.[1] In the second painting, done a week later, the bull's head has the appearance of having been flayed alive.[2] Its unprotected eyes stare from a livid mass of red flesh, exposed relentlessly to a crude light which is too strong and too universal to come from the candle.

Picasso soon recovered after his illness and continued to create

[1] Raynal, *Picasso*, Skira, p. 102.   [2] Plate XVIII, 2.

images of people and of animals with great violence and frequent allusions to cruelty, such as the painting of a ferocious cat carrying a lacerated and fluttering bird.[1] The half-human face of the cat with its shifty eyes is a terrifying vision of calculated brutality made all the more powerful by the direct, childlike manner in which it is drawn.

In the spring Picasso had worked in the evenings at the studio of Lacourière. His project was to reproduce in coloured engravings the texts of poems he had written not long before, decorated with drawings in the margins. The difficulties of this complicated technique were exactly what he needed to excite his inventive powers. Sabartès tells us how his ideas became steadily more ambitious as he became enthralled by his work. Vollard was called in as editor. He willingly offered his services, leaving Picasso an entirely free hand in the choice of paper, layout and every other point in the production. To make his work easier, the press was brought back from Boisgeloup and installed under Lacourière's supervision in a wing of the apartment in the rue des Grands Augustins, which was at that time being made more habitable with central heating. Even with all these preparations it would have been a long time before the project could have been completed. As it happened, Picasso became interested by other means of expression which prolonged the process, until one day, irritated by the technical problems of putting his work together as a book, the calculations involved and the interminable length of the whole process he announced to Sabartès that there was no question of the book's being finished. The engravings have so far never been published, they remain stacked away at the present time in the rue des Grands Augustins.[2]

In July the usual urge to leave Paris drew Picasso to the Mediterranean coast. He took an apartment in Antibes, but hardly had he settled in when he heard of the sudden death of Vollard. The next morning Sabartès was surprised to find him back in Paris. Picasso,

[1] Plate XVII, 3.

[2] In a recent conversation in Cannes between Picasso and Dr. Bernhard Geiser (the editor of the catalogue raisonné of Picasso's graphic art), Dr. Geiser asked how he could have access to these and other works which he needed to photograph so as to make his catalogue complete. Picasso with charming nonchalance said, "how is it possible, they are all in Paris, many of them stacked away in a bank, even here I have difficulty in finding things and there no-one could do so without me. It would be easier," he added, "for me to do them all again. How often has it happened that someone has called for a drawing that I had promised to do for him and although it was done, it has been impossible for me to find it, so to put matters right, while out of the room looking for it, I have quickly done another which has been accepted just the same. '

ant reason

however, did not stay long. A few days after the funeral a telegram from a friend in the Midi arrived announcing a bullfight at Fréjus. This was the decisive factor that started him on another hasty all-night road trip with Marcel at the wheel. For the first time Sabartès, overcoming his distaste for travelling, went with him.

The first few days after their arrival at Antibes were spent in showing the attractions of the coast, such as Monte Carlo, Nice, Cannes and Mougins, to his old friend. After that Picasso started work. In bourgeois style the apartment was crowded with tea-tables and depressing ornaments. These suddenly became offensive to him, and with the help of Sabartès and Marcel, the imitation antiques, bibelots and pictures were stacked away, leaving room for him to crowd the room with his own kind of disorder. The large walls stripped to the flowered wallpaper were an incentive to paint another picture of great dimensions. He bought an enormous roll of canvas which he pinned up and began to cover at an incredible speed with a subject that he had found nearby.[1] His evening walks with Dora Maar had led him to discover the little fishermen's harbour where they prepared their boats for the night fishing, which was done at that time with strong acetylene lamps. The purpose of the lamp shining on the water was to attract fish that could be speared with a trident from the boat. By this means, even close in among the rocks, the sea yielded creatures of wonderful colour and strange shapes glistening under the powerful light, while insects such as beetles and large moths flapped about in its glare. This was the scene that Picasso chose for the big canvas and every day he concentrated his energies on its realisation.

The painting did not however hinder him from taking his morning bathe. As I was also in Antibes, we met daily on the beach and exchanged views on the political situation. The surrender of Barcelona and the defeat of the last faint hopes of the Republicans had filled us all with an intense depression, which was in some degree relieved by the arrival of Fin and Javier Vilato, two of Picasso's nephews, who after crossing the Pyrenees with the defeated army, had escaped from internment by the French. Their joy at finding their uncle and the antics they played on the beach in their irrepressible high spirits helped temporarily to disperse the increasing gloom.

Although no-one could be mad enough to feel optimistic about the future, the news of ultimatums and mobilisation came as a sudden shock a few days later. Picasso came every evening to sit with his friends at the café in the main square of Antibes, and enjoy for an hour

[1] Plate XVIII, 7.

or so in the cool air his abstemious choice of coffee or mineral water. The conversation which formerly had been varied and amusing from then on had only one theme. Plans for departure were being discussed on all sides. Within a day most of our friends had gone and the town began to fill with troops, while on the rocks close to the fashionable hotels and bathing pools Senegalese soldiers had already set up their machine guns.

Picasso remained undecided. He was particularly annoyed to have been interrupted just as he had begun to see more clearly the path his new work was to take. Joking with us he said they must be making a war just to annoy him when he was starting on a good line. As Sabartès said pertinently: "What he dreaded in war was its menace to his work; as though peace were indispensable to this being who cannot live without mental strife."[1]

The evening after the announcement of Hitler's invasion of Poland I went up to Picasso's flat. The new painting of the night fishing seemed finished but other large panels of canvas pinned to the walls remained untouched. In the centre of the picture two fishermen in a boat, one peering with a hideous grimace into the water and the other making frantic efforts to secure their catch, were being watched by two girls in gay frocks. One of them, wheeling her bicycle along the quay, licked a double ice-cream cone with a sharp blue tongue like a bee drinking honey from a flower. The decoy lamp, to the fish a treacherous substitute for the sun, hung ambiguously on the horizon. Over its yellow surface Picasso had drawn a red spiral, his early symbol for a source of nourishment. As I looked out of the windows, the towers of the palace of the Grimaldi stood out faintly, coloured with tenebrous blues, purples and greens, against the sky, just as they were in the picture. From the balcony could be seen the old town with its street lighting partly dimmed as a first measure of defence. The angular shapes of the stone walls lit from the street-corners had a striking resemblance to analytical cubist paintings. The architecture of these ancient buildings seemed to have grown to look like these pictures, just as Gertrude Stein was said to have grown to look like her portrait.

We said goodbye, consoling ourselves with promises to keep in touch, and left Picasso to his packing. He had decided to risk a crowded train journey back to Paris, leaving Marcel to return with the car loaded with extra petrol, trunks, boxes and the picture, *Night Fishing at Antibes*, rolled up on the back seat. Six years were to pass before Picasso saw the Mediterranean again.

[1] Sabartès, *Portraits*, p. 148.

CHAPTER XI

SECOND WORLD WAR—ROYAN AND PARIS
(1939–1945)

Royan

WHEN PICASSO reached Paris after the discomfort of an all-day
journey in a desperately overcrowded train in intense heat, he found a
changed city, and for the second time in his life a war with Germany
imminent. Again his French friends were on the point of being
mobilised. Some like Eluard had already left Paris to join their regiments. Faced with the terrors of immediate bombing, upon which he
had meditated so thoroughly in painting *Guernica*, and realising the
futility of staying in a city where rumours and preparations for
hostilities occupied everyone's thoughts, he set out by road for Royan.
Three days of anxious conversations with friends had convinced him
that he had better seek shelter outside the city. This little port at the
mouth of the Gironde some seventy-five miles north of Bordeaux
seemed a place sufficiently remote and yet near enough to keep in touch
with Paris.

Sabartès describes how after leaving in the Hispano about midnight
they arrived at Saintes, close to their destination, in the early morning
to find there the same preoccupation and anxiety. After a breakfast
served by waiters already in uniform they continued to Royan.
Picasso was relieved to find himself back in the sunshine and again
by the sea. They found rooms for his party, which included Dora
Maar and the hound Kasbec, on the outskirts of the little port near the
station. In the haste of their departure it had been impossible to bring
the materials required for painting, but unable to remain idle Picasso
ransacked the local shops for paper and sketchbooks until he had found
what he wanted. The following day, returning to the only activity
that could bring him some comfort, he was again at work.

The first drawings he made were of horses. In traditional style,
France mobilised her forces from the fields as well as her manpower.
Everywhere on the road they had seen processions of requisitioned
horses, which, as Picasso remarked to Sabartès, certainly understood
that they were not going towards their usual work, in spite of their air
of submission. Once more the horse was the victim of a calamity
brought upon it by the incomprehensible behaviour of its masters.

But Picasso was not allowed to find tranquillity even at this distance from Paris. Within a few days he was troubled by the announcement that as a foreigner he required a special permit to stay in Royan. His fear of finding himself in the wrong with official regulations induced him to hurry back to Paris with Sabartès to obtain the permits that had become necessary. During the day they spent there Picasso had his first taste of an air-raid warning which kept him immobilised for at least an hour. Even so he had time to collect the permits and a few precious objects from the rue la Boètie before taking the road back to the coast.

The rooms in which he lived for the next few months were cramped and badly lit. The town itself apart from its harbour had few attractions. Accepting the situation, however, he settled down to a regular routine in which the main factor, work, was punctuated with meals and walks round the town, accompanied by Dora Maar, Sabartès and the docile Kasbec. As they visited the harbour and explored the markets one of their main pleasures was to search among the mysterious piles on the stalls of the junk merchants, an endless occupation which yielded unexpected finds.

The spasmodic preparations for the defence of the town were watched by them during their wanderings along the beaches. When Sabartès remarked one day that they had begun at last to dig trenches as shelters against bombardments, Picasso answered mockingly: "It's only you who would imagine such things. No, mon vieux, no . . . you don't understand. These are excavations to see if they can find trenches, nothing else. You'll see all right. As soon as they find one, they'll take it off to the museum and if there's no museum for it, they'll make one especially."[1]

The same lack of respect for those who were professionally in charge of the fortunes of the state was expressed more tersely in a conversation with Matisse, whom he met by chance some months later in Paris, when the war had suddenly taken an alarming turn for the worse. It was in May 1940 and the two painters, who had not seen each other for some months, looked anxiously into each other's faces. Matisse reported their conversation in these words:

' "Where are you going like that?" said Picasso.

"To my tailor," I [Matisse] replied. My reply surprised him, he seemed scared.

"What! but don't you know that the front is completely broken through, the army has been turned upside down, it's a rout, the

[1] Sabartès, *Portraits*, p. 222.

Germans are approaching Soissons, tomorrow they will perhaps be in Paris?"

"But even then, our generals, what about our generals? What are they doing?" I said.

Picasso looked at me very seriously: "Our generals, that's the professors of the Ecole des Beaux Arts." '[1]

From the experience of both artists, no more complete condemnation of the military leaders as stubborn and slavish followers of a decayed tradition could have been made.

Discomfort and the shortage of painting materials did not hinder Picasso during this first autumn while the war hung fire. Squatting on the floor for lack of an easel, as he had done in the days of the Bateau Lavoir, he painted on planks or hardboard when canvas was lacking; and for palettes used ready-made wooden seats of chairs, which he liked better for the purpose than the conventional type. The paintings could not be large in their dimensions, but before the end of October he had produced an astonishing portrait of Sabartès in a ruff as a courtier of Philip II;[2] a portrait of Dora Maar, powerful in its arrangement of simultaneous profile and full face; paintings of nude women and women seated in chairs; and still-lifes of fruit and fish. He had also filled many sketch-books with drawings, including some careful studies of the skinned heads and jawbones of sheep.

The portrait of Sabartès was again full of ironical good humour, a mixture of teasing and affection which was a well-established relationship between the two friends.

"The next one", he told Sabartès, "will be bigger, full length, life size and in oils of course, to season this kind of frizzled lettuce collar round your neck, as well as salt, pepper &c. to taste, [there will be] the nude woman, the greyhound, and the complete costume you wore when you strutted valiantly in the corridors of the Escorial. That's a long time ago, but we can still picture it."[3] The patient unassuming Sabartès quietly enjoyed these extravagant but lifelike versions of himself in fancy dress.

The melancholy of autumn in a small seaside resort, thoughts which continually took him back to his friends, and the vast quantities of pictures and other things precious to him that he had left in Paris, compelled Picasso to return once more to the rue la Boétie in October.

[1] André Verdet, 'Picasso et ses environs', *Les Lettres Nouvelles*, Paris, July-August 1955.
[2] Plate XVIII, 8.
[3] Sabartès, *Portraits*, p. 212.

On this occasion he took the time necessary to sort out the canvases and objects he valued most and to place them in the strong rooms of a bank, where they were housed in safety during the rest of the war. Some in fact remained there very much longer owing to his reluctance to bring out all his treasures and his uncertainty as to where to house them.

When he returned to Royan after that visit, bringing with him a heavy load of canvases and an easel, he found that his quarters were hopelessly inadequate, and after further search he rented rooms on the top floor of a villa called 'Les Voiliers' which later in the war was destroyed by Allied bombs. Looking out to sea, it had a splendid view over the port. His motive in taking this apartment was not however the view—"that would be fine for someone who thought himself a painter", he explained to Sabartès—but rather the light which had been lacking in his former lodgings. Although he spent hours watching the coming and going of the ferry boat, the changing reflections on the water and the long curving sweep of the bay with its hotels and villas gilded by the sun, he felt uneasy about being the only one to enjoy a scene which was not essential to him for his inspiration.

Hardly had he installed himself in his new quarters and got used to the more spacious, well-lit room he had taken over as his studio, than he was seized by a fresh desire to return to Paris and arrange his affairs. The greater part of the month of February 1940 was spent there, and after a fortnight in March when he was in Royan, he settled in again at the rue la Boètie until 16 May. The war had slowed down all intellectual activities in Paris. Although in April some water-colours and gouaches by Picasso were shown at the Galerie M.A.I., very few exhibitions were being held, and publications such as the one Eluard had planned with Picasso, of a book of his poems called *Fleurs d'Obéissance*,[1] failed to materialise. In America, however, the great retrospective exhibition planned by Alfred Barr at the Museum of Modern Art for the autumn of 1939 opened in New York. This impressive collection, which included *Guernica*, made a great impression on the thousands of visitors who saw it there and later in other cities throughout the United States.

A few friends still remained in Paris. Zervos continued his activities in a limited way. Man Ray, Georges Hugnet and a few other surrealists, who for one reason or another had not been called up, re-

[1] In a letter to me dated 31 Mai '40 Eluard, then stationed at Mignères (Loiret) says: "Je comptais publier les *Fleurs d'Obéissance* avec Picasso. Celà paraît compromis, c'est le moins qu'on puisse dire."

mained engrossed in their work and met Picasso frequently on his daily visits to the cafés of St. Germain des Prés.

A review edited by Hugnet and published by Zervos[1] appeared during the winter. To the third and last number, in company with Miró, Arp, and Chagall, Picasso contributed a vignette as a decoration to poems by Pierre Reverdy. These small consolations, and occasional visits to Paris from Eluard and others on leave, provided moments when Picasso could renew his friendships. They were however of short duration. Hitler's blitzkrieg was at hand. Having already occupied Denmark and Norway in April, on 10 May the Nazi troops marched into Holland, Belgium and Luxemburg and the military situation rapidly became catastrophic for the Allies. From day to day the German divisions drew nearer to France until on 15 May news of the break-through at Sedan made it obvious that Paris was in danger. The day after, which was the same day he had met Matisse in the street, Picasso left on the night train for Royan.

The German Occupation

After the disastrous ending of the Spanish Civil War hardly a year before, Picasso was now to witness the defeat of his adopted country, France, by forces similar to those that had overcome the Republican Government of Spain. The chaos brought about by military defeat and the misery of thousands of refugees culminated for him with the arrival in Royan of the German troops. From the windows of 'Les Voiliers' Picasso saw the arrival of the round steel helmets of their scouts followed by the sinister paraphernalia of tanks, guns and dust-covered lorries. They filed past to their new headquarters on the quay nearby. As he watched he said to Sabartès: "At bottom, if you look carefully, they are very stupid. All those troops, those machines, that power and that uproar to get here! We arrived with less noise. . . . What nonsense! . . . Who was preventing them from acting like us?"[2]

The absurdity of the arrogance that led these invaders to believe that because they had conquered the French armies they had also conquered the spirit of France served as a stimulus to Picasso in taking the only path left open. By returning to his work with even greater concentration he affirmed his contempt for those who had openly declared that they considered his influence to be degenerate and evil. During the two months after his return to Royan on 17 May, he filled many

[1] *L'Usage de la Parole*, Editions Cahiers d'Art, Paris, December 1939–April 1940.
[2] Sabartès, *Portraits*, p. 229.

sketchbooks with drawings which contained a new violence and a power equal to that of his fury over *Guernica*. One such book, reproduced later by the *Cahiers d'Art*, contains some very moving pen-and-wash drawings, in which the head of a girl inspired by Dora Maar goes through a series of permutations. The head is in varying degrees split in two, seeming to look both out into the world and into itself with apprehensive tear-filled eyes. While one part of the face is full and tender, with soft lips and cheeks, the other, with its long-drawn-out nose ending in curling nostrils, resembles Kasbec's elegant snout.[1]

This marriage of woman and beast in one image culminated in a large canvas, for which there are drawings in this same book, known as *Seated Woman dressing her hair*.[2] In spite of an earlier date on the back of the canvas the picture was actually painted between 4 and 19 June. By restricting his colours severely to mauve, purple and green, Picasso presents us with a firmly constructed, monumental form of aggressive appearance. The nude female squatting on the floor has a sphinx-like presence. The anatomy is built of shapes that, like petrified fruit, are both swollen and hard. Two monstrous feet in the foreground are thrust out in front of a body in which belly, buttocks and breasts make the four corners of a construction which seems to pivot like a swastika round a point on the breastbone. Above it towers a ruthless head, with human lips on one side and on the other the snout of a beast. Its double personality is united at its apex into a small forehead with two insensitive squinting eyes and two hands tugging behind at its black mane of hair.

Other drawings express a mood of increasing vehemence. On 28 June, four days after the last fighting had taken place not far from Royan, Picasso filled a page with diabolically distorted female nudes and heads.[3] At the top is a row of skulls constructed with his own invented anatomy. The fleshless bones of one, crowned with a luxuriant shock of black hair, make one of the most ghastly and heartbreaking images he has ever produced. Skulls, scenes of rape and demented faces, distorted with diabolical invention, fill the rest of the book nearly to the last pages. Here towards the end of August there are signs of a more gentle mood. Distortion is allied to charm and the smiling eyes and lips of Dora are again recognisable. From these days also dates a landscape, the *Café at Royan*,[4] which glows with sunlight, a reminder of his previous saying that he was not always occupied with gloom.

[1] *Carnet de dessins de Picasso* (Facsimile), ed. Cahiers d'Art, Paris, 1948, 24 July 1940.   [2] Plate XIX, 2.   [3] Plate XIX, 1.   [4] Plate XVIII, 5.

Return to Paris

With the signing of the armistice between Hitler and Pétain there was no further reason for Picasso to remain in voluntary exile at Royan. Invitations came from the United States and Mexico offering an escape from the uncertainty of life in occupied France. He refused them all, however, and as soon as travel was again permitted, late in August, he left Royan for good and returned to Paris.

To begin with he settled in at the rue la Boètie, returning daily to the rue des Grands Augustins to work. The great room where he had painted *Guernica* was now emptied of all that could be safely stored away, and the monumental stove with its complicated chimney standing in the centre was the only remaining ornament; a feature which as fuel became scarce was to turn into a useless relic. The difficulty of finding any means of transport between the rue la Boètie and the rue des Grands Augustins, however, soon induced Picasso to shut up the apartment and install himself as best he could in the rooms adjoining his studio. He remained living and working in these surroundings, noble in proportions, but lacking in comfort, for the duration of the war.

Throughout the Nazi occupation Picasso was unmolested by the invaders. His reputation as a revolutionary could alone have been enough to condemn him. He was the renowned master of all that Hitler hated and feared most in modern art, the most formidable creator of the 'Kunstbolschewismus' or 'degenerate art' which for years the Nazi régime had tried to suppress. In addition, though at this time he had made no allegiance to communism, he had clearly shown his hatred for Franco, the dictator whom Hitler hoped to gain as an ally. However, the invaders took no action against him. Possibly from fear of criticism from America or from French intellectuals, whom the Nazis at that time believed they must make some attempt to woo, Picasso was allowed to return to Paris and to live there with the same limited degree of freedom as the French. The policy was to attempt a liaison with French artists, but any such ill-timed advances as offers of tours of Germany or even extra allowances of food and coal were steadfastly refused by Picasso, though in some cases they were accepted by artists who had formerly been his friends. He told them, "a Spaniard is never cold".

It is significant that Picasso was forbidden throughout the occupation to show his work in public. The most serious attacks that were made on him came not directly from the Nazis but from those

collaborationist critics who under the new régime found places of
authority and ample encouragement for their reactionary thoughts.
To quote André Lhote, who had been a cubist from early days and
who now took a stand with Picasso: "Never, never was independent
art . . . exposed to more idiotic annoyance or ridiculed in terms more
absurd. . . . 'To the ashcan with Matisse!' and 'To the loony-bin with
Picasso!' were the fashionable cries."[1]

Picasso remained unmoved, nor was he overawed when members
of the Gestapo searched his apartment and Nazi critics and officers
called on him. During one visit a remark from an inquisitive Nazi
officer brought a retort from Picasso which has become famous. Seeing a photo of Guernica lying on the table the German asked: "Did
you do this?" "No . . . you did."

Of other callers, Picasso said later, "Sometimes there were some
Boches who came to see me on the pretext of admiring my pictures.
I distributed among them postcards reproducing my canvas Guernica
and I told them, 'Take them away. Souvenir! souvenir!' "[2]

Towards the end of the occupation high-ranking officers who before the war had visited Paris to collect impressionist paintings called
on him. They arrived in civilian clothes and announced themselves
politely, although they were fully aware of Picasso's reputation and
sympathies. They asked suspiciously after Paul Rosenberg, whom
Picasso said he believed to be in America, and made him uneasy by
commenting on the bronzes they saw in the studio. Picasso said
nervously, "they won't help you make your big guns." "No," one
of them answered, "but they could make little ones." Nothing however came of this threat, and Picasso's clandestine supply of bronze
through loyal friends continued.

Picasso as Playwright

One effect of Pétain's armistice was that some friends could now
return to Paris to help refill the void caused when others had fled.
With the demobilisation of the French army, Eluard was released,
and with other poets and painters he found his way back. Picasso's
uncompromising yet detached attitude made him the centre of their

[1] The attacks on Picasso came notably from the painter Vlaminck in an
article in *Comoedia* 6 June 1942; from Vanderpyl in the *Mercure de France*,
autorisation No. 64460/9-42; from the old art critic Camille Mauclair in *La
Crise de l'Art Moderne, imprimerie spéciale du C.E.A.*, Paris, 1944; and from
the aged American pro-fascist expatriate, John Hemming Fry.
[2] 'Picasso n'est pas officier dans l'armée française', interview with Simone
Téry, *Lettres Françaises*, Paris, 24 March 1945, quoted in Barr, *Picasso*, p. 226.

activities and their hopes. Without taking an active part himself, he became a symbol to those who secretly and precariously, in face of constant dangers, began to think of the future and organise a resistance which would lead eventually to the liberation of France.

Restriction of movement and shortage of food heralded a period of severe privation. Thrown on their own limited resources and obliged to invent a new way of life within the artificial boundaries of occupied France, many artists remained for a while stunned and inactive. For Picasso, however, the necessity to react against an atmosphere which oppressed him urged him to find ways in which he could create, even though destruction was the order of the day. His zeal to create was in a sense dependent upon destruction. Who had dared to dismember the human form more completely than he? Yet such acts of violence in art led to a new creation. They gave to Picasso the destroyer the means to evoke life. And so when disillusionment and despair were in the ascendant they too had to be destroyed by the healing power of his art.

Although Picasso claims that he writes only when for some reason he is unable to draw or paint, at Royan he wrote poetry in spite of his fertile production as a painter. Again, on Tuesday 14 January 1941, during the long cold evening which followed a vigorous day's work on his canvases, he picked up an old exercise book and started to give his friends a surprise such as none had dreamed of. Systematically he began with the title *Desire caught by the tail*, and, as a frontispiece, a pen and ink portrait of the author, seen as a fly on the ceiling would see him, seated at his table, his glasses protruding from his forehead and his pen in hand.[1] He then began to write a play which he had conceived either as a tragic farce or a farcical tragedy. Act I scene 1 begins with a drawing of a table laid for a meal which consists of ham, fish, wine and a man's head on a plate. Beneath the table dangle the legs of the characters whose names are inscribed down the side of the page. The hero of the play is a certain Big Foot, writer-poet who lives in an "artistic studio". His friend called the Onion is also his rival in his passion for the heroine, the Tart. She has a Cousin and two friends, Fat and Thin Anxiety. The other singular characters are Round Piece, the Two Bow-wows, Silence and the Curtains.

This strange company is almost entirely preoccupied with three things—hunger, cold and love. Their conversation, which is often charged with poetic metaphor, is at other times brutally crude. The action which centres round love and feasting ends inevitably in

[1] Plate XIX, 7.

disappointment. For instance, their great 'déjeuner sur l'herbe' ends badly. Here are the stage directions. "The two Bow-wows, yelping, lick everybody. They jump out of the bath-tub, covered with soap suds, and the bathers, dressed like everybody of this period, come out of the tub. The Tart alone gets out stark naked except for her stockings. They bring in baskets of food, bottles of wine, tablecloths, napkins, knives, forks. They prepare a great picnic lunch. In come some under-takers with coffins, into which they dump everybody, nail them down and carry them off. Curtain." But the play does not end here. All the characters reappear in the next act as though nothing had happened. A similar anticlimax comes at the end of the last act when after a prizegiving Big Foot says these last heroic words: "Light the lanterns. Throw flights of doves with all our strength against the bullets and lock securely the houses demolished by bombs." Then follows the entry of "a golden ball the size of a man which lights up the whole room and blinds the characters. . . . On the golden ball appear the letters of the word: NOBODY."

Cold, hunger and love make themselves felt in a variety of ways. One scene is set in a corridor of "Sordid's Hotel" where "the two feet of each guest are in front of the doors of their rooms, writhing in pain". In turn they wail a monotonous chorus: "My chilblains, my chilblains, my chilblains. . . ." There are frequent mentions of stoves and chimneys and icy temperatures which serve merely to increase the pangs of hunger. Food is their main preoccupation. In the last act a splendid feast is served "in the main sewer-bedroom-kitchen-bathroom of the Anxieties". The sisters boast of the fantastic viands they have prepared. Thin Anxiety exclaims: "I shall help myself to the sturgeon, the bitter erotic flavour of these delicacies keeps my depraved taste for spiced and raw dishes panting eagerly." Big Foot as he writes love poems meditates: "When you think it over, nothing is as good as mutton stew." Even his desire for the Tart is translated into such terms as "the melted butter of her dubious gestures", or when he addresses her, "your buttocks a plate of cassoulet and your arms a soup of sharks' fins".

Finally with her infatuation for Big Foot leading nowhere, the Tart speaks these moving lines from her heart: "You know, I met love. He has all the skin worn off his knees and goes begging from door to door. He hasn't got a farthing and is looking for a job as a suburban bus-conductor. It is sad, but go to his help . . . he'll turn on you and sting you. Big Foot wanted to have me and it is he who is caught in the trap. . . ."

Play

Picasso's habit of finding his material close at hand or from memories that spring up again vividly in his imagination provided the flood of images with which the play is inundated. Fat Anxiety talking of some newly-born kittens says: "We drowned them in a hard stone, to be exact a beautiful amethyst." This strange evocative metaphor was inspired by a large amethyst belonging to Picasso and of which he is particularly proud, because in a cavity enclosed within it water can be seen. His characters also have similarities with those around him, but it would be fruitless and impertinent to search for consistent descriptions. Just as in his painting he enjoys seeing his models in mirrors that distort them so thoroughly that only certain features are recognisable, so he destroys or decomposes his characters before building them again. When Big Foot soliloquising says of the Tart: "the roses of her fingers smell of turpentine", we can see an allusion to Dora Maar who spent much of her time painting. He continues, "I light the candles of sin with the match of her charms. The electric cooker can take the blame." It would be impossible to explain the last sentence unless it were known that the electric cooker installed in Dora Maar's flat was, jokingly, always given credit for any specially good dish cooked by her.

Raymond Queneau notices that there are surprisingly few allusions to painting in the play.[1] Apart from a mention of the "demoiselles d'Avignon" who "have already had a private income for the last thirty-three long years", there are frequent phrases which are obviously from a painter's or a sculptor's vocabulary, such as "the blackness of ink envelops the saliva of the sun's rays", or "I beat my portrait against my brow", or again "the whiteness and hardness of the gleaming marble of her pain". The purely visual images are possibly outnumbered by those which appeal to other senses. The predominant appeal to the sense of taste is followed closely by that of smell, which wafts its way in, not only as the fumes from chip-potatoes which completely suffocate the actors at the end of the fourth act, but in reference to the Tart who melts "into the fragrant architecture of the kitchen" and attracts Big Foot by "the sweet stink of her tresses". Sound also is by no means absent. "The noise of unfastened shutters, hitting their drunken bells on the crumpled sheets of the stones, tears from the night despairing cries of pleasure", or again, "the feasting will burst all the strings of the violins and guitars"—such passages clearly result from an enjoyment of music.

There is one short act which brings in numbers in an extravagant

[1] Raymond Queneau, 'Une Belle Surprise', *Cahiers d'Art*, 1940-44, Paris.

way. The entire cast are trying their luck at the big wheel of a lottery. As it comes to a stop, each of them shouts out in turn the fantastic sum that has become his prize. In the end they all, even the Curtains, 'win the jackpot, but this avails them nothing for it is at this moment that the fumes of fried potatoes asphyxiate the lot. As well as making appeal to all the senses and to erotic desire, Picasso here adds the unaccountable fascination that numbers have always had for him, which was noticed as early as his first examination in Malaga.

On Friday 17 January 1941, four days after he had started, Picasso drew a line at the bottom of the last act and wrote: "Fin de la pièce". The friends he allowed to read it found its humour irresistible. The contrasts between Rabelaisian wit, evocative imagery and macabre situations were unlike anything they knew. Three years later, in the spring of 1944 when the Nazi occupation still made such things danger-ous, a reading was organised in the apartment of Michel Leiris who lived nearby. Leiris read the part of Big Foot while other parts were taken by his wife, Louise Leiris, Jean-Paul Sartre, Simone de Beauvoir, Raymond Queneau, Georges and Germaine Hugnet, Jean and Zanie Aubier and Dora Maar. Camus offered his services as producer. It would have been difficult to find a cast who could interpret Picasso's intentions with more understanding and delight. The rendering of the play was so excellent that this single performance in occupied Paris is talked of by those who were there as an event as memorable for its accord between poets and painter as the banquet in honour of the Douanier Rousseau some forty years before. In addition it savoured of a clandestine orgy, an insult to the preposterous invader who had imagined that he could govern Paris. "Never has our freedom been greater than under the German occupation", wrote Jean-Paul Sartre, ". . . since the Nazi poison filtered even into our minds, every just thought was a victory; since the omnipotent police tried to force us to silence, every word became as precious as a declaration of principle; since we were at bay, our very gestures had the weight of vows."[1]. [2]

[1] *Les Lettres Françaises*, 9 September 1944.

[2] After the war, performances were given in London. The most successful were those which did not attempt any staging. The stage directions in some Rabelaisian details are impossible to act, and since they are eloquent in them-selves they are best understood when read. A reading such as this, in which Dylan Thomas took part, was organised by the Institute of Contemporary Arts. *Desire caught by the tail* shared the bill with *The Island in the Moon* by William Blake, making an unexpected parallel between two plays written by painter-poets. Picasso's play was first published in *Messages II Paris, Risques, Travaux et Modes*, 1944, with four illustrations, and later as *Le Désir attrapé*

"Portraits" of D.M.

Since Picasso began to draw portraits of Dora Maar when he was staying at Mougins in 1936, her face became more and more an obsession at the basis of his inventions and reconstructions of the human head. Among the early versions there are many lifelike portraits, exact studies of the first direct impression of her features. Treating her appearance with great tenderness and often combining her features with poetic fantasies, he explored every line and every surface, watching her expression and her gestures. Dora Maar, as I have said before, appears as a water nymph, as a chimerical bird-like creature with the regular oval of her head crowned with horns, or in more distorted forms, with her features composed of flowers.

The faces of other women and small children whom he saw frequently during these years also appear in portraits. Nusch Eluard, Ines the maid who had come from Mougins to keep house for him, his daughter Maïa, and friends who called frequently at the rue des Grands Augustins were often his models. However, paintings in which the features of Dora Maar can be traced are the most numerous, though the degree in which they can be said to be portraits varies greatly. For Picasso the subject, ever since the revolution which occurred in the *Demoiselles d'Avignon,* has been the victim of his will to destroy appearances. Vision rather than subject-matter becomes supreme. The cubists had all destroyed the form of objects such as guitars, bottles and even the human body when reorganising their shapes in still-lifes or figure compositions, but none had had the same courage as Picasso to demolish the human head. What is more, he did not confine this disruptive process to his male friends, as he had done in the early cubist days, when he had scrupulously avoided making any reference to Eva except as a symbol. The face of his closest and dearest woman friend was eligible to suffer the same violence. The face of Olga had not been exempt, nor was the face of Dora Maar.

Picasso uses the features of a face as raw material. He knows them intimately from long observation and from frequent studies made either from life, or from an equally visible mental image. Sometimes they become complicated by the intrusion of features of another origin, as when he creates composite heads of dog and woman, or, as

par la queue, 62 pp., Paris, Gallimard, 1945 (Collection Métamorphoses, XXIII), without illustrations. A facsimile of the manuscript was also made for private distribution.

in the Minotaur series, heads which are the aggregate of features from man, bull and dog.

As early as the autumn of 1939 we find a 'portrait' of Dora Maar in which distortion is carried so far that it might be expected that all resemblance to the human head had been forfeited and in consequence no-trace of likeness to the model could possibly remain. However, in this painting[1] which Dora Maar had seen for several weeks in the studio, she suddenly realised that an isolated bulbous shape between the eyes had an uncanny likeness to her own forehead.

The vision of Picasso seems to know no prejudice and no taboo which will limit its penetration. He does not allow sentiment, tenderness or any convention to stand in the way of his creation. Such liberties will be considered by some an unpardonable indiscretion, an outrage on what is sacred and beautiful, whereas for Picasso it is a necessary process, a process which makes his creation fertile with associations.

To describe the variety of ways in which the presence and intelligence of Dora Maar nourished Picasso's inspiration exceeds the scope of this book. There are some portraits painted during the war which however must be mentioned. The first dates from the autumn of 1939.[2] In a small, simple and yet monumental painting Picasso has seen his model from the least advantageous angle, from behind. With the desire characteristic of the cubists to see her from more than one viewpoint, he had given the head two profiles, one on either side of a black torrent of hair. Later he used the same device in his treatment of a nude,[3] where although the sleeping figure lies prone, the face and body are opened out in such a way that both profiles and breasts are made visible at either side of the back. The frustration caused by never being able to see both back and front at once has been subtly overcome. Once more he had preferred a cubist solution to the old problem, which, if we consult history, we find had caused long discussions during the renaissance. In comparing the relative merit of sculpture and painting, sculptors claimed that the superiority of their art lay in the fact stressed by Cellini that sculpture does not confine itself to one, but can give eight different views of its subject. Giorgione according to Leonardo, in answer to this, "to the utter confusion of certain sculptors . . . painted a Saint George in armour standing on the banks of a stream and between two mirrors reflecting the figure at various angles".[4] Picasso was not ignorant of this method. He had used the

[1] Plate XVIII, 4.   [2] Plate XVIII, 6.   [3] Plate XIX, 4.
[4] Leonardo da Vinci, *Paragone*, note by Irma A. Richter, Oxford University Press, 1949.

reflection in the mirror in the moon-like nudes of 1932. Those were purely visual solutions; the splitting of forms such as he was practising here had a more tactile quality. It was closer to the conception of a sculptor, who wishes to manipulate form as well as merely contemplate it with his eyes.

Another painting, a gouache, of the Royan period is powerful in invention though small in size.[1] A gnarled twisted female nude stands with windswept hair against the void of a grey sky. It would be verging on an insult to call this, as Paul Eluard does, *Portrait de Mademoiselle D.M.*, were it not that even in this extreme case, there is still in every detail a reference to the life Picasso was sharing with his friend and to the experiences, visual and emotional, they had in common. Though I am unable here to clarify this suggestion any further it is undoubtedly true because the intimate communion between Picasso, his friends, his surroundings and his work is always at the root of its variety and its success.

There is one more portrait of Dora Maar which should be mentioned because it differs from all others.[2] The stark almost naïve appearance of the sitter against the plain background of a blue wall, as she stares with troubled eyes from the canvas, seems in this case reminiscent of certain portraits of the Douanier Rousseau. She is wearing a green dress with red stripes and in the flesh tints of the face are echoes of these colours. The red glows in her sensitive nostrils and the green and blue shade her cheeks in Cézannesque modulations. In spite of a pronounced asymmetry in the drawing of the nose, which evokes a profile though it is seen full face, there is a relentless realism about the portrait which classifies it as a more austere descendant of the portrait done five years earlier, to whose flowerlike charm I have already referred.

This portrait is dated 9 October 1942. Three months later, in the depths of a bitter wartime winter, Picasso was visiting Dora Maar in her nearby apartment one Sunday afternoon.[3] He had with him a copy of Buffon's *Histoire Naturelle* which, in spite of the war, Fabiani had managed to publish. It contained Picasso's thirty-one illustrations for which the first aquatints had been made five years before. On other occasions Picasso had amused himself by transforming the spots of paint flicked accidentally from Dora Maar's brush on to the white walls of her studio. He had made of the little stains a population of insects—beetles, moths and flies—which were so realistic that visitors tried to squash them. This time, however, he settled down with ink, pen and brush to decorate the copy of the book he had brought as a

[1] Eluard, *A Pablo Picasso*, p. 161.   [2] Ibid., p. 156.   [3] Plate XIX, 9.

present. Turning the pages, he added in the margin the bearded heads of classical heroes, horses, donkeys, cats, rams, bulls, eagles, or doves. When he came to a blank sheet he took the opportunity to fill it at random with a large head of a man or woman or a creature suggested by the text. As a frontispiece he again drew Dora as a bird, her eyes sparkling and her talons grasping a leafy branch. Then on the page opposite he signed and dated his dedication, written round the name Buffon with his usual delight in puns—"per Dora Maar tan rebufond!"[1] On several blank pages the drawings were significant of grim pre-occupation with external events. On one of these, round a skull crowned with the skeletons of snakes, he drew two shrieking gorgons' heads and on another the skeleton of a bird flapping its wings, its head again being a skull. The drawings were made one after the other with unchecked energy. By the end of the afternoon he had filled the book with forty drawings in which he had gone through moods ranging from macabre fantasies or buffooneries to drawings which prove his acute understanding of the animal kingdom.[2]

Still-life and Figure Paintings

The same sinister background of war and privation makes itself felt in many of the still-lifes of this period. Just as music in the form of guitar-playing and songs had been the theme of many cubist paintings in the days before the first World War, so food in its more humble forms, such as sausages and leeks, together with the skulls of animals and the dim light of candles and shaded lamps recur throughout Picasso's wartime paintings. Even the cutlery, sharp-pointed gleaming knives and hungry forks, repeats the same uneasy theme.[3] There are two terrifying paintings of the skull of a bull set on a table in front of a closed window, painted two days apart in April 1942.[4] In the earlier one, raw flesh still hangs to the bone and the horns are silhouetted against the crude dead light of the glazed window. In the other it is night, the whitened bare bone of the skull grins horribly beneath the semicircle of the horns set against the darkness outside. Both are deeply moving in their expression of death, but there is no sense of putrefaction and de-liquescence of form, as there is in the Still Life with Bull's Head of 1938.

[1] "For Dora Maar your rebuffoon! . . ."
[2] The sheets of this copy of Buffon, edited by Henri Jonquières, have been published in facsimile by Fabiani, Paris, 1957, *40 dessins de Picasso en marge de Buffon*.
[3] Plate XIX, 6.
[4] *Skull of bull on table*, 5 April, 1942, Janis, *Picasso: the Recent Years*, Plate 101.

The emphasis is rather on the crystalline durability of structures that lie beneath a perishable surface. There is geometric order in death, which appears in these still-lifes and gives them a distinction which is fundamentally Spanish. It is totally unlike the painting of the German expressionists, in which both form and colour are subjected to palpitating feverish decomposition.

As the kitchen table became deserted by palatable foods, there appeared in Picasso's still-lifes that reminder of our own mortality, a human skull, its bared teeth grinning among the clawing roots of vegetables, the black sockets of its eyes looking blankly at the swollen belly of an empty pitcher.[1] The menace of disaster was continually on the threshold. News frequently arrived that friends because they had the misfortune to be Jews had been deported to the supreme horror of concentration camps or that others had been tortured or put to death because of their clandestine activities in the resistance movement. With all the evil uncertainty that goes with military occupation, Picasso however kept his buoyant, cynical sense of humour. In paintings such as the *Child with Pigeons*,[2] *Seated Woman with Cat*,[3] *Woman with Bouquet*,[4] *Woman in a Rocking-Chair*,[5] *Little Boy with a Crawfish*,[6] *Woman seated in an armchair with a hat adorned with three feathers*,[7] and the *Mother and Child*[8] in which an anxious mother teaches her son his first steps, there is a mocking and yet compassionate attention to the familiar fundamentals of human life.

Sculpture

Among the diverse resources in his nature Picasso found the means of balancing the angry cynical mood evident in much of his painting with a new outburst of activity in sculpture. The open space afforded by the studios on two floors of the rue des Grands Augustins was highly suitable for this purpose.

Since the period fecund with new inspiration at Boisgeloup, he had contented himself with making small sculptures often inspired by lucky finds among bones and pebbles. On these he had engraved classical profiles or the heads of horned gods and monsters. At Royan he made some small-scale painted bas-reliefs in cardboard on the backs of cigarette boxes which are astonishingly successful as a tour-de-force with limited means, but it was not until 1941 that sculpture again

[1] Plate XIX, 8.
[2] Plate XIX, 5.
[3] Janis, *Picasso*, Plate 71.
[4] *Cahiers d'Art*, 1940-4, p. 54.
[5] Plate XXI, 3.
[6] *Cahiers d'Art*, p. 22.
[7] *Cahiers d'Art*, 1940-4, p. 71.
[8] Plate XXI, 1.

became a major activity. The first works of this period show a great variety of methods. There are small female figures modelled in clay; a plaster head of Dora Maar;[1] and a bird made of a broken piece from a child's scooter placed so aptly on a tall metal stand that the illusion of a tall bird of dignified bearing is a delight.[2] After some contemplation it suddenly becomes apparent that the beak of the bird is nothing more than the fork that once held the front wheel. Again with no visible effort Picasso has made a magical transformation from an insignificant piece of scrap to a creature endowed with the nervous tension of a life. In the same way, bent wires or lead caps from wine bottles or old cigarette boxes come to life as dancing forms, a rooster, a fish or a fluttering dove. Even something as fragile as a piece of soiled paper with holes burnt by a cigarette for eyes gains the strength to claim attention as an evocation of the face of someone.[3]

Of all these discoveries, that which has become the most famous because of its disconcerting simplicity is the object made out of the saddle and handlebars of a derelict bicycle, which when put together by Picasso became a lifelike head of a bull.[4] The metamorphosis is astonishingly complete. Such transformations are a simple game, but for them to become significant it requires a rare perception of the varied and subtle implications in the form in question. Picasso once told me after the war that people frequently brought him stones of curious shapes and interpreted them in various ways, "but," he said, "they often make mistakes—two boys arrived yesterday with a pebble which they said was the head of a dog until I pointed out that it was really a typewriter".

When seen in this way the identity of objects becomes uncertain and changeable. This possibility prompted Picasso to question the shape of things around him. Borrowing their forms, he found the means of using them in ways such as I have described, or by making an impression of their surfaces on clay or plaster he captured their surface patterns. He used a lemon-squeezer pressed into clay to make a head, round like a sun, for the figure of *The Reaper*;[5] a leaf printed on the body of a cock gave the texture of its feathers;[6] the impression of corrugated paper served as a dress to a female form.[7] Picasso's ingenuity,

---

[1] This portrait bust now cast in bronze has been offered by Picasso as a monument to Apollinaire to be erected in the St. Germain des Prés quarter in Paris. Plate XX, 3.

[2] Kahnweiler-Brassai, *The Sculptures of Picasso*, Plate 119.   [3] Plate XX, 4.

[4] Plate XX, 6.   [5] Kahnweiler-Brassai, *The Sculptures of Picasso*, Plate 173.

[6] Ibid., Plate 174.   [7] Ibid., Plate 168.

combined with his sense of the right time and the right place, worked together to bring to life from the humblest sources a new kind of sculpture, in fact, a new art. Eschewing craftsmanship, he gave life with a magic touch where life, to casual observers, was apparently absent; and with bewildering assurance he succeeded at a time when such a miracle was most precious to all. Those who came to his studio laughed from a profound sense of joy and gratitude that someone could halt the general march towards destruction. When Michel Leiris congratulated him on the complete transformation he had achieved in the *Bull's Head*, he replied with modesty: "That's not enough. It should be possible to take a bit of wood and find that it's a bird."[1]

In the summer of 1942 Picasso began to draw a subject which held his attention for over a year and resulted in the most important work in sculpture that he has yet completed. Zervos has reproduced a choice of fifty of the preliminary drawings from the vast quantity that were produced.[2] In general, the reputation that Picasso has gained for rapid spontaneous creation and the speed with which he can pass from one manner to another, lead us to forget the continuity of his effort and the thoroughness of his preparation. The theme of the bearded shepherd carrying a frightened restive sheep began with a series of sketches. The two bodies, the one captive and dependent on the other, which stands in firm equilibrium, are studied in general terms, contrasting their volumes and relationship to each other. They are given detailed attention individually, together and from a great variety of angles as Picasso pursued his intention of developing the idea into a life-size statue.

The following summer Picasso asked a Spanish friend to bring him sufficient modelling clay, which at that time was not easy to find, so that he could start on his project. The Spaniard however, in his zeal to help the master, arrived with a mountain of clay, which was more than sufficient for ten life-size statues. When he had removed the greater part, Picasso set to work one morning, and with energy intensified by the knowledge of his subject, he completed the statue before night.[3] With Paul Eluard, who happened to be there, sitting beside him at a table writing, he began to construct his statue with incredible speed. As he worked it became top-heavy for the fragile armature on which it was being built. It began to topple and had to be steadied with ropes. Later the lamb fell out of the shepherd's arms and

[1] Kahnweiler-Brassai, *The Sculptures of Picasso*.
[2] *Cahiers d'Art*, Paris, 1945-46.   [3] Plate XX, 2.

had to be wired back in position, but with ingenuity which overcame these minor calamities as they occurred, the figure continued to come to life and at nightfall it was complete. Seeing that the reinforcement was hopelessly weak, soon afterwards he got a friend to make a plaster cast from the clay figure. When the plaster had set Picasso made some modifications and it remained in this condition dominating all else in the studio until after the war, when it was cast in bronze. The startling rapidity with which the *Man with the Sheep* was finally made, after a long period of reflection, is typical of many of Picasso's major works. In this way he never sacrifices his spontaneity.

The *Man with the Sheep* stands alone in the canon of Picasso's work. It is difficult to define its style since there are no obvious influences that can be traced, nor has he profited from the inventions and metamorphoses which abound in other sculptures of the same year. Its appeal is largely due to its humble simplicity. The naked man stands rigid, grasping the sheep firmly by its legs and looking resolutely straight ahead, whereas the sheep with hysterical struggles is an unwilling captive. The theme is ancient and archetypal, and similarly the manner of its execution is readily understood by all. It is as though Picasso had wanted for once to speak directly to his human family in familiar terms, and to do so he used the vast wealth of his experience and talent. When at the end of the war, visitors of all nationalities crowded into his studio, the tall white figure greeted them as a symbol of Picasso's humanity.

Among the other outstanding sculptures that marked his wartime activity there is a skull, or rather a flayed head, which contrasts strongly with the serenity of the great statue.[1] Its appearance is particularly arresting owing to the macabre hollows of the eyes and nose and the absence of any suggestion of bone on the surface. There is a frightful implacable hardness about the smooth surface of this head. Whereas the *Man with the Sheep* attracts the light by the lively irregularities of the surface, beneath which there seems to exist a muscular tension, in the *Skull* the light is reflected from the hard lustre of the bronze as though nothing but death lay below. It was thanks to the devotion of certain friends, who enjoyed secretly diverting the metal from the German war effort, that the skull and several other modelled sculptures were cast in bronze.

Death of Max Jacob

"Picasso paints more and more like God or the Devil", wrote Paul Eluard in his first letter to me after the liberation of Paris in 1944. "He

[1] Plate XX, 1.

has been one of the rare painters who have behaved well and he continues to do so", he added. He referred to the way in which certain artists had allowed themselves to be seduced by honours or consolations offered by the Germans, and to how Picasso had always been willing to help the resistance movement by sheltering anyone sent to him by his friends, whether he knew them or not.

Though in general he made no display of his loyalties, Picasso did not hesitate to appear in public at the memorial service for Max Jacob in the spring of 1944. The poet had been arrested, for no other reason than that he was born a Jew, at the Abbey of Saint-Benoît where he had lived as a lay brother for many years. He was sent to a concentration camp at Drancy where he died shortly after. There had been little in common between him and Picasso for many years except their memories, and an enduring respect which was kept alive before the war by visits Picasso paid him in his retreat on the Loire. However the death of a friend, particularly in such atrocious circumstances, has always affected Picasso deeply. It robs him slowly of his links with the past and, as it were, tolls in his ears the hated remembrance of his own mortality.

Landscapes of Paris and a Still-life

As the four years of misery drew to their close, the studio became once more overcrowded with canvases piled high against the walls, and sculpture which had invaded most of the floor-space. To add another activity to the richness of his production, he had painted landscapes of Paris. The buildings that he passed daily as he walked along the river where it flows past the Ile de la Cité were his subjects. Notre-Dame seen from the quay, framed by the arch of one of the stone bridges,[1] or the statue of Henri IV among the trees at the end of the island, were his favourite motifs. Still nearer home, he painted the window of his studio looking out across the roofs, sometimes placing in front of it one of the tomato plants grown for its welcome fruit.[2] These familiar scenes were painted with sober feeling for the grey stones and angular patterns of walls and roofs which in his hands give to the city the facets of a diamond.

A little restaurant a few doors away in the rue des Grands Augustins, named 'Le Catalan' in honour of its distinguished neighbour, was the daily rendez-vous of painters, poets and friends. For some Picasso showed his interest in their work by making drawings to accompany their poems. For Georges Hugnet, who came there frequently for his

[1] Plate XX, 9.   [2] See *Cahiers d'Art*, 1940–44, p. 60.

meals, Picasso made drawings for three books published between 1941
and 1943; and for Robert Desnos, who was killed by the Germans
shortly afterwards, he made a remarkable etching as a frontispiece to
Contrée, a collection of Desnos' poems. The seated nude that it represents, seen from both front and back, is built up in line by a pattern
of arabesques which give her monumental volume.[1] Throughout the
book, sections of the plate are used again as tail-pieces for each poem.
Even so, the disconnected fragments are so strong and rhythmical in
their detail that cut up, they reappear with new significance.

Robert Desnos, formerly a surrealist, had written brilliantly about
Picasso more than ten years before. In his last essay before he died he
recounts a story Picasso told him: "I had lunched at the Catalan for
months," Picasso said, "and for months I looked at the sideboard
without thinking more than 'it's a sideboard'. One day I decide to
make a picture of it. I do so. The next day, when I arrived, the sideboard had gone, its place was empty. . . . I must have taken it away
without noticing by painting it." "An amusing story, of course",
Desnos remarks, "in spite of or rather because of its veracity; but it
illustrates like a fable or a proverb the relationship between the work
and the reality. For Picasso what matters, when he paints, is 'to take
possession' and not provisionally like a thief or a buyer, just for a
lifetime, but as himself the creator of the object or of the being."[2]

Liberation

On the morning of 24 August 1944 the whole of Paris was roused
by the noise of sniping from the roofs and gunfire from the retreating
German tanks. A fever of excitement ran through the city as Parisians
realised that their day of liberation had at last come, and as they took
a hand to hasten it. Divided from the Prefecture only by the Seine
and a few roof tops, Picasso found himself in the centre of a battle.
Friends crept in and out telling him of its progress while explosions
and gunfire shook the windows of his studio. In this tense atmosphere
Picasso chose to forget the immediate danger by submerging himself
in his work. He returned to methods he had used at the end of the
1914-18 war. Taking photos or reproductions as his models, he could
draw from them with less strain and yet continue to work. First he
made a careful interpretation of a photo of Maïa,[3] whom he had

[1] Robert Desnos, *Contrée*, Godet, Paris, 1944.
[2] *Picasso Peintures*, 1936-1946, Ed. du Chêne, Paris, 1949; also see *Cahiers d'Art*, 1940-4, p. 61.
[3] See Barr, *Picasso: Fifty Years of His Art*, p. 242.

installed with her mother some while before in an apartment overlooking the Seine at the far end of the Ile St. Louis. Later, as the noise and
the anxiety increased, he took a reproduction of a painting by Poussin
and began to make from it in gouache a version of his own.[1] While
he worked he sang at the top of his voice to drown the din in the
streets. The picture he chose was a scene of wild bacchanalian revelry,
The Triumph of Pan, which hangs in the Louvre. Its spirit of ritualistic
abandon in an Arcadian setting was in keeping with his optimistic
mood. Retaining the essentials of the composition and the movement
of the ring of dancers, he reinterpreted the figures with freedom and
gave the colour a gaiety which makes Poussin's revellers look demure.
Once more he was working with a brother from the past, one of his
familiars from the *Chef d'Œuvre Inconnu*, for the poets and painters
with whom Picasso shares a timeless intimacy are situated in the past
as well as the present, united with him in a brotherhood of genius.

Hardly had the rattle of automatic weapons ceased when friends
serving with the Allied armies began to arrive. The news that had
reached the outside world about Picasso had been scarce and unreli-
able. Even those who knew him only as a name were anxious to find
out what had happened to him. It was a race to see who could find
him first. A few who had the advantage of having known him before
the war hurried through streets littered with smoking tanks and hila-
rious crowds who sang and wept for joy, to the rue des Grands
Augustins in the hope of finding him still there. The first to climb the
narrow winding staircase and reach the door of his studio was Lee
Miller, who was at that time war correspondent for *Vogue*. With
tears in his eyes he welcomed her, astonished to see that the first Allied
'soldier' he should meet was a woman. Every day more friends
crowded in and news was eagerly exchanged about those who were
absent or dead. Picasso's survival through the perils of war became
a symbol of victory; applied to him the word 'liberation' was synonymous with his work and his life.

The excitement was so great at finding what seemed to be a miracle
—Picasso not only alive but unimpaired in his vigour—that the number of the visitors who pressed around him became almost overwhelming. Every day old friends reappeared to express to him their
admiration and affection. Every morning the long narrow room
leading to the studio on the lower floor became an antechamber filled
with dozens of new arrivals crowding together and waiting for him
to appear. They were invited in groups into the sculpture studio on

[1] Plate XX, 8.

the same floor, and when he felt inclined, they were taken up to the floor above, which he used for painting.

This unsolicited homage Picasso was forced daily to receive. He was besieged by enthusiasts in a variety of uniforms and often unable to make themselves understood in either French or Spanish. Standing firmly with a cigarette perpetually smoking, small but radiating vitality from his black eyes, his voice, his gestures and his enquiring smile, he left a deep impression on the thousands who visited him during the first months of liberation. Even when they were insensitive to or shocked by the paintings, the sculpture and the atmosphere of an alchemist's den, they were never disappointed in him.

In the first months of liberation, the novelty of finding he had so many admirers, after the solitude of four years of musing, fascinated him. He even allowed himself to be invaded by organised parties of forty to fifty service men and women who bombarded him with questions, and shot thousands of views of him and his studio with their cameras. But even so he managed to arrange his life so that he could think his own thoughts and see his own friends. The rejoicings, and the abundant presents of food and other necessities of life that had become rare, were offset by long conversations about more lasting problems. After all, the liberation of France had not brought about the liberation of his own country. His friends in Spain were still the prisoners of Franco. It would take more than the spectacular victories of the Allies to make him forget that injustice and stupidity were still rampant.

Picasso, the Communist

The majority of those who had shared with Picasso the years of anxiety and suspicion and who had shown the greatest courage in the resistance movement were members of the French Communist Party. The party had grown greatly in strength. Its members had earned admiration for their courageous devotion to the cause, even among their former political enemies in France. Among the new adherents who had joined, believing that communism was the only path which could lead the world away from catastrophes such as they had witnessed, and found a new society based on human dignity and the rights of man, was Paul Eluard. He had taken this step in 1942, at a time when it needed special courage to do so, since with Hitler's attack on the U.S.S.R. communism was an unforgivable crime to the Nazis. His motives were idealist and humanitarian; he acted not as a politician but as a poet, a philosopher, and one who was willing to fight to the death for the liberation of his country. To this end, he accepted a party discipline which formerly his love of the rights of an individual would not have allowed him to tolerate.

The prestige of the French Communist Party was very high. Many intellectuals and artists of distinction had joined its ranks. Soviet Russia herself was a gallant and victorious ally. As an act of faith and with the fervent hope of creating a better world, Eluard had become a member, and burying his former animosity he even became reconciled to the poet Louis Aragon, who also had been occupied in dangerous underground activities.

"I have great news for you," Eluard whispered in my ear when I was visiting Picasso in his studio a month after liberation, "in a week it will be announced publicly that Picasso has joined the Communist Party." Indeed, when this became known it aroused speculation on all sides as to what would be the consequences. The question of greatest importance was whether Picasso would retain his right to paint as he wished or whether he would find himself obliged to change his style and adopt a form of 'social realism' palatable to Soviet doctrines. In addition a strange confusion between art and political creeds had become apparent. The diehards of academic art, who were almost without exception the enemies of communism, had for many years realised that the modern movement was revolutionary and in consequence they ignorantly labelled it 'bolshevik'. Soviet ideology had in this matter seen eye to eye with Hitler in condemning the modern movement and with it Picasso as its greatest leader. Who would now win? Would the Communist Party accept the unpalatable style because of Picasso, or would he be compelled to denounce his former discoveries?

If the scene had been laid in Russia the outcome might have been very different. In France, however, the situation was influenced by the great traditions of French art and culture. It was not the politicians but the intellectuals, proud of the liberties they had won by their own revolution in the past and had regained by their recent courage, who now tempted Picasso to join. It was the politicians, however, who had convinced the party leaders that the prestige gained by his acceptance would be immense.

Untroubled by the dangers that others saw for the future of his art, Picasso willingly accepted the invitation. The offer coincided with many of his deepest humanitarian hopes. He was taking the same step as many of his closest friends, and it was a further gesture of defiance against his old enemies, Franco and Hitler. So far as his painting was concerned he was not surprised that Soviet doctrine did not approve. "From past experience I would have been suspicious," he said, "if I had found they did appreciate my work." Wishing to make his motives clear to the world at large he made a statement to Pol Gaillard which was published in New York and Paris almost simultaneously[1] late in October 1944.

With simplicity he said many things which help to explain not only his feelings towards humanity and his art, but also his loneliness as a person and the unity between his work and his life. "My adhesion to the Communist Party is the logical outcome of my whole life. For I am glad to say that I have never considered painting simply as pleasure-giving art, a distraction; I have wanted, by drawing and by colour since those were my weapons, to penetrate always further forward into the consciousness of the world and of men, so that this understanding may liberate us further each day. . . . These years of terrible oppression have proved to me that I should struggle not only for my art but with my whole being." He then speaks of his friends who had long known of his convictions and with whom he was happy to prove his allegiance to the same cause, adding, "I was so anxious to find a homeland again, I have always been an exile, now I am one no longer; until Spain can at last welcome me back, the French Communist Party has opened its arms to me, I have found there all those whom I esteem the most, the greatest scientists, the greatest poets and all those faces, so beautiful, of the Parisians in arms which I saw during those days in August, I am once more among my brothers."

There is no doubt from the emotional tone of these words that Picasso's action came from a profound desire within himself to enter into a pact of friendship with those around him. His art had led him often into isolation; the rare atmosphere of the heights, to which his genius had climbed, could not readily be shared by more than a few. Others if they were to understand needed time to become accustomed to the significance of his discoveries. His hopes of establishing a family had grown dim, but here he could enter into a new comradeship, sharing the same idealism as his friends and those who worked and fought in the streets. He had in his own words found his family.

[1] Pol Gaillard's interview was published in a condensed form in *New Masses* (New York) on 24 October 1944 and appeared in the original in *L'Humanité* (Paris), 29-30 October 1944. This version is printed in Barr, *Picasso: Fifty Years of his Art*, p. 267.

Exhibitions

Six weeks after the liberation of Paris the Salon d'Automne opened its doors. Instead of following its usual routine, which had been despised by Picasso in the past so that he had always refused to participate, it became a great manifestation of French art after four years of German domination. Traditionally a well-known French painter was invited to exhibit in a gallery allotted exclusively to him. On this occasion, however, as an unprecedented tribute to a foreigner, Pablo Picasso was honoured, and for the first time in an official salon. Seventy-five of his paintings and five of his sculptures were shown, most of them being those he had been compelled by the animosity of the Nazis and the partisans of Vichy to paint behind closed doors.

The effect of this tribute to Picasso on a public whom the Germans had attempted to train to admire only Hitler's choice in art was electric. It aroused violent protests from those who considered that the honour should have gone at such a historic moment to a French painter, and from those who disapproved not only of his art but also of his new allegiance to the Communists. On 8 October, two days after the opening of the exhibition, a party of hotheads shouting: "Take them down! Money back! Explain!" besieged the gallery and threatened to destroy Picasso's work. It was not clear, however, whether they were more influenced by the political issue or by their hatred of Picasso as an artist. André Lhote, who was present, described it as a Royalist manœuvre, but it is also possible that the demonstrators were students from the Ecole des Beaux-Arts, who, like their masters, had a thorough dislike for Picasso's work. There were, however, plenty to stand by Picasso and praise his work with even greater enthusiasm in face of the attack.

The following spring there was a similar exhibition of paintings at the Victoria and Albert Museum in London. The recent work of Picasso was shown with a retrospective exhibition of Matisse. With the exception of the great painting of the *Night Fishing at Antibes*, which, with several other important pictures, had been hidden throughout the occupation in Zervos' apartment in Paris, all Picasso's work dated from the spring of 1940. This gave an atmosphere of violence and anxiety to his part of the exhibition which was overpowering in comparison with the "Luxe, calme et volupté" of the Matisse paintings.

The London public was greatly disturbed by this exhibition. Daily it was crowded by people who found themselves divided into those who were passionately appreciative and those who felt themselves insulted at being exposed to such powerful and unaesthetic expression. Many still in uniform who had so recently been trained to commit acts of violence saw an interpretation of the world that startled them. They had expected from the arts a soothing influence and were unwilling to admit that these pictures should be allowed to have such power over them. Whether they liked what they saw or not, Picasso was teaching them to see.

In the summer of 1945 Picasso began another great painting reminiscent of *Guernica—The Charnel House*.[1] The picture was exhibited at the Salon d'Automne in the following autumn, after the war had at last come to an end. It had been painted at the time when the appalling horror of Nazi concentration camps had been revealed to the world. It was unfortunate that it was unfinished at the time of the London exhibition, for it would have helped the public to understand more clearly that Picasso's distortions were the outcome of his state of mind and not of a frivolous desire to shock the public.

Unlike *Guernica*, it is not a symbolic picture, prophetic of coming events, but rather an epilogue to the catastrophes that had lately occurred. A heap of mangled, trussed and putrefying humanity has collapsed beneath a table on which food and water have been placed. Their plight, unrelieved by the few symbols of hope that still remain hidden in the explosive violence of *Guernica*, makes this picture the most despairing in all Picasso's work. Again he avoided the aesthetic distraction that colour might have brought, and restricted the whole painting between the limits of white and black.

Painted in the hour of victory, the picture shows us nothing but the stark reality of our murderous, suicidal age. "This picture", says Barr, "is a pietà without grief, an entombment without mourners, a requiem without pomp", and quoting Picasso he continues: " 'No, painting is not done to decorate apartments. It is an instrument of war . . .' against 'brutality and darkness.' Twice in the past decade Picasso has magnificently fulfilled his own words."[2]

A dialectical process made itself felt; Picasso had been led by his daemon through channels not easily understood by all to this moment when his means could give expression so completely and comprehensively to a current event.

[1] Plate XXI, 6.   [2] Barr, *Picasso: Fifty Years of His Art*, p. 250.

CHAPTER XII

ANTIBES AND VALLAURIS
(1945–1954)

Return to the Mediterranean

IT WAS NOT FOR many months that the exaltation of liberation began to fade, and a stocktaking of losses as well as gains could be made in a more sober light. The ravages of the war and Nazi terror had been appalling in the sufferings they had caused. So many victims had disappeared unaccountably that it was an intense pleasure, a triumph, to welcome the unexpected reappearance of an old friend. Among those who had survived, many found their health weakened by anxiety and privations. In the last months before liberation Dora Maar herself suffered acutely, and Nusch Eluard, whose health had always been precarious, died suddenly of exhaustion in the autumn of 1946. Victory and the future were stained with the blood that had flowed.

In August 1945 Picasso at last managed to escape for a while from Paris. He returned to the Mediterranean for the first time since the flight from Antibes six years before. At Golfe Juan he found a small hotel overlooking the port that suited his habits, and once more he was able to enjoy the sun and the beaches. From here he made an expedition inland to visit an ancient house which had taken his fancy in the Provençal village of Menerbes. A friend in Paris had recently shown him a photograph of this house, built into the ramparts of the little town. It stood perched up above terraces of vines and olive trees looking out across the valley of the Durance. This had been sufficient to persuade Picasso to barter one of his recent still-lifes for the property and as soon as the deeds were signed he handed them to Dora Maar as a present.

For the purpose of seeing the new acquisition they set off together accompanied by Madame Cuttoli, the collector and patron of the arts, who was staying at her villa at Cap d'Antibes. To their satisfaction they found that it was all they had hoped for, and Dora Maar was happy to find in this remote place a landscape which was to offer inspiration to her painting and a future retreat.

A New Medium and a New Model

Since making the invitation card for his exhibition with Paul Rosenberg in 1919, Picasso had made no more lithographs. The scope offered by etching and aquatints had been sufficient for his graphic art. In the autumn of 1945, however, he found a printer in Paris, Fernand Mourlot, whose efficiency in his craft and amiability tempted Picasso to start again on a technique which has since become one of his favourite means of expression. Among his first lithographs appeared the portrait of a girl in full face. The regular olive-shaped outline of the head, and the straight nose, have classical proportions, and the well-formed mouth set in the cup of a firm but graceful chin is the clue to an independent character.[1] The model was Françoise Gilot, whom he had met through other painters in Paris. Her youth and vivacity, the chestnut colour of her luminous eyes, and her intelligent and authoritative approach, gave her a presence which was both Arcadian and very much of this earth. Another quality which attracted Picasso was her interest in painting, for which she already showed considerable talent. The following spring, when he left Paris for a prolonged stay on the Mediterranean coast, he took Françoise Gilot with him.

The disorganisation caused by the war made it difficult to find a suitable place for him to work. The little hotel on the harbour at Golfe Juan, to which he returned, was far too cramped to paint as he wanted. A chance conversation on his return led however to an offer which solved this problem for the moment at least and provided him with as much space as he could desire. The conversation was with Monsieur de la Souchère, the director of the Antibes Museum, which is housed in the ancient palace of the Grimaldi, an old Genoese family. It is a splendid medieval building whose towers crown the small fortified town and harbour. Before the war it had contained a dusty collection of plaster casts and objects relating to local history. In his desire for improvements the director hoped originally to obtain from Picasso a painting such as the *Fishermen of Antibes* which could hang appropriately on its walls. Picasso agreed vaguely that he would do something, and then began to complain that he had never been offered large surfaces to work on. At once, seeing his chance, Monsieur de la Souchère made a generous offer, which, as it turned out later, was to be highly profitable to his museum. Picasso was given the keys of the old palace and was asked to use it as his studio.

[1] Plate XXII, 5; see also Mourlot, *Picasso Lithographe*, Vol. I, pp. 110-20.

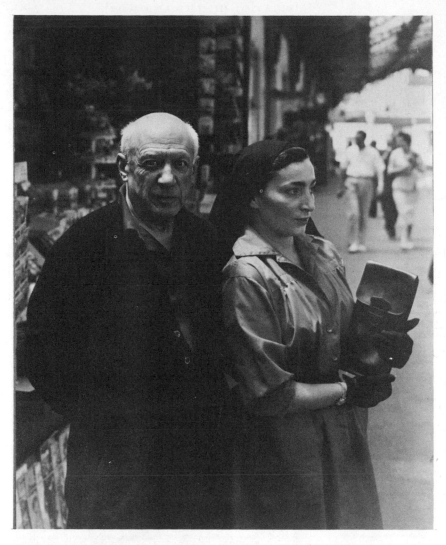
Picasso and Jacqueline Roque at Cannes, 1956

Picasso's studio at La Californie, Cannes, 1958

No time was wasted in ordering large sheets of hardboard, since canvas was still unobtainable, and in laying in stocks of whatever paint could be found. For the next four months the ancient fortress became his headquarters. With its high ceilings, pink tiled floors, and the sunlight reflected from the sea piercing the closed shutters, it provided an atmosphere which inspired him. Stones with bold Roman lettering and dusty casts of Michaelangelo's slaves were his companions as he started work on the new panels, painting pictures which contained, more than those of any other period in his life, an atmosphere of Arcadian joie de vivre. The medieval splendour, the elegance of the Renaissance and the glory of Napoleon which lurked in the surroundings did not influence him. His attachment to his native Mediterranean was rooted deeper in antiquity. He found echoes of ancient Greece around him in the landscape and the people. The mythical population of nymphs, fauns and centaurs lived again among his friends, and the fishermen and other local inhabitants he met in the harbour, the market and the cafés. They were again the daemons and the demigods. The centaurs now walked on two legs instead of four and the nymphs and satyrs were decently dressed, but they were the same population who had lived among the same pine trees, rocks and dwelling-places when the same winds filled the sails of the Argo.[1]

The new pictures and their accompanying drawings reflect the classical Mediterranean tradition with a new vision, both childlike and complex. The colours are tender; blues, pinks, ochres and greens dominate, and their dancing, flute-playing mood gives the great panels an echo of a golden age. One of the largest paintings, *Ulysses and the Sirens*,[2] in soft colouring, is like an allegory in which the sun bathes in the sea among those to whom it gives life—fish, men and sea maidens.

Few visitors came to disturb Picasso in this new-found happiness in which the presence of Françoise Gilot was a factor of great importance. Earlier in the year he had made a series of lithographs, large in size and splendid in the precision of their line. They all showed the lovely oval of her face and her gleaming eyes; all were extraordinarily true portraits and yet no two were alike. In the eleven portraits made on 14 and 15 June 1946 (ten in one day, and the eleventh on the next) he had many different versions of her; he saw her as woman or flower or the sun with her face as the source of light.

In the first half of 1947 Picasso continued his spate of lithographs,

[1] *Cahiers d'Art*, 1948, No. I, and *Verve*, Vol. 5, Nos. 19 and 20, Paris, 1948.
[2] Plate XXII, 1.

completing over fifty in eight months. His subjects were still Arcadian, fauns and centaurs, naked dancers, bulls, goats and the recurring theme of the two lovers, the one seated in contemplation while the other lies asleep. A new or rather very old appearance is that of the owl.[1] This bird is to be found at the feet of the picador (*El Zurdo*)[2]—Picasso's first etching—but for years it had been absent from his work. During his stay in Antibes an owl had been brought to him slightly injured, and keeping it beside him he began once more to be fascinated by its strange aloof behaviour and to introduce it into his paintings, his lithographs and later his ceramics.[3] Now, ten years after this, he has another small owl in a cage in his studio in Cannes. He tells how recently, while he was painting at night, a large bird of the same race flew in at the window and after battering itself against the glass, perched on top of the canvas on which he was at work. It had come, he thought, to prey on his pigeons that fly at liberty from the terrace outside the window during the day. Owls and doves, two birds of such different nature, have both been his lifelong companions. They both have significance for him which borders on superstition. The owl with its rounded head and piercing stare seems to resemble Picasso himself. As a joke he recently took an enlargement of a photo of his eyes and placed over it a white sheet of paper on which he drew the face of an owl, cutting out holes to fit his eyes like a mask. Nothing unnatural seemed to have taken place except that the bird now possessed the vision of a man whose eyes could not only see but also understand.

Picasso and the Museums

   While Picasso was in Paris in 1947, he was approached by a friend, Jean Cassou, who had recently been made the director of the new Musée d'Art Moderne. He was anxious to fill serious gaps in its collection owing to the lack of works by the greatest living painters. As Cassou realised, an absurd situation had grown up in France. In early days the rebels, Picasso, Matisse, Braque, Léger, and others had been banned from all official collections by their enemies in the academic world. But for this, in those days when they were relatively little known, their paintings could have been bought even with the limited funds at the disposal of the museums; now that fame had raised the prices, the museums found that neither did they possess

---

[1] Mourlot, *Picasso Lithographe*.
[2] See Geiser, *Picasso: Fifty-five Years of His Graphic Work*, Plate I.
[3] Plate XXII, 4.

any important works nor had they the money to purchase them. In his determination to build up an important collection, Cassou had visited the artists whose work he needed and bought to the limit of his funds, still keeping enough in hand for essential purchases from Picasso. When it came to his turn to be asked, Picasso welcomed the idea, but with the astuteness in such matters which comes to his aid at the appropriate moment, he offered ten paintings as a gift rather than allow them to be bought and find later that he owed the purchaser, in this case the French Government, a sum rivalling the price he would have received. The cubist paintings had already passed into private hands, but Picasso was able to save the French museums from their embarrassment by presenting them with these important works of more recent years.

In Antibes for other reasons something similar has happened. The Palais Grimaldi has become the Musée Picasso. When he found other places to work, he decided to leave on permanent loan the entire production of the idyllic months spent there, and later he added a collection of his ceramics, drawings and lithographs which transform the museum into one of the most enchanting places to visit anywhere in France. In a fresh and luminous atmosphere the walls display delight, humour, playfulness and a timeless image of human love and human life.

Since the war, other provincial towns have also made efforts to gather together Picasso exhibits. The little town of Céret, where the memory of cubist days had been kept alive until recently by the former museum curator Pierre Brune, has a room devoted to ceramics and drawings, and the new curator recently appointed is Picasso's old friend Havilland. In addition to permanent collections, exhibitions have been arranged in provincial galleries, notably in Lyons in 1953 and in Arles in 1957.

Outside France, in countries where the purchase of works of art for museums is on a more lavish scale, competition has greatly increased in the last few years. Paintings of the cubist period are very much in demand, so much that the rise in their value over the last ten years is the envy of all speculators. Some pictures of this period are now worth more than one hundred times their value twenty years ago, which was then about ten times the price that Picasso would have been paid for them when they were painted. The United States has acquired the largest quantity, and as he continues to produce, the flow of his most recent work to America continues. The time has come when no important art gallery and no collection of modern art throughout the world considers itself complete without an example of Picasso's work.

Ceramics at Vallauris

1947

In a valley surrounded by pine forests there lies, among vineyards, olive groves and terraces where lavender, jasmine and other sweet-scented plants are cultivated, the small town of Vallauris. From its pink tiled roofs smoke has risen for a thousand years. It belches intermittently in great black clouds as the potters light pine faggots to fire their kilns.[1] The town itself has no particular charm and there is no view out to sea to attract the tourist. Its main industries are the manufacture of scent and ceramics, but although the perfume is still sweet, the ancient traditional style of the ceramists had become so debased and the demand for their produce so reduced that at the end of the war Vallauris was far from prosperous.

Remembering his visit with Eluard to the old potter before the war, Picasso again took the three miles trip up the hillside behind Golfe Juan where he was then staying, and made friends this time with the ceramist Georges Ramié and his wife, whose enterprise 'Madoura' defied the general decadence around it. On his first visit he took some clay in his hands and amused himself by modelling a few small figures. It was not however until a year later, in the summer of 1947, that he returned, and was delighted to find that his work had been fired and carefully preserved. From that moment Picasso began to interest himself seriously in ceramics, and round him grew up a new activity in which a host of young artists followed his lead. Within ten years prosperity has come back to the little Provençal town, thanks to the presence and example of Picasso, for ten years ago he bought a small villa on a hill near the town and made Vallauris the centre of his activities.

The idea of conquering new territory, or rather of finding a new medium of expression, once more enthralled Picasso. In this case the art of the ceramist offered scope for various urges that he had always had in mind. Traditionally it combined the arts of painting and sculpture and in addition it had a basis of utility. Picasso's love of the esoteric, which found its culmination in analytical cubism, is balanced by a desire for his art to enter into life in the most humble sense as well as the highest. Pots, jugs, compotiers and plates, formerly the subject-matter of his still-life paintings, were now to be made by him not as rare treasures but as things which could be of daily use or serve as

[1] Plate XXII, 8.

familiar objects in the house. The collaboration of Georges Ramié and his expert potters opened a wide field of possibilities. Picasso's original designs could be copied faithfully by them and sold like etchings, although they could never have the exactness of prints since they were copies each made by hand. The project for reaching a wider public made Picasso enthusiastic. It gave employment to the local craftsmen and greatly increased the numbers of those who could enjoy his work. However, as time has passed, the utilitarian aspect of ceramics has been submerged by delight in the medium as a form of art which combines the elements of polychrome sculpture, painting and collage. In the exuberant vanity of his most recent works, there is little or no attention given to the possibility of their practical use in the household.

He astonished, even terrified those around him by his bold treatment of the material. Madame Ramié warned him day after day that in the firing such unreasonable experiments were bound to fail, but as she had to admit, he proved almost every time that he could do things that were impossible to others. Taking a vase which had just been thrown by Aga, their chief potter, Picasso began to mould it in his fingers. He first pinched the neck so that the body of the vase was resistant to his touch like a balloon, then with a few dexterous twists and squeezes he transformed the utilitarian object into a dove, light, fragile and breathing life. "You see," he would say, "to make a dove you must first wring its neck."[1] It was a delicate process; if the squeeze went wrong there was no remedy but to roll it all up and start again, but Picasso's touch was so sure that such a thing scarcely ever happened. Squeezing firmly but gently with his thumbs he could convert a vase more than a yard high into the most graceful female form with only a few touches. With extraordinary speed he learnt to judge what it was possible for him to do in using clay, glazes and fire. Always he listened to the advice of experienced craftsmen and then always acted in his own way.[2]

Rapidly there appeared on the shelves of the Madoura store-rooms rows of pitchers in the form of doves, bulls, owls, birds of prey, heads of fauns and men with horns or beards, their surfaces decorated with an incredible variety of patterns; some fierce and barbarous in their rhythms, some orderly and classical. Other shelves were spread with casseroles whose traditional Provençal form had been untouched but on which Picasso had painted animals, bullfights or Arcadian scenes.

[1] Plate XXIII, 7.
[2] *Cahiers d'Art*, 1948, No. 1, and *Verve*, 'Picasso à Vallauris', 1951.

From the bottoms of others stared grotesque faces, which often made children shriek with delight as he did a dance for them, holding one of these casseroles as a mask in front of his face.

In Vallauris Picasso had found a new playground where anything could be seduced by him into becoming a delightful toy. The long solitary concentration necessary for painting could be relaxed among his family or craftsmen who were his friends. Every morning he would appear dressed in shorts, sandals and singlet. His small, muscular, well-shaped body tanned by the sun and his alert carriage showed little sign of his age. Only his hair now thinning and becoming white, so that his eyes seemed even blacker than before, and the deep furrows in his face which emphasised his expression, gave indications that he was approaching his seventieth year. Otherwise, at work or bathing, he expressed in every movement the agility and strength of youth. To see his hands as he moulded the clay, small and feminine yet strong, gave a pleasure akin to watching a ballet, so complete was the coordination in their unhesitating movements. It seemed impossible for the clay not to obey: in such hands its future form was certain to become impregnated with their life.

Among all Picasso's inventions, those into which he instils a maximum of life and emotion are inspired by the female form, and since in pottery the ovoid form of pitchers and jugs prevails, he readily found materials which lent itself by modelling or decoration to a great variety of representations of women. As scale has never presented any difficulty to Picasso he was equally happy to transform small pots only a few inches tall with a few rapid squeezes into little goddesses, or to mould great vases of a metre high into a female form. The handle and spout changed into the braided hair of a girl. A simple egg-shaped bulge became her head, poised on a long thin neck springing from a base in the shape of breasts. The unity between the form of the vase, the painted lines that portray the features and the idea that lies therein is of startling perfection.

Vallauris suited Picasso admirably in that it offered wide facilities and an atmosphere in which he could indulge his wish to experiment with everything that came into his hands. Picking up tiles he turned them into owls; the supports used by potters to stack the biscuit pots in their kilns became limbs, trumpets or bones. The amusement of giving life to banal objects never failed because it was so often the origin of new discoveries which led to new achievements. The origin of his inspiration is in fact in play, and his never-ending game with objects and ideas is an essential part of the process of creation.

Picasso and the Cause of Peace

In his retreat in Vallauris Picasso was not isolated. He received visits from Paul Eluard and kept closely in touch with the activities of the Communist Party, particularly in its efforts to organise international opinion against war. In spite of controversy that sprang up as to the value of their endeavour and the sincerity of their aims, a large number of intellectuals in all countries joined forces, and Picasso was asked to support them. He had already made his position clear in the press at the end of the war. Meetings of intellectuals for Spanish relief and for peace had taken place in his studio in Paris. He was now asked however to appear in public and throw in the weight of his reputation in favour of the communist-sponsored Peace Congresses, the first of which was held in Wroclaw in August 1948.

It is a proof of Picasso's sincerity that, with his distaste for travel, he should have left Vallauris in the height of summer for Paris and embarked from there with Paul Eluard on a flight to Poland. Public demonstrations of this nature were completely foreign to him, and in addition, he was expected not only to make his appearance as a distinguished delegate but also to deliver a speech. His arrival was acclaimed with great enthusiasm, and before he left Poland, where he remained for a fortnight visiting Warsaw and Cracow, he was decorated by the President of the Republic with the 'Cross of a Commander with Star of the Order of the Polish Renaissance'. This was not the first of such honours. The day before he left France he had received the 'Médaille de la Reconnaissance Française' for services rendered to France, a sign that there was no disapproval of his action in support of the congress on the part of the French Government.

The following year a similar congress was organised in Paris in April. Picasso was asked to design a poster for the event, and choosing a subject familiar to him, a white pigeon such as he kept in a cage at the entrance to his studio in the rue des Grands Augustins, he made a lithograph which has since become famous for more than one reason. Not only was it used to advertise the congress at the Salle Pleyel which was attended by Picasso and his friends, but afterwards it was reprinted and appeared on the walls of many cities throughout Europe, acclaimed by some as a time-honoured symbol of peace and sneered at by others as an inept form of Communist propaganda. Later in the same year the Philadelphia Museum of Art leaving politics aside awarded his lithograph the Pennel Memorial Medal.[1] In more recent

[1] Mourlot, *Picasso Lithographe*, Vols. I and II.

years, Picasso's doves of peace have literally flown all round the world. Versions of several of his drawings have been reproduced on postage stamps in China and other communist countries.

In November 1950 the third congress which Picasso attended as a delegate was held at Sheffield. Although the former assemblies had incurred nothing worse than hostile criticism, in this case the British Government decided, since war had recently begun in Korea, that it was a dangerous form of propaganda and that it must be kept in check by refusing entry to a large number of delegates from abroad. As there were many distinguished intellectuals among the party arriving from the Continent, including Professor Joliot-Curie, the president of the congress, the discourtesy of this decision and of the manner in which it was carried out was remarked on in Parliament, by no less an anti-communist than Winston Churchill.

It so happened that at the same time an exhibition of recent paintings and ceramics by Picasso, organised by the Arts Council, was being held in London, and either for this or for some other reason never yet divulged, Picasso was allowed into the country. Having been warned that he was on his way, but not yet knowing what had happened to his companions, I hurried to Victoria Station to meet him. The night-ferry was unaccountably late and to my surprise, when I finally caught sight of the small figure of Picasso dressed in a grey suit and a black beret carrying his suitcase, he was alone. As soon as we met he explained that his friends, almost without exception, had been turned back from Dover as dangerous revolutionaries, "and I," he said with anxiety, "what can I have done that they should allow me through?"

Picasso's stay in England was brief. Plans for the congress had been thrown into confusion and the press was anxious to ridicule any victim connected with the affair as a deluded pawn of communist propaganda. To dodge the reporters I invited Picasso to come with me for the night to the country, a plan which suited him because, thinking that he would be with his friends, he had sent his car over with Marcel, the chauffeur, by way of Newhaven which is near my home. The following day we returned to London and Picasso left next morning by train for Sheffield, where the emasculated congress was to be held in spite of its unfortunate start. The City Hall was filled to overflowing and among the speakers Picasso received by far the greatest ovation, although his speech was the shortest. Speaking in French for not much more than a minute, with a delivery which showed his lack of experience in elocution, he characteristically made no reference to politics. Instead he explained how he had learned to paint doves from his father and from that beginning had taken his place in "the family of painters". He finished with the simple declaration: "I stand for life against death; I stand for peace against war." His personality made him popular and his presence as the lonely delegate carried weight.

On his return to London he was met by a large party of art students who welcomed him with wholehearted enthusiasm, but this was not enough to soften his annoyance at the action of the Government and he refused to accept an invitation that afternoon to visit his exhibition, which was crowded with hundreds of expectant admirers. In this case politics strengthened his habitual desire to keep away from such manifestations. It might have been thought that once the congress was over, or rather transferred to Warsaw, Picasso would be allowed to disappear from England without further comment. This would most likely have been the case had not a section of the press considered that this was the moment not only to ridicule him but also to attack those who wished to honour the visit to London of a great artist. Comments were made on the presence of a cabinet minister at a studio party given to welcome him. "It is an odd thing that a British Minister should wish to honour Picasso", the paper announced, and added, "it is now becoming well known that out of the money he receives for his works, the wealthy Picasso makes large contributions to the Communists."[1]

There was nothing however that could upset Picasso in attacks and distortions in the press. He was used to such things. They were not limited to one section of the press nor to England. During his visit he had been greeted by hundreds of his admirers and although he was not at his ease in the crowds around him whose language he could not understand, the novelty of finding himself isolated from his own circle of friends and the excitement of being back in England, the country which had inspired his earliest dreams of adventure, was sufficient to please him. He was astonished and awed by the scars of the blitz in London, and he enjoyed the English countryside as he saw it in the cold autumn sunlight, saying, "I am surprised young English painters do not make more of it".

The rebuff to the congress that Picasso had witnessed in London did not, however, deter him from attending a fourth congress held in Rome in 1951. He spent four days performing his duties, and found time to visit the Sistine Chapel, about which he later remarked to Kahnweiler that it was like a vast sketch by Daumier. On his way home he stopped to admire the Piero della Francescas at Arezzo and enjoyed,

[1] *Evening Standard*, Wednesday 15 November 1950.

but without much enthusiasm, the Giottos at Assisi. This however was his last journey as a delegate. These episodes in a life which has been so little occupied with group activities were remarkable proof of Picasso's disinterested loyalty to a cause in which he believed.

Family Life

The ungracious little pink villa, 'La Galloise', perched on the terraced hillside near Vallauris, had been chosen by Picasso, for lack of something better, as his home. Two mulberry trees too small to screen the childish geometry of its gable front shaded a small terrace, and its bleak rooms provided enough space for Françoise and their newly-born son, Claude. At the bottom of the garden was a garage where the new Chrysler given to Picasso by an American friend could be kept side by side with the old pre-war Hispano—the only car of which he has ever been really proud. After some adventurous years, Paulo had settled at Golfe Juan, and with his passion for cars, he turned out to be an excellent chauffeur for his father at a time when there was an urgent need for someone to replace Marcel.

Two years after the birth of Claude, a daughter was born in 1949. In accordance with her father's passion for doves she was appropriately named Paloma. Yan, a boxer puppy, joined the family and took his place in paintings of the children at play with their mother. With the advent of the new dog, the first to replace Kasbec, the elongated features of the Afghan hound appeared no more in Picasso's paintings. The shape of the children's faces in the new pictures reflected rather the round snub-nosed head of Yan.[1]

Picasso became very much absorbed in his new family. There are many drawings and paintings in which the children can be seen intent on their toys and games, clothed in gay colours, fearless, ruthless and overflowing with energy.[2] He entered into their play, and made them happy with dolls fashioned from scrap pieces of wood decorated with a few lines in coloured chalk; or taking pieces of cardboard he tore out shapes of men and animals and coloured them, giving them such droll expressions that they became fairy-tale characters not only for Claude and Paloma but for adults as well. He had amused himself in the same way before at Le Tremblay with Maïa and earlier had entertained Paulo with similar delights, even painting decorative themes with a few touches on his nursery furniture. Paulo, however, remembers one disconcerting occasion when his father took his toy motorcar after he had gone to bed. In the morning he found it painted in

[1] Plate XXII, 3.   [2] Boeck-Sabartès, *Picasso*, pp. 293, 307.

bright colours, with imitations of cushions on the seats and a gay check pattern on the floor. But to everyone's surprise Paulo burst into tears saying that his motor-car had been ruined—that cars never had check patterns on their floors.

At Vallauris throughout the summer the nearby beach was the main playground. The morning bathe would extend into the afternoon, while Picasso taught Claude how to swim and how to pull gruesome faces. It became widely known to friends who were spending their holidays on the coast that the whole family could be found on a certain beach at Golfe Juan nearly every day, and in consequence there was usually a large party to lunch with Picasso at the beach restaurant before he returned to Vallauris to work.

In spite of this apparent idleness the Madoura pottery overflowed with his production in all its rich variety, and it became necessary at an early date to find a studio where Picasso could paint and continue his sculpture. The solution presented itself in the shape of a disused scent factory near by, with vast tiled workrooms providing all the space required for the time being. The large barnlike workshops could serve as studios for painting or for sculpture and still leave room for future expansion. There was even a place for another painter, Pignon, to live during the summer in one of the rambling outhouses.

In this fertile and friendly atmosphere Picasso inevitably resembled the chief of a tribe—a tribe which had as its nucleus the family at 'La Galloise' and extended to the community of craftsmen at the potteries, not only the Madoura potters but also many other young ceramists who had started their own kilns, as well as painters who came from Paris to try their hand. The tribe also embraced many local tradespeople and artisans, the barber, the carpenter, the baker, and the fishermen from Golfe Juan joined the throng, all sharing admiration and affection for the little man with black eyes and white hair who had come to live among them and to whom the new celebrity of their town was due. He became a legend among them. A roll which the bakers of Vallauris had made for longer than can be remembered, with four points like short stubby fingers, became known as a 'Picasso' because he amused everyone by placing it at the end of a sleeve. The clan ate its 'Picassos' daily.

In Vallauris the legend was based on his daily presence, but elsewhere in France the name of Picasso was also to become symbolic just as at one time in Spain the name of the poet Gongora had been. The obscurity of his sonnets made his name a byword even among the illiterate. Particularly if the sky became black or the darkness impenetrable the peasants would call it a 'Gongora'. Similarly in France today the name of Picasso has come to signify a force that is incomprehensible and capricious. In a crowded street in Paris a taxi driver who has nearly come into collision with another car has been heard to shout "espèce de Picasso!" For those who judge him from a slight knowledge of his painting and from the disapproval, tempered with astonishment at his success, that they read in the press, the legend is less benign than at Vallauris. The name for many has become synonymous with anything grotesque, which can provoke the remark, "On dirait un Picasso". But those who meet him and get to know him think of him otherwise. Even if they do not understand his work they are conquered by his personality.

The Man with the Sheep *and the Vallauris Chapel*

To complete the collection of his works at the Palais Grimaldi in Antibes, Picasso made the generous suggestion that he should add a cast of the *Man with the Sheep*.[1] But difficulties arose, and in annoyance at the delay he withdrew the offer. Having done so, he had the idea of offering it instead to the Municipal Council of Vallauris. The councillors were at first taken aback. They asked with some alarm what sort of a statue it was, and when told that it really looked like a man with a sheep, only the blacksmith was heard to say, "what a pity if it looks just like any other statue". Apart from its value as a work of art, and even the reputation of its author which was not yet fully appreciated by all of them, it was in itself a valuable piece of bronze and would help to attract tourists, as they realised after some persuasion. They were grateful for the solidarity Picasso showed in supporting their interests, but again they had some misgivings when Picasso told them that he wanted to see it set up outdoors in a square where the children could climb over it and the dogs water it unhindered.

Finally the offer was accepted and the statue set up in the central square of Vallauris. A leader of the Communist Party, Laurent Casanova, was invited to unveil it in the presence of the mayor and a large gathering of friends which included Paul Eluard and Tristan Tzara. As a sign of gratitude the town of Vallauris made Picasso a citizen of honour. In the local press it was acknowledged that "Picasso is not only a great artist, he is also a man with a heart", and after speaking in general terms of the artistic value of the gift the article went on ". . . the permanent presence of this statue in our town will

[1] Plate XX, 2.

draw a new influx of visitors for the great good of the economy of our city".

Picasso's popularity in Vallauris was assured. In addition, the municipality offered him a deconsecrated chapel of the twelfth century to decorate as he thought fit. The invitation came at a time when several painters of repute had been using their talents for religious decorations. Léger had made a large mosaic for a mountain church at Assy in the Jura, and Rouault had designed a stained glass window for the same church. Matisse was at work decorating his chapel at Vence, while Braque had contributed to the restoration of a small church near Dieppe. To Picasso, however, in agreement with his communist friends, the idea at that time of seeing his work introduced as an ornament to the Catholic faith was distasteful. "What do they mean by religious art?" I have heard him say. "It is an absurdity. How can you make religious art one day and another kind the next?" However, with the Vallauris chapel the same objection did not arise, since it had been turned over to secular use during the French Revolution. He was therefore free to practise his art as he liked and to develop an ideology of his own in which the cardinal factors could be his profound desire for peace and his horror of war. He has always insisted that it is not a chapel that he undertook to decorate but a Temple to Peace.

During the summer of 1950 a clash between communism and the Western powers brought about the war in Korea. Picasso, primarily for humanitarian reasons as one who hated war, again felt himself involved. His communist friends had grown to expect a gesture from him condemning this new outbreak of violence, and it was hoped that he would paint a picture which could be used to blame the Western powers as aggressors. The painting Picasso produced was one of the few pictures to which he deliberately gave a title, calling it _Massacre in Korea._[1] It shows in unmistakable terms a squad of semi-robots receiving the order to fire on a group of naked women and children, but there is no clue as to which side is guilty of massacre. Picasso remained faithful to his hatred of military force used against defenceless human beings, and by so doing he saved himself from becoming a partisan propagandist and proved the validity of his painting. At the time it was first exhibited in the Salon de Mai of 1951 the communists made free use of it for their cause, but five years later in Warsaw a large reproduction of it was set up in the streets as a symbolic protest against the action of the Soviet armies in Hungary.

[1] Plate XXI, 7.

After *Guernica* and the *Charnel House*, the *Massacre in Korea* makes an appeal which is more easily understood by the public in general. In its composition it owed something both to Goya's execution scene .of 1808 and to Manet's *Execution of Maximilian*. Picasso has never been closer to anecdote in any of his major works since the Blue period. Even so, the picture attains universality by leaving undetermined the identity of the aggressor.

War *and* Peace

It was during a banquet given in honour of his seventieth birthday by the potters of Vallauris at tables spread in the nave of the little chapel, that Picasso, looking once more at the masonry of its vault, promised finally that he would decorate it. The nave consists of a solid stone barrel-vault without windows, open at one end to the chancel which for many years had been used as an olive press, and at the other to the street. Picasso's idea was to cover it completely with a great painting which on one side would have for its subject war, and on the other peace.[1] To do this a prepared surface had to be insulated from the damp stones. The task was put into the hands of the local carpenter. Skilfully he fixed an armature to the rough stone which was to receive the painted panels when they were ready. Picasso's first problem was to find a studio large enough and to erect a movable stage from which he could work on the panels. Fortunately an adjoining part of the scent factory provided sufficient space, and with the aid of Mr. Batigne, an American who had a house in Vallauris, the technical difficulties of lighting and scaffolding were overcome.

In the summer of 1952 Picasso began his task. He had already made great quantities of drawings, but contrary to his practice in painting *Guernica* he made no sketch for the whole picture. Two themes had been occupying his attention. The first he described as centring round "the tattered, jolting procession of those provincial hearses, miserable and grimacing, that one sees passing in the streets of small towns".[2] In the drawings the funereal chariot took a variety of shapes, its black plumes were transformed into the turrets of engines of war, and the macabre vehicle was drawn sometimes by decayed nags, at other times by camels or even pigs. The images made it clear that in his view war is not only ugly but also stupid and insane. During the previous year Picasso had made a series of light-hearted drawings and paintings of knights in armour sallying forth from castles,

[1] Plate XXIII, 1 and 2.   [2] Claude Roy, *La Guerre et la Paix*.

accompanied by their pages.[1] He had amused himself by elaborating the armour of the knights with fantastic excrescences and draping their Rosinantes in rich trappings. These same inventions now took a sinister appearance and medieval skirmishes gave way to the demons of modern war.

In contrast to the preparations for the panel, *War*, Picasso had also been indulging himself at the same time in a very different theme, a series of idyllic drawings of girls dancing. Decked in garlands, with graceful charm they joined hands, skipped, and turned summersaults, tossing flowers in the air and abandoning themselves to their games.[2] He had also found the time to write a second play in six acts which he named *The Four Little Girls*. With the same verve that he had expended on *Desire Caught by the Tail*, but in a more lyrical mood he wrote it to the music of the crickets during the summer nights at 'La Galloise'. It is a fantastic rambling picture of the desires and antics of four charming and precocious children. In the spontaneous joy of their games, their ecstatic dances and their erotic songs, the instinctive violence of their desires breaks through. Disquieting screams season the sweetness of their kittenlike play, in which the claw is scarcely hidden beneath the softness of the fur.

As a painter, Picasso makes continual references to colour and to its ambiguous nature: "The yellow of blue, the blue of blue, the red of blue." The little girls speak a language which reflects on one side the invented words and puns made by Claude and Paloma and on the other his own thoughts about vision, life and death. For instance, with innocent wisdom they speak in turn like a Greek chorus:

"*Little girl II*   Only the eye of the bull that dies in the arena sees.
Little girl I   It sees itself.
Little girl IV   The deforming mirror sees.
Little girl II   Death, that clear water.
Little girl I   And is very heavy."

As in the earlier play soliloquies are important, and the action is described in stage directions which, as in the earlier play, would often cause trouble if they were to be carried out literally. For instance, at the end of the fourth act we read: "Enter an enormous winged white horse dragging its entrails, surrounded by wings, an owl perched on its head, it stands for a brief moment in front of the little girl and then disappears at the other end of the stage."

[1] Plate XXIII, 6   [2] See Claude Roy, *La Guerre et la Paix*.

Picasso's imagery continues with persistence. Characters that appeared at the time of the curtain for *Parade* or before, like the white horse dressed up as Pegasus, reappear in new circumstances. Images that he had formerly realised in his paintings change their medium and become poetry.

When the new studio with its scaffolding was ready, Picasso shut himself off from everyone and only emerged, locking the door behind him, for meals and sleep. For two months the only person who was allowed in was Paulo. His instructions were that if at any moment his father should weaken and inadvertently invite someone to see what he was doing, Paulo like the crew of Ulysses was to turn a deaf ear and refuse to let the visitor in. Picasso's days began with a visit to the pottery. He would make two or three pots as a start until he felt in the right mood, then he would disappear into the studio.

Finally one day in October, apparently on the pretext of fetching some cigarettes, the doors were opened and a few friends were allowed in for the first time. The panels were finished. On a table by the door stood an alarm clock and a calendar on which the date of his beginning was marked and two months mapped out in advance. To the astonishment of all, for no-one had ever realised that he was capable of such precision in timing, he had kept his programme to a day. In addition to the two great panels, there was a large number of drawings round the studio and also some six or seven portaits, as well as landscapes and still-lifes, created as a sideline to vary the tension of his work.

Speaking later of *War* and *Peace* Picasso said: "None of my paintings has been painted with such speed, considering its size."[1] Starting with *War* he allowed the compositions to grow. "The laws of composition," he said, "are never new, they are always someone else's", and to work with the liberty he needed he preferred to trust the storehouse of his own experience to furnish him with solutions when the time came. Like a matador who must judge the right moment and the correct movement for his pass, Picasso said, to explain his method: "In modern painting each touch has become a task of precision."

As the great panels faced each other in the studio it was difficult to appreciate Picasso's ultimate intention. During their visit to Italy for exhibition in Rome and Milan they were shown separately, and it was not until they finally returned to Vallauris in the autumn of 1953 to be installed in the chapel, that anyone but Picasso realised the conception he had in mind. They had been planned to fit the low vault,

[1] Claude Roy, *La Guerre et la Paix.*

lining it from floor to floor, so that, meeting at the top, they made one picture. When at last they were put together, although he had taken no measurements, the joins in the painting met exactly as he had intended. This faculty of judging distances precisely by eye has frequently been put to the test. Picasso tells proudly how during the war, when making a drawing for the *Man with the Sheep*, he found that his paper was too small for his intentions. Having drawn the figure to the waist he took a second sheet, and without looking at the first he drew the rest of the figure. When he put the two halves together, not the slightest adjustment in either drawing was necessary. The same accuracy in his judgement was commented on by his producer when a few years later he was at work on a film with Georges-Henri Clouzot.

With the closing of the west door from the street, the vault of the old chapel, lit only from the chancel, had the effect of a cave. Picasso had toyed with the idea that visitors should see his murals by the flickering light of torches, in the same way that primitive man saw the magic paintings hidden in the depths of the caves of Lascaux. He wanted the time-honoured theme of *War* and *Peace* to be seen in intimacy; its universal appeal was also to be personal. He had contrived that the two contrasting subjects should meet overhead with the menacing sword of war balanced by a multicoloured diamond-shaped sun rising to the zenith, thus enclosing the spectator in two contrary worlds which are one.

Picasso had begun his great panorama with *War*. Its demons breathing fire, burning books and distributing loathsome poisonous insects formed a symbol of the insidious incalculable horrors engendered by war. The tawdry pomp and insane clamour moving from right to left were brought to a halt by a serene god-like figure facing them with the image of the dove on his shield.

The task of creating the image of peace after such spectacular material could have defeated a less resourceful painter. Picasso based his thoughts on what he knew to be the most enjoyable and most permanent in human society, the love that he knew in his own family. For *Peace* he painted a scene in which Pegasus driven by a child is harnessed to the plough. Amidst dancing figures there are feats of equilibrium in which a juggler balances a rod supporting at either end a goldfish bowl full of swallows and a cage containing fish. Thus he makes it clear that happiness is not easily maintained, that like the acrobat the happy man runs a daily risk of calamity. With scathing violence on the one hand and gentle, enigmatic humour on the other, Picasso in this microcosm created the symbols of his philosophy. As

Eluard wrote: "He wants to defeat all tenderness with violence and all violence with tenderness."

Today the vault of the Temple to Peace is complete, and a lighting system has been installed. It still remains however for Picasso to paint the panel which is to cover the wall at the end once the door on to the street has been bricked up. When he will do this no-one can tell.

Paris: Books and Paul Eluard

During these years Picasso's activities extended beyond Vallauris. His visits to Paris were frequent. The house in the rue des Grands Augustins became animated each time with visitors. At times he painted, but much of his energy went into his graphic art. More than a dozen books published by his friends contained lithographs or etchings by him, and he also illustrated several important volumes. The most remarkable of these are the *Twenty Poems* of Gongora, illustrated with etchings and marginal drawings in the text, which is written in his own hand;[1] *Le Chant des Morts*, a volume of poems in manuscript by Pierre Reverdy, boldly illuminated with 125 lithographs;[2] and Mérimée's *Carmen* with Picasso's engravings.[3] Shortly after these he produced with Iliazd, the poet and typographer, an illustrated edition of the sixteenth-century poems by Adrien de Monluc;[4] a book of poems by Tristan Tzara;[5] and another by the Guadelupian poet Aimé Césaire.[6] In 1950 Paul Eluard brought to him a book of short poems he had written, for which Picasso made page by page drawings of the human face, to which he gave the form of a dove. It was published with Eluard's title, *Visage de la Paix*.[7]

In the production of these books, many of which were published as de luxe editions, expert craftsmen from the workshops of Lacourière and Mourlot were eager to give their help. Shifting with ease from one medium to another and keeping them constantly employed, Picasso still found time between their visits for his friends. Kahnweiler had again taken his place after many years as the main agent for Picasso's sales, and Sabartès continued to be his faithful support in business matters. The younger generation was also constantly around him, not only members of his own family but young painters and sculptors in

[1] Gongora, *Vingt poèmes*, Les grand Peintres Modernes et le Livre, 1948.
[2] Reverdy, *Les Chant des Morts*, ed. Tériade, Paris, 1948.
[3] Mérimée, *Carmen*, La Bibliothèque Française, Paris, 1949.
[4] de Monluc, *La Maigre*, ed. Degré, Paris, 1952.
[5] Tzara, *De Mémoire d'Homme*, ed. Bordas, Paris, 1950.
[6] Césaire, *Corps perdu*, ed. Fragrance, Paris, 1950.
[7] Eluard ,*Visage de la Paix*, ed. Cercle d'Art, Paris, 1951.

whom he took an interest and to whom his encouragement was precious. Picasso is generous in his praise, he continually looks for talent and is delighted when he finds it. Even on those not infrequent occasions when he finds himself trapped by an uninteresting young painter asking for advice, he is considerate, knowing how deeply heartless criticism can wound. I have heard him say firmly and finally to a young man who showed no originality in his work: "But what does it matter what I say? The essential thing in all this is inside you, it's for you to decide if you should continue to paint or not."

The political activities to which Paul Eluard devoted an increasing amount of his energy were shared in a more detached way by Picasso, who continued to enjoy his company. To him the great value of Eluard above all other poets, including even Apollinaire, was his understanding of painting. Eluard was as passionate about painting as he was about poetry and he saw in Picasso the man who had liberated the arts and brought them again into contact with reality. In a lecture that he gave in London in 1951 entitled "Today, Pablo Picasso, the youngest painter in the world, is 70", he spoke of the way in which he was affected by his work. Describing some of the night landscapes lately painted by Picasso at Vallauris[1] he said: "He copies the night as though he were copying an apple, from memory, the night in his garden at Vallauris—a sloping garden, ordinary enough. At one side of the house there is a reservoir, lit by a lamp, and plenty of grass and weeds. I realise from the start that these nights at Vallauris will have nothing of the facile grace of Provence, but I am certain that after seeing them I could never live through a Provençal night without feeling it in the way it exists in his pictures. All Picasso's models resemble their portraits. In a drawing by Picasso, things are reinstated in their true light; from an infinitely variable appearance, with a thousand considerations he releases a constant, he renders permanent a sum total of images, he totalises his experiences."[2]

On 14 June 1951 Picasso with Françoise Gilot attended the marriage of Paul Eluard and Dominique Laure in the town hall of St. Tropez. Together with the Ramiés they had come over from Vallauris as witnesses of an event which after the death of Nusch was at last to bring happiness back to Eluard. His new life with Dominique however was to last little more than two years, for in November 1953 Eluard

[1] Plate XXII, 6.
[2] Extract from a lecture delivered by Paul Eluard at the opening of a retrospective exhibition of drawings by Picasso at the Institute of Contemporary Arts, London, 11 October 1951.

died. His death brought to an end the longest of the intimate friendships of poet and painter that Picasso had known.

At the time of the wedding no-one could have suspected such an abrupt finish for a man who overflowed with energy and enthusiasm, in spite of his precarious health. The celebrations had been enlivened by the gift of a tall and magnificent vase, decorated with nude girls and acrobats, from Picasso, who at lunchtime made drawings of those round the table.[1] Soon afterwards he returned several times to St. Tropez to enjoy the company of Eluard and visit other friends. Françoise, however, was not always with him on these occasions and it was whispered that an estrangement between them had begun.

Towards the end of the summer Picasso was forced to return to Paris. Owing to the shortage of housing the authorities were evicting him from his apartment in the rue la Boètie, which since he had left it to live in the rue des Grands Augustins during the war, had become no more than a storehouse where everything remained in a state of abandon. Picasso however resented being told to move out; as he said, if he had been running a conventional business he would have been allowed all the space he needed to store his wares, and he felt it unjust that painters were not treated with the same respect. In any case, the idea of delving into the disorder that had accumulated over so many years and been covered so deeply in the grime of Paris was more than he could bear. In consequence he delegated Sabartès and Marcel, the chauffeur, to do it for him while he waited at the rue des Grands Augustins for reports of their progress. The housing of Françoise and the children, who had outgrown the little rooms above the studio, was however solved by taking another apartment in the rue Gay-Lussac.

The size of Picasso's family and those dependent on him was by now considerable. Olga, whom he saw occasionally, was in poor health and had settled in Cannes. Although the tension which had led to such violent encounters and made her unwelcome in the thirties had died down with time, Picasso's new family and new friends had made a final barrier, and Paulo was now the only link between them. In 1953 she died, but according to Alice B. Toklas, who had always remained her friend and who visited her in hospital, she spoke with great emotion of both Picasso and her son, who, she said, had been very good, doing all they could to comfort her in her illness. Before his wife died Picasso had become a grandfather and Paulo had affectionately named his son Pablo.

[1] Plate XXIII, 5.

Sculpture and Painting at Vallauris

The great empty spaces of the old scent factory were rapidly filled in every corner with paintings and sculpture. Among them stood the piece of sculpture that has become the most widely known of those made since the move to Vallauris in 1948—the *Goat*.[1] Like most of the others, it is a composite construction pieced together from objects in which Picasso found new possibilities. When we examine it we find that its fertile belly is a wicker basket, its backbone and ribs are a palm branch, pieces of scrap iron protrude from its shoulders and its udders are made from clay pots. At the same time it is so essentially a goat, so much the quintessence of goat that it becomes surprising to think that goats can be made otherwise. It is the sleepy, brooding heaviness of the animal soon to give birth that makes it impressive. This greedy friend of man, capricious and yet generous with its gifts, is set solidly before us. Compared with the black and white animal that grazes beside it in his garden, with its chain attached to its sister's bronze tail, it is more permanent and can evoke a more lasting vision of a goat in our minds than the millions made of flesh and blood that come and go.

Other sculptures of animals, constructed in the same collage technique, are also impressive. There is a life-size monkey with her baby hanging at her chest which provokes a sense of astonishment when it is realised that its head is a toy motor car.[2] The shock it causes is more than a temporary sensation. It recurs in other sculptures; the tail of the *Crane*[3] is a spade and its crest a small tap, the horns of the bull, in the *Still-life with Bottle and Candle*, are handle-bars, and the rays of light from the candle are nails. In each case the metamorphosis is complete and appropriate. The joke is not forgotten at first sight in an instantaneous guffaw, it lives on as the inexplicable comedy played between forms which apparently have no affinity, and which yet, in juxtaposition, sacrifice their former identity. By doing so they give birth to a new and vital image, as when equating the motor car with the ape's head, Picasso creates a modern version of the Minotaur. The implications are endless; they remind us of the *Temptation of St. Anthony* of Hieronymus Bosch, where we are shown a confusion of identity which has become universal and so dangerous that the saint hides his face from it. Picasso however is not frightened to approach the frontiers of madness, knowing that without taking this risk it is impossible to question the reality of what we see.

I was once at Vallauris when Braque paid him a visit. At that time

[1] Plate XXIV, 3.   [2] Plate XXIV, 1.   [3] Boeck-Sabartès, *Picasso*, p. 439.

Picasso had begun a sculpture, the first elements of which were a child lying in a derelict baby carriage. Again it was made up from the most unlikely material: he amused us by adding to it pieces of pottery, a gas ring or anything that came to hand to make the effect all the more entertaining, and finally taking the infant in his arms, he kissed it. Braque who is inclined to be shy of Picasso's buffoonery laughed with us all and then said: "We laugh, but not *at* you, we laugh *with* you, in sympathy with your ideas." Our laughter had not been trivial. It was of the kind of which Baudelaire said ". . . laughter caused by the grotesque has about it something profound, primitive and axiomatic, which is much closer to the innocent life and to absolute joy than is the laughter caused by the comic in man's behaviour".[1] The alliance of the grotesque with Picasso's ability to metamorphose objects at will is a key to the power of these composite inventions.

Some other sculptures of this period do not rely on the collage technique. There are several versions of owls cast in bronze, some of them painted so that their cantankerous scowls are accentuated and their feathers made light and fluffy. The application of bold patterns in black and white on the bronze, completely eliminates the heavy quality of the metal. This mixing of the effects of painting and sculpture has come about through Picasso's desire to speak simultaneously in more than one medium and reduce the conventional barriers between them. In the figure of the *Pregnant Nude*,[2] however, his preoccupation is different. In this case it is the swollen forms to which he draws attention by polishing the bare bronze surfaces of breasts and belly as though they had been caressed by devotees like those who polish St. Peter's toes with their kisses. This figure standing stark and proud of her fruitfulness is one of Picasso's most human and most moving achievements. At the present time he keeps a plaster cast high on a table, presiding over the corner in his studio where he is most often at work.

More Paintings and New Versions of Old Masterpieces

Among the many paintings that crowded the studios in Vallauris, the winter landscapes, the scenes of his children at play with their mother and the paintings of the summer nights, there was the series of twelve portraits, painted in the spring of 1954, of a blonde girl, Sylvette Jellinek, whose nordic beauty attracted him as he saw her walking with her English husband round Vallauris. Although in fact she was French, he enjoyed thinking of her as an incarnation of his dream of English beauty, and taking her as his model he painted many

[1] Baudelaire, *The Mirror of Art*, Phaidon Press, p. 144.   [2] Plate XXIV, 5.

versions of her seated with her blonde pony-tail coiffe crowning her head.[1]

Yet another diversion had become increasingly important in his recent work. His continual interest in the work of others had tempted him on several occasions in the past to take as his theme a painting that he admired, such as Poussin's *Bacchanale*, and reinterpret it according to the feelings it provoked in him. At this time two great paintings, the *Demoiselles de la Seine* of Courbet and El Greco's *Self-Portrait*,[2] had attracted his attention, and he painted two large canvases, rearranging them in his own manner. In both cases it is possible to trace in detail the original work, but by the way in which they have been transformed they have become completely his own. A careful comparison between Picasso's versions and the works of his predecessors is the best possible guide to the revolution he has brought about in painting and to its significance.

In the portrait of El Greco, for instance, his admiration for the master of Toledo and his interest in the fact that it is a self-portrait have not restrained him from making fundamental changes, although at the same time he has kept faithfully to the spirit of the work. He has treated his subject, the original painting, as formerly he treated a guitar, analysing it and making a statement of its essential qualities without failing to take every detail into account. The head of El Greco, surrounded by a white ruff, is greatly enlarged, and the features, instead of presenting an almost photographic likeness, are formed, rather than deformed, in a way which changes their static appearance into one of movement. El Greco's right hand, with little finger raised, holding the brush, is spread out nervously like a flower and El Greco's small rectangular palette, held in his left hand, is unchanged in shape, but it becomes unmistakably the less tidy palette of Picasso. El Greco's portrait with its Renaissance conception of realism prepared the ground for photography. Picasso's version some three hundred and fifty years later opens our eyes to a new vision in painting, and a new attitude towards reality.[3]

The Death of Friends

The death of Paul Eluard was the first of several blows in quick succession that carried off old friends. André Derain had for many years ceased to be an intimate friend, but the news that he had died

---

[1] Plate XXII, 9.   [2] Plate XXII, 7.
[3] See John Lucas, 'Picasso as a Copyist', *Art News*, New York, November 1955.

from the effects of an accident was disturbing to Picasso, especially as the news of the death of another companion of the days of the Bateau Lavoir, Maurice Raynal, who had recently completed his second book about Picasso, came soon afterwards. Picasso told a friend who was staying with him when he heard the news of Raynal's death that he had a habit of going over the names of his most intimate friends every morning, and added with a sense of guilt that that day he had left out Raynal. "But you didn't kill him," said his companion. "No," said Picasso, "but I forgot him this morning."

Shortly afterwards came more bad news. Matisse was dead. Since the war, Matisse had been living in Nice, and although bedridden most of the time, had continued to work on plans for his chapel at Vence and amused himself by cutting out decorative patterns from coloured papers. Picasso had made a habit of paying him frequent visits and they exchanged paintings and other objects, including an alarming life-size female figure from the New Hebrides which Matisse presented to Picasso. Unfortunately no-one was present to make notes of their conversations, for Matisse was a fascinating talker and any exchange of views between them after long years of experience could not have been without interest.

A year later, in 1954, yet another death, that of Fernand Léger, came as a further shock. Picasso was outliving his generation. One of the four great names in the evolution of cubism, Léger had developed his own vigorous interpretation. In his attempt to popularise his art he applied strictly formal limitations. His paintings were so indicative of his strong simple personality that Picasso's verdict on seeing an exhibition of his work a year before his death was: "Léger never makes a mistake."

Separation

The winter of 1953 was one of extreme bitterness for Picasso. The situation between him and Françoise Gilot had become increasingly difficult, and at the end of the summer she returned to Paris with the children, leaving him alone in Vallauris. Apocryphal stories in the·press that she did not wish to spend the rest of her life with a 'historical monument' and other prejudiced gossip helped to widen the breach. It would be indiscreet to try to establish the reasons for the break-up of a liaison which to all appearances should have been a very happy one for her and for Picasso in his old age. That he had been in love with her is obvious from the many tributes he has paid to her beauty in his work. The children she had borne were adored by them both and their life in common as painters brought satisfaction, though the talent of Françoise was bound to suffer a partial eclipse in his proximity.

The isolation in which Picasso found himself was to some extent relieved by the arrival of an old friend, the widow of the sculptor Manolo who had died a little while before, with her daughter. They saw to his domestic needs, but the bitterness of his solitude could be relieved only by his own efforts.

A Season in Hell

It was in mid-December that Picasso found the outlet he needed for his troubled spirit. In quick succession he made a series of drawings on which he worked with feverish concentration through the lonely nights until the end of January. 'Picasso and the Human Comedy' is the title that Michel Leiris gave to the brilliant preface he wrote for the volume in which these drawings, 180 in number, were reproduced.[1] The artist had turned to the universal reality of his own particular plight to free himself from his obsession, and sometimes making as many as eighteen drawings in a day he set down a visual account of his own thoughts. It became an autobiography in which we find reappearing the actors—clowns, acrobats, and apes—his companions in the work of his early years. Like him they have aged, and holding masks in front of their wrinkled faces, they try to enchant or deceive us with an appearance of classical serenity or obscene grimaces.

The theme of the painter and his model recurs in masterly style with new and more intimate implications. It is still primarily the theme of love; the love of the artist for his model and by transference the love of his own creation, the painting. The ageing artist crouching over his work becomes more absorbed than ever in his picture and takes only fleeting glances at the beauty of his model. The fierce wit with which old age is belaboured and exposed in its ugliness, doting, and myopic stupidity speaks of Picasso's own consciousness of the approach of the 'last enemy'. At the same time he pays generous homage to youth in the most moving terms. Old age and fatuity stand dazed by its radiant beauty as with leering eyes or the obscene grin of Silenus they contemplate the naked body of a girl standing before them.

It is Picasso's most complete confession of his love for women. Drawn with a rapid unerring line, which shows no trace of an afterthought, they appear triumphant and integral in their female nature,

[1] 'Suite de 180 Dessins de Picasso', *Verve*, Vol. VIII, Nos. 29-30, Paris, 1954.

not within the frozen limits of classical beauty but with movement that brings them to life and hides nothing of the irregularities and the imperfections which can make their attraction even more personal and compelling. Picasso's remark, "you don't love Venus, you love a woman", is borne out in these drawings by the accuracy with which he has noted the variety of their charms. To those to whom he has said that he has never yet fallen in love this may be the answer. It gives an indication of the depth and quality of his love. It may be a generic love of women more than the love of one particular woman, but his passion proves to be so intense that one fraction of it may be of greater richness than the entire affection of another man.

The painter's problem, which springs fundamentally from the same source and becomes in its own right the rival of erotic emotion, received equal attention. The place usurped from reality by the image grows in importance through this enthralling series. We are shown the old bearded dry-as-dust painter scratching away at his canvas, oblivious of the model and intent on his 'chef d'œuvre inconnu'. The critics around him examine every detail of his work, and return to admire the least blot made by him on the canvas, just as in other drawings they watch the lady painter who regards the youthful body of her model with a jealous eye. The whole world of the painter's studio is passed in review, and then the make-believe of painting is transferred to games between the artist and the model themselves as they hide their own features, hers behind a bearded mask and his covered by the profile of a beautiful girl. The last drawing, added as a final comment, shows us the model wearing a mask of classical beauty sitting before her muddle-headed bewhiskered painter, who discovers on looking at his canvas a portrait, not of her but of himself mocking him with a toothless grin. Picasso had exorcised the misery which was threatening him by remembering what he had always known, that art being a product of sadness and pain could rescue him from his melancholy because suffering lies at the root of life.

CHAPTER XIII

'LA CALIFORNIE'
(1954-1958)

Tauromachia

AFTER THE first World War, the more sophisticated art of the ballet had superseded the circus in Picasso's affection, but later on, after the death of Diaghilev in 1929, his interest waned. His only contribution since that date was a drop curtain he designed for *Le Rendezvous*, a ballet written by Jacques Prévert for the Roland Petit company in 1945. He found once more, however, that the bullfight, as a spectacle of agility and rich colour, could more than compensate for his former passion for the ring and the stage. Moreover, it brought back memories of his early youth.

In the years after the war, a new interest in bullfighting had sprung up in Provence, and corridas in which famous Spanish matadors took part had become frequent in the ancient Roman arenas of Nîmes and Arles and elsewhere in the neighbourhood. On such occasions it was rare not to find Picasso occupying a place in the front row, surrounded by a party of his friends and receiving the ceremonial honours of the fight. Not infrequently, improvised entertainments offered by his Spanish friends prolonged his visits. Toreadors, gypsies, and the guardians of herds from the Camargue would celebrate the event till dawn with flamenco singing and stories which, if they ceased to be concerned with bullfighting, at once took on a Rabelaisian flavour.

At such times, warmed by the animation of his compatriots, Picasso's voice seems to conceal a laugh. Its tone becomes more robust as he grows more eloquent in his native language. When suddenly he does break into a laugh it is high-pitched and so infectious that it inevitably spreads to his companions. His enormous eyes, which even in daylight show scarcely any difference between the iris, which in fact is of a very dark chestnut colour, and the jet-black pupil, become almost swamped by the deep furrows of his smile, and from the corners of his eyes wrinkles radiate like black rays from two black suns. His sparse crop of short white hair bristles and sparkles like hoar frost. Smaller in stature than those around him, he is always the centre of the group. With tense expression they listen as he talks eagerly, leaning forward to prod the arm of a friend to whom he wishes to emphasise his meaning. His moods, however, can change rapidly with instant effect on his expression. The exuberance fades and a look of sadness crosses his face, seeming to reveal some deep incurable disquiet, or again a penetrating look of enquiry, often tinged with anxiety, demands a reply which will restore his composure.

During the spring of 1954 he had been absorbed by his portraits of his new model, Sylvette. When summer came he stayed on as usual in Vallauris, where he was joined by Claude and Paloma who had been brought by their mother from Paris in spite of their parents' estrangement. The holiday season culminated in a bullfight which Spanish friends, experts in this matter, organised in his honour. In the main square of the town an arena was built specially for the occasion. The corrida that followed was locally a much-publicised event, known to all Picasso's friends on the coast. Jean Cocteau, Jacques Prévert and André Verdet, frequently to be seen in Vallauris, were among the first to arrive, and they found Picasso in a festive mood. Taking part in a procession to rouse the town, he was perched on the back of a car playing a trumpet. Accompanying him were Paulo and his friend Pierre Baudouin who had distinguished themselves by shaving one half of their heads from front to back.

In the grandstand Picasso took the seat of the President of the corrida with Cocteau on one side and Jacqueline Roque on the other. He had recently met her in Vallauris, and had painted portraits of her during the summer, emphasising the beauty of her regular profile and her large dark eyes. Round him also were Maïa, now a handsome girl of eighteen, and Claude and Paloma watching eagerly as their mother, Françoise, rode into the ring on a fine horse to perform the ceremony of asking the President's permission for the corrida to begin.

From the point of view of the aficionado the proceedings that followed had little interest. They were no more than comic games in which the bull suffered no harm, but the intimacy among the spectators and the buffoonery of the performers made it memorable. So great was its success that it has now become a yearly event, at which Picasso presides over the festivities like a chieftain surrounded by his tribe.

Apart from these public demonstrations of fraternity, there is a bond between Picasso and the artists, potters and craftsmen of Vallauris. His visits to their workshops are not only an encouragement to them but a meeting between craftsmen. Every year the master potters show their gratitude and affection by offering on his birthday a banquet which is attended by thirty or more of them with their friends. On the last two occasions they have presented him with potters' turntables of a new design, which can hold a pot in such a way that it can be turned round at any angle, thus making it easier for him to work in his own home.

Whatever Picasso enjoys usually finds an echo in his work. Bulls, matadors and picadors are transferred from the arena to the surface of a plate.[1] Large dishes have their oval shape converted into the grand panorama of the bull ring, with its crowds in sun and shade watching the fight. Reminiscent of cubist discoveries, the oval once more aptly places the circle in perspective.

Large lithographs and aquatints, patiently carried through many stages, have been the means of producing vivid images of bullfights in the arena of Arles. At other times his method is to make a great number of rapid drawings in which each stroke of the brush is final. In the summer of 1957 he returned from a disappointing corrida, and with astonishing energy produced some fifty aquatints one after the other. They were in fact inspired not by the corrida he had just seen but by a seventeenth-century book on Tauromachia by José Delgado (known as Pepe Illo) which for years he had thought of illustrating. Suddenly something had happened to make it possible for him to realise this long-standing project in one creative outburst.[2]

Shortly after the Vallauris corrida of 1954, Picasso took Jacqueline Roque and the two children to Perpignan to stay with friends he had known for many years. Comte Jacques de Lazerme had been interested in the arts since his boyhood. Through Manolo, the sculptor, he had known Picasso and the 'Parisians' who had made the nearby village of Céret the centre of cubism for several summers before the first World War. Jacques de Lazerme and his attractive wife lived in a spacious seventeenth-century house in the middle of the town. They welcomed Picasso by giving him several large rooms in which he could live and work as he felt inclined.

Bullfights at Céret and bathing with Claude and Paloma at Collioure were his main pleasures. He enjoyed the change in his surroundings, the coast, and the treeless foothills of the Pyrenees, but he was tantalisingly near his native country. He could see plainly the mountain frontier he had vowed never to cross so long as Franco remained dictator of Spain.

The local people of all ranks greeted him warmly. They hoped he might settle in the region, and as an inducement offered him the old castle at Collioure to use as a studio, as he had used the Palais Grimaldi

---

[1] Plate XXIII, 8.   [2] Duncan, *The Private World of Pablo Picasso*.

in Antibes. They proposed that he should build a temple to Peace on top of a nearby mountain, which could be seen from great distances on both sides of the frontier. Picasso toyed with these ideas, and explored the mountain site which he found magnificent, but although he seemed to agree and talked with enthusiasm of these plans, after he returned to Paris in the autumn they were eclipsed by other more immediate work.

Les Femmes d'Alger

Because of his extraordinary visual memory and his familiarity with the arts in all their variety, Picasso's visits to museums are infrequent. However, when the paintings he had presented to the State in 1946 were assembled in the Louvre before being sent to the Musée d'Art Moderne, Georges Salles, the Director of the Louvre, asked him to come to see them side by side with 'the Masters'. He arrived, feeling acutely anxious, to be confronted by his own paintings set round the walls of the gallery where David's great classical scenes of mythology and heroism are hung. These vast canvases are much larger than Picasso's paintings, which themselves are by no means small, for among them were the *Milliner's Workshop* of 1926,[1] *La Muse* of 1935,[2] *The Serenade* of 1942[3] and several important still-lifes. After a disquieting pause for comparison between two such different styles, Georges Salles was the first to pronounce with conviction that they stood up to the test, and to suggest that they should be moved into the Spanish gallery where they could be seen beside Goya, Velasquez and Zurbaran. Picasso was even more worried this time as his pictures were placed beside the work of his countrymen, but again they held their own through the vigour of their execution and the reality of the life they contain. Having regained his confidence he repeated excitedly: "You see it's the same thing! it's the same thing!"

A few years after this single-handed encounter with the masters, he began in 1954 a series of fifteen variations on the theme of Delacroix's masterpiece, *Les Femmes d'Alger*. This picture haunted his memory. He had not seen it for years, though he had only to cross the Seine and enter the Louvre to do so. I suspect that Picasso was encouraged in a feeling of intimacy with the exotic scene by a striking likeness between the profile of Jacqueline Roque and of one of the seated Moorish women.

Working from memory, he first painted a composition which in its essentials bore some resemblance to the picture in the Louvre. There was only one obvious difference: the negress carrying a coffee-pot in

[1] See Zervos *Picasso*, Vol. VII, p. 2.   [2] Plate XIV, 7.   [3] Plate XXI, 4.

Picasso's picture appears only in the Delacroix version in the Montpellier museum. In quick succession he painted a number of variations on the same theme, some in monochrome and others with brilliant colour. A suggestion of the tranquil atmosphere of the harem with its ladies seated round a hookah in decorous conversation can still be felt in the first paintings. Soon, however, the scene became more orgiastic. Stripped of their silks and jewellery the nude bodies of the women are drawn with bold curves indicating the fulness of their breasts and the roundness of their buttocks. One of the two figures in the foreground lies on her side in abandon with her entwined legs lifted in the air, while the other, in contrast richly clothed, sits erect in hieratic indifference. The discreet eroticism of Delacroix's harem has vanished. In Picasso's summary treatment of anatomy, the seduction of the female form is no longer veiled and segregated, it floods the whole picture, affecting every corner and opening up the scene from a shadowed confinement to the light of the sun.

The more conventional representation of the first paintings made them easy to interpret, but as the series continued Picasso became interested in more abstract qualities of colour and form which were the outcome of his former discoveries. In the last brilliant composition to be painted, he introduced both styles in the same picture.[1] Instead of incongruity he succeeded in achieving an even greater unity, holding the picture together by strong overall patterns of bright colour. The two different styles instead of clashing became complementary, offering different versions of the same reality. The more representational seated figure had the effect of spreading its influence over its neighbours whose forms are less easy to interpret at first sight, humanising their geometric severity and supplying the key to their metaphorical eroticism.

This great canvas had just been painted when one day in February 1955 I climbed up the narrow stairs in the old house in the rue des Grands Augustins. The glow of colour from the paintings was warm enough to make me forget the bleak, grey atmosphere of the streets. The stacked canvases left little space, but in the centre of the room he stood there friendly and smiling. Bringing them out one after another he showed me the rich variety of style and fantasy to which the *Women of Algiers* had been subjected. My first sight of the Moorish interiors and the provocative poses of the nude girls reminded me of the odalisques of Matisse. "You are right," he said with a laugh, "when Matisse died he left his odalisques to me as a legacy, and this is my idea

[1] Plate XXIV, 2.

of the orient though I have never been there." As he continued to bring out more canvases I remarked upon the variations between the representational and cubist styles. I could discover no direct sequence leading in either direction. With an enigmatic smile he told me that he himself never knew what was coming next, nor did he try to interpret what he had done. "That is for others to do if they wish," he said, and to illustrate his point he brought out a large recent aquatint: a group of several figures, some old and grotesque and others young, watching an artist at work at his easel. "*You* tell me what it means, and what that old naked man who turns his back to us is doing there. Everyone who's seen it has his story about it. I don't know what's going on, I never do. If I did I'd be finished."

The planned, methodical development of a theme is as foreign to Picasso as a reasoned explanation. Each painting as it arrived had served as a gateway to the next, the suggestions that had come each time he was at work had not been forgotten, and each had widened the theme rather than narrowed it towards a limited solution. In his perpetual turning over of his ideas, every solution had to be questioned, for the reverse might be equally near the truth. When I asked if he intended to continue to work longer on one of the large canvases towards a résumé of the whole series, he said: "The fact that I paint so many studies is just part of my way of working. I make a hundred studies in a few days while another painter may spend a hundred days on one picture. As I continue I shall open windows. I shall get behind the canvas and perhaps something will happen." This was not an answer but the metaphor suggested that the solution was already present in what he had done. New aspects of it were revealed by each change he had made as if he were turning over a precious stone before our eyes. This in fact became clear when a few months later the fifteen paintings were exhibited together, and their homogeneity as well as their variety became apparent.

However, to guard against giving the impression that he was working with the hope of ultimate perfection, he added: "Pictures are never finished in the sense that they suddenly become ready to be signed and framed. They usually come to a halt when the time is ripe, because something happens which breaks the continuity of their development. When this happens it is often a good plan to return to sculpture." And to express his satisfaction in changing to another medium, he added: "After all, a work of art is not achieved by thought but with your hands."

A few days after this visit, the interruption in his work, which he had sensed as a possibility, occurred. He had to leave for Vallauris where complications in the ownership of property had arisen. The unwelcome break in his work upset his temper, and when he left his face was clouded. Once more, however, the climate that he enjoys and his new love restored his energy.

More Exhibitions

Since the last war the demand for exhibitions, great and small, of the work of Picasso has surpassed that for any other painter's work. A summary of the situation may be useful. Before the war was over a retrospective exhibition was shown in Mexico City, and paintings shown in Paris soon after its liberation were sent shortly afterwards to the Victoria and Albert Museum in London. Smaller exhibitions, less systematic in their selection, abounded during these years.

In 1948 the Maison de la Pensée Française in Paris presented to the public for the first time 149 ceramics of Picasso, which amounted to no more than a tenth of his production up to that date, though he had only begun to work at Vallauris the year before. The following year 64 canvases painted during the four previous years, mostly portraits of Françoise Gilot and Claude, were shown at the same gallery. The Venice Biennale of 1950 organised a relatively small retrospective showing of his work.

1951 was the year of Picasso's seventieth birthday, and in addition to the celebrations in Vallauris, exhibitions were planned in widely distant parts of the world. In Tokyo drawings and lithographs were shown. In London the Institute of Contemporary Arts opened an important retrospective exhibition of drawings, to which he himself had lent more than half the exhibits. But the most memorable event was the large exhibition of sculpture, accompanied by drawings, most of them shown for the first time, at the Maison de la Pensée Française. It was then that the world at large began to realise the greatness of Picasso as a sculptor.

In 1953 an important retrospective exhibition of paintings opened in June in Lyons, and most of the pictures shown there went on in the late summer to Rome and afterwards to Milan. In Italy the display, already considerable in size, was enlarged by work that came direct from Vallauris, including the murals *War* and *Peace*. The same winter an exhibition was held independently at Sao Paolo in Brazil.

A third exhibition at the Maison de la Pensée Française opened in the summer of 1954. The unusual interest it offered was the presence of

thirty-seven paintings loaned by Soviet Russia from the collection
which had been taken over from Shchukine. These had been shown
the previous autumn in a small private gallery in Rome. They were
now augmented by some early pictures such as the 1903 portrait of
Celestina,[1] lent by the artist, and seven paintings ranging from 1905 to
1914 from the collection of Gertrude Stein. This exhibition, including
the paintings from Russia, the earliest dating from 1900, was the finest
collection of Picasso's early work that had ever been seen. All the
pictures were in excellent condition, for although the Russian authorities had kept them hidden from the public as dangerous specimens of
Western decadence, they had seen that they were well cared for.
Among them were the great melancholy paintings of the Blue period,
the *Harlequin and his Companion* of 1901,[2] the portrait of Sabartès
caressing his bock of 1901[3] and the great paintings, *The Old Jew* of
1903[4] and the little girl balancing on a ball—*L'Acrobate à la Boule*—of
the Saltimbanque period of 1905.[5] These were followed by some of the
most powerful examples of the Negro period such as the *Draped Nude*
of 1907[6] and the *Farmer's Wife* painted at La Rue des Bois in 1908.[7] As
we know from Shchukine's reactions to the *Demoiselles d'Avignon*, he
had sometimes been hesitant in his choice, particularly towards the
close of his career as a collector. But seeing this collection, no-one
could question his remarkable discernment. One of the greatest
pleasures was to be face to face with the astonishing cubist portrait of
Ambroise Vollard.

Unfortunately this unique opportunity to see these splendid pictures
in Paris lasted only a few days. The daughter of Shchukine who lived
in France claimed them as belonging legally to her, and in order to
avoid any possible complications, the Russians preferred to close
the exhibition and ship their paintings immediately back to Moscow.
Now with the recent political changes in Russia it is reported that a
number of them are again on view in museums in Moscow and
Leningrad, but it is unlikely that we shall see them again in the West
for many years.[8]

At the time, Picasso was in Vallauris. He told friends who were
interested to know if he would like to have seen his early work again,
that he had no intention of making the journey to Paris and that they
must understand that he still disliked seeing exhibitions of his own
work. "In the past I refused for many years to exhibit and even would

[1] Zervos, *Picasso*, Vol. I, p. 5.   [2] Ibid., Vol. I, p. 46.   [3] Plate II, 1.
[4] Plate II, 7.   [5] Plate IV, 2.   [6] Zervos, *Picasso*, Vol. II*, p. 25.
[7] Ibid., Vol. II*, p. 46, No. 92.   [8] Some of them exhibited Brussels, 1958.

not have my pictures photographed," he said in a conversation with Pierre Baudouin. "But finally I realised that I had to exhibit—to strip myself naked. It takes courage. Even a whore when she strips naked needs courage. People don't realise what they have when they own a picture by me. Each picture is a phial filled with my blood. That is what has gone into it."

The exhibitions continued. Two were held in Paris in the summer of 1955, in honour of his arrival in Paris the year before and his seventy-fifth birthday in the following year. In that part of the Louvre known as the Palais de Marsan, a retrospective exhibition containing 143 works was planned to show Picasso's fabulous career from 1900-55; that is from the end of the Blue period to the studies for the *Dames d'Alger*. From America came many important pictures belonging to private collectors, and also *Guernica* which had been on loan since 1939 at the New York Museum of Modern Art. The *Demoiselles d'Avignon* unfortunately was lacking in this important manifestation; though as we know, this picture had been seen in London in an exhibition organised by the Institute of Contemporary Arts in 1948, and, more recently, in Paris at the Cubist Exhibition.

The second exhibition in Paris in the summer of 1955 was held in the Bibliothèque Nationale. It was a very ample survey of the graphic art of Picasso, in which for the first time the public could see the rare prints of the Vollard suite. The same exhibition was shown the following spring in London by the Arts Council. Many other exhibitions of drawings and ceramics, and of the great canvas of *Guernica* with its studies, have been organised throughout Europe during these years. They have included a small exhibition in Barcelona in the autumn of 1957, the first for more than twenty years. At the time of writing, however, the most important display of Picasso's painting and sculpture yet held has been arranged this year (1957) by Alfred Barr at the New York Museum of Modern Art. From there it will travel to Chicago and Philadelphia.

Cannes

Picasso's fame weighs lightly upon him. His thoughts are always sufficiently occupied with his work and his simple enjoyments with his family and friends for him not to be burdened by it. He takes it as a matter of course that visitors should nearly always wish to take his photograph, and he is sometimes surprised if he is not asked for his autograph. In general he accepts with grace the position he has earned. He likes to complain about the time taken up by visitors in the summer, at the same time a lack of visits or enquiries as to whether a caller will be welcome would at once worry him.

In Paris, however, in the spring of 1954 he found himself being overwhelmed by callers and family affairs. In addition, he began to find it impossible to visit cafés and restaurants without being pestered by tourists. One day when he walked to the end of the rue des Grands Augustins to see the floods, which were then reaching alarming proportions, he was trapped by journalists who asked senseless questions and wanted to take photographs when he was not in the mood. Feeling depressed at the changed atmosphere in Paris and seeing no other solution, he set out again for the Mediterranean. The little villa at Vallauris, however, had lost its attraction since the break with Françoise and also it was far too small for his needs.

He therefore decided to move house, and with Jacqueline Roque he started looking about in the neighbourhood. One evening, in the hilly inland part of Cannes, they were seeing over a large ornate villa, 'La Californie'. He knew suddenly in the dusk that it would suit his purpose. Its clumsy 1900 style, its pretentious wrought-iron staircase and the stylised carvings round the windows, did not deter him. He was not looking for an old house of fine proportions, nor did he want an artist's studio. He remembered how once before he had taken a villa with a studio in Cannes for the summer, the only time he had ever done such a thing, and as a result, he said, he hardly did any work at all. He knew that what he had found was ugly, but its vulgarity was something that he could dominate and even use, for the house had the attraction of well-lit rooms with high ceilings and space which would take even him some years to fill. A high black iron fence with a lodge for a guardian at the gate provided the defences needed to keep the curious and the unwanted at a distance. Terraced gardens with some fine trees, including palms and a gigantic eucalyptus, isolated the house from neighbouring villas and a view out to sea gave a pleasant feeling of space.

Picasso soon cleared the house of curtains, carpets, grand pianos and the furniture of the rich industrialists who had used the villa before for their sumptuous entertainments. The drawing-rooms, bathroom suites, kitchens and extensive basement were now to be used very differently. The mirrored doors of the entrance halls soon became hidden behind cases of belongings brought out of store in Paris. Bronzes, ceramics, canvases, easels and furniture, including the eighteenth-century English chairs left to him by his father, crowded the ground floor, while the kitchens were transformed into workshops for lithography and engraving. Into the first-floor bedrooms were brought the bare necessities for comfort and the top floor remained relatively empty. The rugs and curtains were not replaced, and he preferred to let the worn-out silk covers on the armchairs, which brought with them an echo of the rue la Boètie, continue to split until they looked like the slashed doublets of medieval knights. No thought was given to redecoration—such considerations do not interest Picasso. His house is his workshop and a place to store his belongings rather than something to be admired for its elegance and comfort. On the walls, unframed canvases and rare specimens of masks from the South Seas and Africa found themselves hanging between the plaster mouldings wherever there happened to be a nail, interspersed with photos or scraps of paper with messages written boldly in crayon. With haphazard finality objects took their places round the rooms.

After three years, in spite of the attentions of Jacqueline Roque, the situation has not changed much. Incongruous objects, crowded together, become more deeply hedged in by a forest of newcomers. Packing-cases are opened to see what is inside, then left packed. Flowers stand desiccated in their vases. Food, clothing, toys, books, lamps, presents of all descriptions, and objets d'art pile up on top of each other like the crusts of the earth.

Yet strangely enough, in spite of all this, there is no squalor. As the visitor grows used to the disorder, details of fascinating interest catch the eye. A Sicilian marionette in golden armour hangs from a lamp standard, a cage of noisy tropical birds can be seen among books and papers, a small self-portrait of the Douanier Rousseau and a night landscape by Max Ernst emerge from piles of ceramics. These are a few of the finds that become visible to the prying eye, but there are a thousand treasures locked away in a back room or submerged and forgotten.

The quality essential to every object in this heterogeneous collection is its value to Picasso in his work. Everywhere there are signs of his activity, everything has gone through his hands and been scrutinised by him before taking its place in this agglomeration. Canvases, ceramics, tiles, plates, bronze and plaster sculptures, bulging portfolios crammed with drawings and engravings mingle with things that have been brought there intentionally or by chance. All have their significance and their place in the alchemist's den in which he lives.

The ground-floor rooms are connected to each other by wide doors. Large french windows, open in summer, bring the scent of pine and eucalyptus in from the garden. In this atmosphere Picasso works, receives his friends, plays with his goat or his dogs and amuses himself as he feels inclined. Meals are cleared from the dining-room table to make space for him to draw or to work on his ceramics. His life, his work and his play are never separate. Picasso the painter, the sculptor, the engraver, the ceramist, the poet, coincides with Picasso the friend, the father, the sage, the magician and the clown.

In this multifarious dwelling Picasso has the company of Jacqueline Roque who is always present, attentive and charming. She is quick to assess his wishes and provide for rapid changes of plans. She guards jealously against intruders, sees to his comforts and provides excellent meals. During the hours that Picasso is at work, if she is not with him she enjoys herself listening to music, reading or playing with her young daughter, who lives with them. Inspired by the variety of subjects at hand she is also an observant and successful photographer.

Many of the paintings produced in the new house are portraits of Jacqueline. In some of them she is wearing a Turkish dress reminiscent of the *Dames d'Alger*. The classical lines of her profile and the large dark eyes that Picasso has given her are impressive in their likeness. In others, representation has been sacrificed to gay improvisations with flat brilliant patches of colour, which recall the most daring inventions of Matisse.

In the winter of 1955-56 the portraits of Jacqueline were accompanied by paintings of nudes, in particular two large canvases in which the figures are constructed in monochrome geometric facets. Their proportions are monumental and they appear to be so solid that one figure, crouching, seems to offer shelter like a cavern, her breasts hanging like spherical lamps from its roof. There are other smaller nudes quite different in their effect. Their realism is more direct and the appeal of their voluminous forms so strong that they seem to convey even the odour of flesh.

When Picasso bought 'La Californie', though he had seen it only by twilight, he realised that its most precious asset to him, in addition to its nearness to Vallauris, was the light that penetrates into every corner of the house. He was happy at once in the luminous atmosphere of the lofty rooms, and as he had done before, he began to paint pictures inspired by the objects that lay around and the tall windows with their art nouveau tracery, through which a yellow-green light is filtered by the branches of the palm trees. Day after day he saw his studio anew. Sometimes the main feature to be placed in the composition was Jacqueline seated in a rocking-chair in front of stacked canvases on which could be seen former versions of the same studio.[1] In other paintings the pattern of the windows dominated everything, towering high like a cathedral nave; or again cool recesses led the eye deep into the picture, past chairs, sculptures, easels and the Moorish charcoal-burner which looked like another relic of Matisse.

The last paintings of this series have an austerity of colour and arrangement which strongly recalls the atmosphere of Spain.[2] Picasso explains that they were begun on Easter Sunday 1956 when torrential rain prevented him from going to a bullfight. Strong contrasts of black and luminous white give a sensation of the whitewashed passages and the solemn seclusion of Spanish houses. They evoke a bittersweet taste, and the contrast between the burning sun and the freshness of sheltered interiors, of white wine and black olives. From the magnificent disorder of his surroundings Picasso has resolved in these paintings a masterly plan of light and space in which everything takes its place with serenity.

Although the general rhythm of his life is the same from day to day, Picasso keeps changing the forms of his activities. There is the constant coming and going of ceramics brought by car from Vallauris for him to paint or ornament with designs incised or in relief. On the large platters he makes bold images of owls, goats, bulls or the calm profile of Jacqueline, and then without warning he is likely to transfer his attention to the tall thin sculptures that stand like sentinels to watch over the turmoil. These strange figures built by him with material such as planks, driftwood and canvas stretchers are then sent to be cast in bronze in Paris, so that their hybrid nature becomes unified and transformed in the more permanent material.

With such variety around him and such mastery in so many techniques it is impossible for him to be idle. The passionate energy which goes into his work infects those who come into contact with him. Although he takes no pupils, his example spreads to others and gives them the means of producing works of art themselves. It is not only the engravers with whom he works, the publishers, the ceramists, the makers of tapestries and mosaics, the bronzecasters and iron-founders, but also those who work in gold and silver who have been provided with new and unconventional ideas. It was not in the rue de la Paix that Picasso was introduced to the jeweller's craft but in that fearful place, the dentist's chair. His capacity for detecting new resources leads him to discoveries in regions where others would find

[1] Plate XXIV, 4.   [2] Plate XXIV, 6.

it absurd or indiscreet to look. As he noticed the dentist's instruments, the idea came to him of engraving in gold with dental drills and making gold ornaments from models with the same precision with which the dentist crowned his teeth. As a result, by using dental material, Picasso made a necklace so magnificent in its effect that it rivals the gold ornaments of ancient Mexico.

Among others who have found a new impulse in their craftsmanship, the designer of jewelry, François Hugo, has recently begun making copies of some of Picasso's large platters with designs in relief. Beaten out of solid silver they make splendid replicas and to many of them Picasso has added drawings chased into the surface.

Although the infectious influence of Picasso both as a man and as an artist is immense, it is not surprising to find that there are those who react violently against it. His power is also recognised by those who disapprove. One day I was present when he opened a letter addressed to him by a French painter, in which the author, who remained anonymous, began by saying: "Monsieur, the harm you have done is incalculable." As he read it, Picasso said quietly, "who knows, perhaps he is right." In the impulse of his creation Picasso is not conscious of doing good or evil. Power is inherent in his work, and we are in the habit of judging the greatness of a painter by the strength he has to affect ourselves and others.

Films

When the producer Georges Clouzot came to Cannes during the summer of 1955 to propose to Picasso that they should make a long film together, several films of his work had already been released to the public. The first had *Guernica* as its title and a commentary by Paul Eluard. The story of the great painting was seen in relation to Picasso's work from his earliest years and the tragedy of the bombing was accentuated by Eluard's poetry. Later the Belgian producer Paul Haesaerts produced a film in which the most interesting sequence was made in Vallauris. It showed Picasso drawing on a sheet of glass so that his movements could be seen like a dance through transparent images of smiling mythical creatures, fauns and goats. Haesaerts later made a second film, *From Renoir to Picasso*, which makes comparisons between these two modern masters and a third—Seurat. He stressed the emotional violence of Picasso in contrast to the sensuality of Renoir and the intellect of Seurat. These other qualities are, however, so evident in Picasso, too, that the argument at times seems oversimplified.

In 1953 Luciano Emmer, known for his films on Carpaccio, Bosch and other old masters, came to Vallauris to take pictures of Picasso at work. He needed scenes taken from life to complete an ambitious film describing the evolution of his art from the Blue period to the present time. Two sequences of considerable interest were filmed. In one Picasso is shown making a huge drawing on the vault of the Temple of Peace in Vallauris (the panels of *War* and *Peace* were away on exhibition). The agility with which he moves about on ladders to complete the drawing is impressive, and even more astonishing is the precision of the long sweeping curves that never lose their meaning in spite of this acrobatic feat. Climbing from one position to another, he completes before our eyes a drawing covering the whole wall, representing a gigantic birdlike demon meeting its destruction at the hands of a hero of classical nobility. In the second episode Picasso constructs on the floor of his studio a statue made up of a great variety of materials discovered while the work is in progress. As a description of his methods in making collage sculpture it is of value, but the feeling that his actions have been rehearsed haunts the whole sequence. The film as a whole is important as a record of Picasso's work. Emmer took advantage of the presence of the paintings assembled in Rome for the exhibition of 1953, including the pictures from Moscow that later had their brief showing in Paris. The colour reproduction is as faithful as possible; the commentary, however, is biased by theories of social realism which seriously distort Picasso's motives. It is only the most representational paintings that meet with the author's approval, the others are shown with condescension as the temporary aberrations of a great man.

Picasso himself has experimented with film making on a small scale. He used paper cutouts of animals and figures, animating them with coloured chalk, but he is modest about the results which have never been shown in public. Although he is intrigued by the possibilities of the cinema as a medium he is nervous of appearing to the public on the screen. In 1950 I went with him to see a film of Matisse. The producer had induced the artist to say a few halting phrases about his own work, and had later suggested to Picasso that he might be able to do something similar. But the reply was emphatic. "Never will you make an ape of me like that," said Picasso, and in spite of attempts at persuasion the film was never made.

This made it all the more surprising that when Clouzot came to Cannes to suggest making a long colour film in which Picasso was to be the only star, his proposal should be taken seriously. The idea was to record the actual creative process of Picasso, in so far as it can be watched, by filming him making drawings and paintings from start to finish. Its success, however, would depend on making a sequence out of the action and on its presentation to a public without specialist knowledge or even an interest in painting, in such a way as to capture the imagination. A vital factor was Picasso's reaction to the exacting and complicated demands of cinema technique. He would be obliged to work surrounded by technicians instead of alone, to start and stop drawing as they required, and to work long hours in the scorching heat of the lamps. All this, it seemed, would combine to kill spontaneity. Discussing it beforehand, Picasso remarked that he would feel like a matador about to enter the arena, a sensation that he knew already in some degree every time he started a canvas, but this time it would be much more intimidating with a crowd of spectators.

Clouzot had both the tact and the imagination to make it possible for Picasso to go through this ordeal. Contrary to his habits, Picasso was forced to rise early every day for two months during the summer so as to get to the film studios in Nice. There he had to work with great patience and persistence in a heat which "made the sun outdoors seem like Iceland". As time went on, he became more and more interested and cooperated fully in the awkward processes demanded of him, such as stopping after each stroke of a painting for it to be photographed and announcing in advance when he would be ready to start again.

It was not until late in the following spring, at the Cannes Film Festival, that the film was shown publicly. Meanwhile Picasso had spent a whole winter suffering at intervals from the fatigue that his exceptional effort had caused. When he is ailing, Picasso goes through great mental torment and his thoughts turn to old age and death, two facts with which he refuses to make his peace. The idea that he is not feeling well enough to work torments him and his dejection increases when he is told by the doctor that the best cure is rest. His motto could be, like Don Quixote's, "my combat is my repose", for unless he is able to work he becomes miserable and begins to brood. Yet that winter, work, the one cure which he knew would be effective, was forbidden him.

It was some weeks before he managed to break completely out of this vicious circle. The day of the private view of his film, *Le Mystère Picasso*, he was going through another spell of despondency. He stayed in bed all day and insisted that he could not go to the opening. Everyone was unhappy and in particular Clouzot and his old friend, Georges Auric, who had composed the music. At the last moment, however, thanks largely to the tactful persuasion of Jacqueline, Picasso appeared dressed in an elegant dinner jacket which still fitted perfectly although he had not worn it for more than twenty years, and another relic, his favourite hat, an English bowler.

To the delight of all, his drawings spread across the screen as if by magic. Clouzot had devised a technique by which the drawings could be filmed from the back of an absorbent paper through which the coloured inks penetrated immediately, with the advantage that the artist's hand did not hide his work. Each line as it appeared seemed right and inevitable once it was made, and there was a feeling that it was predestined, in fact that it had already been there, but invisible to all but the artist. I have had this sensation before when watching him make a drawing, though in the film it is accentuated because he is hidden. The movement of his crayon in obedience to an unseen presence and the lack of hesitation give proof of complete accord between the inner eye of the artist and the realisation of the vision on the paper. Picasso had overcome his misgivings and was enjoying the wonderful display that he could give of the visible side of his creative process.

The film also is tense with the excitement of wondering what he will do next. His actions are enthralling, like the actions of a tight-rope walker who compels his audience to follow every movement of his perilous dance and applaud his prowess when it comes successfully to an end. At one dramatic moment, after a long sequence in which he has made many astonishing changes in a large painting of a beach scene, he exclaims to Clouzot: "This is going wrong—all wrong", and then proceeds to wipe out the composition and start again, this time benefiting from his failure. His performance throughout is a triumph not only of his artistic talent, but of his personality, unassuming, powerful and sincere. With Clouzot's ability to hold his audience in suspense added to Picasso's brilliant display, the film becomes a rare and valuable account of the workings of genius.

Politics

In his retreat, Picasso has often received visits from officials of the French Communist Party. Frequently they come to ask him to contribute a drawing to some party cause, or to add his signature to a manifesto. He considers them as politicians and assumes that as such they are capable in their own profession. He knows that they have not much understanding of his painting nor does he expect that of them. So long as they allow him his freedom in his art he is willing to support them for ideological reasons. This mutual arrangement has worked reasonably well in spite of a temporary disagreement arising from a portrait of Stalin, which he had made as a 'bouquet of flowers', at the death of the man who was then their hero. This gesture met with official disapproval because it was said that the drawing was not sufficiently realistic.

In the autumn of 1956 the brutal suppression of the rising in Hungary troubled many intellectuals in the French Communist Party. Picasso was greatly disturbed by the news and signed a letter with nine others, including his friends the painter, Edouard Pignon, and his wife, Hélène Parmelin, addressed to the central committee of the party. In it they complained that although "the weeks that have just passed have posed burning problems of conscience for Communists, neither the central committee nor L'Humanité [their newspaper] have helped to resolve them", and they demanded the summoning of a special party congress. The reply, published in L'Humanité, was not reassuring. It gave a lengthy defence of the official line and concluded by saying: "The signatories . . . may have another opinion! They may even become obstinate in spite of the facts, but they have not the right to attempt to impose their point of view on the party by illicit means." Here the public exchange of views came to an end, though Picasso received further visits from the highest ranking members of the party, who were anxious not to lose so distinguished a member.

Recently Picasso explained his attitude to the American art critic, Carlton Lake, who had told him in an interview that he thought many admirers would be happy to hear that he had resigned from the party. "Look," said Picasso, "I am no politician. I am not technically proficient in such matters. But Communism stands for certain ideals I believe in. I believe Communism is working towards the realisation of those ideals."[1] He went on to make it clear that though he had no intention of resigning from the party his attachment to communism was not political. So long as the party in France continues to represent the aspirations of a large portion of the working classes it is unlikely that he will resign. He feels that by remaining a member he keeps a link which he needs with the common people. He meets them in his contacts with the artisans, craftsmen and technicians with whom he enjoys working, and his communism helps to

[1] Carlton Lake, 'Picasso Speaking', The Atlantic Monthly.

establish confidence between them. His faith in them is part of his fundamental humanism.

Visitors and Friends

All the year round in Cannes, but particularly during the summer months, there is a continuous flow of visitors wishing to call on Picasso. 'La Californie', however, is well hidden among trees on the hillside, and its remoteness helps to check an invasion which might easily become intolerable. Among others in a different category who pay visits in or out of season are his old and intimate friends, Sabartès and Kahnweiler. Their help in business matters combined with a life-long understanding of his habits continues to make them welcome. Since he has not returned to Paris for nearly three years his Parisian friends must make the journey to see him. As in the past he enjoys the company of poets. Michel Leiris and his wife, Jacques Prévert, Tristan Tzara and André Verdet enliven his voluntary exile. Jean Cocteau is still unfailing in his attentions. 'Mon Maître Picasso' was the title he gave to a recent article in the press. When two years ago Cocteau became a member of the Institut Français, Picasso made burlesque designs for the sword hilt which is part of the insignia of an Academician.

Musicians such as Francis Poulenc and Georges Auric call from time to time, while dealers from all parts of the world, collectors, publishers, film stars, fashion experts, photographers, and architects swell the numbers of those who come to pay their respects. Many painters spend their summer on the coast but few of them share Picasso's intimacy. There are those in consequence who accuse him unreasonably of making himself inaccessible. When he meets young artists, as he does frequently, he is always tolerant, and if he finds talent in their work he is generous with suggestions and recommendations. At times Picasso is depressed by the lack of understanding of his own discoveries and the lack of revolt and individuality among the young. As he says: "There are miles of paintings in the manner of . . ., but it is rare to see a young painter work according to his own style."

A painter whose company he has enjoyed since the last war is Edouard Pignon. During his stay in Vallauris, working nearby in the old scent factory, Pignon remembers one day leaving an unfinished study for a picture of a mother and child. During his absence Picasso came in and painted another version of the subject in the same manner, which he left on the easel. His exit was followed by the arrival of friends looking for Pignon, who became enthusiastic about this latest

painting. When they met shortly after they congratulated him warmly
and Pignon innocently told them it was just a small study of no
importance. It was not until they returned to the studio that they all
realised what had happened and that the new Pignon was in fact a
Picasso.

An understanding grew between the stolid good-natured painter
who had broken loose from the mining areas of Northern France and
the unfathomable, volcanic Andalusian. Pignon is a talented painter
and a good talker, his knowledge of the arts is wide and his tastes are
decided. While he speaks in the language of painters of his latest
intentions in his work, Picasso listens intently and breaks in suddenly
with ideas which excite and surprise at the same time. Pignon tries to
explain his motives with clarity, whereas Picasso speaks in metaphors
without any thought of justification. As you listen you realise that
Picasso appreciates that truth is never easily accessible. Direct statements imply falsehoods too often for them to be trusted. The truth can
be better understood by subtle manœuvres which catch it alive instead
of trampling it to death. His short eager interruptions are like well-
aimed gunfire which not only tears breaches in conventional defences
against possibly disconcerting revelations, which but pierces a way to
a more profound understanding of life and the arts.

To record these conversations would be difficult. They rely on
glances, expressions, gestures, a quick laugh which introduces a
relevant absurdity, and above all on the reactions of his listeners to
ambiguities and paradoxes which can become the threshold of new
ideas. The pleasure Picasso takes in presenting the reverse side of a
problem can reduce the over-serious questioner to despair. "You
mustn't always believe what I say," he once told me. "Questions
tempt you to tell lies, particularly when there is no answer." Friends
have sometimes offered to make recordings, but Picasso laughs at their
naïvety. Divorced from its surroundings such talk loses its meaning.

The ambiguity of words warms Picasso's sense of humour. Their
insufficiency as labels and their variety of interpretation tempt him to
juggle with them. French words, Spanish words, even English words
exchange meanings with each other just as colours can change in value
according to their surroundings. You can play with words and make
puns just as you can play with colours and shapes. "After all", he
enjoys saying, "the arts are all the same; you can write a picture in
words just as you can paint sensations in a poem. 'Blue'—what does
'blue' mean? There are thousands of sensations that we call 'blue'. You
can speak of the blue of a packet of Gauloise and in that case you can

talk of the Gauloise blue of eyes, or on the contrary, just as they do in a Paris restaurant, you can talk of a steak being blue when you mean red. That is what I have often done when I have tried to write poems."

Paterfamilias

It is easy to see from his work and his way of living that Picasso is very fond of children. For many years there have usually been children, his own or those of friends, around him. We have seen also how more than once he has been tempted with the idea of establishing a family, but this does not mean that he accepts willingly the rôle of father. Now his four children are dispersed. Paulo, who has now provided him with grandchildren, lives his own life, though he frequently returns to 'La Californie'. Maïa is in Spain and Claude and Paloma live with their mother in Paris. These two children however spend long holidays with their father. They are perhaps the only people alive who can distract his attention from his work. They spend long hours on the beach and devise games together in which the dogs, the goat, the doves and the owl may be required to take part.

In Picasso's earliest self-portraits his love of disguise is to be found. The game of changing one's personality continues at 'La Californie'. Claude is shown how to wear the hat and cloak of a toreador and with Paloma they try out the effects of faces made by their father from a torn sheet of paper or a ceramic tile. On the sideboard there is a store of comic masks, hats of all descriptions and even a cutlass which provides for any emergency that may arise.

Picasso receives Visitors

The moment when disguises are called for most urgently is on the arrival of visitors, especially those from abroad. The less known or the more intimidating his guest may be, the more likely it is that he will find himself confronted by the master not as he expected to find him but as a burlesque little figure wearing, perhaps, a yachting cap with horn-rimmed spectacles, a red nose and black side-whiskers and brandishing a sabre. When this grotesque dance has effectively removed the first embarrassment of meeting, Picasso emerges from behind his mask, his eyes shining with laughter and his expression still enigmatic.

A visit to Picasso is always a new adventure. Those who call expecting any fixed routine are disappointed. At the same time those who manage to penetrate the defences of the front gate are well received, and when they leave their pulses have been quickened and their thoughts set moving by the presence of the little white-haired man whose black eyes have stirred their emotions like a red-hot poker sizzling in a pot of mulled wine.

The trivial and the serious live well together. During a visit that begins with clowning and progresses to an improvised performance on an African musical instrument, the final reward may be a showing of some of his latest canvases. The visitors stand round or sit on the floor for lack of chairs, while Picasso himself does all the moving. Choosing among the paintings that are stacked deeply round the walls, he brings them out one by one and props them against each other, fitting big and small together into a patchwork. Their appearance is greeted with signs of admiration by the cosmopolitan group of spectators in languages often incomprehensible to him, while those who are most deeply moved by the power and the rich variety of display often wait for some time before expressing their enthusiasm. With their approval the look of anxiety which is always in his face when he begins to unveil his recent creations disappears, and he listens intently to their remarks.

That Picasso enjoys such visits while they last and even finds them necessary seems certain. When friends who know his taste for strange objects arrive with presents, such as a Western six-shooter and a cowboy hat from Gary Cooper, or an elegant photometer and comic spectacles from Alfred Barr, he does not hide his pleasure. His power of astonishing them with the variety of his talents and the profusion of his work gives him equal satisfaction. At the same time these visits often set up a conflict within him. He finds it difficult to put up for long with anything that distracts him from his work and interrupts the atmosphere in which his own inclinations are unchecked. Yet when recently I remarked that none the less he had done an extraordinary amount of work during the summer, he answered, "yes, who knows? It may be *because* of the interruptions."

Projects in Store

In addition to the work which before long will leave the studio to be dispersed among dealers, museums and collectors, there are signs of future projects, some of which will again demand exceptional efforts from Picasso. In 1957 he accepted an invitation to make a gigantic mural for the new UNESCO building in Paris, and although he has given some thought to this, nothing has materialised. Recently, delegates arrived to talk the matter over again. They measured out on the front of the house a space comparable to that offered to him in the building in Paris. The area, 33 feet square, was so vast that Picasso became worried about the physical effort involved in covering the surface. "I am no longer twenty-five," he said. "It can't be done." At the same time, refusing to admit defeat, he began discussing methods which might make it feasible. The idea of providing a design which would be executed by an expert in murals or a scene painter did not please him. He said, "I want to *live* this picture myself just as I do all my other paintings, otherwise it will become a mere decoration." Then, turning to the delegates who were searching their brains for fruitful suggestions, he said firmly, "Au revoir! There is a solution, but I must find it myself."[1]

Talking about the problem later, he pointed out a fundamental difference between the methods of the fresco painter and his own. The Renaissance artists painted a small area on a newly prepared surface every day, and knew from their sketches where the joins were to come, but he himself liked to extend his painting at any time over the whole surface and without restriction, working either on details or on the overall effect as he felt inclined. The sheer size of the UNESCO mural forces him to invent other methods.

Another project which Picasso has recently been offered pleases him greatly. He has been asked to design four gigantic figures in bronze for the entrance to a new skyscraper in New York. In this case he is prepared to delegate the execution of the sculptures to craftsmen in America. He will make the models, he says, and allow them to be carried out across the Atlantic where a mechanical process of enlargement will be appropriate.

A third equally monumental task is that of designing stained glass for the sixty-two windows of the sixteenth-century Cathedral of Mézières in the Ardennes, to replace the glass that was destroyed during the war. The plans lie against a table in his studio and Picasso talks with enthusiasm of the proposal. As his views on religious art and his assertion that there is no 'bon Dieu' are well-known, both the offer and its acceptance are a surprise to all. When he painted the small violent scene of the Crucifixion in 1930 he had thought of it as of any other subject which has captured his interest. It was not an illustration of a religious subject but a symbolic representation of human suffering. The original subject was submerged in eagerness to state a savage and agonising event in the new language of his painting. For Mézières, will he not interpret his emotion in a similar way? To these projects Picasso will give his attention when his 'daemon' tells him that the moment has come; meanwhile other tasks present themselves more vividly to his mind. [1] Mural completed 1958.

Work in Progress: Las Meninas

In the centre of the ground-floor studio, enthroned on a chair, sits one of Matisse's last gifts to Picasso; a monstrous female effigy from the New Hebrides. Her presence is made especially imposing by the startling stripes, blue, white and pink, with which she is painted from head to foot. This ugly goddess stuffed with straw has recently become the presiding genius in a room where a live occupant also sits, immobile all day—a small owl in a cage, to whom Picasso pays periodic visits with food. Although the walls are lined with canvases, some finished and turned to the wall, others, of enormous size, still virgin, awaiting his attention, he is not working here this autumn.

Since midsummer the work in progress has taken place on the top floor, hitherto uninhabited except by the tame pigeons. Even the pet goat was not allowed to go higher than the corridor of the first floor where at night it slept outside Picasso's bedroom door. The pigeon house, looking not unlike a cubist construction, was built by him on the balcony of the largest of the empty rooms that he has now invaded. There is nothing to distract him but his doves and the view over the palm and eucalyptus trees towards the Lerins Islands that lie just below the horizon. Here, he can work isolated and undisturbed by day or late into the night.

None of the treasures from the rich haphazard assortment below has yet been elevated to this level, nothing breaks the bleak severity of torn and faded wallpaper and the marble mantelpieces of abandoned luxury. He works at night by the light of a high-powered electric bulb hung from the middle of the ceiling. "What does it matter?" Picasso says, "if it looks good by that light it will look good at any time." Furniture is absent except for two small tattered armchairs and a packing case turned upside down surrounded by a mob of paint tins. Scraps of smooth board or tin lying on top of the case serve for mixing his colours. His brushes are mostly worn to a stump with the violent scrubbing on the canvas they receive and the great distances they are made to travel while he is painting. Though in many cases hardly a bristle remains he still finds no difficulty in making them perform exactly as he wants. By day, to the accompaniment of the cooing and fluttering of pigeons, or by night with Jacqueline silently watching every movement, he covers canvases of various sizes with tremendous speed and astonishing control.

Two themes have developed concurrently. One is a series of jubilant paintings of his immediate surroundings, in which the chief actors are the pigeons flying from the shelter of the improvised dovecote, tumbling into the blue sunlit air with the sea as their background. All that is visible from the room where he works is eligible for a place in the pictures. If we compare the paintings and their subjects it can be seen how each detail, pigeons, palm trees, islands, dovecote and terrace has been considered on its own account before being knitted together into the unity of a composition, like flowers of different kinds arranged in the same bouquet. Each has found its place in the sparkling sunlight and yet everywhere there is an exuberance of movement. Not only do the pigeons strut and flutter, but we feel also the movement of the painter himself as he shifts his viewpoint and looks behind walls and round corners. The sense of life, of an airborne dance, that animates the subject is transposed directly into the pictures.

For the second theme on which Picasso is at work, his model is not present in the same way. Once more he has taken a subject from the work of one of the great fraternity of painters who live permanently in his thoughts. After using paintings by Le Nain, Poussin, Cranach, Courbet, El Greco and Delacroix, he has now turned to *Las Meninas* (The Ladies-in-Waiting) of Velasquez as the picture which is to feed him with new ideas and to become the source of innumerable variations.

This painting has been known to Picasso ever since he visited Madrid with his father at the age of fourteen. He learnt then to admire it for the qualities of its composition, drawing and lighting and for the acid harmonies of its colour. Since then he has considered the virtues and understood the anatomy of this masterpiece, and with time his love of the painting has grown for many reasons. "What a picture! what realism! . . . what a marvellous achievement!" he said to Kahnweiler more than twenty years before he decided to make a thorough investigation of the complicated scene that it presents.

Velasquez' painting contains some very strange and subtle relationships between the painter, the model and the spectator. "Look at it," said Picasso recently when we were discussing *Las Meninas*, "and try to find where each of these is actually situated." Velasquez can be seen in the picture, whereas in reality he must be standing outside it, he is shown turning his back on the Infanta who at first glance we would expect to be his model. He faces a large canvas on which he seems to be at work but it has its back to us and we have no idea what he is painting. The only solution is that he is painting the king and queen, who are only to be seen by their reflection in the mirror at the far end of the room. This implies incidentally that if we can see them in the mirror they are not looking at Velasquez, but at us. Velasquez therefore is not painting las Meninas. The girls have gathered round him not to pose but to see his picture of the king and queen with us standing beside them.

Such complicated relationships between the reality implied inside the picture and its relationship with the reality of the world outside raise problems which delight Picasso. He has always enjoyed involving the spectator in the web of his picture, and here in fact the spectator finds himself caught in no ordinary sense. He had been drawn into the royal apartments of the King of Spain, and Picasso intends to keep him there and show him not only a whole gallery of incongruous associations but also how the great traditions of Spanish painting can find a new orientation in his hands. Into such surroundings anyone might stray. Don Quixote might appear, or El Greco, burying the Duke of Orgaz. Goya could stroll in, dressed in his trousers with stripes which are horizontal instead of vertical like those worn by Courbet in the painting of his studio. Picasso has had made a similar pair to complete the trio, he too has taken up residence with Velasquez and his other companions in this lofty Spanish palace into which the sunlight is only allowed to penetrate with discretion. From the hooks in the ceiling to which the chandeliers are hitched at night, he will hang hams and sausages. The painted characters, as his companions, will enter into his disrespectful games.

A large canvas, six feet by nearly nine feet, painted in monochrome, occupies most of the wall in Picasso's top-floor studio.[1] It is the first of the *Meninas* series. All the main features of the original painting by Velasquez remain, though the composition has been changed from vertical to horizontal. Picasso has opened the shutters of the royal apartment to let in more light, at the same time he has not diminished the dramatic effect of the Chamberlain's silhouette in the open doorway at the far end of the room. Velasquez had organised the effects of lighting and perspective according to the established rules, convincing us of the great distance between us and the Chamberlain. Picasso also succeeds in convincing us, but by quite different methods. He creates a sense of space so great that you feel you would have to shout to call the Chamberlain's attention. It is done in the later versions by means of angular facets of cubist origin, planes which link together and disappear into the depths of the scene aided by strong contrasts of light and dark. The light no longer comes from a fixed direction, it spreads throughout the picture and the eye is led from facet to facet deep into

[1] Plate XXIV, 7.

the painting as if it were exploring the inner depths of a crystal. Velasquez, tall and lost in thought, is given the authority of an inquisitor. The two ladies-in-waiting, standing in the shadow, become rigid and observant like two sinister officers of the guardia civil, their features outlined in red, like warning signs on the road. The Infanta and her two attendants receive special attention. Many studies of them of various sizes have been made in greens, yellows, whites and greys, the figures treated individually and as a group. A combination of tenderness and violence used in close proximity in their treatment plays on the emotions. He transforms the carefully modelled surfaces of flesh and silk of Velasquez into a language of signs, a calligraphy in which, however, flesh and silk are still present. We recognise at once their qualities, incorporated into a new and powerful reality, brutally and yet lovingly portrayed. By these bold devices we are drawn in to enjoy and to share the life and surroundings of these children.

For two months during the summer Picasso worked in isolation. Again he refused to allow anyone but Jacqueline to see what he was painting. The canvases multiplied rapidly during the long summer evenings and the nights when the black curtainless windows reflected his work, their uneven surfaces changing and distorting his pictures as he moved. Such ready-made deformations proved once more to be an amusement to him, just as the distorting mirror on the floor below never fails to make him laugh at its weird versions of reality.

When in the early autumn Michel Leiris and Pignon were finally allowed up to Picasso's sanctuary they were confronted with an astonishing sight. He had taken possession of *Las Meninas* in some twenty paintings, large and small. The realism of Velasquez that he had so much admired had been transformed into the life of Picasso and his surroundings. Even the phlegmatic dog of the Velasquez had been changed into the dachshund Lump that Picasso had received not long before as a gift from the photographer, David Duncan, and other more significant changes had taken place.

The game he plays with reality leads him to question everything and to place even those things that are held most in respect in situations which can make them seem ridiculous. It is a risk taken in the interests of penetrating the complex ambiguities of the world rather than a heartless mockery. By a reversal of standards even those things which we love can gain in value rather than lose. The ruthless parody to which *Las Meninas* has been subjected cannot fail to bring a smile, and the laughter that it provokes is of the kind defined by Baudelaire when he wrote: "Laughter is satanic, it is thus profoundly human and . . . essentially contradictory; that is to say, it is at the same time a sign of infinite grandeur and infinite misery."[1] In his study *Of the Essence of Laughter*, Baudelaire went on to define national characteristics, saying: "The Spaniards are very well endowed with the comic. They are quick to arrive at the cruel stage and their grotesque fantasies usually contain a sombre element."[2] The story that Picasso imagined for the little Italian buffoon who enters on the right of Velasquez' picture is an example. As he pokes the good-tempered dog with his foot the boy's hands seem to flutter nervously. This tempted Picasso to think that he might be playing an invisible piano, and to paint a study of him seated at a piano well lit with candles. He also noticed in the original a black line in the panelling that rises from the nape of the boy's neck. This in turn suggested to him a cord by which the young pianist was hanged like a helpless tinkling marionette.

"I saw the little boy with a piano," he said to me. "The piano came into my head and I had to put it somewhere. For me he was hanged so I made him hang. Such images come to me and I put them in. They are part of the reality of the subject. The surrealists in that way were right. Reality is more than the thing itself. I look always for its super-reality. Reality lies in how you see things. A green parrot," he continued, "is also a green salad *and* a green parrot. He who makes it only a parrot diminishes its reality. A painter who copies a tree blinds himself to the real tree. I see things otherwise. A palm tree can become a horse. Don Quixote can come into *Las Meninas*." Velasquez' picture had become the pretext for a new human comedy in which Picasso had many unforeseen rôles for the actors.

"And yet the 'subject'," Picasso went on, "no longer exists in our time. When you look at the *Last Judgement* of Michaelangelo you don't really think of the subject, you think of it as a painting. When people look at devils in medieval sculpture they are no longer frightened."

The subject as such has indeed lost much of its significance for us. Now it is no more than a nucleus clothed with assets which belong more strictly to the domain of painting. The treatment of the subject rather than the subject itself has become increasingly important. It is not the haystack in Monet's painting that makes his picture a good one, any more than the presence of the figures of Apollinaire and his Muse made the portrait by the Douanier Rousseau a masterpiece. Even if we take the example of *Guernica*, the greatness of the picture

[1] Baudelaire, *Œuvres*, N.R.F., Paris, 1939, Vol. II, p. 171.
[2] Ibid., p. 177.

does not depend entirely on the subject matter. Then Picasso had adopted a symbolism of his own to convey the original idea. The symbols by proxy became the subject-matter and even so it is the manner of their treatment which is the source of the picture's power to touch off chain reactions in our imagination.

Attempts to rid painting completely of subject-matter are of little interest to Picasso, although his work contains a wealth of purely visual delights. To prove that such pleasures are not absent, it is only necessary to isolate a detail and enjoy it for its abstract qualities. In one of Picasso's studies for *Las Meninas*, for instance, there is a triangular patch representing the hair of one of the ladies in waiting to the Infanta. The qualities present in it that excite the eye are produced merely by green paint brushed thinly with sweeping curves on to white canvas. The mysterious depth and movement contained in the brush stroke has been achieved by a combination of chance and Picasso's knowledge of what he can do with the materials he uses. If this detail were cut out of its context and framed, it could, stripped of the subject to which it belongs, still give satis-faction though it would be of the kind which depends only on the arrangement of shapes and colours. When the detail is restored to its surroundings it becomes once more the flowing hair of a girl, green like grass and moving in sensuous undulations. You may ask, why should Picasso want the Menina's hair to look like grass? It is not certain that he does, but by such suggestions he widens the scope of his image, and his painting gains a new power over our emotions.

In his attachment to a subject, however distant, Picasso remains in spirit nearer to Velasquez than to those of the present generation who have become hostile to that quality in painting which has many names—subject-matter, literary content, realism—and which he always uses as an asset to his work. In other ways, Picasso the rebel and the liberator also shows his appreciation of past achievements. In his tech-nique we can often trace traditional styles that have been transformed by him. His contemporary versions are a kind of shorthand. They can be read as a translation into modern terms of more laborious methods. In his *Meninas* variations the bold movements of the brush of Picasso are the descendants of the careful modelling of Velasquez. They are as sensitive and deliberate, but they belong essentially to our century with its accelerated tempo and its apprehensions, rather than to that more contemplative age three hundred years ago. His work is addressed to the sensibility of the time in which he lives, a new perception which he has given to us and to the generations to come.

In his seventy-seventh year Picasso is working with projects in view that are on a greater scale than anything before. It is the excitement of discovery that keeps him at work, the challenge of unsolved problems that still disquiets him. This is the stimulus that keeps his vitality and imagination unimpaired, rather than the determination to arrive at a final perfection which like death he has no desire to face. Picasso presents us with a lifetime of prodigious achievements. He has done more than any artist of our time to liberate the arts and to make more acute our reactions towards them. He speaks to us with eloquence but even more, he speaks to future generations. The generosity of his spirit and the abundance of his creation have established a source which can grow and whose influence can know no limit.

*   *   *

The story of the life and work of Picasso does not end here. His power of regeneration continues to make him the "youngest painter in the world". Never has he allowed himself to become the victim of his own success. The invention of new styles and techniques in rapid succession, often to the dismay of those who had scarcely had time to appreciate his former manner to its full, has saved him from a hardening of sensibility and a weakening of the emotions which herald old age. In his life, his affection for his friends and his enjoyment of simple pleasures has not diminished. When circumstances have brought to an end a passionate romance, his love has been reborn for a new mistress. But his power of regeneration does not imply a fickle discontinuity in his life. In the diversity of his work there is a constant, unifying strain due to the strength of his personality, the firmness of his decisions that finally puts an end to vacillation and doubt and his gift of an accurate and unfailing visual memory.

His work and his pleasures are those he has always loved. To Jacqueline alone he sings Catalan songs and he watches with excitement the passage of the sputnik in the evening sky, but he tells with equal zest of how that evening when he first saw it a bat came and perched on his shoulder.

Picasso was not content to see no further than others had seen. His love of life urged him to question and probe appearances. Before his gaze beauty was stripped of the disguises invented by a tradition which had supposed an antithesis between beauty and ugliness and had separated them like day and night. He has never been the enemy of beauty and the champion of the hideous, as some would have us think. He has shown us the diversity of forms in which beauty resides. "Beauty", he once said to Sabartès, "what a strange thing . . . For me it is a word devoid of meaning, for I don't know from where its significance comes nor to what it leads. Do you know exactly where to find its opposite?" In nature beauty and ugliness are inextricably partners and Picasso's art expresses at every moment his love of nature as a whole. He accepts its principles as did Michaelangelo when he answered the Pope's objections to the indecency of certain figures in the *Last Judgement* by saying: "Let him change the world and after we will change the painters."

Picasso's love of nature is not limited, it extends to qualities that are conventionally despised. It is there he often makes discoveries and brings to light things of unexpected value. He is the scavenger who unearths from the mud abandoned riches, and the magician who can produce a dove from an empty hat. He was born with the philosopher's stone in his hand. There is literal truth in attributing to him the touch of Midas since in recognition of his powers, every time his pencil touches paper the slightest scribble has its market value.

The virtue common to all great painters is that they teach us to see, but few have had a more compelling way of doing so than Picasso. His power has enchanted those who are susceptible and enraged those who resent being disturbed by his brilliance. "It is art itself", said Molière, "that should teach us to free ourselves from the rules of art", and this is precisely what the art of Picasso, unaided by theories, has done. It has freed art and in consequence it has freed us of false conceptions, of prejudice and of blindness. There is reason also to be grateful for the violence that he has used, for in our time when signs of apathy and despair are easy to detect beneath a garish surface, it is only a resounding and decisive challenge that can succeed. As he himself has said: "The essential in this time of moral poverty is to create enthusiasm." Without the awakening of ardent love, no life and therefore no art has any meaning.

How can we judge what honour should be done to a man of such stature? How at such close quarters can we estimate the greatness of his genius? "Picasso is among those of whom Michaelangelo said that they merited the name of eagles because they surpass all others and break through the clouds to the light of the sun. And today all shadow has disappeared. The last cry of the dying Goethe: 'More light!'

ascends from his work sublime and mysterious." This was the estima-
tion of Apollinaire forty years ago. Meanwhile Picasso's disarming
passionate vision and ceaseless energy have continued to widen our
horizons. Today his art enriches us and its prodigious variety will
provide future generations with a profound joy and an understanding
of our human condition.

CHAPTER XIV

POSTSCRIPT
(1958-1962)

SINCE THE PUBLICATION in 1958 of the English edition of this biography, Picasso has added to the long list of his achievements in various ways. I will briefly outline the most important events, knowing that as I do so he continues daily to add to his production and realising that the only prediction that can be made about his next activity is that it will again be astonishingly new.

The Unesco Mural

Picasso's concern about the gigantic size of the mural he had been asked to paint for the new Unesco building in Paris has already been mentioned. During the winter of 1957-58 he meditated on various ingenious solutions put forward by friends all very willing to offer their help, but with his habitual independence he found his own solution. The initial difficulty was to make a plan for a painting of such vast proportions and secondly to find a method of working on so great an area. Seeing that these problems were insurmountable he decided to paint the mural in sections small enough to be placed on the floor in groups of some half dozen at a time. This amounted to forty panels in all. Relying on his ability to imagine it as a whole, he was able to complete the painting and coordinate the colour, the drawing and the composition throughout, without ever seeing all the panels together. Finally the work was assembled and set up under a temporary roof with special floodlighting in the courtyard of the municipal school at Vallauris. With due ceremony Picasso presented it to a deputation from Unesco headed by Georges Salles who came to receive it officially from the hands of the artist.

Exposed by day to the brilliant light of the sun, away from the architectural surroundings for which it had been conceived, the painting had a disquieting effect. Once more it did not turn out to be what the public had expected. There were however those who understood. Georges Salles, who had followed with enthusiasm the mural in process of creation, showed in an inaugural address his confidence that once installed it would take its place triumphantly in the setting for which it was intended.

This indeed proved to be the case. In September 1958 the great painting was placed in the hall leading to the Conference Room, well lit and framed by rough concrete walls and massive columns. It could now be seen that in spite of the unusual difficulties with which he had to contend, Picasso, although he had been given only a small model of the building, had found brilliant solutions. From these sparse indications Picasso had understood the problem and discovered dramatic possibilities in what seemed to be an extremely awkward site. The visitor does not see the mural as a whole until he has passed the columns and a low footbridge, which hides its central area, and has arrived within a few yards of it. But his movement round these obstacles seems to give movement to the composition itself, in particular to the sinister black shape near the centre of the painting, like the shadow of a man head downwards on which his blanched bones are traced. This tattered apparition seems to drop headlong out of a white hot sky into a mountainous blue wave, while bathers basking on the beach nearby remain indifferent to this dramatic descent. Our own movement as we emerge from behind the rough concrete pillars creates a new and dramatic relationship between the painting and ourselves.

The Chapel at Vallauris (War and Peace)

For some years there had been speculations as to whether Picasso would ever decide to finish the one remaining panel which should cover the end wall and complete the chapel in Vallauris. Some thought that he had lost interest in Vallauris since his move to Cannes; others, knowing his dislike of the act of finishing anything at all, prophesied that the chapel would never be completed. Again Picasso did what no one expected; he painted the semicircular panel and it was promptly announced in the press that there would be an inaugural ceremony towards the end of June 1958. This, however, again unexpectedly, did not take place. The authorities in Paris, under whose jurisdiction the chapel had been placed, decided that it would become dangerously overcrowded by the visitors who would come, and in spite of violent protests in some newspapers, the chapel remained closed for more than a year. In the spring of 1960, however, it was opened to the public without ceremony, and it has now become, as Picasso desired, a grotto lit from the ground and sealed at the far end by the new semicircular panel. Its composition of four interlocked figures suggests the reunion of the races of mankind, crowned by the dove of peace.

New Paintings: 1958

There are few events that have the power of dragging Picasso more surely from his work than a bullfight. The reason is clear. The bullfight always provides him with nourishment for his inspiration. In 1958 at Whitsun this happened once again. Excited by an unusually brilliant performance and at the same time worried by the violent political crisis of 13 May that brought de Gaulle to power, Picasso was particularly sensitive to the fragile nature of life, and the picture he produced in this mood was one that shouted defiance. "I painted this with four-letter words", he said as he showed me a large canvas now known as *Still Life with Bull's Skull,* in which the burning reds and yellows, a double reflection of the sun in the open window, and the monumental immobility of a horned head in the foreground, produce a shock like a deadly explosion within the calm of a distant blue sky.

Other large paintings less turbulent in their atmosphere, such as *The Bay of Cannes,* were produced during the same summer. There were also several portraits of Jacqueline which reveal his continual tenderness for her, and a head of amazing sensitivity, *L'Arlesienne,* which he painted with pigeon feathers that lay thick on the floor of his studio. The liquid freshness with which the paint finds its place on the canvas with no sign of brush or knife seems due to an instant of complete spontaneity, but for his own record, and our enlightenment, Picasso has scored up along the side of the canvas a long tally of dates, showing that he started on 8 July and finished on 15 August.

Vauvenargues, La Californie and Notre Dame de Vie

Picasso once asked me at La Californie if I liked his surroundings and to my polite evasive reply he answered bluntly, "Well, I don't." The garden, in spite of some splendid trees, seemed to him artificial, and the architecture of the house, although it provided him with plenty of space and light to work in, still echoed the bourgeois vulgarity of 1900. In addition, the proximity of Cannes with its beaches, over-crowded in summer, and the growing numbers of admirers and auto-graph hunters, hold fewer attractions for him now than in the past. The daily visit to the beach has ceased to tempt him and he had become more impatient at the frequent interruptions by day and the noise of "son et lumiere" at night, wafting across to him the history of the islands opposite his windows.

In August 1958 Picasso once more took his place of honour at the bullfight in Vallauris, but he returned home without festivities when it was over. When in October his friends prepared once more the banquet which by then had become a tradition, he decided at the last moment he could not face celebrations of this kind any longer and let them know that that year at least he did not intend to have a birthday. Leaving La Californie abruptly with Jacqueline and Sabartes he disappeared until the menace had passed.

 Pleasures had become torments and it was not surprising to hear Picasso talk frequently of moving to more remote surroundings, but none of his friends thought that he would easily abandon the amenities of La Californie. It was natural therefore when one day he telephoned Kahnweiler saying "I have bought le Mont Sainte Victoire" that his old friend, thinking of his love of Cezanne's landscapes, should reply, "Congratulations—but which?" Picasso had to convince him that it was not a painting he had bought but a property consisting of more than 2,000 acres, nearly all of it forest, surrounding the ancient Chateau de Vauvenargues on the northern slope of the mountain. It had happened with vertiginous speed. At first sight he had been enchanted by the austere dignity of the ancient building, with its towers and robust masonry perched on rocks in the centre of a wild and beautiful valley. Its noble proportions and its rugged surroundings reminded him of a Spanish castillo, and its remoteness promised to make it the refuge he had dreamt of, far from the frivolities of Cannes. Not more than a week passed before Picasso found himself landlord of this great estate which carries with it the title of Marquis de Vauvenargues.

 During the following winter while that bitter wind, the "mistral", scourged the rocks and the pine forests with its icy whips, Picasso returned at intervals to see how the work of putting his new house in order was proceeding. The old caretaker, who had used her tongue with such efficiency in her attempts to bar his way when he first came to visit the property, opened the iron gates in great trepidation. "Forgive me, Maitre, for having been so rude," she said, expecting those to be the last words before her dismissal. "Not at all," answered Picasso, "you must always do that and even worse for other visitors."

 Once again Picasso had found space in which to expand. Vans arrived from Paris with his pictures, and those that he had collected in the past by painters such as Le Nain, Cezanne, Matisse, Courbet, Gauguin and many others. All of these had been hidden away for years and he greeted them as old friends released from prison. The bronzes from La Californie arrived without their bases and were dumped along the drive just as they came out of the van. The long line of figures looked as though it had been drawn up ready to salute the arrival of its master.

Furniture chosen in the antique shops of the neighbourhood, chiefly for its size and good solid workmanship, arrived to make the great whitewashed rooms habitable. If the chairs needed upholstery he had them covered with plain cloth and then painted them with designs which reflected the colours of a landscape dominated by the sun. He was also very pleased with his discovery of a ponderous nineteenth-century Henri II style sideboard covered with elaborate carving which he placed in the dining-room. This piece, in company with his new Dalmatian hound, found its way into some of the first paintings made at Vauvenargues. There was a common link between the haphazard scattering of black spots on the dog and the inept arrangement of the carvings.

As usual when Picasso moves to a new place, his style changed with his arrival. In the great salon, where the bust of a former mar uis dominates the eighteenth-century overmantel, he began work on a new series of paintings. There were portraits of Jacqueline in violent reds, blacks and deep sombre greens with her features drawn with extraordinary economy and precision. To one of these he added significantly the inscription "Jacqueline de Vauvenargues".

In a series of still lifes, a lute and a large jar seem to court each other in a dance. The jar displays a new sign which might be called the signature of Vauvenargues. It is a sun-face with four curved limbs radiating from it in the manner of that ancient emblem, the swastika, or the astrological sign for Taurus with two horns added. The dominant colours, bottle green and reddish pinks, seem to have filtered in from the reflection of the sun on the bare limestone of the mountain side, the deep shadows of the pines and the lush grass of the meadows below. For there is water at Vauvenargues; two grotesque heads built into the masonry of the terrace spout water into two great stone tanks, one on each side of the steps that lead up to the front door, a handsome feature designed by Portuguese masons in the sixteenth century. "Portuguese or Spanish, it's all the same," commented Picasso thinking probably of Velasquez and wishing to insist on the Iberian character of his new house.

The nobility both of the chateau and the landscape at Vauvenargues is such that the casual visitor, or more certainly, a new owner would be likely to become the victim of its grandeur, devoured by nostalgic thoughts about its ancient traditions, but Picasso entered as though it were his birthright, both as a peasant and a grand seigneur, and above all simply as an artist moving into a new studio.

For a while the influence of Vauvenargues revived in Picasso his most Spanish vein. When Kahnweiler warned him of the melancholy that could be overpowering in this lonely place, he replied calmly that since he was born a Spaniard he was not frightened. In the spring of 1959, the first spent there, the paintings, whether they were portraits or still lifes, echoed the severity of his native land and without doubt revived his earliest impressions of light and colour. There are also a few small landscapes of the village seen across the ravine, sheltering against the steep mountain side, which have nothing of the gentle restraint of French landscape painters and nothing easily recognisable of his great predecessor in this region, Cezanne.

But as Maurice Jardot remarks in his preface to the catalogue of the exhibition in Paris in January 1962, when over thirty paintings of this period were shown: "The exaltation ceased suddenly: Picasso was to paint only four more pictures at Vauvenargues between May 13 and June 24 and only five during the years 1960 and 1961." (Peintures [Vauvenargues 1959-1961] Galerie Louise Leiris, Paris 1962).

Le Mas Notre Dame de Vie

Picasso now had two homes some fifty miles apart, or rather two places for work, very different in atmosphere: one comfortable but overrun by civilisation, the other austere and solitary. When the stimulus of Vauvenargues died down he returned to Cannes. But the constant expansion of the tourist trade was by now encroaching on the Villa la Californie itself. Gigantic apartment blocks rose up between it and the sea, cutting off the view and even menacing the privacy of the garden and the house itself. For a while Picasso watched the siege with curiosity; the tall red cranes perched high on the great towers that would soon make his life intolerable appeared in some large paintings of the view seen by night and day from his windows. He did not seem annoyed that the idyllic landscape with the islands which he had painted only three years before was slowly being blocked out. With characteristic willingness to see things from every angle he said, "Who knows?—perhaps they are beautiful."

However, as the overcrowding became intolerable another solution offered itself. A villa in the Provencal style, providing ample space, came into the market and was bought without hesitation by Picasso. Situated on a hill near Mougins, it had the advantage of being sufficiently isolated although it was only some five miles from Cannes. Unlike Vauvenargues it was already in good repair and its position, at the top of a hill, gave it an impregnability which La Californie lacked. The slopes of the surrounding hills, covered with pines, oaks, vineyards and villages, stretch down to the sea on one side and rise to the bare ramparts of the lower Alps on the other. On the crest of the hill above the villa is the ancient chapel of Notre Dame de Vie which appropriately gives its name to the property.

Apollinaire

The tedious controversy among Apollinaire's friends as to what would be the most appropriate monument to his memory[1] was finally resolved by the decision to accept Picasso's offer of the large bronze head of a girl, inspired by Dora Maar in 1941.[2] All formalities and permits from official quarters were at last complete in the spring of 1959, and with due ceremony and emotion a group of the poet's old friends, including Madame Apollinaire, Andre Salmon and Jean Cocteau, assembled to unveil Picasso's gift. The site chosen was the corner of the churchyard of St. Germain des Pres facing the street, one of the shortest in Paris, which had been named "rue Guillaume Apollinaire" a few years before. So at last Picasso's tribute to the most eloquent and revolutionary friend of his youth stands modestly shaded by chestnut trees, backed by the walls of the old monastery and surrounded by children at play.

Figures and a Fountain

For several months Picasso had enjoyed making a series of sculptures which should form a group of figures playing together. One of the figures was in fact to function as a fountain in the same way as the Mannequin Pisse fountain in Brussels. They were originally constructed with batons of wood from packing cases, empty canvas stretchers, broom handles and other scraps of material chosen from pieces lying about his studio. For many weeks these tall thin figures with semaphore gestures had stood around at La Californie, exchanging signals with each other. Then in the autumn of 1958 they reappeared cast in bronze and grouped as Picasso had intended round an imaginary pool in the centre of the Galerie Louise Leiris. Later they were shown in an exhibition in New York where critics, excited by their originality and humour, gave them an unusually enthusiastic welcome. Again, in the summer of 1960 they were exhibited in Battersea Park in London. Here the group was placed by the lake. One of the figures appropriately had its feet in the water but the organisers had not the courage to follow out all Picasso's instructions and the fountain failed once more to function as he had intended.

1 see p. 206.   2 Plate XX, 3.

More Exhibitions

In recent years there have been many important exhibitions to add
to the long record. Kahnweiler's unique position as an intimate friend and
Picasso's dealer has kept the Galerie Louise Leiris well stocked with a
flow of work which he could show to the public for the first time.
Picasso's continuous output provided the material for five major exhibitions in the years 1959-62. In the first, the entire series of the Meninas variations (see pages 370-376) was shown, together with the landscapes with doves, those jubilant observations made from the balcony
of his studio. The careful hanging made it possible to follow the sequence of Picasso's thought and to enjoy on the one hand, his playfulness in response to the subject matter—the child princess surrounded
by her attendants—and on the other, the depth of his insight into pictorial problems. It became clear that the series should not be considered
only as a critical study of Velasquez's style but also as a panorama revealing new conceptions of time and space in relation to our vision.

Next came an exhibition of great vigour and gaiety, "Forty-five
engravings on linoleum", the result of experiments and discoveries that
Picasso had made in the simple process of lino-cuts. With the aid of a
young printer in Vallauris, whose craftsmanship became transformed
by Picasso's powers of transmission, new methods of enriching this
otherwise coarse technique were invented. We were presented with
idyllic scenes: fauns, bulls and maidens dancing in upland pastures and
swirling clouds, or the secluded intimacy of lovers. Following this,
in the autumn of 1960, there was an exhibition of drawings made during the two previous years. The main themes were the "gallant picadors, favourites of the great ladies" and "the encounter between the
bull and the heavy horseman".[1] Slender ladies with towering mantillas,
witchlike peasant women and flamenco dancers surrounded the impas-
sive picador, centre of all admiration, in an aura of flying skirts and
provocative gestures. The drawings, masterly in their creation of movement and suspense, were once more a brilliant proof of Picasso's
nostalgia for Spain and the ease with which he could communicate his
passion to us. Never had the skill of his hand as a draftsman and the invention of his wit been used with more cunning and with more brilliant
success.

In 1962 two more exhibitions were added to this brilliant series. The
first consisted of the paintings from Vauvenargues (1959-61) which I

[1] Michel Leiris, Preface to Picasso catalogue, *Dessins 1959-60*, Galerie
Louise Leiris, Paris.

have already described, and the second was a series of 27 paintings begun at Vauvenargues and continued at the newly acquired Mas Notre
Dame de Vie. Picasso had once more taken a painting he admired and
used it as the starting point of successive variations. This time he had
picked the *Dejeuner sur l'Herbe* of Manet, a subject which could easily
have taken place in the sunlight and shade of the water meadows of
Vauvenargues. The composition of this landscape with figures had already been borrowed by Manet from Giorgione's painting in the
Louvre, "La Fete Champetre". But as usual the scene became increasingly transformed by Picasso's imagination, and except for the dominant greens, the allusions to the original painting gave way to playful
inventions. Manet's characters lived a new life improvised for them by
Picasso.

It is not possible for me to mention here all the exhibitions that have
taken place continually in many countries, but there are some major
events that must not be forgotten. In the summer of 1959, thanks to the
initiative of M. Gaston Defferre, senator and mayor of Marseilles, an
important selection of some sixty canvases covering all periods was
shown in that city, the choice having been made by Mr. Douglas
Cooper with Picasso's cooperation. The day before the opening Picasso
overcame his aversion to seeing exhibitions of his own work. He found
among many paintings he had not seen for years the portrait of a
woman he had painted in Madrid in 1901, which had spent many
decades in the vaults of the Bellas Artes museum. So many years had
passed that even he had forgotten the colour of the lady's skirt.

The following year, 1960, it was London that honoured Picasso with
the most representative exhibition of his paintings that had yet been
assembled. The Tate Gallery gave up more space than it had ever before
allowed to a single artist and the 280 paintings, ninety of which were
lent by the artist, included early works such as the *Girl with Bare Feet*,
painted when he was fourteen, the *Demoiselles d'Avignon*, the great drop
curtain for *Parade*, the entire *Meninas* series and ten superb canvases
dating from 1900 to 1909, lent by the Russian Government. The response of the London public was overwhelming. Almost half a million
visited the exhibition. Their reactions and those of the critics were in
fact very different from the violent antagonism that had been aroused
when the wartime paintings were shown only fifteen years before at
the Victoria and Albert Museum. The press now acclaimed Picasso as
a great genius and the Queen herself during a private visit spoke of
Picasso as the greatest artist of this century. There was only one disappointment. In spite of the persistent encouragement of his friends

Picasso could not be persuaded to come to London. It was impossible
to discover whether he dreaded more the acclamation and publicity
that he was bound to receive or the formidable sight of his whole life
work presented to him in one great sequence. His own explanation
however was summed up when he said: "Why should I go? I know
them all, those paintings. I did them myself."

A New Spanish Period

In recent times there has probably been more Spanish spoken at La
Californie than French, owing to a notable increase in visitors from
Barcelona, Malaga and Madrid. Old friends such as Pallares and Vidal-
Ventosa have called on him. Architects, publishers, dealers, museum
directors and poets have come to pay their respects and frequently
found that there were ways in which they could appeal to Picasso's
persistent love of Spain and obtain his cooperation in new projects. The
faithful and indispensable Sabartes has been active in arousing enthusiasm and support in Barcelona for the foundation of a Picasso Museum
for which he has obtained a Gothic palace in the Calle Moncada, in the
quarter where Picasso spent his youth. As a sign that he is not insensitive
to this gesture Picasso has announced his gift of the whole series of the
Meninas paintings to the Museum. In Malaga a plaque has been placed
on the house in the Plaza de la Merced where Picasso was born and the
installation in an ancient palace nearby of a well-documented collection
of Picassiana is well advanced.

Barcelona has always been the city in Spain for which Picasso has
felt most sympathy and when a group of young architects asked him
for designs for the decoration of a new College of Architecture that
was being built in the old part of the city close to the cathedral, the
quarter in which he had lived in his "blue period", he agreed to help.
The designs he produced were large line drawings inspired by the traditional Catalan dances and festivals in which he had taken part in his
youth. They were drawn to scale, so that they could be reproduced on a
wide band of concrete that extends across the facades of the building.
The lines were incised into the surface by sandblasting—a technique
perfected and executed by a young Norwegian artist, Karl Nesjar, who
is now busily producing more sandblasted sculptures and reliefs from
Picasso's designs. The decorations at the College of Architecture were
unveiled in April 1962.

Picasso's new Spanish period has also led to the publication of three
fragments, the first to be printed in Castillian in Spain, from a long
poem, *Trozo de Piel,* written by him during the winter of 1959-60. The

publisher, Camilo Jose Cela, himself a poet, has other similar projects in progress. Also, Picasso has for the first time since the Spanish war lent paintings from his studio to an exhibition in Spain. This took place at the Sala Gaspar in November 1960 and gave the people of Barcelona their first opportunity to see some thirty of his paintings representative of many different periods.

A Secret and a Public Celebration

When it was announced in reputable newspapers on 14 March 1961 that Picasso had married Jacqueline Roque, most of his friends including those who had long wished that this might happen, believed it to be no more than a rumour. They were wrong. It was in fact on 2 March that the marriage had taken place without ceremony at the Town Hall in Vallauris and for ten days no one but the communist mayor, a devoted admirer of Picasso, and two witnesses had any hint of what had happened. For once the flood of publicity and congratulations had been successfully kept in control.

Six months later however Picasso was to celebrate his 80th birthday and for this occasion he decided to enter wholeheartedly into the festivities that had been planned for him. In spite of rumours that he was sick and confined to bed which kept visitors at a respectful distance until the day arrived, he set out to enjoy it all to his full capacity.

The little town of Vallauris gave itself up to rejoicings on a scale which might be compared to a holy feast in Renaissance times. Four thousand invitations in the name of M. Paul Derigon the mayor were sent out, announcing events which began in Nice with a Festival of Music, Song and Dance. Among the performers were the Russian musicians Svjatoslav Richter and Leonide Kogan, Gloria Davey of the New York Metropolitan, Antonio the famous Flamenco dancer, and other stars from various countries, such as the conductor Marcovitch. In an atmosphere which remained intimate in spite of the 6000 spectators and the profusion of distinguished guests the acts and the applause went on till early morning.

The following day, Sunday, Picasso arrived before noon in Vallauris escorted by helmeted motor-cycle police with white gauntlets. With difficulty a path was made for him through the crowd, to enable him to visit an exhibition of some fifty of his own paintings. They had been carefully selected by his friends so that he could again see pictures which had been hidden from him in museums and collections for many years. The streets were crowded with admirers of all descriptions. In addition to those who understood his greatness as an artist were many who loved him as a man. Parties who had come from neighbouring villages with guitars to serenade him found themselves shoulder to shoulder with distinguished foreigners from all parts of the world.

At midday Picasso was honoured at a lunch by the sea where a hundred of his friends acclaimed him with speeches in various languages and great quantities of presents. By this time the road back to Vallauris had become so hopelessly blocked that a long detour had to be made so as to arrive in time for the bullfight that was given in his honour in the spacious Place des Ecoles. The matadors were his friends the famous Miguel Dominguin and Ortega. Four bulls were killed by them with full Spanish ritual and in deliberate contravention of French law.

The official programme came to an end in Cannes where a great reception at the Palm Beach Casino was followed by a display of fireworks fit for royalty. After all this activity Picasso was still in splendid form. Throughout he had showed his appreciation and enjoyment of this amazing display of affection and admiration. When it came to an end he was loth to let his friends disperse. Several were obliged to cancel reservations so as to accompany him in further conviviality. Finally when they had all said goodbye he at once shut himself up in his studio and returned to his work.

The homage paid to Picasso was not only local. In various parts of the world exhibitions were held and special numbers of magazines were dedicated to him. Of these the most important was the organisation in New York galleries of nine concurrent exhibitions entitled: "Picasso, an American Tribute". Each gallery presented a different period or medium of his work from 1895 to 1961, and the Museum of Modern Art put on an all-summer showing of its great collection of Picassos. At the same time that these events were bringing together magnificent displays of paintings, drawings, and sculpture in New York, it was announced in Moscow on May 1 that Picasso had been awarded the Lenin Prize: a prize intended "to strengthen the bonds of peace between all peoples."

The relationship between Picasso and Russian officialdom has always been equivocal. Although his affiliation to the French Communist party and its respect for him, as well as his international fame, have made him for many years a desirable asset, and in spite of the immense attraction that an exhibition of his paintings in Moscow in 1956 proved to be, there has always been violent antagonism from official and academic quarters. On this occasion some fifty paintings were borrowed from Picasso, thanks to the initiative of the poet Ilya Ehrenburg; the response of the younger generation was one of great curiosity mingled with admiration. It is said that the exhibition attracted about a million visitors. Yet five years later officialdom seemed not to have progressed. Mr. Khrushchev and his suite greeted with scorn the "decadent" art of Picasso when they visited the exhibit of his work in the French Exhibition in Moscow as recently as the summer of 1961. However by placing the onus of his fame as a painter on the judgement of foreigners and praising his opinions and his conduct as a man, Pravda was able to explain the official party line in these terms: "All people of good faith will welcome with enthusiasm the award of the Lenin Prize to Pablo Picasso, the celebrated French painter and the great humanist, whose name is known to hundreds of millions of people. His work can be seen in the museums of almost all the capital cities in the world . . . For Picasso, painting can be likened, as he himself says, 'to a weapon both of defence and of attack in the war against the enemy': and this enemy is Fascism."

In contrast to this I will quote the headlines of an interview published in *France-Soir* at the time of his 80th birthday in which he is quoted as saying: "Love is the only thing that is worth while." Whatever the means, Picasso has in fact made his conquest of the world.

With the new defences of his privacy now well in control Picasso enjoys with more assurance the cool spacious rooms of Notre Dame de Vie with its terraces of vines, olive trees and cypresses. The sculptures that had never found their final places at Vauvenargues have been brought there and are now crowded together on the steps on the entrance hall, joined by many others, big and small, that have come from Vallauris or been made by him recently. Above them hangs an immense spiral collage of the drawings of 1000 school children made for him in honour of his 80th birthday. Sculpture has again become one of Picasso's chief preoccupations. New forms emerge constructed out of sheets of three-ply bent like the sails of a ship and painted, but fundamentally human in their form. The new house has become a series of spacious and well-lit studios animated by the voice of a grey parrot that talks Spanish and the silent tread of an Afghan hound that moves neatly between the easels and stacks of canvases on which the paint is still fresh. With unobtrusive devotion Jacqueline is quick to follow Picasso's needs and desires and above all nothing is allowed to hinder him during the long hours when he is working. As the prospect of life becomes inevitably shorter the imperative need to use every possible moment for work increases. At the same time nothing impairs the freshness and power of his vision. As a symbol of this, I remember an incident which happened recently when Jacqueline noticed with alarm that Picasso was looking straight at the afternoon sun. To her timely warning Picasso replied casually: "That's all right. I have always looked the sun straight in the eye since my childhood."

ACKNOWLEDGEMENTS

BIBLIOGRAPHY

PLATES

ACKNOWLEDGEMENTS

IN WRITING this book I have drawn largely on information derived from conversations with friends, of whom the most important is M. Pablo Picasso himself. I am deeply grateful to him for his patience during many days spent in his company, and for the hospitality shown to me in Cannes by him and Madame Jacqueline Roque.

Other members of his family have also helped me. I am indebted to M. Paul Picasso for his friendly assistance, to Señora Vilato Ruiz, M. Picasso's sister, for her welcome in Barcelona, and to her sons, particularly MM. Fin and Javier Vilato whose friendship I have enjoyed for many years.

Among those who have supplied me with valuable information are MM. Daniel-Henri Kahnweiler and Jaime Sabartès who have taken a special interest in this book. To them and to many other friends my thanks are due. I wish to mention in particular Mr. Alfred H. Barr, Jr., M. Pierre Baudouin, Mr. Clive Bell, M. Georges Braque, Professor Douglas Cooper, Mmes. Dominique Eluard, Françoise Gilot-Simon, Valentine Hugo, Manolo Hugué, M. Maurice Jardot, Lady Keynes, M. Michel Leiris, Mlle. Dora Maar, Mr. Man Ray, Baron Jean Mollet, Mme. Fernande Olivier, Mme. Valentine Penrose, Sir Herbert Read, Mr. John Richardson, MM. Henri-Pierre Roché, Georges Salles, André Salmon, Miss Alice B. Toklas, MM. Tristan Tzara, Patrick Waldberg and Christian Zervos.

For continuous help and advice throughout the writing of the book I am most grateful to my wife and to Mr. John Haywood. I am also grateful for help received from Mr. and Mrs. Terence O'Brien, Mrs. Sonia Orwell, and Mr. John Russell. In compiling the illustrations I have been assisted in particular by Miss Elizabeth Frank, M. Tériade, the Arts Council of Great Britain and the Galerie Louise Leiris, and in addition I should like to thank the many owners, both private and public, who have kindly allowed me to reproduce works of art in their collections. Finally I wish to record my warmest thanks to Miss Joyce Reeves for the time, patience and devoted care she has given to putting my manuscript in order.

R. P.

Paris, 1958

BIBLIOGRAPHY

THE MOST COMPLETE bibliography of works on Picasso so far published is that printed by Barr in *Picasso: Fifty Years of His Art* in 1946, originally compiled by Beaumont Newhall. The reader is referred also to the bibliography in *Pablo Picasso* by Boeck and Sabartès, 1955; and to that printed by Maurice Jardot in the catalogue of the exhibition, Picasso, Peintures 1900-55, at the Musée des Arts Décoratifs, Paris, 1955. The following list gives a selection of the chief works used in the compilation of this book, and of others considered of particular interest.

Adéma, Marcel. *Apollinaire*. Heinemann, 1954.
Apollinaire, Guillaume. *The Cubist Painters*. (English translation.)
—— Wittenborn & Co., New York, 1944.
—— and Cerusse, Jean (editors). *Les Soirées de Paris*. Monthly Review, Paris, No. 18, 15 November 1913—Nos. 26 and 27, July-August, 1914.
—— *La Femme Assise*. Gallimard, Paris, 1948.
Aragon, Louis. *La Peinture au Défi*. Corti, Paris, 1930.
Argan, Giulio Carlo. *Scultura di Picasso*. Alfieri, Venice, 1953.
Barr, Alfred H., Jr. *Picasso: Fifty Years of His Art*. The Museum of Modern Art, New York, 1946.
—— *Matisse: His Art and His Public*. The Museum of Modern Art, New York, 1951.
Bataille, Georges. 'Soleil Pourri', *Hommage à Picasso, Documents*, No. 3, 2e Année, Paris, 1930.
Bell, Clive. *Old Friends*. Chatto and Windus, London, 1956.
Billy, André. *Max Jacob*. Pierre Seghers, Paris, 1953.
Braque, Georges, and Vallier, Dora. 'La Peinture et Nous', *Cahiers d'Art*, Paris, October 1954.
Breton, André. *Le Surréalisme et La Peinture*. La Révolution Surréaliste No. 4, Paris, 15 July 1925.
—— 'Picasso Poète', *Cahiers d'Art*, No. 10, Paris, 1935.
Boeck, W., and Sabartès, J. *Pablo Picasso*. Thames and Hudson, London, 1955.
Cirici-Pellicer, A. *Picasso avant Picasso*. Cailler, Geneva, 1950.

Cocteau, Jean. *Le Coq et l'Arlequin*. Editions de la Sirène, Paris, 1918.

—— *Picasso*. Stock, Paris, 1923.

Crastre, Victor. *La Naissance du Cubisme*. Ophrys, Paris, undated.

Duncan, David Douglas. *The Private World of Pablo Picasso*, Ridge Press, New York, 1957.

Elgar, Frank, and Maillard, Robert. *Picasso*. Fernand Hazan, Paris, and Thames and Hudson, London, 1955.

Eluard, Paul. *A Pablo Picasso*. Trois Collines, Geneva/Paris, 1944.

—— *Selected Writings*. Translated by Lloyd Alexander, Routledge and Kegan Paul, London, 1952.

—— 'Je Parle de ce qui est Bien', *Cahiers d'Art*, Paris, 7.10, 1955.

Fagus, Felicien. *Gazette d'Art*, quoted in *Cahiers d'Art*, 1932, Nos. 3-5.

Geiser, Bernhard. *Pablo Picasso: Fifty-five Years of His Graphic Work*. Thames and Hudson, London, 1955.

Gonzalez, Julio. 'Picasso Sculpteur', *Cahiers d'Art*, II, Nos. 6-7, 1936.

Hugnet, Georges. 'Dada and Surrealism', *Bulletin of the Museum of Modern Art*, New York, November/December 1936.

Jacob, Max. *Correspondance*. Editions de Paris, Paris, 1953.

Janis, Harriet and Sydney. *Picasso: The Recent Years, 1939-46*, Doubleday & Co, New York, 1946.

Kahnweiler, Daniel-Henry. *Picasso: Dessins 1903-1907*. Berggruen et Cie., Paris, 1954.

—— *The Rise of Cubism*. Wittenborn, Schutz Inc., New York.

—— Preface to *The Sculptures of Picasso*. Rodney Phillips & Co., London, 1949. (Photographs by Brassai.)

—— Questionnaire in *L'Œil*, No. 1, 1955.

Larrea, Juan. *Guernica*. Curt Valentin, New York, 1947.

Leiris, Michel. *Miroir de la Tauromachie*. G.L.M., Paris, 1938.

Level, André. *Picasso*. Crès, Paris, 1928.

Loeb, Pierre. *Voyages à Travers la Peinture*. Bordas, Paris, 1945.

Melville, Robert. *Picasso: Master of the Phantom*. Oxford University Press, London, 1939.

Mourlot, Fernand. *Picasso Lithographe*. Vols. I and II, Editions du Livre, Monte Carlo, 1949 and 1950. Preface by J. Sabartès. Vol. III, 1956.

Nicolson, Benedict. 'Post-impressionism and Roger Fry', *Burlington Magazine*, January 1951, London.

Olivier, Fernande. *Picasso et ses Amis*. Stock, Paris, 1933.

d'Ors, Eugenio. *Picasso*. Paris, 1930.

Penrose, Roland. *Portrait of Picasso*. Lund Humphries, London, 1956.

—— *Homage to Picasso*. Lund Humphries, London, 1951.

Penrose, Roland. 'Picasso', *L'Œil*, October 1956.

Picasso, Pablo. Statements and Interviews:

(1) 'Picasso Speaks.' Interview with Marius de Zayas, printed in *The Arts*, New York, May 1923, reprinted by Barr in *Picasso: Fifty Years of His Art*, p. 270.

(2) 'Pourquoi j'ai adhéré au Parti Communiste', *l'Humanité*, Paris, October 29-30, 1944. Interview with Pol Gaillard, reprinted by Barr, *Picasso*, p. 267.

(3) 'Picasso Explains.' Interviews with Jerome Seckler, *New Masses*, 13 March 1945, reprinted by Barr, *Picasso*, p. 268.

(4) 'Picasso n'est pas officier dans l'armée française.' *Lettres Françaises*, Paris, Mar. 24 1945, reprinted by Barr, *Picasso*, p. 269.

Le Désir attrapé par la Queue. N.R.F. Collection Métamorphose No. 23, Gallimard, Paris, 1949.

Raynal, Maurice. *Picasso*. Crès, Paris, 1922.

—— 'Panorama de l'Œuvre de Picasso.' Le Point, 'Picasso' (Revue Artistique et Littéraire) XLII. Souillac (Lot) and Mulhouse, October 1952.

—— *Picasso*. Albert Skira, Geneva, 1953.

Read, Herbert. 'Picasso's *Guernica*', *London Bulletin*, No. 6, 1938.

—— *Art Now*. Faber and Faber, London, 1933.

Roy, Claude. *La Guerre et la Paix*. Editions du Cercle d'Art, 1954.

Sabartès, Jaime. *Picasso: Portraits et Souvenirs*. Louis Carré et Maximilien Vox, Paris, 1946.

—— *Picasso: Documents Iconographiques*. Pierre Cailler, Geneva, 1954.

—— Preface to Mourlot, F., *Picasso Lithographe*.

—— See also Boeck, W., and Sabartès, J.

Salmon, André. *Souvenirs Sans Fin*. Gallimard, Paris, 1955.

Serna, Ramon Gomez de la. 'Le Toreador de la Peinture', *Cahiers d'Art*, 1932, Nos. 3-5.

Soby, James Thrall. *Modern Art and the New Past*. University of Oklahoma Press, 1957.

Sprigge, Elisabeth. *Gertrude Stein*. Hamish Hamilton, London 1957. (Yale Collection Letters.)

Stein, Gertrude. *Autobiography of Alice B. Toklas*. John Lane The Bodley Head, London, 1933.

—— *Everybody's Autobiography*. Random House, New York, 1937, and Heinemann, London, 1938.

—— *Picasso*. Scribner's, New York, and Batsford, London, 1938.

Sweeney, James Johnson. 'Picasso and Iberian Sculpture.' *Art Bulletin*, 23, No. 3, New York, September 1941.

Tériade, E. (editor). *Verve*, Vol. V, No. 19-20, Picasso at Antibes. Paris, 1948.

—— *Verve*, Vol. VII, No. 25-26, Picasso at Vallauris, Paris, 1951.

—— *Verve*, Vol. VIII, No. 29-30, Suite of 180 drawings of Picasso, Paris, 1954.

Tzara, Tristan. *Picasso et la Poésie*. De Luca, Rome, 1953.

Uhde, Wilhelm. *Picasso and the French Tradition*. Editions des Quatre Chemins, Paris; Weyhe, New York, 1929.

Vallentin, Antonina. *Picasso*. Albin Michel, Paris, 1957.

Vollard, A. *Recollections of a Picture Dealer*. Constable, London, 1936.

Verdet, André. 'Picasso et Ses Environs', *Les Lettres Nouvelles*, Paris, July-August 1955.

Zervos, Christian. *Picasso*. Editions Cahiers d'Art, Paris. Vol. I (1932) to Vol. XII (1961). The monumental catalogue of Picasso's painting, sculpture and drawing with reproductions of most of his work. In course of publication.

—— (editor). *Cahiers d'Art*. Many volumes of this series contain important articles on Picasso, some of which are referred to above. See especially No. 3-5, 1932, and the No. for 1945-46.

—— *Catalan Art*. Heinemann, London, 1937.

ADDITIONS TO BIBLIOGRAPHY

des Champris, Pierre. *Ombres et Soleil de Picasso*. Gallimard, Paris, 1961.

Duncan, David Douglas. *Picasso's Picassos: The Treasures of La Californie*. Harper & Brothers, New York, 1961.

Penrose, Roland, and Wilenski, R. H. *Picasso*. 2 Vols. The Faber Gallery, London, 1961.

Penrose, Roland. *Pablo Picasso: Four Themes*. The Folio Society, London, 1961.

Penrose, Roland. *Picasso*. Modern Sculptors. A. Zwemmer Ltd., London, 1961.

Picasso, Pablo and Villers, Andre. *Diurnes,* Decoupages et Photographies. Texte de Jacques Prevert, Berggruen, Paris, 1961.

Picasso, Pablo. *Toros y Toreros*. Texte de Miguel Dominguin avec un etude de Georges Boudaille. Thames & Hudson, London, 1961.

Picasso, Pablo. *Trozo de Piel*. Les Ediciones de los Papeles de son Armadans. Madrid—Palma de Mallorca, 1959.

Picasso, Pablo. *Carnet Catalan*, Facsimile of sketchbook of 1906. Preface and Notes by Douglas Cooper, Berggruen, Paris, 1958.
Picasso, Pablo. *Le Dejeuner sur l'Herbe*. Preface by Douglas Cooper, Paris.
Zervos, Christian. *Picasso*. Editions Cahiers d'Art:
Vol. IX 1937-39 Paris, 1958.
" X 1939-40 " 1959.
" XI 1940-41 " 1960.
" XII 1942-43 " 1961.

The Picador. Earliest known painting by Picasso. 1889-90. Oil on wood.

2. Girl with Bare Feet. 1895. Oil. ($29\frac{1}{2} \times 19\frac{1}{2}$)

3. Diploma drawing. 1895. Pencil. ($19\frac{3}{4} \times 12$)

4. Science and Charity. 1896. Oil. (c. 60×80)

5. Self-portrait. 1901. Pen and coloured crayon. ($7 \times 4\frac{1}{2}$)

6. Scene in a Tavern. 1897. Oil. ($7 \times 9\frac{1}{2}$)

7. Harlequin. 1905. Oil. ($39\frac{1}{2} \times 39$)

8. Moulin de la Galette. 1900. Oil. ($35\frac{1}{4} \times 45\frac{3}{4}$)

9. Burial of Casagemas (Evocation). 1901. Oil. ($58\frac{3}{4} \times 35\frac{1}{2}$)

PLATE I

1. Portrait of Jaime
Sabartès. 1901. Oil.
(32 × 26)

2. The Blue Room. 1901. Oil. (20 × 24½)

3. Self-portrait. 190
Oil. (32 × 23½)

4. La Vie. 1903. Oil. (77½ × 51)

5. Two Sisters. 1902.
Oil. (60 × 39¼)

6. Maternity. 1901. Oil. (44¼ × 38½)

7. The Old Jew. 1903.
Oil. (49¼ × 36¼)

8. The Blind Man's Meal. 1903. Oil.
(37½ × 37½)

9. The Courtesan with a
Jewelled Necklace. 1901. Oil.
(25¾ × 21½)

PLATE II

1. The Actor. 1904-05. Oil. (77¼ × 45¼)

2. Salomé. 1905. Drypoint. (16 × 13¾)

3. Meditation. 1904. Watercolour. (13¾ × 10)

The Jester. 1905. Bronze. (16¼ high)

5. The Soler Family. 1903. Oil. (59 × 79)

6. The Old Guitarist. 1903. Oil. (47½ × 32)

7. Acrobat's Family with Ape. 1905. Tempera. (41 × 29¼)

8. Nude. 1905. Gouache. (19 × 11½)

9. Boy leading a Horse. 1905. Oil. (87 × 51¼)

PLATE III

1. Portrait of Gertrude Stein. 1906.
Oil. (39½ × 32)

2. Acrobat on a Ball.
1905. Oil. (57½ × 37).

3. Self-portrait. 1906. Oil. (36 × 28

5. Two Nudes. 1906. Oil.
(59¾ × 36½)

4. Family of Saltimbanques. 1905. Oil. (83¾ × 90½)

6. Woman with a Fan. 1905. Oil.
(39½ × 32)

PLATE IV

2. Negro Dancer. 1907.
Oil. (24 × 17)

1. Les Demoiselles d'Avignon. 1907. Oil. (96 × 92)

3. Head. 1908. Oil.
(24½ × 17)

4. Nude with Drapery. 1907.
Oil. (60 × 39¾)

5. House in Garden. 1908. Oil.
(28¾ × 23½)

6. Two Nudes (Friendship).
1908. Oil. (59¾ × 39¾)

PLATE V

1. Nude on Beach. 1908. Oil.
(51 × 38)

2. Fruit Dish. 1908-09. Oil.
(29¼ × 24)

3. Portrait of Clovis Sagot.
1909. Oil. (31¾ × 25½)

4. Head of a Woman. 1909.
Bronze. (16¼ high)

5. Seated Woman (Femme en
vert). 1909. Oil. (37¾ × 31½)

6. The Reservoir, Horta. 1909.
Oil. (31¾ × 25½)

7. Portrait of Vollard. 1909.
Oil. (36¼ × 25½)

8. Portrait of Uhde. 1910. Oil.
(30¾ × 22¾)

9. Portrait of Kahnweiler.
1910. Oil. (39½ × 28½)

PLATE VI

1. Girl with Mandolin. 1910.
Oil. (39½ × 29)

2. The Torero. 1912. Oil.
(53¼ × 32½)

3. Seated Nude. 1909 or 1910. Oil.
(36¼ × 28¾)

4. Pipe, glass and apple. 1913. Oil.

5. "Ma Jolie" (Woman
with zither or guitar).
1911-12. Oil. (39½ × 25¾)

6. Still-life with Gas Jet. 1912.
Oil. (27 × 21)

7. Violin, bottle and glass. 1912-13.
Charcoal and pasted papers.
(18½ × 24¾)

8. Head. 1914? Charcoal
and pasted papers. (17 × 13)

9. Still-life with Chair-caning.
1911-12. Oil and pasted oilcloth.
(10½ × 13¾ oval)

PLATE VII

1. Guitar on a Table. 1913. Oil on wood, with plaster reliefs. ($26\frac{1}{4} \times 17\frac{3}{4}$)

2. Girl in an Armchair in front of a Fireplace. 1914. Oil. ($51\frac{1}{4} \times 38$)

3. Woman in a Chemise. 191? Oil. ($58\frac{1}{4} \times 39$)

4. Vive la France. 1914-15. Oil. ($21\frac{1}{2} \times 25\frac{3}{4}$)

5. Glass of Absinthe. 1914. Painted bronze and silver spoon. (8 high)

6. Still-life. 1914. Painted wood wit upholstery fringe. (18 long)

7. Card Player. 1913-14. Oil. ($42\frac{1}{2} \times 35\frac{1}{4}$)

8. Harlequin. 1915. Oil. ($72\frac{1}{4} \times 41\frac{1}{2}$)

9. Guitarist. 1916. Oil. (51×38?

PLATE VIII

1. Portrait of Max Jacob. 1915.
Lead pencil. $(13 \times 9\frac{3}{4})$

2. Portrait of Apollinaire.
1916. Lead pencil.

3. Portrait of Stravinsky. 1920.
Lead pencil. $(24\frac{1}{2} \times 19)$

5. Portrait of Olga Koklova.
1917. Oil.

4. Drop Curtain for *Parade*. 1917. (11 yards × 17 yards)

6. Horse and Bull. 1917. Lead pencil.

7. Diaghilev and Selisburg *c.*
1917. Lead pencil.

PLATE IX

1. The Bathers. 1918. Pencil. ($9\frac{1}{4} \times 12\frac{1}{4}$)

2. Table in front of Window. 1919. Gouache. ($8\frac{3}{4} \times 12\frac{1}{4}$)

3. Mother and Child. 1921. Oil. (38×28)

5. Two Seated Women. 1920. Oil. ($76\frac{3}{4} \times 64\frac{1}{2}$)

4. Three Musicians, 1921. Oil. ($79 \times 87\frac{3}{4}$)

6. Seated Woman. 1923. Oil. (36×28)

PLATE X

1. Still-life, Dinard. 1922. Oil.
(13 × 16¼)

2. Three Dancers. 1925.
Oil. (84½ × 56¼)

3. The Studio, Juan-les-Pins.
1925. Oil. (38½ × 51½)

4. Mandolin and Guitar. 1924. Oil
with sand. (56 × 79¾)

5. Drawing. 1924. Pen
and Indian ink.
(11½ × 9)

6. Guitar. 1926. Floorcloth,
string, nails and newspaper.
(38¼ × 51½)

7. Head. 1926. Oil. (8½ × 5½)

8. Painter and model knitting. 1927. Etching.
(7½ × 11¼)

9. Paulo as a Toreador.
1925. Oil. (63¾ × 38¼)

PLATE XI

1. Bather (Cannes). 1927. Charcoal.

2. On the Beach (Dinard). 1928. Oil. (7½ × 12¾)

3. Woman's Head and Self-portrait. 1929. Oil. (29 × 24)

4. Metamorphosis. 1928-29. Bronze. (8¾ high)

5. Project for a Monument (Woman's Head). 1929. Oil. (25¾ × 21¼)

6. Sculpture. 1928. Iron wire. (about 30 high)

7. Crucifixion. 1930. Oil on wood. (20 × 26)

8. Painter and Model. 1928. Oil. (51½ × 64)

PLATE XII

1. Woman in an Armchair. 1929. Oil. (76¾ × 51)

2. Sculpture. 1931. Bronze. (39½ high)

3. Seated Bather. 1929. Oil. (64 × 51)

4. Girl seated in a red armchair. 1932. Oil. (51 × 38¼)

5. Girl before a Mirror. 1932. Oil. (63¾ × 51¼)

6. Nude on a Black Couch. 1932. Oil. (63¾ × 51¼)

7. Pitcher and Bowl of Fruit. 1931. Oil. (51¼ × 64)

8. Anatomy. 1933. Pencil.

9. Composition with butterfly. 1932. Matches, drawing pin, leaf, butterfly, etc. (9½ × 13)

PLATE XIII

1. Head. 1931-32. Bronze.
(22¼ high)

2. Figures. 1931.
Wood, later cast in
bronze.
(*left* 17 high, *right*
20 high)

3. Bullfight. 1934. Oil. (38 × 51)

4. Heads. 1932. Plaster,
later cast in bronze.
(*left* 34 high, *right* 30¾
high)

5. Two Girls Reading.
1934. Oil. (32 × 27½)

6. Sculptor's Studio. 1933. Etching. (7¾ × 10½)

7. The Muse. 1935. Oil. (51¼ × 63¾)

8. Minotaur carousing. 1933. Mixed process.
(11½ × 14½)

9. Dying Minotaur. 1933. Etching. (7¾ × 11¾)

PLATE XIV

1. Bathers with a Toy Boat. 1937. Oil, charcoal and chalk. (51 × 76¾)

2. Portrait of Dora Maar. 1937. Oil. (36¼ × 25½)

3. Portrait of Nusch. 1937. Oil.

4. Nude with Night Sky. 1936. Oil (51½ × 63¾)

5. Portrait of Eluard. 1936. Pencil.

6. Grand Air. 1936. Aquatint. (16½ × 12¼)

7. Blind Minotaur. 1935. Mixed process. (9¾ × 13¾)

8. Minotaur with a Boat. 1937. Indian ink and Ripolin on cardboard. (9 × 11)

9. End of a Monster. 1937. Pencil. (15 × 22)

PLATE XV

1. Portrait of Marie-Thérêse.
1937. Oil. $(39\frac{1}{2} \times 32)$

2. Still-life, Le Tremblay. 1937-38. Oil.

3. Still-life with Horned God.
1937. Oil $(27\frac{3}{4} \times 23\frac{1}{2})$

4. Woman with Cat. 1937. Oil.
$(c. 32 \times 23)$

5. Portrait of Maïa. 1938. Oil.
$(28\frac{3}{4} \times 23\frac{1}{2})$

6. Portrait of Lee Miller. 1937.
Oil. $(32\frac{1}{2} \times 23\frac{1}{2})$

7. Dream and Lie of Franco.
1937. Etching. $(3\frac{1}{2} \times 5\frac{1}{4})$

8. Signature to Dream and Lie
of Franco. 1937.

PLATE XVI

1. Guernica. 1937. Oil. (11′ 5″ × 25′ 5¾″)

2. Weeping Woman. 1937. Oil.
(23½ × 19½)

3. Cat and Bird. 1939. Oil. (32 × 39½)

4. Minotauromachie. 1935. Etching. (19½ × 27)

5. Girl with a Cock. 1938. Oil.
(57¼ × 47½)

PLATE XVII

1. Woman in a Garden.
1938. Oil. (51×38)

2. Still-life with a Red Bull's Head.
1938. Oil. (37¾×51)

3. Man with Lollipop. 1938.
Oil. (24×19)

4. Portrait of D.M. 1939. Oil.
(36×25½)

5. Café at Royan. 1940. Oil. (51×38)

6. Woman's Head. 1939. Oil.
(25½×21¼)

7. Fishermen of Antibes. 1939. Oil. (6′ 9″×11′ 4″)

8. Portrait of Jaime Sabartès.
1939. Oil. (23¾×18)

PLATE XVIII

Page from Royan sketchbook.
1940. Pen, ink and wash.
$(16 \times 11\frac{1}{2})$

2. Nude dressing her hair. 1940.
Oil. $(51 \times 38\frac{1}{2})$

3. Head, Royan. 11 June
1940. Oil on paper. (25×18)

4. Sleeping Nude. 1941. Oil.
$(36 \times 25\frac{1}{2})$

5. Child with Pigeons. 1943. Oil.
(64×51)

6. Still-life with Sausage.
1941. Oil. $(36 \times 25\frac{1}{2})$

7. Self-portrait from *Desire
Caught by the Tail*. 1943. Pen
and ink.

8. Skull and Leeks. 1945. Oil.
(35×51)

9. Portrait of D.M. as a bird.
1943. Pen, ink and wash.

PLATE XIX

1. Skull. 1943. Bronze. (11½ high)

2. Man with Sheep. 1944. Bronze. (7' 2" high)

3. Head of D.M. 1941. Bronze. (31½ high)

4. Head. 1943. Paper. (5 high)

5. Nude. 1942. Oil. (51 × 76½)

6. Bull's Head. 1943. Bicycle saddle and handlebars. (16 high)

7. Still-life with Candle. 1945. Oil. (33½ × 43)

8. Bacchanale after Poussin. 1944. Watercolour and gouache. (12¼ × 16¼)

9. Paris Landscape. 1945. Oil. (28¾ × 36½)

PLATE XX

1. First Steps. 1943. Oil.
($51\frac{1}{4} \times 38\frac{1}{4}$)

2. Seated Woman. 1941. Oil.
(51×38)

3. Woman in a Rocking Chair.
1943. Oil. ($63\frac{1}{4} \times 51$)

4. Serenade. 1942. Oil. ($6' 4\frac{3}{4}'' \times 8' 8\frac{1}{4}''$)

5. Pastoral. 1946. Oil on fibro-cement. ($47\frac{1}{4} \times 98\frac{1}{4}$)

6. The Charnel House. 1945. Oil.
($78\frac{3}{4} \times 98\frac{1}{4}$)

7. Massacre in Korea. 1951. Oil on wood. ($43\frac{1}{4} \times 82\frac{3}{4}$)

PLATE XXI

2. Spiral Head of Faun.
($c.$ 12×10)

1. Ulysses and the Sirens.
1946. Oil on fibro-cement.
(about 177×118)

3. Mother and Children with
Orange. 1951. Oil on wood.
($45\frac{1}{4} \times 34\frac{3}{4}$)

4. Owl and Sea Urchins. 1946. Oil
on wood. ($31\frac{1}{2} \times 30\frac{1}{4}$)

5. Françoise. 1946. Lithograph.
($24\frac{3}{4} \times 19$)

6. Night Landscape, Vallauris
1951. Oil. ($57\frac{1}{2} \times 45$)

7. Portrait of a Painter, after El
Greco. 1950. Oil on wood.
($40 \times 32\frac{1}{4}$)

8. Chimneys of Vallauris. 1951. Oil.
($23\frac{1}{2} \times 28\frac{3}{4}$)

9. Portrait of Sylvette. 1954.
Oil. ($39\frac{1}{4} \times 32$)

PLATE XXII

1. War. 1952. Oil on isorel. (15′ 5″ × 33′ 6″)

2. Peace. 1952. Oil on isorel. (15′ 5″ × 33′ 6″)

3. Woman Vase. 1948. Ceramic. (c. 18¾ high)

4. Model and Monkey Painter. 1954. Ink and wash. (9½ × 12½)

5. Vase. Ceramic c. 1951. (c. 18 high)

6. Knights and Pages. 1951. Oil. (18 × 24)

7. Three Doves. 1953. Ceramic. (8-12 long)

8. Plate with Bullfight. c. 1957. Ceramic. (11 × 26)

PLATE XXIII

1. Ape with young. 1951.
Bronze. (21 high)

2. The Women of Algiers, after Delacroix.
1955. Oil. (45 × 57½)

3. Goat. 1950. Plaster, later
cast in bronze. (47 × 55)

4. Jacqueline Roque in the Studio. 1956.
Oil. (18 × 21½)

5. Pregnant
Woman.
1950. Bronze.
(41¼ high)

6. The Studio. 1956. Oil. (28½ × 36)

7. Las Meninas, after Velasquez, 1st version. 1957. Oil. (5′ 10″ × 8′ 6″)

PLATE XXIV

INDEX

INDEX

Daumier, 45, 53, 329
David, 350
Degas, 45, 64, 68, 71, 73, 109, 110, 133, 185
Deharme, Lise, 262
Delacroix, 64, 72, 192, 350, 351, 371
Delaunay, 174
Denis, Maurice, 121
Derain, André, 102, 126, 127, 129, 130, 139, 140, 148, 150, 157, 180, 181, 187, 193, 208, 210, 212, 343, 344
Diaghilev, Serge, 195, 196, 200, 201, 210, 213-215, 230, 347
Doucet, Jacques, 130, 229
Duchamp, Marcel, 174, 175, 207, 228
Dufy, Raoul, 101, 147
Duhamel, Georges, 106
Durio, Paco, 99, 100
Duthuit, Georges, 277
Dutilleul, Roger, 223

Eluard, Cécile, 262
Eluard, Dominique, 339
Eluard, Gala, 254
Eluard, Nusch, 254, 259, 262, 263, 278, 279, 283, 284, 303, 319, 339
Eluard, Paul, Title-page, 179, 180, 227, 228, 230, 254-255, 256, 259, 260, 261-3, 277, 278, 279, 280, 282, 283, 284, 294, 295, 298, 309, 310, 314, 315, 324, 327, 332, 338-340, 343, 360
Ernst, Max, 173, 182, 208, 227, 230, 254, 357
Errazuriz, Mme., 208
Eva (Marcelle Humbert), 169-171, 180, 181, 187, 188, 189, 194, 201, 245, 303
Exhibitions mentioned in the text:
1896 Barcelona, Municipal Exhibition, 44
1897 Madrid, National Exhibition of Fine Arts, 44
1897 Barcelona, 46
1901 Barcelona, Sala Parès, 67
1901 Paris, Vollard Gallery, 71-76, 83
1902 Paris, Berthe Weill Gallery, 83
1909, 1911 Munich, Thannhauser Gallery, 174, 175
1910-11, 1912 London, Grafton Galleries, 175
1911 New York, Photo Secession Gallery, 175
1912 Barcelona, Dalman Gallery, 176
1912 London, Stafford Gallery, 175
1913 New York, Boston, Chicago, Armory Show, 175
1916 Zürich, Cabaret Voltaire, 207
1919, 1920, 1921 Paris, Rosenberg Gallery, 222
1921 London, Leicester Galleries, 212, 222
1925 Paris, Galerie Pierre, First Surrealist Exhibition, 229
1931 New York, 244
1931 London, Reid and Lefevre, 244
1932 Paris, Galerie Georges Petit, 244
1936 Barcelona, Bilbao, Madrid, ADLAN group, 255, 256
1936 Paris, Cahiers d'Art Gallery, 256
1936 Paris, Renou et Colle Gallery, 256
1936 Paris, Paul Rosenberg Gallery, 256, 257, 259
1936 London, International Surrealist Exhibition, 259
1937 Paris, Guernica, 268-278, etc.
1938 Norway, 286
1938 London, New Burlington Galleries, Whitechapel Art Gallery, 286; Leeds, Liverpool, 286
1939 Paris, Paul Rosenberg's Gallery, 265
1939 New York, The Museum of Modern Art, 287, 294
1940 Paris, Galerie M.A.I., 294
1944 Mexico City, 353
1944 Paris, Salon d'Automne, 317
1945 London, Victoria and Albert Museum, 317, 353
1945 Paris, Salon d'Automne, 318
1948, 1949 Paris, Maison de la Pensée Francaise, 353
1950 London, Arts Council of Great Britain, 328
1950 Venice Biennale, 353
1951 Paris, Salon de Mai, 333
1951 Tokyo, 353
1951 London, Institute of Contemporary Arts, 353
1951 Paris, Maison de la Pensée Francaise, 353
1953 Lyons, 323, 353
1953 Rome, Milan, 336, 353
1953 Sao Paolo, Brazil, 353
1954 Paris, Maison de la Pensée Française, 353, 354
1955 Paris, Bibliothèque Nationale, 355
1956 London, Arts Council, 355
1957 Arles, 323
1957 Barcelona, 355
1957 New York, The Museum of Modern Art, 355; Chicago, 355; Philadelphia, 355

Fagus, Felicien, 72, 73, 104
Falla, de, 210
Fauconnier, Le, 174
Fauves, Fauvism, 102, 121, 128, 130, 140, 147, 171, 173
Férat, Serge, 194, 206
Films on Picasso: with Georges-Henri Clouzot (Le Mystère Picasso), 337, 360-363; with Luciano Emmer, 361; Guernica, music by Guy Bernard, 360; with Paul Haesaerts, 360
Forain, 73, 109
France, Anatole, 185
Franck, César, 38, 39